what we want is free

what we want is free

CRITICAL EXCHANGES IN RECENT ART

SECOND EDITION

EDITED BY TED PURVES AND SHANE ASLAN SELZER

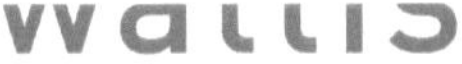

CCA Wattis Institute for Contemporary Arts

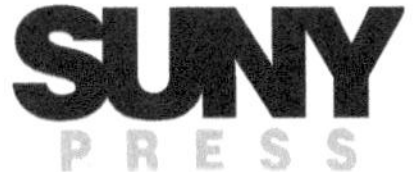

STATE UNIVERSITY OF NEW YORK PRESS

Original cover concept by Nancy Nowacek, © 2013

Unless noted, all images appear courtesy of the artists

Published by State University of New York Press, Albany

Printed in the United States of America

For information, contact State University of New York Press, Albany, NY
www.sunypress.edu

Production by Jenn Bennett
Marketing by Kate McDonnell

Library of Congress Cataloging-in-Publication Data

What we want is free : critical exchanges in recent art / edited by Ted Purves and Shane Aslan Selzer. — Second Edition.
pages cm
Revised and expanded edition of What we want is free: generosity and exchange in recent art. 2005.
Includes bibliographical references and index.
ISBN 978-1-4384-5313-2 (hardcover : alk. paper)
ISBN 978-1-4384-5314-9 (pbk. : alk. paper)
1. Generosity in art. 2. Social exchange. 3. Interactive art. 4. Artists and community. I. Purves, Ted, 1964– II. Selzer, Shane Aslan, 1977–

N8217.G43W48 2014
306.4'7—dc23 2013044074

10 9 8 7 6 5 4 3 2 1

CONTENTS

ACKNOWLEDGMENTS

The second edition of this book feels like a continuing conversation among friends. We are deeply grateful to all of the artists, curators, and writers involved in the first book who set in motion a conversation that we are still deeply engaged with. The research for the second book began with a call for recommendations that went out to a handful of curators and artists. We are deeply thankful to Michelle Grabner, Greg Scholette, Bisi Silva, Caroline Woolard, Mabel Wilson, Kianga Ford, Heide Fasnacht, Kalia Brooks, Sarah Robayo-Sheridan, Elizabeth Thomas, Kate Fowle and Oksana Chepelyk. for the outpouring of relevant projects this call generated.

Institutions are crucial partners for arts research, and we would like to offer special thank you to California College of the Arts for supporting this book's development from the first symposium in 2002, through their continued gift of research grants, including the Chalsty Fellowship for Aesthetics, granted in 2006. We also are grateful to Parsons, The New School for Design for hosting a roundtable panel in 2011 that addressed ideas of collaboration and exchange between artists and institutions. The resulting dialogue allowed us to more fully flesh out the criteria for the final selection of projects that we chose to include in the book. We want to extend our gratitude to the panelists, Caroline Woolard, Kianga Ford, Hen-Gil Han, Athena Robles and Anna Stein.

We are especially thankful to our new contributors; Matthew Rana, Ignacio Valero, and Elyse Mallouk, as well as to Peter Coyote who allowed us to print the keynote lecture he delivered at the first Generosity Symposium at CCA in 2002. As makers ourselves, we are in debt to Jacob Wick for his sharp research and editorial assistance and to Nancy Nowacek for designing the book cover just because she really cares.

If this book is a conversation among friends; then it is decidedly a book dedicated to our families, both given, chosen, real and imagined. Major thanks are due to James Peltz of SUNY Press, who has edited and managed this book in its various forms for well over a decade. We could not have finished the book without Susanne Cockrell's thoughtful readings of the chapters in progress as well as Oliver's inquisitive social energy and Sekou's wide-eyed arrival. You are all the reason we are doing this work.

CANDIES IN ENDLESS SUPPLY

FROM GENEROSITY TO CRITICAL EXCHANGE

Ted Purves

Why return to a book? Why make it again, when it might be just as simple to start out fresh? How can we still talk about art under the banner of "free," in terms of generosity and gifts, when the last decade has thrown enough hardballs to dislodge such utopian thoughts from our wary, critical minds? These questions have been continually on my mind throughout the last year, as I have endeavored to transform a book originally published in 2005—*What We Want is Free: Generosity and Exchange in Recent Art*—to the current edition that you are reading now, which now bears a new subtitle, *Critical Exchanges in Recent Art*, and welcomes a second editor, Shane Aslan Selzer. The first edition came directly from a symposium, projects series, and graduate practicum, which I organized at California College of the Arts. This second edition, however, comes neither from a symposium nor a class, but draws instead upon ten years of observations within the field of contemporary art, as well as ongoing engagements with curating, writing, and producing projects within it.

When I was approached to make a revised edition, there were many good reasons to undertake the project. The research for the initial book was largely undertaken in the 1990s, and the symposium was developed in early 2001. All of the projects that were presented at the symposium and researched for the book took place in what now seems to be a different world, before 9/11 and the ensuing decade of ongoing war in the Middle East, before the advent of Web 2.0 and the rise of social media, before the collapse of the financial markets in 2008 and the continuing global recession. To build an editorial view, as the original book did, on ideas of alternative exchange or gift economies was timely then, as it provided at least a theoretical alternative to the emergent globalized capitalism that encompassed the world at the end of the Cold War. However, this focus, from the vantage point of 2010, was beginning to seem a bit rose-tinted.

By returning to a book, however, rather than writing a new book, one assumes something of a responsibility for the earlier material. Any book, after all, has a history and a path that it has made in the world. Making a second edition, then, should be seen as an opportunity to refine and continue that path, rather than raze it from existence and go in a different direction. However, many of the recent artists' projects that emerged in our research contained a markedly different tone, one that was not entirely generous. They had sharper edges and markedly different tactics. Given this, when we surveyed the majority of the material in the first edition, we reached the conclusion that while much of it was still relevant, it was very much in need of a new editorial lens. This lens would not only provide a larger context by which this material could be understood, it would also create a framework through which it could be aligned with the newer artists' projects, and grow to include the contemporary social theory that we had been researching.

The new lens that emerged considered the "critical exchanges" within a given project, and it connects the underlying methodologies of projects done since 2003 with the works that were considered in the prior edition. Confrontational generosity, the possibilities of *detournement* through the tactical use of gifts, or the democratic gesture of redistributing your own privileges as an artist to an audience or community—all of these can be read in light of critical exchange. This lens also builds on work that has occupied both Shane and myself for the last decade in our individual scholarship. For Shane, this has been research into ideas of criticality and failure both in the studio and in the community. For my part, it builds on my recent investigation of theories of social form, which, in my view, provides an intriguing framework from which one can consider the capacities of contemporary art to leverage relations in the world. Both of our lines of research are brought together in the initial chapter of this edition, and it sets the stage for the three sections that follow.

Section one builds on the critical essays of the prior edition and adds two chapters to its mix. The first, by Matthew Rana, brings a consideration of the relatively recent writings in the field of object-oriented philosophy into dialogue with the exchanges inherent in material and immaterial artworks. The second, by Ignacio Valero, investigates the historical relations that emerged during the European Enlightenment that conflated an enclosure of the "commons" with an elevation of the both the individual and "the free." While section 1 has expanded to include some more current scholarship, section 3, in many ways, works to preserve the original debates within the first edition of the book. Comprised solely from chapters derived from presentations given at the original Generosity Projects symposium, this section provides a "snapshot" of the early discussions around this area of artistic investigation. One chapter has been added to this section, "The Arts, Generosity, and Politics," by Peter Coyote. This text was originally delivered as the keynote address which opened the symposium, and it was not available at the time the first edition went to press. We are grateful to the author for letting us include it in this edition, as it allows for the symposium to be seen with a greater appreciation of its scope.

Section 2, which contains the project histories of dozens of artworks, has been significantly expanded and almost entirely rewritten. While many of the projects from the prior edition are still profiled, their number has more than doubled, to accommodate the many works that have been created since the first edition (and a few older ones that were missed the first time around). In this edition, this section also lost the few "historical" projects that were previously included, while it adds a significant body of research into the alternative institutions that have emerged in parallel to the art projects. These institutions incorporate many of the same tactics of critical exchange into their structures, and they demonstrate the ways in which the more temporary strategies employed by the art projects can be extended into more lasting cultural forces. The section closes with a visual examination of some of the ephemera that these projects leave behind in the world.

The paragraphs above should serve to outline what has changed between the first edition of this book and the present one. While it gives some insight onto the editorial direction that we took with it, it does very little to reveal the more fundamental "why's" that compelled this book to be redrawn into the present. On first blush, the reasons are very straightforward. The first edition of the book has "done well." It has been widely read, and has been of use to the art community, especially to the emergent curriculums of social and public practice that have cropped up over the last decade; as such, an update would continue to build on that usefulness. But on further reflection, it's possible that some of the reasons "why" I would undertake a second edition are quite personal and founded on a very discreet and idiosyncratic experience of the last decade.

One of the fundamental "drivers" for undertaking this project in the first place was based around an experience that I had encountering a candy-pile sculpture by Felix Gonzalez-Torres sometime in the mid 1990s. This experience with a sculpture that, literally, gave itself away and yet was replenished by an institutional structure, pushed me to look farther afield. It led me to discover the works of artists like Jorgen Svensson and make thematic connections to the works of Rirkrit Tiravanija. It also provoked a small piece of preliminary writing (one that did not make it into the first edition of this book). The other day I came across this piece of writing. A short excerpt, where I had written about encountering Gonzalez-Torres's candy sculpture, follows:

> . . . The piece itself is an embodied idea. It does not refer to meanings or concepts, but rather it enacts them. It is an act-field. This is not to say it is devoid of larger meanings, but rather than state them, it allows its meanings to arise from the various interactions within the act-field that is the work . . . It needs the artist to provide the initial collectability and worth to supporting the idea of the piece. It needs a complicit buyer. This buyer must understand that buying the piece really means buying into an idea of supporting

> a space wherein the action of dispersal must continue for the piece to continue to be the piece. It needs an audience willing to consume it, and it needs attention from an institution to maintain its availability. It, in short, requires a constant expenditure of money, resources, and time. The works needs a great deal of support, like many works of "public" art, and yet I can think of no better example of a work of art which so immediately justifies the artworld's network of support and money as this one.

I found this piece of writing around the same time that I made the decision to not include some of the more historical projects in the project sections of the handbook for this edition. This included leaving out the entry for the Felix Gonzalez-Torres candy pile, the very work that inspired the project in the first place. While I do not regret that decision, I also do not want it to go by unremarked.

It also provoked a need to know where that sculpture is now, in 2013. Who owns this "act-field"? Is it on display? What audiences get to take its offerings and eat them, piece by piece? It turns out that it is in the permanent collection the Museum of Modern Art in New York. One can read about it on their website, and also learn that it is not currently on display. It's unclear how often (if ever) it is on display, but in some ways this is irrelevant, as the registrar's notations for the work were equally illuminating.

"Untitled" (Placebo)

Felix Gonzalez-Torres (American, born Cuba. 1957–1996)

> 1991. Candies, individually wrapped in silver cellophane (endless supply), Dimensions vary with installation. Ideal weight: 1,000–1,200 lbs (454–544 kg). Gift of Elisa and Barry Stevens. © 2013 Felix Gonzalez-Torres[1]

It is all right there. The moment in which I first encountered this work, the now in which I write these words. *Candies, individually wrapped in silver cellophane (endless supply)* . . . When I first saw this work the promise of such an endless supply seemed possible. Such sweetness was intoxicating. From the vantage point of today it's hard to even know why one would write (or believe) such a thing. How can there ever be an endless supply of candies, even if the museum were willing to purchase them, even if Elisa and Barry Stevens bequeathed their entire fortune to the museum? One imagines the lines that would form at the museums door, and how they might snake through Manhattan were such an "endless supply" possible. Would anyone, a museum, a donor, an artist have enough resources to provide such a thing? Would the factories roar to life each time the candy pile went below 1000–1,200 lbs.? It seems so impossible now, so filled with hubris and hype.

And yet there is something there, still, locked up, within the proclamation that the structural medium for an artwork could be something, anything, in endless supply. Such a thought still beguiles. Whether it's merely rhetoric, or a utopian impulse, the story is worth contemplating, with its thought of everlasting sweetness emerging at the same time we realize that nothing is further from the truth. There are things in endless supply these days. Sadly, candy is not one of them. What there is we have yet to see.

Notes

1. Taken from the permanent collection area of the New York Museum of Modern Art website. www.moma.org

NO LONGER NORMAL

CRITICAL EXCHANGES IN THE LANDSCAPE OF ART

Ted Purves and Shane Aslan Selzer

Dinner

On any given day, we navigate constantly through shifting landscapes of exchange. Sometimes we are aware of our passage, but more often than not our navigation occurs without a great deal of thought. For many of us, this daily navigation of complex territories of exchange is simply normal and unremarkable—something we are socialized to understand almost intuitively.

We pay our rent from our checking account. We pay for clothes online using funds we borrow through a credit card. We borrow a book from the library for a few weeks and return it when we have finished reading it. We read an article on the Internet and send it to a friend by pressing a button that says "share." We sit and share an orange on a bench in a city park. While it is somewhat obvious to say that these exchanges are all quite different from one another, it is perhaps less obvious to say that the differences between them are best understood not by looking at what in particular was exchanged, but by considering the systems of exchange that governed each of them.

Try to imagine it this way.

You have a child, and one afternoon you discover that you are in need of groceries to prepare the dinner that you had planned for the two of you to eat that night. Time is short, so you ask your neighbor to drop you off at the grocery store on her way to work. At the grocery store, you select the food you need for the evening and pay the cashier. When you leave the store, you notice that it has started raining, so you decide to wait for the city bus to take you home, spending a dollar for the fare, rather than walk in the rain. When you get home, you and your child prepare dinner. You sit at the table. The meal is eaten together.

In this simple story, the main character has made a series of exchanges, but what is significant about them is that the specifics of each of those exchanges were governed by a rotating array of economic systems. What compels your neighbor to say yes when you ask for a ride to the grocery store? Why would you spend time and effort to prepare a meal and then give half of it away to a child, who did nothing to help produce it? Such questions reveal the workings of what is arguably the first, and oldest, economic system that we participate in, which is termed a *traditional* (or *social*) economy. This is a system governed, first and foremost, by participants who live in ongoing association with one another, originally in a village or a tribe, now, more commonly, in a family, or circle of friends, or a neighborhood. Such institutions as barter, favors, and filial obligations govern the primary mechanisms of exchange in a traditional economy. In our story above, this system of exchange is what sanctioned (and structured) the request of a ride from the neighbor, and it is the framework upon which the protagonist, as a parent, takes the responsibility to provide food for his or her child.

Why would a city or community have a bus, which drives along the street whether anyone is riding it or not? Why can someone ride it for miles and others for a few blocks, while both pay the same fare? These questions reveal a second system, which is termed a *redistributive* (or *command*) economy. In this system, resources, goods, and services are taken or levied from those who produce them by a state or governing entity, which then redistributes them to various areas of the society in accordance with goals and policies. In our story, it this redistributive economy that provided a city bus service (likely built with the proceeds from taxes) and set the price level for the one-dollar fare.

Why is a grocery store (which, for example, neither raises vegetables nor produces its own milk) able to concentrate so many varied foods into a single location? What determines the price that is paid for these varied goods, and why might these prices shift as products go on or off sale. A shop, or a market, exemplifies the system of the *capital* economy, where resources, goods, and services are exchanged in relation to abstract systems of exchange, such as money or currency. In capital economies both the resources and the currency can shift in value in relation to each other, due to either speculation and/or supply and demand. This "fluidity" of capital economies is what creates the possibility for investment, loaning, and wagering, as the shifting prices of the market allow for profits to be made simply by guessing which way values might shift. Again, we can refer to our story above, where the lone capital transaction was the purchase of food at the grocery store. Its price was set in relation to both the cost of the food for the market as well as the "overhead" costs associated with running the store (employee salaries, utility costs, etc.), and it also contained a certain level of profit added in, which is taken by the owner of the market.

It is generally agreed that the above systems are the three primary economic systems (or systems of exchange) that have evolved over the course of human history. As seen in our examples, an economic system is a method for producing, distributing, and consuming goods and services. No country (or city, or state) is governed by just one; most are controlled by a mixture of the three. It is important to note that economic systems not only encompass the *mechanisms* of exchange (e.g., currency or barter goods), but also incorporate the social institutions that govern and manage the production, distribution, and consumption of goods and services. This can mean tangible institutions such as a market, a bank, or the Federal Reserve, as well as intangible institutions such as marriages, community services, or a birthday party.

While the story details a series of fairly straightforward exchanges, it is worth noting that the shifts between economic systems means that even this simple set of encounters contains complexities of great interest as we move forward. The food, which is bought with currency, is later shared with another without any subsequent repayment. The trip from the store is the same distance either way, but it is "paid for" quite differently. Each of these systems contains its own rules, and the terms of exchange in one do not really transfer to any of the others. You would not usually consider charging your child money for the meal you prepared, any more than you would tell the bus driver that instead of paying the fare that you will give her a ride tomorrow.

Basketfill

These systems of exchange are the ground upon which the artists' projects assembled and investigated in this book are constructed. It is the landscape that they occur within, as well as what they are attempting to make meaning of and from.

One such landscape can be found in the town of Nsukka, in southeast Nigeria. Once a small town, Nsukka has grown to become a cultural zone of over a million people, and the pressures of a rapidly shifting economy have resulted in a massive influx of internal migration as the population has moved from rural villages to urban areas in search of work and opportunity. It is there in this bustling town, the home to the University of Nigeria, that Amuche Ngwu-Nnabueze initiated the Sculpted Basket Project (SBP). In the most straightforward sense, SBP is an ongoing project that takes the form of workshops and community organizing while producing woven objects for exhibition, use, and exchange. Ngwu-Nnabueze wanted to address the potential overlap between the disappearance of traditional basket weaving and a major issue facing her community: waste removal. The growth of population in this area has far outpaced the local government's ability to provide basic infrastructure, which has resulted in a proliferation of open waste dumps full of unsorted throwaway materials, some degradable and some not.

Following an intensive series of meetings, first with the local community and subsequently with such institutional forces as the university and the municipal administrators, Ngwu-Nnabueze started holding workshops to teach traditional methods of basket weaving using reclaimed waste material, which would simultaneously raise awareness about environmental waste problems. The result is an ongoing social project that fuses waste separation, composting, and basket weaving, one that presents baskets as traditional, sustainable, functional replacements for plastic bags, plastic seats, and other items generally made from imported or unsustainable materials. It also proposes the revival of a somewhat dormant tradition of producing locally woven baskets as transporting vehicles, made from repurposed fabrics, plastics, wood, and metal found in the local dumps.

Ngwu-Nnabueze conceptualized the project to interpenetrate a variety of social groups as well as various local institutions. She first considered who the project might impact, and how those impacted might become personally involved in the project. This was largely determined by the population attending the initial workshops, and extended to the many roundtable meetings SBP held to pull in schools, churches, civil authorities, and public service agents. She then considered the various public institutions that the project would both intersect with and draw upon: sanitation systems, traditional methods of basket weaving, workshops, radio stations, and church bulletins. These forms were deliberately chosen to reflect and respond to the needs of those who were becoming personally involved in the project through regular attendance at the workshops. Out of these gatherings a campaign was launched to begin the sorting, recycling, and composting of waste.

SBP can broken down into a number of separate parts: a civic organization, a lobbying group of concerned citizens, as well as a craft project producing woven baskets using traditional techniques. But separating these elements of the project undermines its conceptual premise and devalues the leveraging of the various local systems of exchange that the project navigated between as it went from inception to action. By fusing the removal (or nonremoval) of waste, generally considered to be a part of a functioning redistributive economy, with a community-based workshop (part of a traditional/social economy), in the service of producing baskets (which are both reusable and saleable, and thus have an impact on the local market economy), the project attempts to harness together a series of disparate interests to create a tangible physical and social result. The fact that the project is also created as an art project adds an extra dimension, as the Sculpted Basket Project also has the potential to be considered by a nonlocal audience, through critical institutions of the art world such as exhibitions and publications (including this one). In this framework, the project also has the potential to be seen in a larger, critical discourse, one where its varied exchanges and the objects it produced also function symbolically.

#criticalexchanges

This pulls into focus one of the key lenses of this book: *critical exchanges*. What are critical exchanges and what criteria might we put forward for understanding how they operate? Critical exchanges occur within works in which the participants (audience/collaborators/institutions) are made consciously aware of the *transfers* that occur within the work. They make visible the conditions and stakes that are required for the production of the work, and, at times, the participants may have a voice within the process and that voice could affect the ultimate outcome of the project. This awareness of the transfer(s) of power, of material, of resources, or knowledge, forms a core aspect of both the work itself and its attendant meanings. Rather than emphasizing process or production as the outcome, the exchange itself becomes the most important outcome identified through the project.

In 2002, Santiago Sierra initiated a new work entitled *Person Saying A Phrase*, in Birmingham, England. For this work, he hired a person begging for money on a busy shopping street to be filmed stating the following phrase: "My participation in this project could generate $72,000 profit. I am paid £5" One point of this project is possibly to expose the myth that most participatory artworks are inherently generous, by showing ways that they are potentially self-serving and often profoundly unequal in terms of who benefits from their production. But there is a more pressing issue that is poetically brought to the surface by this work, namely, the terms or social contract engaged to produce works that are dependent on social interaction. When Sierra makes these terms transparent, he also puts them at the center of the work itself, asking questions about how value is determined during an exchange.

By asking his hired participant to recite the script about payment, Sierra ensures that the participant is also fully aware of the discrepancy in how his "work" is compensated, versus how Sierra's "work" may be later rewarded. Sierra does nothing to rectify this problem, and no solution is proposed. But the issue is made public, and that becomes the core of the work. The video produces an uncomfortable scenario for its viewers about privilege and access. It points back to Sierra himself as a conscious party to this inequality and the hired participant as a disempowered subject, one who is participating in the exchange for small monetary gain rather than refusing the terms of the exchange based on the inequities of the agreement.

Critical exchanges look at the power dynamics in relationships (those within the art world and those beyond), but they aren't necessarily focused on representation; they are less interested in interpreting or constructing meaning and more concerned with demystifying power relationships through an active encounter. In this respect, critical exchange is a way of practicing what Cornel West terms "demystification," for it attempts to understand not only why something is the way it is, but also all the historical and social forces that have made something act the way it does today.[1] During a critical exchange, the conditions of the exchange itself are highlighted in such a way that they provide an expanded view of the cultural, historical, and sociopolitical forces at play. In this respect, we are using the word *critical* not simply within its most common definition, where it is understood to mean careful (or even disapproving) judgment or evaluation, but in its alternate definition, where the word critical describes a crucial juncture or turning point, a place where a situation or fact may suddenly change or transform.

You've Got Form

Part of understanding how criticality operates within these projects comes from an understanding of the forms that these projects occupy. While it might sound somewhat traditionalist, when it comes to artworks, there is an integral relationship between form and content, and any assessment of a work's efficacy is incomplete if there is no acknowledgement of the form by which it manifested. That said, it's certainly the case that most, if not all, of the projects considered in this book do not manifest in forms that we would readily identify as artworks (e.g., there are few paintings and sculptures detailed in these pages). However, this does not mean that these works do not have form; rather, it means that we have to turn to other frameworks to understand the forms that they do have. This leads us to bring forward the concept of *social form*.

In his essay "The Problem of Sociology," the German-born philospher and sociologist Georg Simmel defined social form as the mode of interaction among individuals through (or in) the shape of which specific content achieves social reality. Simmel positioned these social forms as being distinct from social content, which is considered to be the interest, purpose, or motive of an interaction.[2] As such, a social form could be something like a street vendor's cart, a protest march, a meeting at work, a trade union, or a wedding. For the purposes of this book, the concept of social form has far-reaching implications, not simply because it extends a familiar art-historical concept of form to a large group of artists' projects that, at first glance, might not have an obvious form, but more importantly because the consideration of social forms gives us an added ability to talk about the mechanics of criticality that operates within these projects.

An example might serve at this point. Consider the work *Untitled (Beauty)* (1994), by the artist Rirkrit Tiravanija. For this project, the artist, and others, cooked Thai curries in the Jack Hanley Gallery of San Francisco for a month, and served them for free to anyone who came into the gallery. This work was one of a long series of such projects that Tiravanija performed in galleries during the early 1990s. Considered in terms of its basic content and its structure as a participatory artwork, *Untitled (Beauty)* and similar works by Tiravanija have been widely discussed within the field of art criticism as a utopian gesture. They are generally credited with carving out a convivial space in the gallery wherein participants were drawn together, lured by a free meal, and (together with the artist) generated an ongoing social space where their relations were both open to experience and also (due to the work's location in a gallery) "framed" as a social sculpture. However, when the work is considered in terms of social form, it is possible to read somewhat different meanings in the work.

Commercial art galleries, as social forms, can be thought of as a particular form of "shop." However, unlike most shops (where members of the public become customers or shoppers upon entering the shop, whether they actually purchase something or not), in most commercial art galleries, members of the public are not generally considered to be potential buyers of the wares that the gallery/shop is offering. If you work in a gallery, you quickly learn to call these people "visitors," such as you would have at a museum or a zoo. What happens within this space when there is no artwork on display, and the gallery is required, through the "rules" of the artwork that they have commissioned, to serve free food to those who come into the space? Of course many things can (and do) happen, but on a structural, or formal, level, the gallery is no longer able to treat these people simply as "visitors." You do not feed free meals to visitors, after all; such people are usually called guests. Through this sequence of modifications to the social form of the gallery, it is possible to see how critical relations arise: What changes for the worker in the gallery (who is now a host), and for the visitors (who are now guests)?

Centering the consideration of social projects from the vantage point of form shifts the central questions from ones centered on ideas of a project's meaning to a consideration of a project's capacity: How does it operate within the social world, and for whom? How does it interact with the surrounding social forms that form its immediate social context? What is the work's agency? After all, we do not encounter social forms in a vacuum—they are adjacent to (and interpenetrate) other social forms, as much as they are discrete unto themselves.

In a landscape of social forms, the recognition of the forms we are within are of ongoing importance. We enter someone's home for a dinner party as a guest. In the Tiravanija example *Untitled (Beauty)*, we enter a gallery as a visitor who then is asked to become a guest by sitting down and being served a free meal. Both of these points of entry are something that we know almost sub-intellectually; they are parts of the world of social forms that we have been raised within, things that we have an almost inherent grasp of. This learned familiarity with social forms is, obviously, similar to the familiarity that we have with systems of economic exchange, as discussed in the first section of this essay.

While this brief discussion of social form has focused on the form of the gallery/shop, critical exchanges can occupy any number of social forms—from dinner parties to potlucks, from community meetings to online encounters, quite literally any social form wherein we would normally expect to find one or another system of exchange in play. When such social forms are taken up by artists and subsequently altered to achieve more idiosyncratic or subjective ends, it is possible to become disoriented, to have a moment of adjustment that requires a shift in thinking and reaction. It is in this moment of realignment that a possibility of critical exchange arises—where the form is seen not just for the moment when it is strange, but for all of the prior times we have entered it when it was "normal."

+1 Add Friend

At this point it is useful to look outward to the landscapes of exchange within which we, as a people, as societies, are living. As has been discussed, there is, in each of us, almost an inbuilt sense of order to the shifts in systems of exchange that we encounter as we go through our daily lives. But if we look back at the last twenty five years (which is roughly the timeframe for the projects that this volume considers) or even the last ten years (which is the amount of time that elapsed between the bulk of the writing in the first edition of this book and the present edition), it is clear that that the exchanges we live within on a daily basis aren't quite as ordered as they once were. They are no longer normal, and the ground under us has changed.

While exchange systems morph and evolve over time,[3] it is difficult not to look back over the periods of time covered by this book and imagine that the rate of evolution for economic systems has somehow had a finger pressed firmly on the fast-forward button, so fast that they seem to collapse into each other as each permutation is explored by global enterprise. It is this period that John Berger summarized (beautifully, as always) in his essay "Where Are We":

> Might it not be better to see and declare that we are living through the most tyrannical—because the most pervasive—chaos that has ever existed? It's not easy to grasp the nature of the tyranny, for its power structure (ranging from the 200 largest multinational corporations to the Pentagon) is interlocking yet diffuse, dictatorial yet anonymous, ubiquitous yet placeless. It tyrannizes from offshore, not only in terms of Fiscal Law but in terms of any political control beyond its own. Its aim is to delocalize the entire world. Its ideological strategy . . . is to undermine the existent so that everything collapses into its special version of the virtual, from the realm of which—and this is the tyranny's credo—there will be a never-ending source of profit.[4]

While details of this drastic shift are beyond the scope of this essay, a single example might serve as instructive. Ten years ago, at the time when we were writing the last edition, the world (or at least the digitally linked or "wired" world) was just beginning to glimpse what would come to be collectively called "Web 2.0," a nest of innovations that included social networking, free webmail, blogs, and photo-sharing. The first rush of the arrival of Web 2.0 could be seen in the emergence of user-driven websites such as YouTube, MySpace, Napster, and FlickrWeb, among other offerings. The basic idea of Web 2.0 represented not just a new mode of internet technology, it also represented a totally different outlook on how to harness creative energy to create meaningful (and meaningless) content. Unlike earlier websites, which created their content "in-house" and then "uploaded" it to the web for people to see, these websites created a platform that grew somewhat organically, primarily using the creative energy of their users, who uploaded their own content at the same time they were seeing and reading content generated by others.[5]

This shift represented not just a break from a traditional model of producer and consumer; it also demonstrated an entirely different economic model for production, wherein content is produced entirely off of the creative surplus of the "wired" populace. Of course, the users of sites like Flickr and YouTube are (by and large) not paid for their creative efforts, and one of the initial notions around these sites is that they actually represented something of a high-tech version of a traditional economy, specifically a barter economy with a user-community at its heart. In this economy, users got free email, free access to a larger public, free opportunities to exchange thoughts and information, in exchange for which they supplied their creative energy (and watched a small amount of advertising that was placed on the sites) to generate both content and "traffic" (which was a tracking of how many visits a site had over the course of a day).

This system of production came to be called "crowdsourcing,"[6] and it represented a significant innovation in terms of both exchange and creative production. This innovation was viewed with great optimism by the "wired" public, who invested these various platforms for user-interaction and exchange with a belief that they might create an almost global system of "free" personalized communication and information exchanges. However, within a few years, as one after another of the companies supporting this technology "went public" with multi-billion-dollar IPOs, many users realized the truth in what was quickly becoming a new maxim: When you get something for free, you are not the customer, you are the product.

Consider the example of Facebook. Launched in 2004, Facebook, initially offered a nominally free platform for college students to create an online representation of their social "self," where they could post pictures, communicate with friends, build networks, chat with each other, and share their lives, as well as their "likes." The site was gradually opened up to the general population and exploded in popularity. Over this same period, Facebook was collecting staggering amounts of data from all of its users, not just in terms of the content they uploaded, but also information on what other websites they visited, what they might buy or look at after they left. In May of 2012, Facebook went public, trading about 490 million shares in its first day, and raising sixteen billion dollars for the company. What is particularly instructive about this for the purposes of this essay is not simply the staggering amount of capital that was raised, primarily through monetizing the digital production of billions of social exchanges (which were by and large not created for any form of monetary payment); the thing to note is that this public offering completed a transfer of the product of one economic system (information and content arising from the social economy of Internet users) into another (the monetized information capital). All of those discrete and personal likes, all of the friendings and unfriendings, all of the shared photos and games of Scrabble spawned countless shares of Facebook stock.[7]

There remain, however, signs that this collapse between systems (and cultures) of exchange does not simply collapse in one direction. For example, one of the more interesting aspects of this new economy that converts crowd-sourced content into data for advertising and marketing is that, despite the disparity between the gift economy of its producers and the monetizing power of its owners, it must still (somewhat) rely on open access to continue to make profits. New veins of information must be continually laid down, like sediment, into the oceanic server farms that underlie the information economy, from where it can be productively mined for yet more data. This has created a situation where continuous need for content is turned to surprising (and startling) ends. One can spend an hour on YouTube and see, literally, almost anything. Homemade videos of cats sleeping are only a single click away from a political rant filmed in a bedroom in Holland or an illegal upload of a Bollywood drama.

A more dramatic and visible example of the forces at play in this situation was seen in early 2010, when the "Arab Spring" protests, fueled in part by tactical use of Facebook and Twitter, spread across a dozen countries in the Middle East and North Africa. In many cases, these new social media platforms were used to facilitate, very quickly and on a mass scale, a "low-tech" strategy that has served the masses for centuries: gather in great numbers in a public place and refuse to leave until someone in power responds. In the fall of 2011, Occupy Wall Street, a viral, populist array of long-term protests that emerged in many cities across the United States in the midst of an ongoing recession, took many organizing cues from the disparate revolutions of the Arab Spring, using a similar formula of combining sophisticated communications with persistent, physical intransigence. In the Greater New York area, the network of protestors and the communication strategies that linked them were reorganized as Occupy Sandy in order to put to use the organization and distribution tactics employed during the Occupy Wall Street protests in the wake of a natural disaster, Hurricane Sandy, which struck the area in the fall of 2012. Again, a mix of high-tech and age-old strategies was found to be effective. Occupy Sandy was able to network with local churches to help them function as distribution hubs,[8] and was able to harness the ingenuity of texting, cellphone cameras, and Twitter to act as contemporary versions of SOS signals.

Horizon

While it is important to look at the forces at play in this collapsing realm of exchanges and economies, it is naive to imagine that artists' tactical uses of critical exchanges will "solve" the problems that have arisen, or redress the mendacity that lies behind them. Nonetheless, they remain full of possibility. Learning how to speak about the times we are living through is vital. In his essay "The Subject and Power," Michel Foucault wrote: "Maybe the most certain of all philosophical problems is the problem of the present time and of *what we are* in this very moment." This sentence builds upon his reading of a question raised by Kant almost two hundred years prior, "Was Heist Auflklarung?" which Foucault elaborated to mean, "What is going on just now? What is happening to us? What is this world, this period, this precise moment in which we are living?"[9]

One of most pressing tasks is for us to understand *how we are* (and *who we are*) within these hyperglobalized realms of exchange. If the projects in this book can be seen as critical exchanges, and we can see this process of critical exchange being furthered by tactical uses of existing social forms, there is then a substantial framework in place to understand how their criticality has an integral relationship to the social and economic world that forms their context. There is the possibility that they can slow down a moment of exchange long enough for us not just to see it fully, but to ask *why*. Why am I giving this away, what is the encounter that forms this moment? It is more than possible that this slowing, this consideration, can form a benchmark from which we navigate our way . . . somewhere. To home. To market. To dinner.

Notes

1. West considered the practice of demystification to be a more forceful (and, in his view, prophetic) mode of critical practice, one that not simply deconstructs but builds a framework for future action. See "The New Politics of Cultural Difference" in *The Cornel West Reader* (New York: Basic Civitas Books, 1999).

2. For a thorough introduction to Georg Simmel, readers are directed to Georg Simmel, *On Individuality and Social Forms*, ed. Donald Levine (Chicago: University of Chicago Press, 1971).

3. This morphing over time is one of the central questions addressed by Marcel Mauss in his landmark book *The Gift*. For more on the historical evolution of exchange systems, readers are directed to chapter three of this volume.

4. John Berger, "Where Are We," from David Levi Strauss, *Between the Eyes: Essays on Photography and Politics* (New York: Aperture Books, 2003).

5. By most accounts, the term Web 2.0 appeared in Darcy DiNucci's article "Fragmented Future," *Print* 53.4 (January 1999), 32.

6. Interestingly, the term *crowdsourcing* was coined largely as a play on a much more negative word, *outsourcing*, which was a term used by corporations to describe the process by which they got rid of their workers as employees and formed one of the primary modes of globalized capitalism.

7. As we write this, at market close today, January 30, 2013, each share is worth $31.64.

8. It is worth noting that this tactic, which rests on the inbuilt community connections of churches, echoes those used by 1960s civil rights organizations, such as the Student Nonviolent Coordinating Committee.

9. "The Subject and Power," Michel Foucault, *Critical Inquiry* 8.4 (Summer 1982), 785. Foucault goes on to say that an even more pressing problem for philosophy might be to "refuse who we are." In the context of the following projects this might be an even more meaningful goal.

I

FROM MARKETS TO LOBBIES

CONSIDERATIONS OF OBJECTS, EXCHANGES, AND VALUE

SURE, EVERYONE MIGHT BE AN ARTIST . . .

BUT ONLY ONE ARTIST GETS TO BE THE GUY WHO SAYS THAT EVERYONE ELSE IS AN ARTIST

Bill Arning

An understanding of art practice as a generous act might well start with Joseph Beuys's celebrated pronouncement that "Jeder Mensch ist ein Künstler." In those few words, with their frustratingly fugitive meaning, resides the possibility of works of great art that treat their audience members as equal participants in a shared experience, and thereby attempt to resist reiterating troubling hierarchies. The question of how to honor "genius," and give due respect to creativity, without unintentionally creating and reifying inequalities that cause actual communication and fellowship to dissolve between makers and receivers of culture, is the task before us. To do this we must examine our romantic attraction to those hierarchies, what fruits we enjoy by maintaining and protecting them, and what we gain by forsaking them, at least occasionally.

This argument is based on two unproven "facts" that will not be proven here:

1. Art is ideally a communicative medium.
2. Communication between or among equals is the most significant, purest, and most meaningful form of communication.

While point one seems self-evident, point two is more debatable. I believe that the greatest teachers are those that learn from their students. Similarly groups like Alcoholics Anonymous work better than other treatment programs because the teachers are always also the students. There are exceptions I cannot easily explain. What of great orators, spiritual and political leaders of the people, who speak wonderfully yet are rarely seen publicly listening? I wonder what explains them.

The standard response to great art of the past has been to imagine its creators as otherworldly beings possessed of divine gifts. There are many times when that is not only the appropriate response, but a highly pleasurable one as well. My last trip to Washington, D.C., on contemporary art business luckily included a half-day spent in one of the temples to mankind's greatest achievements, the National Gallery. When revisiting Leonardo da Vinci's portrait of Ginevra de' Benci, I felt myself in the presence of an artwork of positively superhuman origin, and allowed myself to settle into a worshipful swoon. Whether because of the extraordinary virtuoso skill, the romantic patina of the intervening centuries, or merely the synonymy of the author's name with the role of artist as superhuman, I felt privileged to be in the presence of such a work. (It is perhaps unfair to use Leonardo as an example, because his existence beyond the human limits of achievement is so unassailable, but were I to try to make this case with a more recent make and model of "genius," be it Picasso, Pollock, Warhol, or Richter, the debate might veer off into the relative merits of the choice.)

That the otherworldly genius model—so deeply rooted in our psyches by the drug-like pleasure of encounters like mine with Leonardo—is uncritically and anachronistically carried over into looking at contemporary art has its positive and negative side. The positive is practical—without that model we could not get government coalitions and privileged folks to spend millions on building the museums that allow us scopophiles our regular visual fixes at pretty reasonable prices. The negative is that in worshiping art we end up denigrating everything else, including our lives and our own creativity. Hierarchies form and communication is muted.

The last century of progressive art has as one of its main progress narratives the attempted erasure of clear boundaries between art and life. This is by definition a project that it is impossible to complete. The preservation of art history in museum displays cannot, and probably should not, allow too much of the chaos of actual life to intrude. The inherent contradictions of artworks that are by their nature and intent against the art/life divide achieving canonical status, and thus reinforcing that divide, can madden the purist. Still, learning how to live with necessary contradictions and treating them as a form of koan to contemplate, in order to understand how little we can know or control, should make regarding a Duchamp "Fountain," with a million-dollar-plus reserve price, a form of learning similar to a Dharma study session with a Zen master.

In the art world post–Beuys's dictum, the exemplary "artist" has become an individual with certain skill sets, which may or may not include making objects, who still fulfills a useful social role that is often, but not always, bound to a facility for innovative thought. The art object today is best understood not as wondrous, but rather as a catalyst for a set of stimulating relationships that make up the art experience. At least that is one utopian vision for how art of our times functions.

It is amazing, therefore, how easy it is to fall back into a way of thinking more appropriate to da Vinci than Beuys. Even an artwork that seems to intrinsically question the beatitude of mastery, be it by Warhol, Richter, or Koons, can still induce aesthetic swooning when well installed in a gleaming museum or gallery cube. The pleasure those experiences give is immense, and I would hate to see them vanquished for consistency's sake. That a Sol LeWitt wall drawing or a set of Allan McCollum's surrogate paintings provide a similar pleasure seems patently absurd, and therefore implies a serious rupture between concept and reception in current art practice. Yet it is in that rupture's contradictions that things get juicy.

That rupture can lead us towards cynicism when it compels us to focus on aspects of artworks as commodities, as failed fetishes traded by the wealthy, as decadent and extravagant ways of expending surplus energy, or sociopathic gamesmanship to amuse the jaded. The attraction of those more cynical responses is serious and as addictive as crack. After indulging in a can-you-imagine-payinghalf-a-mil-for chortle, one is left feeling vaguely superior, one's ego and one's self reassured by how clever one has been in seeing through pretenses one might otherwise feel coerced into honoring. That feeling is fleeting, however, as it leads up a dead end path. It is better to work though the contradictions and to look for the good in art.

We are often left with two models of what constitutes the contemporary artist, for which I use the shorthand comparison of "Shaman" versus "trained monkey." The first posits the artist as superhuman oracle dispensing mystic truths—thank you, Bruce Nauman—in whose presence we are unworthy of being. The second is the artist as trained monkey providing a sophisticated entertainment, no more fulfilling than a good night of sitcoms, yet leaving us feeling superior for our understanding of obscure humorous or cultural references. Opposite sides of exactly the same coin, one role produces its needed correction in the other, but neither is healthy.

It has occasionally been my privilege to be involved with artists as they staged situations in which those hierarchical relations were at least temporarily vanquished. As when a stale room is aired out after being closed up for along time, a revivifying air filled the room. Some, but not all, of the works I will describe were performance-based, which in itself may tempt us to put them in an altogether different category from the genius-based art history I have discussed. That would be a mistake, however, for the art categories we have today encompass multiple histories. It is in their reintegration into standard visual art history where the promise of these works is most profound. The lesson of how to have a nonhierarchical relation to an artist and artwork—a conversation among peers—is ultimately fully translatable into all forms of art.

In my role as a curator I have often been called upon to lead "studio tours," usually as a fundraising tool for some not-for-profit organization. Most people that pay to visit up-and-coming artists' studios are comfortably well off, but by no means rich, and most enjoy the pleasure of buying art. Hence they tend to expect and desire paintings and photographs, which is understandable, as those can be lived with most easily. They are not on the whole closed-minded, but on the whole, shopping is what they have in mind.

One group had a very different experience when Jim Hodges agreed to host them in his studio. Understanding that the conventional studio-visit format could be transformed with a little imagination, Jim had said he wanted to do something different. When we arrived at his Chelsea basement studio, none of his works were on view. He was at this point a rising artist, known by anyone who pays attention to such things, and the group seemed a little disquieted by there being nothing to look at right away. There was a slide projector, which—please forgive my amateur mind-reading—I believe may have led them to worry that a mere slide talk was all they would see instead of the "authentic" experience of newly birthed studio creations. Instead they were offered a big box of colored pencils, and told to pick out their favorite colors. The mood transformed—it was a big box with lots of colors, and the choosing soon became quite a fun game.

There was a large piece of paper on the wall and the next instructions were simple, "stand against the paper and have someone mark your height with your favorite color"—as one marks the height of growing children on a doorjamb. This also caused the normal awkwardness of strangers in a group to vanish, as you had to ask someone to draw your line and to touch the top of your head in so doing. Then we were asked to write our names to claim our marks and color choices. This collective drawing was in fact quite beautiful in an unplanned way, twenty something brightly colored lines at zigzagging heights, infused with the collective high spirits of a successful group project.

Then the slides clicked on and we were shown houses in Spokane, Washington. Jim had photographed them because they had been painted interesting colors. Far from any high-art sphere, these homeowners had been to the paint store and decided they would be happier in their houses and lives if they made a somewhat unusual choice. We were nudged in a very gentle way to view the creative choices people who do not consider themselves artistic, ourselves included, make many time a day as being worthy of the respect we give those that do consider themselves artists. (I learned later that Jim Hodges has given similar slide presentations in museum and school settings, although this descriptive term may sound anachronistic when describing such an expansive project.)

Our group then walked a few blocks to the studio of Elaine Tin Nyo, who greeted us with homemade ice cream. It was a hot day and we were already feeling like giddy children from our collective drawing, so ice cream seemed perfect. Then the video player clicked on and we understood that food was Tin Nyo's vehicle for her storytelling art. When we are eating, or smelling food being prepared, we are enculturated to listen well.

In an earlier work Tin Nyo prepared curried eggs while telling the story of her family's political exile from Burma. It seems the recipe had been passed on to her and had come to represent childhood memories of Burma. Yet when correctly executed, the taste of the dish brought forth no Proustian flood of images. It was revealed in the course of the narrative that the dish she had eaten as a child was always slightly burnt and the bitterness of the charred egg taste was what was missing. As she told the tale live and on video we could smell the dish cooking, and we were ready to swallow Tin Nyo's lessons of identity, memory, and politics wholeThere is a central contradiction we cannot avoid, and it was suggested to me while teaching Joseph Beuys's work, and discussing his "Jeder Mensch" dictum with bright students. One said, "Sure, everyone might be an artist, but only one artist gets to be the guy who says that everyone else is an artist." True, and the one time I got to see Beuys speak in person, the charisma of this very theatrical man was undeniable. That his presence made him "different from," or "better than," his worshiping audience was clear, even though he was speaking against such distinctions. Jim Hodges and Elaine Tin Nyo are both similarly charismatic. If they had different presences perhaps they would not have been the catalytic agents for the joyous nonhierarchical artist-audience relation that our group experienced.

I must let this contradiction remain, and accept it as is. High culture foregrounds authorship and has done so since the European elevation of the artist to a different category from the talented craftsman in a guild. While there have been attempts to circumvent that distinction, this is not my intention, and the works I have discussed are bound to unique individuals happily fulfilling their role as authors.

I would like to suggest that a reversal of cause and effect has taken place. It might not be true that we are willing to accept these works because their makers are charismatic, but rather that we are drawn to generous individuals, particularly ones who urge us to stop and be grateful for our own gifts of creativity. In fact I think the next time I visit that Leonardo painting in D.C. my experience will only be more profound if my heart remains filled with the gratitude for that creative spirit—da Vinci's, Beuys's, Hodge's, Tin Nyo's, yours, and mine.

EXCHANGE—THE "OTHER" SOCIAL SCULPTURE

Francis McIlveen

The last two decades have seen an increase in artworks that use generous gestures and non-capital exchange systems as the primary medium for social sculptures. Artists such as Felix Gonzalez-Torres, Rirkrit Tiravanija, and Ben Kinmont provide excellent examples of this medium in action—questioning the role of the artwork in the context of the art economy, and the role of each participant in that economy, including those typically left on the margins. Their works have brought these questions into the rarified atmosphere of the high-art world and its holy inner sanctum, the gallery. Historically, Joseph Beuys's concept of social sculpture was an example of the broadened definition of art that encompasses—among other things—various social activities, exchanges, and relationships. This "new" type of art looks at social reality as a dynamic flux, a moving network of rules/morals and social groupings/alliances that changes and responds to itself. The art in question draws viewers into a focused space to experience this reality, to question/change it, and to integrate it into their understanding of self-in-context to the larger social reality.

This investigation will outline the history and context of contemporary artworks that employ methods of gifting and exchange. These methods include drawing attention to facts of giving, establishing obligations of implicit reciprocity, using rituals (implicating religion) that developmentally precede disinterested monetary exchange, and shifting the relationships/assigned roles of participants in these exchanges. To better understand the rich cultural context for such works, it is useful draw a theoretical (if not historical) line of development for such systems of exchange—and thus the complex morals and customs that are attached. These are what shape our individual and collective prejudices and responses to giving, receiving, buying, and selling.

On its surface the act of giving an object or performing a service for another without a negotiated price seems like an act of generosity and easily becomes associated with altruism and related moral principles of charity. However, the complex network of morals, motivations, and functions underlying such deceptively simple acts beg a look into the history of non-monetary systems of exchange in order to better understand their role in art practices employing such "generous" exchanges as the focus of the work.

Perhaps the most fundamental (or "primitive") motive for exchanging gifts and hospitality is to integrate and bind together the giver and the recipient and by extension those associated with them (e.g., members of different families, clans, or communities).[1] This takes place through the establishment of an obligatory bond wherein reciprocity is implicit. This bond of obligatory reciprocity seems most evident in cultures where monetary exchange is either absent or very rudimentary. These cultures exhibit less evident yet elemental systems of exchange transactions that preceded the forms of contract, sale, and money essential to Western economy—for example, some Polynesian cultures, and the Tlingit and Haida of the American Northwest. In such societies, social commerce is carried out through a system of total services: elaborate acts of politeness and community building such as banquets, festivals (or markets), and so forth, wherein economic transactions are only one feature of a broader social contract of obligatorily reciprocated goods and favors between different clans, villages, or similar social groups. These reciprocated services and exchanges appear to be voluntary, but are obligatory on pain of social expulsion, ostracism, or warfare. In many of these societies there is a discrepancy between the common belief that groups or tribes have the right to refuse the tool services and goods (which reinforces the appearance of generosity) and the more likely reality that they have neither the right to nor an interest in refusing.[2] For not only is there an obligation to reciprocate, but also an obligation to give and receive—that is, to participate in the gift-giving economy and enter into bonds with other groups, to foster friendly feelings between potentially rival groups. The importance of this mutual relationship of giving and receiving has left clear traces in the Indo-European vocabulary. As Calvert Watkins notes, "The [Indo-European] root 'do' of Latin 'donare' means 'to give' in most dialects, but in Hittite means 'to take.' The root 'nem' is 'to distribute' in Greek (nemesis), but in German it means 'to take' and the cognate of English 'give' (ghabh) has the meaning 'to take' in Irish." Additionally, "several roots specify the notion of 'bond': bhendh-, ned-, and leig-, all of which have derivatives with technical legal meanings in various languages.[3]

Thus the "bond-forming" motive behind gift exchange and obligatory reciprocity could be otherwise expressed as the will toward peace "imposed, in wellorganized work (e.g., trading and banquets), alternately in common and individually, in wealth amassed and then redistributed, in the mutual respect and reciprocating generosity that is taught by education."[4] In fact it is the will to make peace between ambivalent, or at worst hostile, parties (see Kant's "perpetual peace" below) and to create society that is the motive behind the systems of exchange and obligation at the historical root of gift-giving economies.

Hierarchy of Exchanges

Many so-called archaic societies offer examples of clearly delineated hierarchies of exchange. This is no wonder, since they serve as the social glue between potentially warring groups and socioeconomic classes. For example, Melanesians make clear distinctions between *gimwali*, which is the trade for everyday useful items, in which hard bargaining is the norm, and *kula*—meaning "circle"—which is trade only between chiefs of different clans from the various islands. Kula refers to navigating the circles of islands and binding them together through trade. Kula maintains the appearance of disinterested reciprocal gift giving—even for things that are asked for. Kula exchange mandates that participants do not hoard the wealth but continually pass it on to trading partners at some future kula. Among the goods traded in kula are *vaygu'a*—especially valuable bracelets or necklaces imbued with virtues that cannot be acquired by owning one. This hierarchy of exchanges is nested: a more important trading forum, such as kula, enables a lower (or more pedestrian) one, such as gimwali, by creating a social space within which it may happen. A further example is the giving of pari—inducements or smaller gifts put on display before being given in order to induce the initial vaga gift that officially initiates the special kula trading relationship between chiefs and their respective clans. The motives for giving pari are competition, rivalry, ostentatiousness, the seeking after the grandiose, and the stimulation of interest. In a similar vein, Fijians give tambua, sperm whale's teeth, as inducements. To give them constitutes a request, and to accept them is to commit oneself. While tambua function similar to money, they are admired and polished, and thus imbued with inherent virtues.[5]

In these Polynesian cultures there is a tautological relationship between authority and wealth—property (particularly tonga, which are ritual gift items traded through the maternal side of the family) is a talisman conferring honor, prestige, and mana (authority). Trading partners are under absolute obligation to reciprocate these gifts under pain of losing that mana, that authority—the talisman and source of wealth that is authority itself.[6] A more elaborate, indulgent example of gift-giving to "buy" prestige and authority is the potlatch of the Tlingit and Haida of the American Northwest. However, in this system of reciprocal giftand banquet-giving between clans and tribes, honor, prestige, and thus power are won only by repaying the potlatch with inflated interest. These feasts are characterized by mad extravagance, ostentatious consumption, and destruction of precious objects. The whole system of exchange is based on a range of principles: from antagonism and rivalry to gaining prestige, honor, and authority. However, when this "generosity" is carried out in the spirit of immediate gain, it becomes the object of marked scorn. These political impulses persist in contemporary Western culture in the form of irrational spending, such as the non-utilitarian buying of items of pleasure and luxury, further evoking this concept of buying authority and prestige. Yet, there is also a sense of aesthetic emotion informing these acts of potlatch and ever-escalating gifting—the implication of pleasure (purely sumptuary, deliberate spending for its own sake) as motive.

Yet another example of the hierarchical nature of gift giving is the practice of giving gifts to gods—and receiving gifts from gods. Many of the world's religious traditions have elevated the practices of sacrifice and charity to the ultimate reciprocal exchange: buying spiritual transcendence. However, there are also the more banal purposes—success in the hunt, for example, or a good crop. In many religions, this transaction between humans and gods has been transformed into one between the rich and the poor (and children). Sadaka in Islam and zedaga in Judaism (originally, "justice") champion the idea that God is appeased by giving superabundant wealth to the poor instead of sacrificing it.[7]

Almsgiving subsequently developed into a part of the preparation for incorporation into a higher spiritual level. Brahminism has most efficiently professionalized this institution: The Brahmin's role is to receive the riches of the rich, in exchange for rites and prayers. Brahminism also lends a spiritual interpretation to the notions of the obligation to "pass along the wealth": in this world and in the next, what is given away is acquired once more. In fact, "to not share food is to destroy/poison its essence,"[8] notion extended to our interpretation of charity and hospitality. Alternatively, many traditions offer gods who become incarnate and offer their bodies "as the gift that establishes the bond between man and the spiritual state to which the god pretends."[9] Examples are Jesus Christ and the Buddha (as the Wise Hare in the Jataka collection). Thus the Christian God bought the spiritual salvation of all believers and followers of his religion with the sacrifice of his son, or rather of he himself incarnate.

Even in so-called primitive or archaic societies, the exchange of gifts and favors form merely a part of the complex network of total services exchanged between social groups in an effort to establish important political and economic bonds within many institutional contexts. Moreover, these systems of exchange are nested within one another, creating social (and physical) spaces for their existence (potlatches, Indo-European festivals and fairs, and the gimwali and kula of Melanesia). The structural nature of these phenomena can be seen in the various religious, economic, political, and legal institutions that persist today.

The Problematic Movement towards "Disinterested Exchange"

The movement towards market economy and monetary exchange for goods and services required a cooling down of the exchange itself—that is, that the burden of the system of obligations and reciprocities be lifted from the act of giving and receiving and restricted to remuneration. The object had to be disengaged and disassociated from the person selling it. This was initially effected through elaborate rituals—and eventually through contracts—performed to dissolve the moral bond between the seller and buyer.

To facilitate this, Roman law formally recognized the distinction between the incorporeal web of social relationships inherent in the concept of ownership and the thing or object being "owned." Mancipium or mancipation was a formal public ceremony by which the incorporeal legal title of the thing being sold was symbolically passed to the new owner.[10] Under this law of buying and selling—mancipatio (and later emptio venditio—the first possessor, the tradens, displays his property, solemnly detaches himself from it, hands it over, and thus "buys" the accipiens. He who receives the thing takes it in his hand (manus) and not only acknowledges it as accepted, but acknowledges that he himself is "sold" until payment has been made.[11] Even under this monetary system of commerce, the power of the obligatory reciprocal bond between giver and receiver is still implicated through the symmetrically corresponding acts of taking possession of things and persons. A similar example is the giving of the Wadium, a pledge in ancient Germanic law, which is a personal item of little value that will be returned when payment is made. It is a challenge, a wager, thrown down at the feet of the creditor.[12] It is a contract (like the roman *nexum*) symbolized by the small pledge. Implicit in this challenge is the mistrust of exchanging things or services with a stranger (*hostis*)—of potentially risking entering into an obligatory reciprocity. It is perhaps this risky business that accounts for the ironic difference in the meanings of the word "gift" in German and English (*Gift* being German for "poison").

In later Roman law came the distinction between *res* and *personae*—things and people belonging to a household (*familia*). Modern society understands this division as the distinction between "real" and "personal" law (laws dealing with property vs. laws dealing with persons). It was through this distinction that the exchange of things became disengaged from the exchange of persons (such as slaves, or children, or daughters in marriage), and therefore from the sphere of "total services" or "total social obligations." Even linguistically, that this "law of the household"—in Greek *oikonomia*—bears such a significant importance to the formation of economy should be readily apparent. By legally separating persons and things into separately exchangeable categories—and reinforcing this through distinct rituals—exchange shed the emotional and spiritual content, and thereby severed that type of obligation. Thus the origins of economic—or exchange—value, and of market activities in general, lie in the rituals and ceremonies employed to sever the obligatory bonds of the gift economy (a veritable mythopoetic gold mine for future exchange-based art).

In attempting to understand the cultural context for exchange-based art, it is important to look also at the historical and theoretical lines of resistance to disinterested, economic exchange and its impact upon the societal distribution of wealth and ownership of land. For as long as there has been power and wealth concentrated in the hands of one or few, there have arguably always been struggles to depose that power and reclaim that wealth.[13] It is useful to start with the peasant rebellions of Europe of the 1500s and 1600s as a backdrop. The most widespread and well organized was the German peasant rebellion of 1524–25. In what was not simply a local uprising, thousands of peasants across northern and central Europe took up arms to demand an end to the increasingly intolerable and impossible conditions imposed by the landed aristocracy. Members of the rebellion drafted a pamphlet of twelve articles—known as the Memmingen Articles—which was widely distributed. Among other things, it called for an end to serfdom (that peasants and wage laborers were to be considered as free individuals and not property of the landed nobility); an end to the usurpation of "commons" and "wastelands," lands traditionally free to all but progressively taken over by lords for their private use as fishing and hunting preserves; and free access to firewood as needed and the return of expropriated common fields. In other words, the peasants were rebelling against the increasingly excessive exploitation of their labor and the assertion of property rights (often ill-gotten) over human rights on the part of the aristocracy[14]—or the widening material gap between artificially created social castes.

These movements—the Rebellion of 1524–25; the Anabaptists of Muenster, Germany (1534); and the Diggers of England (1649), among others—to varying degrees called for a return to principles of equitable exchange, redistribution of surplus wealth, and to some degree a reversion to pre-contract, pre-monetary economies. The most extreme example was the Anabaptists, a religious sect of mainly Dutch immigrants who took over the town of Muenster in 1534 for more than a year until they were bloodily suppressed by the bishop and his armies. Under Anabaptist rule, all property (including women) was considered to be held by the whole community. All written records of contracts, titles, and debts were ritually burned in an attempt to revert to a state of pure communalism (arguably the historical precedent for modem day anarchists who hack into bank and government computer servers to erase similar records). At the time, these rebellions were justified by, and steeped in, religious principles[15] dating back, at least, to the Catharists of the early eleventh century, and possibly as far back as Manichaeism of the third century CE. These religions were based on the belief in a fundamentally dualistic world, of an evil god (who created the material world) and a good god (who created the purely spiritual world); thus the belief that the accumulation of wealth only perpetuates the valuation of the material world over the spiritual. Catharism in particular evolved in response to the ever-expanding wealth and power of the Church (i.e., the Holy Roman Empire) of the Middle Ages.

No wonder, after centuries of such cyclical social upheavals, that Immanuel Kant at the end of the eighteenth century would propose that conditions for "perpetual peace" would depend upon the "cosmopolitan right" of all peoples, and that cosmopolitan right would depend upon "universal hospitality." For

Kant, "Hospitality [meant] the right of a stranger not to be treated with hostility when he arrives on someone else's territory."[16] Kant established this claim on the assumption that "all men are entitled to present themselves in the society of others by virtue of their right to communal possession of the earth's surface . . . [and that] no one originally has any greater right than anyone else to occupy any particular portion of the earth."[17] Later, at the turn of the twentieth century, Peter Kropotkin sought to find examples in nature of communal right and cooperation, of these relationships giving rise to competitive advantage to the species and subgroups using them. "Mutual aid" then becomes the modus operandi of social groups seeking to thrive and prosper through the exchange of total services, and mutual aid is reinforced through the rituals of obligatory reciprocal exchange.

In contemporary Western society this tension between the moral obligations of gift-giving and the disinterested exchange of the market economy continues to inform many of our beliefs and rituals. For example, the common belief that unreciprocated gifts make the recipient inferior; the tendency to strive to do away with the unconscious and injurious patronage of the rich almsgiver; the belief that invitations and courtesies must be returned; and the need to "up the ante," to not "lag behind" in gift giving.

The Power of the Object over the Person

For most of art history, the tangible, physical object has been the locus of the work of art. It still forms an ineluctable association in the minds of viewers. However, in exchange-based art, the object holds a special paradoxical power—the artwork is activated only by giving the art object away; and this dissipation of that fetishized object scrutinizes the bond between giver and receiver (which the very act of giving and receiving creates): a complex of moral and legal obligations to reciprocate, to further develop the social bond formed, as well as to respect the power relationship implied in the exchange. In Maori culture, this concept has been elaborately codified in the concept of *hau*. Hau is the spirit of any tonga, any object that can be called a "possession—everything that makes one rich, powerful, influential, and everything that can be exchanged, and used as an object for compensating others."[18] When such a possession is given, it exerts not only a legal and moral hold over the receiver, but also a religious and magical one. It exerts a spiritual, magnetic tug on the receiver towards its point of origin, its original possessor, its birthplace, its native soil. This inherent liveliness, this hau, is what imposes obligation, for to fail in reciprocating can bring harm to the new possessor. In Maori law, there is a tie occurring through things exchanged—it is one between souls, since the thing itself possesses a soul.[19] There is thus an intermingling of souls and things (gifts given). Lives are mingled together through gift exchanges and the ritual meanings attached—each emerges from its own sphere and mixes together. This powerful bond is also apparent in the Chinese tradition of the life-long right of the owner, who has sold an item, "to weep for his property."[20]

In modern economy, laborers have typically given the products of their efforts to factory owners for a one-time wage, thus forfeiting claim to future profits made on that object's resale. The object continues to generate increasingly larger profits at each new point of exchange, usually culminating in the end consumer's purchase. Yet, in French law, artists have capitalized upon the fetishistic power of the art object by winning the "right of succession" over the series of additional gains made during the successive sales of their works.[21] The power of the created object is acknowledged in other arenas through the legal and commercial protections for intellectual property rights (e.g., copyrights, patents, etc.).

This vestigial concept of the object's spiritual power informs one of the central challenges of exchange-based art, particularly in the work of Felix Gonzalez-Torres. It is this preoccupation, this fetish, with the art object that is used against itself and used to call into question the attitudes and assumptions about those fundamental social relationships created through reciprocal (or unreciprocated) exchange. In Torres's untitled "passports"—the stacks of posters to be perpetually given away and replenished—and his similar untitled "candy piles," obligation is reimposed upon the recipient (or buyer/collector) of the art piece (despite the assumed washing away of obligation effected by the disinterested exchange of money). However, the buyer's obligation is not to Torres directly, but to the public, the visitor, the stranger (more on this later). The buyer's obligation is to give the piece away in perpetuity, to employ the fetishistic power of the art object against itself in order to dissipate itself. (If the buyer fails to do this, one coud legitimately ask whether she or he continues to truly own the piece.) Perhaps this is one example of transcendence in art. The concrete, the material is turned into a flow, and in the act, expresses the will towards the social bond that must prefigure any "perpetual peace."

> We do not know what hospitality is.
>
> —Immanuel Kant

The "troubled and troubling" origins of the word hospitality provide fertile ground for unpacking the structural nature of reciprocal exchange, which cuts across entire social systems—various institutions of religion, economy, politics, law, and so forth. It is also the most apt lens for viewing those works that invoke the spirit of hospitality or hosting, such as the gallery interventions of Felix Gonzalez-Torres or Rirkrit Tiravanija.

The Indo-European root word *ghosti*—the root for "stranger," "guest," or "host" in various subsequent archaic languages—means "someone with whom one has reciprocal duties of hospitality." Yet the stranger, in an uncertain and warring tribal society, may well be hostile: the Latin *hostis* (a derivative of ghosti) means alternatively"stranger" or "enemy" and forms the root of "hostility."[22] Already in the notion of hospitality (not only a relationship, but also a social space) is embedded the ambiguity, the potential for conflict, and the wariness of engaging in the kind of reciprocal exchange discussed above.

This linguistically prefigured conflict between guest and host must be simultaneously considered with the problematic of the space of hospitality—the question of where the hospitality takes place. By definition, the host is the one who can offer hospitality, a generous space, while the guest, or the strange, is the one who can receive it. Yet the reciprocal nature, the gift between equals necessary for true generosity, is inherently absent: The host is the master of the house—as suggested in the root compound *ghos-pot* (a derivative of the root word *ghosti*), or "guest-master"—and a problematic power dynamic is inherently set up. There can be no unconditional welcome, because the host, the master of the household, sets the rules of household (i.e., the physical structure and persons residing in it, the *familia* in Latin or *oikos* in Greek) and is by extension master of the guest (because now the recipient of hospitality is a resident, and thus, property of the familia or oikos). This is the inherent paradox of hospitality: "It does not seem to me that I am able to open up or offer hospitality . . . without reaffirming: this is mine, I am at home, you are welcome in my home . . . on condition that you observe the rules of hospitality by respecting the being-at-home of my home."[23] Hospitality is therefore self-referential.[24] There is no true room for the other, the stranger in an ontological sense, but only for a compliant "guest," agreeing to the master's conditions. Thus the true hospitality of "a gift between equals" is forever waiting at the threshold, lingering at the door. (If there is a door that can be closed, then there is no longer hospitality.) The door distinguishes the hospitality of invitation and the hospitality of visitation. In visitation there is no "door"; anyone can come at any time and can come in without needing a key for the door: "The visitor is not necessarily an invited guest [but] someone who could come at any moment, without any horizon of expectation."[25] This aporetic paralysis on the threshold is what must be overcome for true hospitality, for hospitality in spite of itself.

In Rikrit Tiravanija's curry cooking project, *Untitled (Beauty)*, the artist, and by extension the gallery, becomes the host through cooking and serving a free Thai curry meal to visitors during gallery hours. There is yet another layer of relationships called into question, and called into being. By utilizing the gift exchange as the aesthetic device of the work, the "hospitality" of such gallery interventions evokes the obligatory reciprocal relationship and poses the questions—already engendered by the problematic root *ghosti*—who is the guest here? Who is the host? Who is the hostile stranger? Literally, the host is made the host by being welcomed by the guest—the uninvited gallery visitor creates the situation of hospitality—is its precondition. The host (as a role) is therefore the hostage of the guest—is forced to stay in order to maintain her or his host-ness.[26]

As one of the earlier successful practitioners of "generous" gallery interventions, Felix Gonzalez-Torres, used gifts such as a pile of free wrapped chocolates or stacks of free posters to shift the relationship of the "visitor" (viewer who is not buying) and "client" (i.e., buyer/collector) to the artist, and by extension the gallery. The mere "visitor"—who is generally seen as useless in the market driven structure of the gallery—is elevated to the status of guest, valued because her or his participation in the piece is essential to complete it, to activate it. This new relationship inherently questions the market determined role of the art piece by equalizing the roles of visitor and client in the success of the piece, its "reception." Furthermore, this shift in the locus of the art work reinforces the notion of art as a cognitive acting out—that is the viewer acts her/himself out and into the work which is a space (at this point, a social sculpture, specifically, an exchange).

A further challenge to the market value of the art piece can be found in Ben Kinmont's work. Besides challenging market value by giving away his paintings in his dealer's gallery in his work: *For You For Me For Painting*, Kinmont also poses "use-value" against "exchange-value" in works such as *Forse (Perhaps)* or *Ich werde Ihr schmutziges Geschirr waschen (I'll Wash Your Dirty Dishes)*. In these pieces, Kinmont agreed to do housework or wash dirty dishes of strangers he met on the street in exchange for the stranger agreeing to be a part of his social sculpture (or "third sculpture," as Kinmont terms it). To the stranger, having someone else do her or his housework is more valuable than the expense of being part of an artwork (e.g., the risk of inviting a potential "weirdo" into one's home, or enduring a conversa-tion about art); to Kinmont, however, creating a "third sculpture" is a bargain at the mere expense of doing an hour or two of housework. By playing off opposing concepts of worth, Kinmont creates an exchange that conceivably invokes the win-win fantasies of postmodern negotiating strategy, and more importantly, opens the door to unconditioned hospitality: equals meeting and exchanging.

There is a poignancy in mining the past for such interpersonally bonding customs that cut against the grain of totally commercialized contemporary reality yet function in the center of the paradox of hospitality—e.g., the impossibility of unconditional welcome, of hospitality, in the power-related and market-driven space of the gallery—particularly where the visitor is worthless, the patron catered to. This paradox forms the context for the space of generosity (hospitality): conditioned hospitality versus unconditional hospitality; the power of the master over the guest versus the hosting space without a threshold, always inviting the unexpected visitor. And despite this paradox, many individuals and institutions strive to establish the social space for such bond-forming exchange, to forge community. While the perpetually inviting space may be as utopian (and unrealistic) as Kant's perpetual peace, it is refreshing—if not heartening—to see artworks that reach a hand across the hostile void to the stranger, cognoscente and philistine alike, even if only temporarily.

Notes

1. Sometimes this integration can even be intrapersonal, to integrate aspects of the psyche (e.g., when different characters in a dream exchange gifts). See Lewis Hyde, *The Gift: Imagination and the Erotic Life of Property* (London: Vintage, 1999), 58.

2. Marcel Mauss, The Gift: The Form and Reason for Exchange in Archaic Societies (New York: W. W. Norton, 1990), 65.

3. Calvert Watkins, "Indo-European and the Indo-Europeans," *The American Heritage Dictionary*, 4th ed. (Boston: Houghton-Mifflin Company, 2000), 2013.

4. Mauss, 83.

5. Mauss, 12–46.

6. Mauss, 8.

7. Mauss, 18.

8. Hyde, 58.

9. Hyde, 58.

10. "Ownership—Duality of Title and Possession," www.snowcrest.net/siskfarm/Dualtitp.html.

11. Mauss, 52.

12. Mauss, 62.

13. The late medieval world in particular was characterized by a whole series of peasant rebelions: in Italy (1304–7), Flanders (1323—28), France (1356), England (1381), Northern Spain (1437), Hungary (1514), and Bohemia (1419–34). Germany itself had undergone earlier insurrections in 1476, in the 1490s, in 1502, in 1513, in 1514, and in 1517.

14. Another demand was the basing of legal judgments—that is, punishments—on customary law rather than on arbitrary new laws (a protest against the long-developing process of judicial centralization, which was overriding local and traditional feudal law and custom and replacing them with an overarching higher law of the land administered by representatives of the territorial princes).

15. Most of the religious radicals at the time, most notably Thomas Muenzer, supported claims to redistribution of wealth on the following passage in Acts:

> All the believers were one in heart and mind. No one claimed that any of his possessions was his own, but they shared everything they had. With great power the apostles continued to testify to the resurrection of the Lord Jesus, and much grace was upon them all. There were no needy persons among them. For from time to time those who owned lands or houses sold them, brought the money from the sales and put it at the apostles' feet, and it was distributed to anyone as he had need. (Acts 4:32–34)

16. Immanuel Kant, "Third Definitive Article of a Perpetual Peace," in *Kant's Political Writings*, ed. Hans Reiss (Cambridge: Cambridge University Press, 1970), 21.

17. Ibid.

18. Mauss, 10.

19. Mauss, 12.

20. Mauss, 63.

21. Mauss, 67.

22. Julius Pokorny, *Indo-European Etymological Dictionary* (Bern: Francke, 1959), 453.

23. Jacques Derrida, "Hostipitality" *Angelaki: Journal of the Theoretical Humanities* 5.3 (December 2000), 14.

24. See Emile Benveniste *Indo-European Language and Society*, trans. Elizabeth Palmer (London: Faber, 1973), chapter 7 of book 1.

25. Derrida, 17.

26. See Derrida's discussion of Pierre Klossowski's "The Laws of Hospitality," p. 9.

LUNCH HOUR

ART, COMMUNITY, ADMINISTERED SPACE, AND UNPRODUCTIVE ACTIVITY

Kate Fowle and Lars Bang Larsen

The visual arts have a long-standing and complicated relationship to generosity—just consider examples of classic philanthropy to public schemes for the promotion of art, or the recent generation of contemporary artists who produce gifts as a cultural statement.

Theoretically the two are entwined within a system rooted in symbolic values as opposed to market worth. An intricate economy has been established by which to make things happen that cannot flourish, or perhaps even exist, within the basic "supply and demand" principles of commerce.

Art production and acts of generosity are fundamentally generative, but nonlinear, expenditures of time and resources. In this way they contradict the accepted functions of production and utility that are associated with meeting society's basic needs, or the process of its expansion. Each could therefore be seen as potential processes of liberation from the inevitable progress of production and, consequently, as associated with an element of speculation or risk. Having undetermined, or at least nonquantifiable, attributes that bear no relation to the functional development of a community, they create a space in which "irrational" behavior is possible. Arguably, it is around this kind of expenditure or value system that culture is defined, arising out of the surplus or excess generated by a society.

Theorists such as Marcel Mauss, Georges Bataille, and Jean Baudrillard[1] have contributed to the argument that communities are actually organized around excess, as opposed to scarcity. In different ways, each suggests that acts of giving, sacrifice, waste, and ritualistic destruction have undermined both Marxist and capitalist structures of production, redefining the basis on which societies develop.

In *The Accursed Share*, Georges Bataille wrote: "On the whole a society always produces more than is necessary for its survival; it has a surplus at its disposal. It is precisely the use it makes of this surplus that determines it: The surplus is the cause of agitation, of the structural changes and of the entire history of society."[2]

In this context, surplus has a stable, though unusual, symbolic value. It is the physical or mental space in which power shifts occur, the vent for transgression, or on another level it could be described as having a fundamental purpose in reasserting community ideals. To "waste" significantly, as in the pagan-influenced festival or a ritualistic slaughtering of a sheep, can be seen as a metaphysical and ideological process of collective renewal and stimulation.

But, while surplus remains a fact of society, its definition and use have changed. This in turn has affected the way that art production and acts of generosity are related.

To cite Bataille again, as the so-called embarrassment of riches has developed, what he calls "unproductive activity" has gone underground. In his essay "The Notion of Expenditure," he claims that: "Everything that was generous, orgiastic, and excessive has disappeared; the themes of rivalry upon which individual activity still depends develop in obscurity, and are as shameful as belching."[3]

What is accepted as unproductive expenditure, or purely social activity, has shifted. Bataille relates this to the rise of Christianity and, later, to the development of the bourgeoisie, which he suggests is responsible for coveting wealth and promoting the necessity of functional expenditure:

> The decline of paganism led to a decline of the games and cults for which wealthy Romans were obliged to pay; thus it has been said that Christianity individualized property, giving its possessor total control over his products and abrogating his social function. It abrogated at least the obligation of this expenditure, for Christianity replaced pagan expenditure prescribed by custom with voluntary alms, either in the form of distributions from the rich to the poor, or (and above all) in the form of extremely significant contributions to the churches and later to monasteries. And these churches and monasteries precisely assumed, in the Middle Ages, the major part of the spectacular function.[4]

In effect, surplus and all its possible manifestations were hereby privatized. Surplus became productive: a vehicle through which to achieve ostensibly materialist desires. And with this came the reappraisal of how culture is generated, defined, and recorded.

Evidence suggests that in western art history, prior to the advent of modernism, the visual arts directly and unambiguously served the powers that be, whether church, state, or king. And in this context, art was enlisted to endow glory and give an impression of generosity in hierarchical terms. The ruling classes utilized the arts to maintain their hegemony, and as a result there was a mutual progression towards a more benign tone. Following this, it is easy to see how the notion of generosity became associated with colonial power or the privilege of nobility, and how spectacles became ways to control rather than inspire community.

The avant-garde artist's struggle against art's collusion with power was expressed by Hugo Ball in one of his Dadaist manifestos: "[The Dadaist] knows that life is a game of oppositions and that his future like no other time is prepared to annihilate all generosity." The generosity that Ball set out to vanquish was an aspect of what he saw as the pathology of bourgeois hypocrisy, and Dada was the weapon with which to execute "false morality and perfection." To this end Ball recommended "any form of cahoots . . . any hide-and-seek that may dupe."[5]

But this approach becomes complicated in late-capitalist society, as it has become almost impossible to distinguish between symbolic and economic value, intertwined as they are in an often-inscrutable manner, particularly with the advent of the service industry. Market forces make full use of the gift economy and vice versa, and the strategies that Ball proposed to reassert life as "a game of oppositions" are now part of mainstream culture. The escalating speed and level of consumption renders almost every activity and terrain productive in economic terms—communication is big business and even virtual space can now be owned.

Within this, the issue perhaps is still art's collusion with power and the use (or misuse) of generosity, as the Danish artist Henrik Plenge Jakobsen suggested in commenting on the structural similarities between the modes of reception and production in contemporary art and the new economy:

> Giving it all away for free, such as when Rirkrit Tiravanija hands out soup to the audience, is another important new economy principle. It is the same generosity that the company Netscape was into when they launched their browser Netscape 1 for the Internet, and made the Internet a platform for free exchange. Investors from the "market economy" saw the interest in passing on services and products for free. As a consequence both Rirkrit Tiravanija and Netscape have become rather wealthy, and thus rewarded for their generosity.[6]

Jakobsen's insights into the mechanics of generosity within the new economic metabolism identify another shift in both the rhetoric and the context for the act. Today everyone is affected by the possibility of having a potentially double-edged presence, or impact, through globally mediated productions. It is almost as if "Greed is good," the credo of the Reagan-era as embodied by financial raider Gordon Gecko in the 1987 film *Wall Street,* has merged with happy philanthropy. While it is doubtful that Tiravanija's private wealth can measure itself against Netscape's turnover, the comparison of their activities starts to describe ways that current art strategies intersect those of business through the exploration of the potential for communication and social exchange.

The curator and theorist Nicolas Bourriaud appears to have taken this intersection as a starting point when he outlined a tendency in contemporary art that he chooses to call "relational aesthetics," which is concerned with creating "new social models" in the public sphere. He suggests that relational artists strike back "within gaps of capitalism," making a case that, in this context, artists like Tiravanija are transgressing the realm of property with their social projects. The gallery is just one of many sites proposed by relational artists as new public arenas that will stimulate "a culture of activity to counteract market-induced passivity." For Bourriaud, the gallery space is not merely a symbol or metaphor for the public realm, but an actualized space accessible to the public body.[7]

While this may be conceptually valid, the reality is that galleries remain owned and occupied sites that are largely uninteresting and too restrictive for the generic public body to be "actively unproductive" within. In the same way, distributing soup is only something "new" in the context of the regulated spaces and discourses of the art institution—which amounts to saying that is only a "new social model" for the art audience and the art world.

One might well ask what has caused contemporary practitioners to turn towards generosity as a goal in itself, when the early twentieth-century avant-garde dismissed it. While the avant-garde once thrived on rebellious discomfort, relational artists today are interested in making social/artistic agents present themselves. When did contemporary art and subversion become sincere and opt for the stability of meaning? Why this need to redeem social practice and generate conduits through which it can be given back to itself? The discussion of these complex questions is beyond the scope of this essay, although noting the general shift in artistic attitudes is significant in this context.

In Bourriaud's relational aesthetics, the nature and sophistication of contemporary society have been misconstrued. There is not necessarily anything to stop the "gaps in capitalism" from being as smoothed over and strategically organized as the spaces they are spanning: the guise of generosity is just one of the tools that is used in this operation. While artistic products cannot be classed as mainstream consumer goods (and are often more intellectually demanding and inspiring), for this reason alone they are hardly exempt from being perceived as part of the stuff that capitalism tries to palm off on us.

If we start to isolate generosity, removing it from the complex systems and economies in which it is entangled, we invariably end up with its colloquial definition as something unequivocally beneficial. On the other hand, the modernist avant-garde struggle with generosity has a tragic dimension, as in Ball's battle against bourgeois repression. The same is true of Bataille, for whom, as Henri Léfèbvre wrote, "the entirety of space—mental, physical and social—is a reality of sacrifice, violence and explosion."[8]

Currently, this tragic dimension relies on dramatic clashes between the symbolic and the economic or political realms, something that does not gel with the way that contemporary society has blurred symbolic and economic values. If one wants to make sense of the concept of generosity today—and particularly its relationship to art—then some portion of the tragic needs to be retained, simply because true generosity resides in giving away something you care about and could have used.

The constituency to which you give is always in the process of evolving, precisely because it needs your donation to make the future better. This "futurist" dimension renders the idea of generosity inherently unstable: it cannot—or should not—have any representational value, because it is uncertain what the generous act will signify over time, as it is utilized by those who have received it.

So, it is a common delusion of the new economy that we, merely because the production and exchange of goods now takes the form of the creation of relationships and acts of communication, are inhabiting a transparent socioeconomic terrain. And it is not just within art practice that this misconception is increasingly evident. It also has consequences for the way the social activity of the broader community is perceived and organized in public space.

One example is the mandatory implementation of public open space in downtown San Francisco, which started in 1986 and continues to this day. Regarded internationally as a progressive government policy, and instigated in the face of public resistance, the scheme has given rise to what could be seen as institutionalized generosity on an unprecedented scale.

For over two decades, environmentalists, neighborhood activist groups, and many individuals fought to control the corporate takeover of the public realm, motivated by growing concerns for the way that high-rise developments were transforming the cityscape and creating a significant reduction of space and potential for community development. As Robert Campbell stated at the time in the *Boston Globe*, "The San Francisco anti–high rise movement started as a radical fringe and grew into a mainstream."[9] The story began with the "freeway revolt" in the late 1960s, when public protests successfully prevented a major road from carving up Golden Gate Park and the waterfront area. Attention then turned to other big construction projects, but many of the ad-hoc campaigns were unsuccessful in slowing developments. Gradually activists became more strategic in adopting political tools and tactics. But the stakes were raised to an all-time high when a sympathetic mayor was assassinated and developers' million-dollar countercampaigns repeatedly thwarted local ballot initiatives.

Despite the protests, businesses continued to work closely with the council to make San Francisco the steel-clad commercial hub for the Pacific Rim. In true Gold Rush spirit, office space doubled between 1965 and 1981, reaching a total of 55 million square feet in a city that is only seven square miles in total. It amounts to a battle over the definition of "progress"—of quality versus quantity and how each is defined in terms of economic worth.

When the activists finally won through, it was by establishing the "Downtown Plan" as a voter-initiative. This was dubbed as "the nation's largest growth cap" by businesses and included the first annual limit on high-rise development in the United States, the "public open space requirement" and laws preserving sunlight in the downtown area of the city.

The legislation for the open space requirement dictates that developers of new buildings, or extensions of greater than 20 percent to existing office buildings, provide one square foot of publicly accessible open space per 50 gross square feet of the building. This notion of inserting public areas within the corporate realm is a conceptually charged gesture that allows for the inherent chaos of a city to seep into the ordered and "owned" confines of business. In reality however, its potential is restricted because it is beset with bureaucratic rules that have to be adhered to by the architect.

The Planning Code contains an eleven-point directive on what constitutes acceptable open space, including size requirements, access, landscaping, service, and sunlight provisions; and wind limitations. It also stipulates that open spaces be maintained at no public expense for the lifetime of the building, culminating in a clause about placing an "informational plaque" in public sight. This ensures that the donor's act remains visible, and that the public who receive the gift, or have access to what could be seen as examples of Bourriaud's gaps in capitalism, are fully aware of its parameters.

Across the downtown area open spaces take on the guise of rooftop terraces, sculpture courts, foyers, and plazas. Together they reveal that when the act of giving is not only enforced but also completely rationalized, the result is nothing more than a representation of the public sphere. As a result many of the sites remain devoid of people. If they are used at all it is by the constituency inhabiting the building as opposed to the public at large, and for good reason.

At the CNET building, completed in May 2001, the plaque recites the requisite information like a grumpy teenager: "The plaza and inside seating area of this building is provided and maintained for the enjoyment of the public. The interior seating area is open to the public Monday–Friday 8 am–6 pm." Directly under this is another notice. "Warning. This building utilizes video surveillance. Any person entering the premises is subject to being monitored and recorded." On walking into the building, the first person you see is a guard at the desk, directly behind the bland, matching seating and sculpture and potted-plants that define the public arena. For about an hour at lunchtime employees come and go, temporarily littering the tables with wrappers and drink cans, before deserting the area again. A year after the space has been made available there are still no signs of wear, or the tell-tale marks that commonly indicate some sense of repeated use and identity.

Situated as a kind of gateway between street and business, the open space is pristinely maintained to the point that it can never be more than an up-market waiting room. It is reduced to a brand in relation to the original aims of the protests that were instigated to retain a sense of community in the city. The Planning Code, defining space as a tangible product rather than a process (just as arts funding bodies define social practice) has effectively restricted any potential for the user to significantly contribute to the outcome. While the plaque is the mask of generosity that hides the twisted arm of the developer, the use of the seating for lunch is a deceptive signal that the receiver has accepted the terms of the gift.

One could imagine Howard, the main protagonist of Nicholson Baker's novel *Mezzanine*, having his lunch here. He is an introspective young Californian office worker who has developed routines for even the smallest things in life:

> Ten minutes of the lunch hour remained. If I wasn't going to read, I felt that I should spend the time replacing my worn-out shoelaces with the ones I had just bought. But the sun was too warm for that: inclining my face toward it, I sat with my eyes closed, my arms outstretched on the bench, and my legs crossed at the ankles in front of me, drawing in my feet whenever I heard a person walking nearby, in case I was blocking the way. My right hand, in the shade, touched the cool dome of a neo-Victorian bolt; my left hand, in the sun, touched hot, smooth, green paint; a current of complete peaceful contentment began to flow from the shade hand to the sun hand, passing through my arms and shoulders and whorling up into my brain along the way. "Manifestly," I repeated, as if scolding myself, "no condition of life could be so well adapted for the practice of philosophy as this in which chance finds you today!" Chance found me that day having worked for a living all morning, broken a shoelace, chatted with Tina, urinated successfully in a corporate setting, washed my face, eaten half of a bag of popcorn, bought a new set of shoelaces, eaten a hot dog and a cookie with some milk; and chance found me now sitting in the sun on a green bench, with a paperback on my lap.[10]

The sunny stretch where we find Howard is the psycho-spatial equivalent to Prozac. In this obsessively mapped terrain, like the tightly administrated surplus of Planning Code spaces, nothing is supposed to happen, apart from perhaps pondering the philosophy of all the contortionist formats modern life makes us fit into. You draw in your feet whenever somebody is approaching.

Translated into art-world terms, this could describe the current, virtually total institutionalization of social practice, or the implementation of a kind of Planning Code for artists. A warped legacy of the so-called alternative strategies used by practitioners in the sixties and seventies, and the outcome of a renewed resistance to blatant capitalist economies of the eighties and nineties, many projects, "happenings," or events feed seamlessly into already established bureaucratic patterns and administrations.

If we are now in a situation where even the gaps in capitalism are smoothed over, there has to be another way to establish vents for transgression, no matter how small, and to engender outcomes that are unaccounted for. Perhaps the answers lie in encouraging those moments or activities whereby the mainstream economy "leaks."

The Copenhagen-based group N55 (Ingvil Aarbakke, Rikke Luther, Jon Sørvin and Cecilia Wendt) explores the concept of putting surplus back into the public domain with their ongoing project, *LAND*. Initiated in 2000, *LAND* is a global non-nation. It is comprised of odd pieces of donated territory in, among other places, an island off the Norwegian coast, northern Jutland in Denmark, and Santa Fe and Chicago in the United States. The principal idea of the project is to counteract the absurdity of land ownership. The legal rights to each piece are retained by the donor, who agrees to keep access and use completely unrestricted, at all times, as a politically motivated liberation of land. The only requirements are that people respect the ways in which others wish to use the space, and that any acts do not detract from the potential for others to add to what happens in the location.

Emphasizing a sort of utopian frontier spirit that opens up a struggle for territory, *LAND* is based on the idea of transforming what you might term "excremental" or wasted space into free space. But it carries with it the proviso that freedom needs a structure or a framework that encourages certain forms of behavior instead of—as when legislating—administrating behavior.

To date, strips of land varying from a hundred to a thousand square meters have been contributed by individuals and institutions. The project works through consensus and shared decision making between people who choose to participate, defying traditional strategies for resolution over how land is used. In the literal sense, N55 are not actually giving anything away; rather, they act more as a catalyst. The generosity resides in the participants' (and N55's) act of setting land free from the concepts and habits of ownership, turning it into a continuous dialogue that, in the process, is made a concrete reality, a cloud of conjecture and a small hemorrhage in society.

In N55's *LAND* project, the temporal aspect of generosity is clearly connected to the tragic space of the modernist avant-garde, in opposition to the Planning Code's defined and certified, static space. However, this land art project is an inversion of Dada's resistance to generosity, where it becomes an artistic agent both subversive and reconstructive, ostensibly taking place outside the physical and administrative framework of the art institution. *LAND* is one space, at once urban and rural, that awaits the agents of its future community to start putting it to use in the spirit it was given. One could object that N55 is merely replacing old habits with new, but in the space between these two positions room is being made in their projects for the formulation of new directions and universal fantasies.

However subversive, the ethical pathos of N55's *LAND* project hardly resolves the question of how to encourage something to happen in an unproductive way—sheer excess, a game of twister with ten thousand people, mass miming in the high street, anything! What kind of disruption to the status quo can be elicited in Howie's square as well as in N55's *LAND?*

The practice of the Austrian collective Gelatin (Wolfgang Gantner, Ali Janka, Florian Reither, and Tobias Urban) willfully defies any "meaningful" purpose or coy attempt at generous acts. In fact it would not be defined as generous in the contemporary usage of the word. But in the Bataillan sense it is all about the significant wasting of surplus, and the creation of a temporary community excess that has both feet firmly planted in unproductive expenditure.

In many of Gelatin's projects there is a fine line between the opposing responses they elicit—pleasure and pain, inspired dreaming and futility, like and loathing—a tension that is integral to the experimentation in their processes. This was taken to its extreme in *Schlund,* which they realized in Munich, Germany, for two days in March 2001. Here, Gelatin developed a transportation device, enlisting the help of thirty overweight people. Using a vertical scaffolding structure, they literally "lined" the inside with the volunteers, who stood on temporary platforms naked and greased up. Participants were invited to undress and enter at the top of the 35-foot shaft, sliding to the ground between the projecting bellies. Ali Janka likened the sensation to "travelling down a hot and steamy esophagus and through a whole digestive system."[11] This intimate journey took about three minutes to complete, but who knows how long it took for the memory of the experience to fade. Witnessing this project, even Bataille may have conceded that everything "generous, orgiastic, and excessive" has not completely disappeared.

When prompted, Gelatin admit that there are things they do that they cannot explain, and their practice willingly extends this predicament to their audience. Perhaps it is not that they cannot explain, but rather that they do not want their practice to represent anything other than, for example, an impromptu digestive system. To analyze or objectify the experiences is to quantify them in ways that head toward the productive, the economic, and the utilitarian. And their approach has a somewhat surprising currency within today's art field; Gelatin are enjoying success by creating projects full of open-ended meaning, which have avoided the trap of accountability, or mandatory generosity. In a small way, giving has been given back its freedom.

Notes

1. For key contributions, see Marcel Mauss, *The Gift: The Form and Reason for Exchange in Archaic Societies*, trans. W. D. Halls (New York: W. W. Norton, 1990);

Georges Bataille, *The Accursed Share* (New York: Urzone, 1988); Jean Baudrillard, *The Mirror of Production*, trans. Mark Poster (St. Louis: Telos Press, 1975).

2. Bataille, *The Accursed Share*, 106.

3. Georges Bataille, "The Functional Expenditure of the Wealthy Classes," in *The Notion of Expenditure*, reprinted in *Visions of Excess—Selected Writings 1927–1939*, ed. Allan Stoekl (Minneapolis: University of Minnesota Press, 1985), 124.

4. Ibid., 123.

5. Per Højholt, *Auricula* (Copenhagen: Gyldendal, 2001), 84.

6. Henrik Plenge Jakobsen, "Spectacle Economy," in *Henrik Plenge Jakobse* (Dresdner Bank AG/Kunst und Wissenschaft, 2001), 2.

7. Nicholas Bourriaud, lecture at the Royal Academy of Fine Arts, Copenhagen, 3 April 2002.

8. Henri Léfèbvre, *The Production of Space* (Oxford: Oxford, 1999), 20.

9. Robert Campbell, as quoted by Dean Macris and George Williams in *San Francisco's Downtown Plan: Landmark Guidelines Shape City's Growt* (San Francisco Planning and Urban Research Association, http://www.spur.org).

10. Nicholson Baker, *The Mezzanine* (London: Granta Books, 1998), 124–5.

11. As quoted by Dick Pursel in "Viennese Art Guys Lift Shame to New Heights," *About Gelatin* (http://listen.to/gelatin).

BLOWS AGAINST THE EMPIRE

Ted Purves

Welcome to the Machine

The Situationist strategy of *detournment* overlaid on the giving of unexpected and unsanctioned gifts creates a double transgression that rips through the fabric of what we have accepted to be a given, a tyrannical and pervasive market of the senses that gives nothing without taking something in return. A gift offered in the midst of the transgressive act not only destroys, it also creates. What it creates is the existence of something altogether different, a community and a bond that is not the bond of bondsman to master or of addict to dealer, but of the giver to the receiver, who then becomes kin and neighbor.

We live in a society more spectacular and pervasive than the Situationists ever thought possible. Acts of resistance to, and dissent against, the monocultural, spreading waistlines of corporate control and capital economies either resound flatly and are lost in the din of the 24-hour media, or they are simply taken on as a style alternative by marketing firms and sold back to the populace as alternative culture. In this time of shrinking public space and growing oversight, the question of how to fight back pales behind the even more modest question of how one, one individual, one voice, responds to the bombardment of press releases, spins, media blitzes, and shrieking advertisements. Or failing that, how is it possible to armor up or walk away?

I would suggest that strategies for responding, and perhaps even fighting back (at least by striking a glancing blow), have come to light in the last few decades in the form of certain contemporary artworks that by choice and definition unfold themselves within the public sphere, rather than on stages and in galleries. Some of the most intriguing and effective of these have combined a complex parentage, which begins on one side with Situationism, and continues through the various quasi-heretical art movements that have followed in its wake (including Fluxus and happenings, body-art-life experiments, living theaters, political protest, punk rock, and other obscure cultural moments). On the other side one finds strains of anthropology and social reform with an abiding interest in alternative economies, gift systems, and precapitalist societies.

This essay neither intends to prove something, nor attempts to establish the primacy or originality of certain artistic acts. Its wish is to tell the stories of certain individuals and their decisions, decisions that have several common reference points, but none more so than their allegiance to the idea that they were in some way a manifestation of artmaking, in its broadest and most contemporary sense. These stories of decisive acts will hopefully form a set of working models with which to highlight certain ideas. These ideas are manifest either in the structure of their conception, in the intent behind them, or are implied by their delivery. It is important to remember that these works are not examples of anything larger, there is no genre of *gift-detournment* performance art. But they could be thought of as signposts or survey markers that describe a territory that is coming to light in the unfolding of this moment and the last few decades.

In the spirit of generosity and brevity, I will list the main points of construction, the axiomatic beginnings that provide a foundation for understanding the works and the context of their specific heresies. They are:

1. The strategy of detournment as a method of social confrontation is successful primarily because it creates a rupture between the expected and the unexpected, even in terms of dissent. When the expected is hijacked, the spectator is forced to confront not just the subject of the dissent, but also the structure that supports the world and worldview that contains both the dissent and the status quo.

2. The nature of gift transactions is fundamentally different from the nature of capital transactions, and where gift-based economies exist, societies utilize the gifting of objects and services to create and receive social bonds and to strengthen social ties. Gifts forge relationships between givers and receivers that are traditionally a part of the transaction of giving and receiving.[1]

3. An act of detournment that incorporates the giving of gifts, or services, into its action structure rips through the fabric of the "spectacle," or of perceived reality conditions. It also holds out the prospect of weaving an alternative fabric, an instant or gradual community, through the inherent power of the gift's ability to create bonds between giver and receiver.

4. The dual practice of gifting goods and services within the context of heretical resistance is an occasional tool of value in the tradition of expanded art. This tool serves the underlying desire of radical art practices to expand and push forward the possibility of greater social and aesthetic freedoms.

Dimension 7

Throughout the writing of this essay, a couplet has gone through my brain endlessly, becoming a mantra as I have attempted to describe communities in resistance, artistic heresies and gift economics. Simple enough, it runs, "it's not the truth I see, it's just a mockery."[2] Penned by an obscure but legendary punk rocker named Greg Sage in the early 1980s, when it is sung in his strangled voice, the final word is almost incomprehensible, drawn out to sound like "mock-a-ree." I have always found its combination of awkward rhyme and underlying sentiment embodies alienation in its simplest form—urgent, artless, and real.

Sage had a lot to be alienated about when he formed his band, The Wipers, in 1978, in the rainy town of Portland, Oregon. His lyrics found their source in his own queerness, and he wove the angry essence of his sexuality into songs that embody larger realms of frustration and exile. These realms were big enough for anyone to relate to; anyone alienated by their youth, by feelings of not belonging, by living far away from like-minded people, by their sexuality, by the constant sense that one is being lied to.

But running through Sage's lyrics is another thread—his absolute conviction in the existence of another world, another place, or society, a place more real, a place with fewer lies. "I'm straight over the edge" is the concluding line to the song that begins with the couplet quoted above. The qualities of this place shift across the body of his songs, but in general, it is a place where human relations are connected and harmonious rather than commodified and treacherous. What one finds when one goes over the edge is a place where "I could be a part of you,"[3] an unscripted place of more direct, real relations, "a place deep inside that seems real."[4] It is perhaps one of Sage's earliest songs that most simply outlines that place and the rage that might provide the fuel to carry one there: "Straight as an arrow, defect, defect, not straight, not so straight, reject, reject, going to leave this region, going to take me with them . . . Dimension 7."[5]

There are parallels here of relevance to the starting points of this essay. There is another world, or there used to be, and that world was the "real" one. What happened to it, and how we arrived at the world we currently occupy is succinctly articulated at the beginning of Guy Debord's *The Society of the Spectacle:* "All that was once directly lived has become mere representation. Images detached from every aspect of life merge into a common stream and the former unity of life is lost forever. Apprehended in a partial way, reality unfolds in a new generality as a pseudo-world apart . . . The spectacle appears at once as society itself, as a part of society and a means of unification."[6] In other words, it's just a mock-a-ree.

Throughout *The Society of the Spectacle*, Debord articulated clearly the roots of contemporary alienation, of the feeling that we are not living in the real world but inside its hollow representation, an illusion so complete that it veils the real world seamlessly. Because it exists so completely, it has actually replaced the real world that preceded it, and it can be penetrated only with difficulty. This state of society arises out of the combination of industrial modernity, capitalist economics, and mediated culture, and is in many ways the perfect articulation of these forces, the end point of their collusion and alliance.

It is possible that the real world, the one that was pulled out like a doormat from under our feet, still exists somewhere. This real world would have to be an articulation of forces opposed to the ones listed above, an articulation of gift economies rather than of capital ones, a place where "I can be a part of you." For when I am a part of you, it implies that we are in a community, a bonded state, rather than a mediated one. And most of all, this world would be a place that contains larger freedoms than the freedom to choose between brands of soaps and careers. Dimension 7, indeed . . .

Return the Gift

> President George W. Bush
> 1600 Pennsylvania Ave NW Washington, D.C. 20500
>
> Dear Sir 11 June 2001
>
> I joined the Marine Corps very optimistic about the opportunities the United States and I would have to make the world a better place.
>
> After serving in Desert Storm and Desert Shield, I was less optimistic about what the United States and I could or would do to make the world a better place.
>
> I am in awe of the responsibilities and opportunities you have to better the United States and the world. I hope you will succeed where others have failed and make real, positive change.
>
> Please accept this bowl I have made as a gift. Sincerely,
>
> W. A. Ehren Tool
>
> —W. A. Ehren Tool, text of a letter sent to President George W. Bush, 2001. (The same letter was sent to Vice President Dick Cheney, Secretary of State, Colin Powell, Secretary of Defense, Donald Rumsfeld, and Secretary of the Navy, Gordon England.)

The letters and gifts of Ehren Tool suggest themselves as starting points, for the shifts that accompany their dispersal as they pass from his studio out into the corridors of power and privilege also contain a lesson on the basic nature of gift economies. In a nutshell, "Tool mails gifts of handcrafted ceramic bowls and cups, decorated with military insignia, toy soldiers cast in clay, and various weapons, to people with power. The ceramics are accompanied by letters connecting the artist's experiences as a Marine in the Gulf War with his present political and social concerns."[7] In each letter, Tool is careful to explain that the bowl is a gift and always asks the recipient to accept it as such. It is this deliberate insistence on the gift status of the bowls that makes me wonder whether the introduction of the tangible gift creates unavoidable manifestations of reciprocal and unrequited debts.

The bowl sent along with the letter gives the message weight. If it were not present, perhaps the letter could be more easily discarded, like so many other public opinions. Once burdened with a gift, a thing, which serves in some ways as a token of the gesture and physicalization of the request and intention of the artist, the letter has to be accepted as well. You read a letter, but you accept a gift. Once accepted, another, different weight is placed on the receiver. What to do with the bowl? Does keeping the bowl imply sympathizing with the thoughts of the sender? Should the bowl be returned if the sentiments in the letter are found to be repellent?

The nature of gifts, both in traditional societies as well as in our personal lives, is to create social bonds, which cement ties between individuals and mark relationships. It is in the nature of a gift to keep moving, to demand from the receiver the action of moving the gift property along. If not the bowl itself, then something else, something equivalent or greater, and if not back to the original giver, then to someone else, someone next in line. Not to do so breaks all the rules about how gifts function. This is one of the clearest points that the anthropologist Marcel Mauss makes in the conclusion of *The Gift*, his landmark study of gift economies in precapitalist societies: "The unreciprocated gift still makes the person who has accepted it inferior, particularly when it has been accepted with no thought of returning it."[8] Things we are given have different meanings from the things we buy.

I don't know what Colin Powell or Donald Rumsfeld think about their bowls. Perhaps they are sent letters of innocent yet explosive political concern every day, mysteriously accompanied by craft objects made by former-servicemen. Whatever they think about them and how they utilize them are issues beyond our concern. What matters is that they have returned the letter with a thank you note to Ehren Tool, effectively declaring acceptance of the gift to its giver. Thus they are now the receiver and the holder of gift property, which falls into its own uncomfortable and noncapitalist sphere of logic.

We are entering territory here most thoroughly examined by Mauss in the early part of the last century. One of the first things to be learned from gift economies is this: Gifts are not free, and neither are they the products of generosity. Gifts are offers. They produce bonds. They are a token through which social relationships are forged, managed and preserved. When we receive the gift we must automatically consider the giver of the gift, the person behind the token. If we accept the gift and do not do this, then a diminishment of the spirit, both our own and that of the community to which we are attached, occurs.

Meanwhile, Downtown . . .

It is said that a fool and his money are soon parted. In this instance, the fool in question might seem to be a young San Francisco artist named Josh Greene, who, among many other works of dispersal, handed out two hundred one-dollar bills to passersby in the city's downtown area. This gesture could be interpreted as staunch anticapitalism, a quixotic Franciscan desire for poverty, an act of minor philanthropy, or else, perhaps more cynically, as a publicity stunt seeking to turn short term loss into long-term gain through an accrual of notoriety. All of this could be true, the latter perhaps the most so. This temptation might always be strong when the artist is evaluated in place of the work, which is often the case when the artist's persona and actions are included in the conception and execution of the work. Temptation aside, we will learn more here from looking at the artwork itself, the actual action, if only because it helps us to look at the work through the eyes of its primary audience: those who received or refused Greene's handout.

The dispersal of money on the street was, like any public performance, carried out beyond the confines of the art world, and thus, from a spectator's point of view, had no art context. To passersby, Greene more possibly appeared as an enigma, or some sort of "reverse panhandler," or simply a fool. Of course the fool is often much smarter than we think. Clearsightedness is often seen as guileless wisdom, and in the case of Greene, the wisdom of the project of handing out money to strangers resides in how he went about it: simply and with an economical innocence. The space of interaction was short and to the point. People either took a dollar or they didn't, and nothing more was expected of them. If they wished to engage Greene in conversation, he would participate, but in no way was interaction beyond taking money required. When this is considered as a fundamental aspect of the piece, this passage from Lewis Hyde's *The Gift* springs to mind: "It is the cardinal difference between gift and commodity exchange that a gift establishes a feeling-bond between two people, while the sale of a commodity leaves no necessary connection . . . The disconnectedness is, in fact, a virtue of the commodity mode. We don't want to be bothered."

What interests me about Green's gesture is how it contrasts with the basic notion of the gift as set forth by Mauss and articulated in the works of William Tool, while on the surface seeming to be about precisely the same thing, giving gifts. If the above assertion by Lewis Hyde is taken to be correct, then Greene's refusal to really engage with the recipients means that there is no real bond established or community forged. Rather, Greene's gesture continues to function in the way in which capitalist economies work, where the exchange of money (and thus the idea of a system of equivalent and transferable worth) necessitates no other action beyond the transaction itself. In this way, and contrary to surface appearances, Greene's distribution of the $200 does not constitute itself as gift giving. It can be seen more as an act of pure and simple detournment, a rupture that creates a moment of anti-economics in the rush of lives that are dominated by transactions. In this anti-economics, one gains a dollar as easily as one spends one. The flow of money is reversed, with few or no strings attached. If there is no real gift exchange present, and there is only a "detourned" capital transaction, then another way to describe the situation is that Greene paid people for the time it took to stop and take a dollar. A very economical wage structure for the working man or woman.

However, when the lucky, or daring, two hundred are next in an economic transaction, buying a cup of coffee or a newspaper, or paying the lot fee for the allday car park, will they find one dollar more in their pocket? Will it be handy? Will they wonder about the circumstances that led it to becoming theirs rather than someone else's? All of this remains unknown. It is the price we pay for having an artwork set loose in the world without marking it as such. We can only speculate (itself an exercise in gambling) about the impact and possible endpoints of this action. We can think about it, of course, as a work of art, performance art to be precise, but we cannot be quite sure of its direct effects, since its status as an artwork was never circumscribed by informing its direct audience that they were in fact just that. No record of their reactions was ever made.

However, and this is a fairly big however, because of Josh Greene's interest in creating a gesture within the context of "art-making," this work, the fugitive performance, gains a stabilizing frame. While we don't know anything about the workings of the piece in terms of its primary audience, the work did not end at that point. Greene created a series of documentation panels (photographs and texts) that sought to present—or represent—this work to a new audience, a secondary audience. This is fairly standard in the practice of performance art, as the demands of making permanent objects, or at least permanent records of impermanent objects, are part and parcel of the system. Tool's letters and photographs of the bowls he sent are similar and are also displayed in such a way, as documents and evidence of the original, direct, fugitive act. Because these presentations are made in the style of documents and are written and coded in such a way that they refer to a primary (and inaccessible) point in time, they end up with a foot in two moments. One is permanently at a remove, the world of the original performed moment, and the other is permanently present, redirecting the secondary audience continuously back to the past.

Where to Eat Cheaply in San Francisco

Dig this:

> Let me explain how we thought. Imagistically, a pedestal, a frame around a picture, or a stage can be regarded as the epitome of private property—space owned and controlled by the artist for their own purposes. A number of us [in the San Francisco Mime Troupe] became troubled by the tensions between our democratic intentions and our monopolization of the stage and dialogue. A dissident movement evolved within the Mime Troupe, seeking to erase the distinction, or more aptly, the imbalance of power between acting and audience, and elicit creative participation from everyone in what we hoped might be newly liberated public space. This internal subset of the Mime Troupe evolved into the Diggers, and led to an eventual fissure in the company . . .
>
> In 1967, a displaced Brooklyn visionary named Billy Murcott and his charismatic friend Emmett Grogan began to preach a digger-like ethos in San Francisco. They papered the Haight Ashbury Neighborhood with cryptic handouts proclaiming, "It's free because it's yours," and criticizing city officials and "hippie" merchants for capitalizing on the new phenomena of the counter-culture without giving anything back. The two soon gravitated into the orbit of the Mime Troupe.
>
> Under their influence, the dissidents in the Mime Troupe advanced their ideas until a spot in Golden Gate Park was established where free, hot food was delivered daily to the hordes of kids scrabbling to live on the streets . . . The Diggers visited the farmers market for donations of day old vegetables, cooked them in friends' kitchens, to produce a hearty stew which they delivered in steel milk containers, accompanied by small loaves of bread, shaped like mushrooms because of rising over the old one pound coffee cans in which they were baked.
>
> At the food site, a yellow wooden frame, six feet by six feet, was assembled. One stepped through this free frame of reference and on the other side was handed a smaller version (about an inch by an inch) attached to cord for wearing. Then you were given free food. The extent of the coercion was the invitation to look at the world from another perspective—a free perspective; a point of view one could assemble oneself, without the intervention of ideologues, scribes, pundits or coercive behavior. It was after all, a free exchange. This free-food program was a great success, not

because it was charity, but because by participating one created a world in which free food was "a fact."[9]

—Peter Coyote; excerpt from a speech, California College of Arts and Crafts, San Francisco, CA, February 8, 2002

What stands out for me now in the rereading of this passage is the idea of the free frame of reference. While I find myself quite sympathetic to its ideals, I am more interested in the fact that they actually made a thing, an object of symbolic intent, to accompany their actions and ideas. They could have simply talked about the free frame of reference and the meaning of shifting one's world vision while they were doling out the stew to the hungry hordes. But they made an actual doorway that people had to cross over.

One aspect of the San Francisco Diggers' decision to construct the "free frame of reference" that is worth examining is the aesthetic deliberateness of it. In the midst of what has been largely characterized as a social activist/theater movement, something so sculptural, so architectural, is an interesting find, and possibly makes a case for the San Francisco Diggers to be seen in a more expansive light, even an art historical one. Their other "Free" projects, which included a free store (where anyone who entered could potentially ask to become the manager), free survival classes, and other undertakings, reveal a shrewd conceptual bent that would certainly brand the Diggers as "relational" artists, were they to undertake them in the context of the contemporary "art scene."

Of greatest interest is their creation of a doorway and the fact that the doorway had to be stepped through in order for the world to change. . . .

Rather than ripping through the veil to find the world behind the world, to find a place where relationships are unmediated and free food is a fact, the Diggers built a door. Not only as a way across for them, but as an architectural structure to render the same service for others. This architectural solution is the first indication that there is community creation at work in the midst of the detournment (for what is more heretical than revealing to the assembled that commodities are not actually scarce at all?). The Diggers' free food and free frame of reference was a manifestation of a start-up gift economy. Through the distribution of free food and the invitation to view the world in another way, the Diggers began to assemble the basic ingredients of a counter economy based on dispersal of goods, and the redistribution of surplus and gifts to all who came forward to claim them. Dimension 7 indeed. . . .

There are still doors and one finds a similar threshold today in San Francisco, twenty-five years and a mile away from the Diggers in the Golden Gate Park Panhandle. *Any Wednesday*, a project initiated by San Francisco artist Diana Mars, will see that you do not go hungry, at least once a week.

Since 1993, Mars has made dinner available, free and without strings attached, every Wednesday at her apartment. She advertises discreetly, by word of mouth and through the distribution of handmade calling cards, as well as in mailings circulated through the networks that 'zines and comic books follow.

Nevertheless, after ten years, the circle of people in the loop has grown fairly large. I myself have been a part of it at different points in my life. Mars's calling cards, which serve as invitations, still say basically the same thing today that they have always said: "At home, Making Good Food, Wednesdays 7:00–10:00 pm."[10]

The rest is filled in by attending, getting to know the work directly, and then coming back and getting to know it again. It is in no way a "potluck," there is no requirement for people to bring food, though one finds that most often they do so anyway. It is an interesting quality of this work that even when something is known to be free, like a free meal, people will very often bring food to share even though it is not asked of them.

The management of such a project in many ways becomes the "work" of art. How does one afford it? How does one account for how many will come? What happens if someone disruptive or simply annoying comes (and then comes back and back again)? Mars means for the structure of the dinners, the availability of food, and the matters of attendance to be self-governing. She rarely steps in to "take" control, either as author or authority, and instead maintains order by continuing to provide dinners as a work and a gift. It is this, in the end, that creates the framework for managing the uncertainties. Because this piece is a long-term project and because what Mars offers is a gift, it creates bonds with the recipients. As they become enmeshed in the work, they become part of a community and in many ways begin to co-create the piece anew. As members of community, with a "feeling-bond" between them, the responsibility for governance is shifted to many shoulders. And if it doesn't work so well this week, they can come back and try again next week.

This is why people bring food to share even though they are not "required" to. Because they are not an audience for very long—they are a part of a community, and must participate as such. After all, the work has unfolded in Mars's apartment. You cannot just show up and eat without interacting with the rest of the guests. The Diggers' threshold allowed entry into a world (located just to the left of this one) where free food is a fact, and exit is possible when one has finished eating. In contrast, when one crosses the threshold into Diana Mars's house on any Wednesday night, one enters into a world where a community has coalesced around a central idea and made an amorphous covenant. Yes it's "free," the food that is, but that is only the beginning. Your freedom to become a partner and responsible co-creator is also brought into play, the result of accepting the initial offer and stepping across the threshold to participate.

The Hot Tub and the People's Park

Near to where I live, on an anonymous, dead end street on the Oakland side of Berkeley, there is a small red house with a gated backyard. On this gate is a fairly high-tech lock with a keypad, similar to the keypad that guards the sliding driveway gates of nearby Black Hawk estates and the mansions of Tiburon. This keypad protects access to a pleasant back yard filled with redwood trees and a very nice, quite warm hot tub. It's simple. The hot tub is free, communal property. If you have a code (and you are supposed to be able to request one from the caretaker) then you can come in and use the facilities. Codes are passed around from friend to friend like tips for quiet vacations. I don't know how many are circulating, but I would assume that there are more than many, since the hot tub has been operating as a social experiment since well before I arrived in the area in 1993. It was instituted by a man who has since moved away, although he gives a caretaker free rent in exchange for the daily maintenance of the property and project. Behind the idyllic redwoods, the codes—how many times they are used—when they were used, are all being tracked by a dedicated computer. The flow of the codes is at the root of the experiment. One could document a whole history of hot tub use by analyzing them.

Inside the little changing/shower room are various messages and notes from the caretaker. In the dimly lit space you learn that there are rules (or, more properly, codes) for behavior. Do not talk, take a shower first, restrain excessive male [!] energy, maintain a meditative spirit, and most importantly perhaps, don't give out your code to people you don't trust. (The last time I was there, there was an addendum to this that recommended that women shouldn't give out their codes to men, even if they are friends; they should only bring them as guests.) The penalty for bad hot-tub behavior is the removal of your code. This occurs when other users register a complaint. The time of the complaint is compared to the computer record, and the offender's code is cancelled.

Another part of the posted message provides a reason for the oversight—wariness. After all, it says, the hot tub is a limited use space; it can't be People's Park.

For those readers unfamiliar with the iconic locations of Berkeley, California, People's Park is a small piece of land that belongs to the University of California. It was claimed in the late sixties by squatters and hippies as a place for free assembly, in defiance of University plans to turn it into a parking lot, and it has become synonymous with the rights of the "people" to accessible, usable, and uncommodified public space. The University has made various attempts over the years to develop the land into dormitories, volleyball courts, sports complexes, or parking lots, but resistance has always been too fierce, and the park today still remains an open commons.

I decided to take a walk there this morning and it seemed the same as always—squatter kids with mohawks hanging around, the bushes filled with the campsites of homeless men and women. The current state of economics and social affairs has taken its toll. The loss of so much other public common space and the shrinking economic sphere have put too much stress on the park; too many people with no where else to go use it as bedroom, living room, and bathroom. There are no kids playing in the playground, no picnics, no soccer games, and no young dog-walkers.

In juxtaposing these two "facilities," my point is not to elevate one above the other, but to point out that the aspirations of each to being free, public, communal property are undermined by tensions between each of those qualities. The hot tub must create a set of rules for self-policing that make it a privileged space, not too dissimilar from a boathouse on a private lake that is shared by several families. This is because in an effort to be communal, and to create a community (albeit one of relative strangers) around intimate space (people are naked after all), one cannot be wholly public. The accountability that members of a community feel towards one another and their shared space is achieved precisely because there is a finite demarcation of who belongs and who doesn't. Conversely, People's Park cannot maintain its premise of being a free public commons by exclusion policies. For a commons to mean something there has to be open access. This makes it difficult to maintain the sort of intimate bonds that knit a community together and allow any thing other than minimum social values to flourish.

It is in the parable of the Hot Tub and the People's Park that we find an analogy to the free meals on offer in San Francisco. The public gestures of the Diggers soon broke under their own weight, moving from the ideal of a liberated and cocreative space, a manifestation of another world, to an overly popular spectacle that changed into a public charity operation and scene as the event became more publicized and popular. Like the People's Park, it has found its end point as another handout, a space that no one else is that interested in having. On *Any Wednesday*, however, those who know, who are somehow invited or in the know, sit down and eat together. Like the Hot Tub, in order to maintain a community, a functioning, respectful one, barriers are erected and/or rules are set in place to create mutually agreeable circumstances.

This is not to lay down a judgment, only to observe a fact. Both the Hot Tub and Diana Mars's apartment are only so big, only so accommodating. When one opens up a pocket, a free space inside or outside the spectacular society, then the weight of that society presses in upon it. Perhaps if there were twenty free hot tubs in Berkeley and several open apartment dinners on any given night, then the weight could be borne, but it is too much to expect any one act by an individual to support a public structure.

The dilemma here is not in the unworkable nature of gift economies (they work quite well in the total social systems that create them), but in the fixed nature of these social experiments. By locating themselves firmly in a place, whether a park or a street address, and attempting to persist over time, these experiments become fixed, and once fixed, they no longer function as detournments. They are too known, too institutional. They can be ignored, coopted or otherwise accounted for. For gift economies to keep functioning as heretical detournments, their emergence must be unheralded and their exit swift, with a reappearance elsewhere similarly unexpected. This is the essence of the Temporary Autonomous Zone (TAZ), a concept developed by the scholar Hakim Bey as a way to envision the contemporary possibilities for social resistance and freedom. Given that fixed utopias and free-society experiments are susceptible either to attack or incorporation by the larger, spectacular society, Bey speculates that spaces of freedom, or autonomy, must arise spontaneously in locations that present themselves in the moment, so that they cannot be predicted and undermined by the pressure of societal forces. While active, these spaces become areas of liberation, alternative economics, and social protest. When infiltrated or discovered, they are easily disassembled. They can re-emerge elsewhere when the conditions are right.

Power in the Darkness

After keeping us, the audience, waiting for more than an hour, the lights went off and the band took the stage. Or did they? No corresponding lights went up on the stage, and the drumming that began didn't seem to have a point of origin. I remember a strobe light and huge explosions as entire bricks of firecrackers were set off in the midst of the audience and suddenly there was light. Still not on the band or the stage but instead emanating from dozens of large wooden torches that were being carried into the milling crowd by almost naked men. The torches were not set up in any spot, since they were not part of a display concept. Rather, the torches were simply handed out to the audience, first come, first served. What the audience did with them varied—some danced, or fought, or held them aloft to illuminate the surrounding area, revealing a crowdscape of seething bodies in various stages of undress, dance, observation, or navigation. There was always more provided for the audience—more fire (the next time it was in the form of 50-gallon drums filled with burning, oil-soaked wood); more huge bags of wine, fruit, and honey; and most intriguingly, as a nervous management turned off the PA system and turned on the warehouse lights, the instruments themselves—drums, cymbals, and blocks. We, the audience, took up the instruments and continued to play for at least another hour until the security guards found a way to remove one thousand people.

The year was 1994, in the lower Mission district of San Francisco, and the band that I "saw" was Crash Worship. From inquiries I have made since that night, this was a fairly typical performance. Comprised of a core set of musicians and a rotating number of friends, instigators, and performers, Crash

Worship was more of a concept than a rock band. What they sought to recreate, in the context of an industrial, apocalyptic, post-punk, and neopagan aesthetic, was a Dionysian space, where libido, carnival, and release were offered to the audience through the most economical of sources: themselves. Crash Worship's decision to turn over the means of spectacle to their audiences set them apart from a whole host of acts that sought to create the style and look of a bacchanalian celebration, by staging the spectacle for their audiences, who paid for the privilege of watching. The project of the band was to enlist the audience as active co-creators of the "work" that was the concert, and in so doing, many of the usual distinctions between the author and the audience became erased.

In many ways, the Crash Worship project fulfills many of the goals set forth by the dissidents in the San Francisco Mime Troupe, as articulated above by Peter Coyote, and in particular the creation of a situation to "elicit creative participation from everyone in what we hoped might be newly liberated public space." But Crash Worship also took that intention into private space, to a paid venue, not only challenging expectations of the role of the audience, but also creating a situation where the audience has to produce its own meaning and spectacle. Given the typical frame of mind and traditional roles in the context of attending rock concerts, this is both a gift and a challenge. Crash Worship's gift to the audience is the provision of a riot of release, flesh, fire, and wine. However, the gift can only be redeemed by an acceptance of the responsibility of co-creation, by taking up the torch (literally) and deciding the best use to put it to.

In the early days of the punk rock explosion, the late 1970s and early 1980s, the U.S. adherents of the movement made and saw much of the concept of DIY (do-it-yourself). This simple acronym expressed both an attitude and a working method for taking responsibility of one's own potential role in the creation of culture and its local context. No punk bands playing in your area? Form one of your own. Don't have an instrument? Start a fanzine instead and send it out to contact magazines or rent out your local community hall and invite some bands to play, paying them from what you take at the door. In some cases, you could and would have to do all of these things yourself to manifest a local "scene," but why not? It was better than waiting around the mall or figuring out a way to move to a city on the coast where it was "happening." Right at the heart of DIY was this thought: why wait for them to give it to you? If you know what you want, or even have a hunch about it, why wait at all?

In part a reaction to the bloated corporate excess of seventies stadium rock and its megastar bands, and a reflection of punk's early ties to Situationist thought, DIY was essentially an optimistic mind-state/culture movement that believed that only money and force of habit keep people from seeing that culture is something you make rather than something you buy. It was based in the belief that creativity was widespread and omnipresent, something that everyone had, rather than an anointed few. All one needed was permission and a "little help from your friends" to make a cultural contribution, to make an act of authorship concrete and real, and to have a place where it could be received. There were contact lists waiting, 'zine's to be traded, phone lists of people in small towns across America to call who would put you up or find you a place to play if you wanted to tour your band. There were independent record stores that would take your 7-inch singles on consignment and cooperative distribution networks to send them to. Behind all of this lurks the presence of Situationist thought, mainly in the easily grasped concept that we have lost our power to the forces of capital and spectacle only because they made us believe that they already had it by constantly stating that it was true. When one can step away from that idea, it is possible to see it simply again as a veil pulled down over the truth, and that the power is there to be taken back, since we were the ones to give to them. This democratic mindset was steadily eroded over the course of the next ten years, as record companies and media outlets figured out how to carve themselves back into the social sculpture. Finding stars within this milieu, elevating them above their peers and their "scenes" through the mechanisms of record contracts and MTV videos, the corporate powers were able to reinsert themselves into the equation.

So by the time that Crash Worship appeared on the stage, the DIY ideals were in need of some fresh inspiration and perhaps higher and more defensible ground. What Crash Worship offered was the creation of a space within the concert, within the performance, where people were not merely encouraged but actually instigated and tempted into doing it themselves. "It," in this case, was not the creation of a scene, a band, and an alternative economy (for these were too easily bought and stolen), but the control of a single night, the control of who watches and who performs in a space of co-creation.

The single night is certainly more defensible terrain than an independent record company. It is more mobile, discrete in time, and doesn't show up on the radar. And yet as a blow, as a defiant action it is perhaps, ultimately, just as effective, since in both cases there are possibilities for the creation of real communities based around the gift transaction.

What We Do Is Secret

Sometimes the work has to be kept under wraps. The very revelation of its existence acts as a special circumstance, a favor. A specific decision is made by the maker to release the idea to someone else. In a way it, and by "it," I mean the thing, the location of information transfer that we can call art, or the site of the art action, is like a germ, which moves surreptitiously and somewhat nomadically from host to host. Maybe in these cases it can only be a story or a rumor of an artwork.

The rumor, the germ, begins for me with an introduction to Johnny Spencer, an artist from the U.K. who has an interest in the process of art as an exchange of information. In June we had a short meeting in a library in Oakland with the specific purpose of him telling me about an undertaking that he called "site-seeing." I will tell you now what he told me.

Johnny was invited in 1997 to attend and partake in an outdoor Thai public art festival called *Chiang Mai Social Installation: Week of Cooperative Suffering*. Enchanted by the title, and with an interest in both subverting it and making it literal, Spencer conceived of an activity, surreptitious and unrecorded, that would serve as his contribution to the event. I should mention that while it was his contribution to the "exhibition," it was not publicized or made in anyway available to the viewing public of the event. Because he was interested in the idea of suffering in the context of artwork and because of an ongoing interest in art as a manifestation of the exchange of ideas, Johnny contacted a school for the blind. He inquired whether any of the students were interested in attending the festival with him. He found two young women willing to take part. For the next three days, they toured the city of Chiang Mai together, visiting the various art projects that were being erected, painted, and performed. With the two blind girls serving as a link/guide for Johnny (talking with him about the local context and their understanding of the town) and he in turn supplying the visual information that they used as a starting point to discuss the artwork being made, *Site-Seeing* unfolded. At one point, one of the girls commented that, "to blind people, talking is art," and this in many ways confirmed some of his initial instinctive thoughts about the work and what he wanted to accomplish with it. The most obvious of these was that he had long held a belief that conceptual works, being concerned with pure information transfer, do not need visual realizations. Circulating through a festival with two blind guides confirmed this. The least obvious was, perhaps, that if they were correct, then he might not actually be the only artist in the piece—the two blind girls had arrived there before him because of their nonvisual understanding of the possibilities of artistic practice.

Of the two confirmations, I am less sure of the truth of the latter. Spencer didn't exactly tell me that it was so. I have woven it into the story from my own mind, but this is perhaps the risk and benefit of making works that aren't works, but rumors. I do know that it should be true enough, because the one statement that Johnny made that has remained with me indelibly is: "with this work, there was no product, no show, not even any artist or any audience. It was not a performance piece, nor an opportunity to make documentation photos and texts to describe the piece. If the piece was anything," Johnny confided, "it was a conceptual gesture, or an exchange."[11] Co-creation again.

What does it mean to tell you this? Does the secret now disappear? This is the essential problem of fugitive work and fugitive practices, since the game is always up when someone like me spills the beans. My sense is that Johnny's decision not to bring forth the piece as an "artwork," or a set of photographs, or an artist's statement, was because he wanted the original experience to remain the primary one, to not create a secondary experience through the mechanisms of the image and reproduction. Johnny didn't want to trade what he had co-created for something that he would have to make himself, that would be only his. To not create something new was the only way for the work, the exchange itself, to remain intact as the primary creation.

It might slightly assuage my conscience to think that I am not the stool pigeon in this case because this description of the "piece" is only my own iteration, my own retelling of what was told to me. Make no mistake, this isn't an artist's text and there is still nothing to buy. In this way, I hold out the hope that the sanctity of the work, as Johnny intended it, has not been disrupted.

By ending my writing with a description of this work, I am perhaps setting out the possibility that I will subvert my whole premise. There was very little subversion and social protest involved in *Site-Seeing*, and Johnny's reluctance to lend it a form that could be easily displayed or disseminated makes the possibility of a secondary impact also quite low. However, I do believe that for the three people directly involved, the experience was life changing. Not in the way that surviving a car accident is, but in the way that a fork in the road can be. You can go one way or the other, and by choosing a path and committing to it, you enter into an experience that cannot be undone. In this case, these three co-creators entered into a new space of their own devising. This space, by virtue of their commitment to the process, contained a spirit of exchange and equality that perhaps can be seen as the hope of a gift in its truest form. Where the gift and the discharge of the debt that it brings on are brought forth simultaneously, there is no real cognizance of the intention and its attendant burden, only an experience of the community that has been formed. Johnny's decision not to "report" on this work in the typical forms of art has also impacted the space they created, in that he did not trade it for something else. He did not circumscribe it as a work and did not seek to make his version of the story the "official" one. In this way, the space the three co-created still exists as it was, perhaps in the past now, and through my own retelling, certainly dimmer and more distant. But that original space is still

By the way, the night after I met with Johnny in the library for our conversation, I had a dream that my wife and I went to Thailand. Perhaps you will, too.

Notes

1. In a gift economy, there is no concept of value-based exchange; only in reciprocity-based exchange. If one gives a feast, what one gets back might be a necklace or a son-in-law or a new social standing, but there is no underlying code that states that these things are equal in value (i.e., a feast is not worth the same thing as a son-in-law;

they are not even thought of as being equivalent). This is because in reciprocal relations, the transfer of gifts produces returns and consequences, rather than value. This is what Lewis Hyde means when he says that gift economies create "feeling-bonds" (Lewis Hyde, *The Gift: Imagination and the Erotic Life of Property* [London: Vintage, 1979], p. 56). In a capital economy, an overarching system of absolute value (monetary systems) is assumed, so that exchanges have no left over relations when they are finished. If you get a donkey for a day's work, it is because both of them were valued to be the same in monetary terms. The transaction is over, and you can move on to the next one. In a gift economy, transactions are never really over, because each one produces more reciprocal ties.

2. The Wipers, "Over the Edge," *Over the Edge* (Seattle: Brain Eater Records, 1983).

3. Greg Sage, "Seems So Clear," *Straight Ahead* (Torrance: Enigma Records, 1985).

4. The Wipers, "No One Wants an Alien," *Over the Edge* (Seattle: Brain Eater Records, 1984).

5. The Wipers, "Dimension 7," *Is This Real?* (Seattle: Park Avenue Records, 1979).

6. Guy Debord, *The Society of the Spectacle* (New York: Zone Books, 1994), 12.

7. Susan Sobeloff, email correspondence with Ted Purves, 2002.

8. Marcel Mauss, *The Gift: The Form and Reason for Exchange in Archaic Societies* (New York: W.W. Norton, New York, 1990), 65.

9. Hyde, 56.

10. Diana Mars, invitation card, self-published, 1995.

11. Johnny Spencer, notes from a conversation, Oakland, 2002.

HOW DO YOU PIN A WAVE UPON THE SAND?

AN INTERVIEW WITH CESARE PIETROIUSTI

Shane Aslan Selzer

The project approach to learning has gained widespread support in the past decade. In progressive early childhood programs, such as the Reggio Emilia Approach in Italy, projects are initiated by the interests and questions of young students. These projects take the form of investigations into very specific queries, and they generate further questions as the research progresses. Project work encourages group collaboration and the utilization of individuals' skills. It allows the researcher to branch off from the initial topic, and often yields unexpected results. The underlying theory is that children's curiosity and motivation will spur research, which allows them to pursue personal interests and take the responsibility for direction and choice.

Many artists have adopted this project model, using the studio as a laboratory to fuel new research and allowing the questions generated to lead them into another vein of a continuing exploration.[1] One such artist is Cesare Pietroiusti, whose practice is broadly based on project work, often taking on and following the judgments and decisions of others, through actions or direct participation. For the *Headlands Project* (1993) Cesare asked visitors to and residents of an area in Marin County, California, to give a written description of a scene they considered to be most characteristic of the drive. Later he tried to meet with these individuals to photograph the site they described.

In 2002 Pietroiusti organized a skills exchange with the community of the California College of Arts and Crafts in San Francisco. Volunteers were asked to teach Pietroiusti a skill, and were taught one by him in return. I thought about the skills exchange in terms of time spent together, rather than time determined by labor. In this case, the skill itself facilitated a social exchange. In its action, the time spent was guided and structured by variants of what was taught and learned. By creating a performative spectacle, a real time/space relationship was relaxed. Through the constructed scenario of teacher/student, an intimate moment between strangers was nourished. In my own practice I think about the visual and kinesthetic connectors that initiate a social response to bodies and space. By entering a specific social grid, certain potentials are released, but outcomes are still relative to the context of a moment of action. This comes back to haunt me when making objects that are required to function both within and against set social structures. Sometimes writing is sculpture and the questions that arise concerning oral and written traditions can also be posed in terms of objects and how they come to function in the world. So ultimately my studio practice also begs the question: where does documentation find its place in the project approach?

Cesare Pietroiusti's work raises points concerning exchange practices as they move from a level of direct experience to a level of symbolization. The apparent dichotomy between socially motivated fieldwork and its gallery representation also brings up questions about our modes of viewing and how the intricate relationships surrounding art, artists, and viewers change and affect each other in new ways. If a primary audience becomes participatory, how do they view the project? And how does the work translate for those who aren't in the participatory audience? This comes back to objects, which are the cause of much contemplation. Can an inanimate object act as a catalyst for furthering specific social exploration, or is it completely dependent upon the physical body to bring politics and meaning to its core?

Using these questions as a starting point, Cesare and I had several discussions between May 27 and June 2, 2002, in his Rome studio about the relationship between specific actions and the residual objects that map or document them. Our meetings were recorded, transcribed, edited, and reread. My additional writing served to develop the transition from live conversation to written text by engaging the internal musings that arise from viewing any documentation. This format has sought to represent the subjective interpretations of a conversation without trapping its meaning. Text in brackets stems from my responses to the initial conversations.

SS Do you see the people that you are interacting with as being the subject of your work?

CP Subject, in psychological terms, means two quite different things. As a connotation of authorship, there's the subject who is personally the author of an action, and, in another sense, there's the subject who is the instrument, thanks to which the theory of another author, the scientist, is proved, or is put on some type of trial. I would say it's pretty much a situation of coauthorship that I am interested in. There can be different levels of awareness, intention, or even interest by the persons involved, but I think to the others as collaborators who help me to get to some critical point. When you put some ideas on a table and different people sit at that table, and they share an attitude, a general interest, then usually what happens is that those ideas become more interesting, and what I like most is that popping up of ideas that wouldn't have otherwise emerged from the individual minds of the participants.

SS Right, but collaboration with an audience goes against current trends in the art world which posit the artist, particularly the international artist, as a sort of progenitor of meaning.[2] [Miwon Kwon defines contemporary practices of site specificity as being linked to nomadism and committed to using site as a "discursive narrative" (Kwon, 51). These practices commonly involve a contractual agreement between an artist and an institution, which depend on the physical presence of the artist in the traditional mode of anthropologist. Here, the body of the artist becomes a service commodity because it guarantees that certain meanings or sociopolitical strategies will be revealed by the artist's insertion into the site. This model of site specificity addresses the basic idea that "home" has shifted from a physical place to an internal set of relationships. However, I have to argue here that the model is misguided in its tendency to seek objectivity and systematic reasoning as the grounds for producing meaning. Unlike the roundtable approach Cesare is exploring, the older model is more structured by specific goals and foreseen outcomes.] I refer to it as an anthropological model, where an artist goes into a community outside of their everyday context and through a series of conversations and research they enact a system, which produces meaning or insight for a site. This model of working tends to overlook issues of subjectivity, and because the artist is no longer the subject, they are no longer at risk in the scenario. These newer exchange practices seem to be more invested in putting the artist back into the game in that way as a subject. But in doing that, it seems to collapse the gaze, the relationship, or the way that we know it, between the artist, the art, and the viewer. As soon as you start to have an interaction with someone, then they are no longer employing an optic gaze, they are inside of it, and they are involved. So they are less capable of being analytical and the artist does well because they are immersed inside of what it is—that thing.

CP My experience with groups is that it's easy for a group to create a mechanism of inclusion/exclusion. Inclusion means defining who is in, even in a temporary circumstance. Immediately, there is an issue of belonging, and at the point where you define belonging to the group, you also define the exclusion as to who is not belonging. This decision creates a barrier, a fence, and what often happens is that there is a shift that is both moral and ideological from which the components of a group start to believe that they are good because they are part of the group.

I see your point, when you are totally into something, you don't have a physical gaze because you are inside it. And you enact a psychological split. You split the good parts from the bad parts and you project all of the good parts inside of the group and all of the bad parts outside of it. And you lose any possibility of a critical approach because to be critical means to see both parts, having some distance from them. In collective practices, some kind of osmosis is always necessary; an in-and-out movement is the only way to avoid the "immersion" you mentioned.

SS Do you think that the point of osmosis, where you can be involved in something and then you can step outside of it, occurs when you begin to document or represent a specific action or activity that has occurred in a real-time parameter?

CP It might happen. When you start thinking of the secondary audience, the ones who are not directly involved in your project, you need to create communication at a symbolic level, and you need to work on the language to convey meanings.

You can use the documentation as a mirror for what you have done, as a confirmation, or as a new source that, starting from your action, gives you the opportunity to go somewhere else, to move aside and explore side effects. Side effects don't confirm the initial assumption of your project, but they open up on things that were not expected. Side effects put out new assumptions, new ideas, new considerations, and will leave discourses and questions open. My general attitude is that it's much better to leave things open rather than trying to find a final solution for a question, or the perfect ending for a project. I don't believe in final endings.

SS Can you give me an example of what you mean by the documentation opening other questions? The moment something that is enacted as a verb, occurring in real time as an action, is captured through photo, video, or text, it becomes a set representation that fixes it in time and inevitably closes down meaning rather than opening it up. I think that's what I'm after: how can the representation of a verb not trap it, but allow it to breathe, to remain fluid and relevant?

[Movement inherently exists as a verb. While pathways may act as a record of the history of movement, they fail to capture "the act itself of passing by."[3] The visible mark may become a commodity while the process of making that mark is free from the structures of our market economy. Again, it is important to realize that the body is present in both of these scenarios and it should be impossible to forget the wholly subjective perspective from which the body navigates. Relativism is crucial to this argument both as an oppressive binary system and also as an empowering agent for change. We can no longer make, walk, or think without accounting for our surroundings and the impact of society upon our choices.

This has been a struggle for language over the centuries. Oral tradition is effective because it is elastic, based on principles of call and response, the oral interaction adapts to the questions and needs, which pertain to its audience, maintaining a connection to the time/place conditions where it occurs. However, oral tradition lacks the power of the written word because it is not fixed: it cannot be distributed or referenced with the same accuracy over lengths of time. Therefore it's susceptible to denial and misinterpreted articulation.]

CP I think this is the core problem of our discussion. Of course, when you say something, when you represent something, you underline a meaning, somehow excluding in the same moment all the other meanings that are not there. When you have an event, when you have a "real time verb," you can have indefinite layers of possible meanings or of possible ways to open meanings. But when I refer to a "side effect," able to pose new questions, I am not thinking of a faithful documentation, but rather of something that was not expected in your initial project, but that comes out of it anyway.

I'll try to give you an example. In the late eighties I was making a series of photographic works of the spaces that were around the gallery space. My idea was to confront how the gallery space was empty of life, let's say, compared to the living places around it, and to criticize the presumed neutrality of the contemporary art "white box." Usually, inside the gallery space, I exhibited photographic "windows" of what was on the other side of the walls, the adjacent spaces, and private apartments, offices, stores, et cetera. In 1991 I was invited to a group show in a gallery in Rome and I decided to directly bring the public of the exhibition to the other apartments in the same building, rather than exhibiting photographic images of them. So I tried to convince the people who were living there to open their places and just let the exhibition visitors enter them. As you can imagine, it was very difficult to convince these people. One of those who agreed to participate told me something like, 'I don't know why you are asking me but, because it seems so important for you, I will let you do it. But I don't want to be bothered in any possible way, I don't want to change my habits and I will continue to do my usual ordinary things in my place while you do your visits.' We agreed on dividing the entrance hall from the rest of the apartment with museum cords, and from the entrance hall the public could look into the kitchen, the bedroom, the bathroom . . . I brought several groups from the gallery, one after the other, to this apartment during the opening. The owner of the flat was preparing a meal, or eating with her son, or watching TV, or ironing, and was completely unresponsive to us. This created a very strong tension, and for me, it was sort of a shock because my intention was to show places, but what actually happened was this awkward relationship between the audience and this woman, particularly the absence of response from her part. This was completely unexpected. To go back to our point, this would be a side effect. With events in real time, there are always side effects that happen and I would try to recognize them and work with them. Usually, when we project something, side effects are considered negative because they are diversions. If you have a goal, you want to get there, and do not want to waste time or be distracted from your point.

I like to think that an art practice is the only work with the freedom to consider side effects as a positive part of a project. At the same time, I think that we cannot expect side effects, nor try to create conditions for having as many of them as we can. On the contrary, if we are not very precise and rigorous in our project's definition, we won't be able to recognize the side effects, because we could be submerged by them and not see anything at all. That would be a naive hippie attitude—easygoing, everything is fine, everything is good . . . If everything is good nothing is good and you won't give meaning to anything whatsoever. When your project is precise and punctual, you can recognize and give meaning to side effects.

SS Going back to your example, when you initially had the photographs inside the gallery, you had created a representation of the space that you wanted to see and that representation became a commodity, because it could be traded, as a discrete object. What's interesting to me is that from that project you made a shift and took people on a tour of the actual space and that is where the side effect occurred because there was a real interaction. Does this mean that something has to stay in a performance realm to maintain its integrity as an action?

CP I don't know if it necessarily has to do with performance, and I don't think

it is a question of integrity here. One could think that, if an artist sells a piece, he loses integrity; to me this is not the point. The point is that if you want to open ways of meanings, put questions, have others' and your own mind working, you have to constantly interrogate and doubt the status quo. This generally is not what the market requires of an artist.

SS But if you don't, at some point, document those side effects in some fixed way, how will the others know, how do you get outside of that circle?

CP Okay, maybe this is the point. I have been always involved in "real time" projects rather than in studio work, but I have to admit that the audience I was addressing was the limited circle of the ones who were directly involved. There's a paradox, here, because I was working on the idea of openness, and I was creating a closed audience, a *private* group of people. Almost ten years after the first shock I just described, I had a second shock—pretty much connected to moving to New York. I realized, in fact, that there is a public out there, and a much wider potential audience for my work. I realized that I cannot get to the point where I know everyone, and everyone becomes my friend and a direct participant in my work. How can I possibly open meanings for all these people I am not directly related to? I don't have a solution for that, but now I know that this is a crucial issue for an artist. Maybe the side effect theory can help us, once again. Maybe we can imagine a situation where a message, working on a symbolic level (so, conceptually, on a different level than a direct "real time" experience), does not determine only the fixity of a specific meaning, but also "side" meanings.

Sometimes, when I document an action, I try, rather than to replicate the experience exactly as it was for the participants (that is something logically impossible), to look into the documentation to find some kind of side effects. I'll give you another example. When I had the studio at the Clock Tower, in New York last year, I enacted a performance on a walkway on Broadway—directly underneath the tower—where I set off in one direction, and each time

I crossed someone who was walking in the opposite direction, I would change my way. So I was constantly just moving back and forth. All this was done several times, and was filmed from above.

When I looked at the filmed material, I noticed that many people turned towards me, probably to realize what was going on—and I had not noticed this, while I was performing. It was usually a very short glance, but to me it could represent the common attention towards subliminal actions or, in general, the relation between the public and the artist's action. Therefore I realized that the video was isolating those little moments of "the other's gaze."

SS Video has become a status quo method of representing fieldwork in a gallery setting. Replacing the photo/text format of earlier conceptual work, video often serves as the new didactic, and I wonder about the potential dangers of its assumed truth and even objectivity.

CP Video gives the artist the sensation of an enormous power that is exactly the power to replicate and give back the experience—the ideal representation of a visual (as with photography) plus sound, and real time. But such a presumption is completely wrong. Or, more precisely, it's dangerous because it has no sense of criticism towards the medium, and makes you become the medium's tool, rather than vice versa.

SS Acknowledging the subjectivity of the medium, its specific gaze and perspective, seems crucial, but it also seems important to note that video is devoid of place. Our society, particularly American society, is more and more reliant on experiencing things through the simulacrum of video and it's rapidly replacing culture, the risk here being that I can go to a museum (as a part of the secondary audience) and see a video of action, of a human exchange, and feel that I understand what spending time with that person would be even though I, as a subject, was never there, I don't have the power of my own gaze. My involvement as a viewer is completely passive, not active in the time and space of looking.

[In their essay "The Smooth and the Striated," Deleuze and Guattari open up the distinctions between these ways of navigating and occupying space. While maintaining that smooth space exists not in relation to other points, devoid of measurement and divisibility, their argument is still framed by placing it entirely in relation to its opponent, striated space. If smooth space is analogous to the patchwork quilt, where connections between pieces are made through accumulation rather than geometric measurements, then how can I as an individual subvert social hierarchies occurring in the striated space of the city by navigating with smoothness in mind? When the power of the gaze is compromised or directed (as in video), it becomes crucial to pull back from a haptic view, to recognize that the representation of action shown is mediated by a specific perspective and personal bias. A simulacrum of movement and interaction becomes a striated space the moment it is marked or captured and therefore removed from its original time/place context. While a call towards smoothness may seem appealing, one should be wary of the ramifications. Spatial order is what creates the opportunity for social interaction, and the haptic view is the uncharted territory that is occupied during that interaction. The void is smooth space and yet that void is dependent on striated order to bring the players to its ground.[4]]

CP Yes! It's exactly that, losing the power of one's own gaze. When you display a video, in a museum exhibition space, for instance, you should always keep some kind of critical/reflective distance towards the medium itself, in order to allow the viewer to reflect on his own real time experience of looking at a screen. Otherwise, he will project himself out, as when looking at TV, and discard ("psychotically," I would say) his own reality. That distance, in general terms, should mark the difference between a regular TV program and an artistic video. I would say the same thing also in relation to the use of computer and "website visiting" . . .

SS When making a shift from an action involving a primary audience (active participants) to a formal representation of that event (to be viewed by a secondary audience), how does memory affect the translation? What strategies can equip us for a critical approach without denying our subjective responses?

CP Earlier in this conversation I mentioned the necessity of having a very clear project in order to get the side effects. My position is in between a minimal approach, where you cut out any subjective interpretation, and an entropic approach, where "everything is fine" and you could go in any direction. I'm interested in recognizing (or even measuring) the distance between the side effects and the initial path of the project, and I need a precise path, in order to have a measurement . . .

Memory is a tool that, together with the mind's functions (sensibility, intentions, logic, etc.), allows me to "see" my own experience from outside (the "critical distance," again!), and not only to "be" in it.

SS The emphasis that these exchange-based works put on local and often bodily interactions seems to directly challenge the assumed viewing relationship we have to social experiences through technology. We've had a massive increase in social interactions through the Internet and television, and recently the "reality TV" trend has hit the United States pretty hard. So, I feel like a lot of these social practices are coming as a way to subvert the power that those media are gaining over human interactions.

CP Yes, you are right. When there is a need there is some kind of response to that need so I think that technology and the Internet create a new need for direct exchanges and artists act accordingly to that need. It is interesting though, that artists use mixed strategies, such as exploiting email to facilitate intimate relationships: the medium which actually encourages physically distant relationships is used to get appointments, to get closer to each other. I am very interested in those kinds of communities where you have extended exchanges through email and also periodical physical meetings and that's the only way these communities can survive and work.

SS [It means accepting a codependent relationship with the systems that govern our society. But how can we find a sense of agency when we're dependent upon those structures, which may be oppressive or manipulative to us? A tactical approach requires a certain amount of fluidity in its movement. In the same way that you speak of the schism between the primary and the secondary audiences, this involvement with technology is also navigated through a tactic of osmosis. The work must remain responsive to its circumstances, avoiding a rigid ideology, which may trap and sterilize its relevance in the world. Only then can we encourage criticality without hanging onto the deconstructivist nature of our predecessors.]

CP The fact is that if you approach something ideologically, you immediately start either celebrating it or disregarding it because it is wrong. You start splitting it the same way you do with the good and the bad parts that are inside of you, so the good is all here, and the bad is all there. This is a psychotic movement and it's very common in history, as well as dangerous. The point is not to be morally or politically correct, or to be generous. Of course being morally correct is better, but it does not really matter here. What matters is to be critical, not to be ideological and celebrative, not to split the good from the bad and pretend to be only good (and most of the so-called relational art has a similar ideological naiveté). This is examined in psychoanalysis. The way psychoanalysis works is to constantly question your sensation to be good. When you feel you are good (and also when you feel good), you have to explore that feeling and ask yourself why. If that guy stays behind you just to confirm you how good you are, you will stay exactly where you were. To question that feeling, as well as the opposite one ("I am bad"), can be effective for you, because it can create a movement. More or less, it is what I mean when I say I would like to have a critical position or promote a critical practice.

Notes

1. It is worth mentioning that in the 1960s many conceptual art practices operated under a pseudoscientific model of laboratory exploration where initial observations lead to extensive research. For historical examples see the descriptions of projects by Palle Nielson (142) and the Diggers (163–64) in this volume.

2. Miwon Kwon, "One Place after Another: Notes on Site Specificity," *Space Site Intervention—Situating Installation Art* (Minneapolis: University of Minnesota Press, 2000), 38–62.

3. Michel de Certeau, "Walking in the City," *The Practice of Everyday Life* (Berkeley: University of California Press, 1984), 97.

4. Gilles Deleuze, "1440: The Smooth and the Striated," A *Thousand Plateaus—Capitalism and Schizophrenia*, trans. Brian Massumi (Minneapolis: University of Minnesota Press, 1987), 474–500.

THE OBJECT OF EXCHANGE

Matthew Rana

I'd like to start this essay with a riddle:

> Once there was rich man who had three children and seventeen ships. The man decided to bequeath his fleet to his children: the oldest child was to receive half as an inheritance; the second oldest, one third; and the youngest child, one ninth. But soon after their father's death, his heirs realized that they couldn't divide the ships evenly. Half of seventeen is not a whole number; neither is a third or a ninth. The three children had resolved to honor their father's wishes, yet none of them would dismantle one of the ships and parcel the pieces out among them. In order to solve this problem, they consulted a magistrate who found a way for each child to receive their share and every ship remain intact. What was her solution?

Some of you may have heard this before. But for those of you who haven't, the magistrate's solution was both simple and elegant: she gave them one of her own ships, making for a total of eighteen. Each child could then have their rightful share of the seventeen—the first receiving nine; the second, six; and the third, two. Afterward, the ship that remained was returned to the magistrate as a token of good will.

Considered as an allegory for exchange, we can take away many things away from this, such as the importance of cooperation, of generosity, or even of respecting patriarchal authority. But if we shift our perspective slightly, it becomes clear that what's really at issue here is the problem of the object. In a crucial sense it is the ships' irreducibility, their ability to remain, that shapes both the problem and the solution. Indeed, it is from this kind of ambivalence, this strange capacity to unsettle and settle, to resist human affairs and force another logic, that the agency of objects emerges.

If most of the texts in this book take exchange for granted, this essay seeks to challenge its givenness. In fact, my argument actually begins with the proposition that exchange is an impossibility—at least, in the sense of one thing being exchangeable or equivalent to another. I realize that this may at first seem like a naive polemic, or even worse, a frivolous semantic argument. After all, commodities are bought and sold, goods bartered for services, trades initiated, gifts given and received. Without a doubt, transactions such as these exist. In fact, for millions of individuals worldwide (artists included) whose livelihoods depend on alternative or parallel networks of exchange, informal economic practices are all too real.

But consider for a moment the following words from Jean Baudrillard: "either a thing is worthless, or it is priceless."[1] At first they too might seem frivolous, but upon further reflection they contain a critical insight. For Baudrillard, in a context where value becomes a kind of general equivalent, a calculus for measuring life itself, all exchange is reduced to commodity exchange. That is to say, life itself becomes economized, with capital providing its regulative ideal.[2] As examples, think of the phrase "time is money" or the notion of an individual's "earning potential." The great theorist of the simulacrum, Baudrillard, therefore urges us to bear in mind that a thing can never be quantified (or, for that matter, qualified) by the abstractions that govern life under capitalism. Irreducible to its worth and its price, the object always exceeds its value within markets and, perhaps most crucially, its evaluation by human subjects. As in the riddle of the seventeen ships, there will always be a remainder, something extra that cannot be fully accounted for and yet which intercedes in our affairs.

What that something might be is, in many ways, the topic of this essay. As a kind of thought experiment, it aims to lay the groundwork for a deeper engagement with objects, while also reconsidering the active role that they have in organizing exchange. Rather than focusing solely on what takes place between human subjects, bringing objects into view allows for a more complex and nuanced view of the social and of exchange. But at stake here is not just a reevaluation of intersubjectivity in art or a vision of political economy in which the fetishized object is newly transformed. It also involves ontological issues, namely, our ability to think of life and agency as such. Recent art may be increasingly relational, dialogical, immaterial, or discursive, but there needs to be an account of the objects swirling at the core.

A first step toward this accounting is to acknowledge that objects, too, have social lives.[3] Citing the historical fluidity between potlatch and capitalist markets as well as their shared characteristics, anthropologist Arjun Appadurai argues in his introduction to *The Social Life of Things: Commodities in a Cultural Perspective* that in order to understand the connection between exchange and value in a globalized world, it is necessary to shift focus from the forms of exchange to the things themselves.

Contrary to the belief that exchange and value are determined by conditions such as scarcity or use, he writes that, "exchange is not a by-product of the mutual valuation between objects, but its source."[4] In this view, value is seen as being embodied by an object even though it cannot be understood as one of its objective properties.[5] The fact that one object is exchanged for another does not mean that the two objects are equal or have an equal value. Nor does it necessarily follow that the resultant transaction is reciprocal or fair. Instead, an object's exchange value can be seen as an expression of the desire that it incites—the price that someone is willing to pay in order to to close the gap between not-having it and having it. Put differently, it is not equality that is being negotiated in exchange; rather, it is degrees of loss and sacrifice.

For Appadurai, the exchange value of an object emerges from the judgments that are made about it by subjects within particular contexts, or what he calls "value regimes." These regimes govern value according to a number of variable relationships. At a national level, these include a country's wealth, history, population, military strength, natural resources, and level of development; they also include factors such as race and religion. Because an object's value—and its signifying value in particular—can be understood as a by-product of the shifting geographies of power in which it is embedded, the link between exchange and value always has a political dimension. But this doesn't just mean that the strength of the US dollar varies in the Eurozone and Japan. In different regimes, objects act differently, with some objects having stronger effects than others. Even in an increasingly normalized world, a bottle of Coca-Cola will "speak" differently in California than it would in Kerala.

In another register, we might even consider the mechanics of a "contemporary art regime" in which objects have the potential to circulate in ways that are too numerous to mention here. But we can easily grasp how the price of a Cindy Sherman print might differ when purchased in a Zurich gallery than when bartered outside a village in post-Soviet Ukraine.[6] Beyond an implicit critique of the art market, these shifts in value also suggest that objects are already socialized inasmuch as they always refer to a certain social logic, the coming-together of a network of relations.[7] From this vantage, the social becomes a broad panorama, an interplay that is not only intersubjective, but also economical, cultural, historical, and geographic.

While adopting a view toward the object of exchange can bring these networks into clearer focus and open them to further inquiry, objects will always be more than the social logic to which they refer, the desires they incite or the values they embody. Objects are never so passive; nor is the concept of value so exhaustive. In a decisive sense, objects always exceed their relations. So, where can we locate this excess; what remains?

For philosopher Graham Harman, "the only way to do justice to objects is to consider that their reality is free of all relation, deeper than all reciprocity."[8] In his view, what remains is an object's reality, which will always surpass the contexts in which it is embedded or its effects on other things. Drawing on the phenomenology of Edmund Husserl and Martin Heidegger, Harman envisions a universe populated exclusively by objects, humans included. Against what he calls the "philosophy of access," which since Immanuel Kant has privileged humanity's relation with the world to the exclusion of all others, Harman proposes an object-oriented philosophy "in which all objects interact with just as much dignity as human and world."[9] For him, objects cannot be reduced to the phantasmic projections of human subjects on the one hand or the objective data of empirical science on the other. Instead, objects must be considered independent of humanity and reckoned with as active agents in their own right. As he puts it, "instead of placing souls into sand and stones" we instead "find something sandy or stony in the human soul."[10]

This rethinking of the subject/object distinction as the basis for a speculative metaphysics implies a fundamental ontological shift. According to this view, humans occupy the same register of being as the Mississippi River, a Volkswagen Beetle covered in jelly, the Hindu deity Vishnu, or Instagram. In this broad spectrum, the way that a human being relates to a stone is qualitatively no different than the way that the Mississippi does. Although their respective encounters with it may be intricate and varied, neither the human nor the river can ever have an exhaustive experience of the stone, whose reality remains inaccessible—even to the stone itself.

While Harman grants that some objects are more complex than others, his point is not that all these things are equal (or equally real), but that all are objects, endowed with agency to produce reality. In this respect, an object-oriented perspective does not imply that humans are the same as ships, coke-bottles, photographs, rivers, stones, cars, gods, or downloadable applications; neither does it make the essentialist claim that all human beings are alike on account of the fact that our objecthood is different from that of, say, a virus.[11] Rather, by underscoring the agency of all objects to constitute a world (including human relations and the embodied experiences that accompany them), it seeks to question humanity's attempts to pacify and subordinate objects, both through our intellectual categories and in our practices. For if we adopt the attitude that the world is full of objects that are dignified, singular, and charged with agency, we must also acknowledge that those agencies are likely to contradict our desires and objectives.

A challenge to notions of the art object as either an expression of subjectivity, an anthropomorphized "quasi-person," or a support for dialogue and face-to-face interaction between people is one way of framing it.[12] In his essay for dOCUMENTA 13, "The Third Table," Harman even suggests that the arts might be a context in which objects are thought along the lines that he proposes.[13] However, this reckoning has implications that extend much further. For example, running contrary to discourses surrounding sustainability, stewardship over nature, or the "sanctity of life," which tend to universalize and gloss over nuance and conflict, an object-oriented approach reinstates difference and the other at the heart of exchange.[14] Here, the social life of objects can be thought to intensify far beyond the threshold of value, of human judgment and mastery. If relations are typically viewed in the dualistic terms of a chess game—that is to say, as a negotiation between two opponents—an object-oriented approach brings a multitude of different players into the fray.

But the purpose of such an orientation toward exchange is not to generate an inventory of what objects do *to* us—or alternatively, what they do *for* us and how this might be done more humanely, efficiently, or with less of an environmental footprint. Although questions such as these are important in considerations of object-agency, from voodoo to hurricanes and the critique of commodity fetishism, they nevertheless tend to demonstrate an anthropocentric bias. In an attempt to avoid treading water, we can reorient ourselves and instead ask "What might objects require *from* us?" While this undoubtedly leads to questions such as "What does my iPhone really want?" it's my opinion that this line of inquiry can have much more profound implications. To begin thinking this through in a serious and non-reductive manner, I find it useful to consider how an object-oriented approach might be extended toward modes of practice that are not strictly art-related, such as urban interventionism. In instances such as these, an object-oriented approach might require that we expand our horizon to consider not simply how an activity such as farming in a former industrial site may benefit, enliven, or beautify nearby communities, but also how this area might already form a dynamic ecology in its own right.

Taken a step further, is it possible, for example, to consider the other nonhuman agents present—such as weeds, insects, feral cats, plastic bottles, syringes, or heavy metals—as constituting an audience? What might such a diverse milieu require? We can easily imagine the conflicts that might emerge between human beings and a clowder of feral cats: noise pollution, the powerful stench of feline urine, perhaps a family pet is attacked or becomes rabid. Aside from euthanasia, the impulse here might be to find "creative" solutions whereby humans and cats can amicably coexist. Perhaps special habitats are constructed, or a spay/neuter program is established to control the feline population; maybe a public debate is staged in which the cats are repositioned as valued members of the community. Adopting a nonanthropocentric stance and asking whether projects such as these might be advantageous from the cats' point of view might end in fruitless speculation. For some, it might even seem too wholesome, eccentric, or trivial to even think about. However, by challenging the givenness of human interests as well as concepts such as resolution, population management, or integration, an object-oriented approach begins to collapse the dividing lines between exchange and antagonism.

More difficult, however, is rethinking the agencies of the heavy metals in the ground, such as cadmium, lead, or mercury. In this case, the metals' ability to seep into groundwater or be absorbed into the tissues of local plant and animal life might already be taken into account and enter into the conversation as hazardous, toxic, or poison. Addressing this in the short-term might involve soil remediation techniques that use special crops to extract the metals and store them for eventual harvest and recycling. But might there also be another way of viewing it, perhaps with shifts in scale or duration in mind? Is there a way of looking at the metals differently—that is, not from the point of view of health or toxicity? From the perspective of development or property value, this would no doubt be seen as disagreeable; from that of wildlife protection, irresponsible, if not disastrous. Indeed, whether or not this approach is desirable can be debated on moral, ecological, or evolutionary grounds. After all, couldn't cleaning-up industrial waste constitute an aspect of human agency?

If there's something disturbing or provoking about these questions, then perhaps this is a good thing. When we reorient ourselves towards issues surrounding life, agency, and equality in such a way, we are forced to rethink not only how the world works but also our place in it. By asking what else might be possible, we ask how objects—broadly construed as anything that can organize and effect life, all the way from a mercury atom to a human being—might in some manner answer to one another.

As the global debt crisis unfolds, barter networks, microgranting organizations, informal gifting, and "black" markets are on the rise. Alternative banking systems such as *Time Bank* by e-flux are being established in the art context. Likewise, as individuals develop a heightened awareness of the financial sector's complex and abstract instruments, a growing interest has emerged in attaching wealth to tangible objects. Art objects increasingly represent stable investments for a range of hedge funds and speculators worldwide, while in the United States a return to the gold standard is promoted by self-proclaimed "99 percenters" and Tea Party members alike. Yet nothing could be further from my point.

An object-oriented approach deals precisely with what *escapes* quantification. When expressed in contemporary art parlance, this should not become an apology for market conditions, or an argument for a return to object-based practices such as painting or sculpture—in fact, even the most "dematerialized" work is an object according to the definition used here. Moreover, it is not a way of saying that artists should not be compensated for their work. Rather, this is to propose that by decentralizing problematics of the subject and taking into account the constellations of objects that delimit any event, we arrive at an infinitely more nuanced, strange, and complex view of the social and of exchange.

Unseating the subject and intersubjectivity as the horizon of a "socially engaged" practice, the object of exchange is both a means and an end. But the movement that it proposes resonates with the uncertainty of a network of forces that cannot find equivalence in terms of a word, a sign, or a shake of hands. Beyond the potential implications this line of thought can have within the field of art, it also poses enormous challenges. If objects, all the way from iPhones to Vishnu and hurricanes, possess agencies independent of the humans that respectively use, worship, and are displaced by them, then how might we rethink our position within this motley armada? Are we even prepared to make concessions? Surely, this is no easy task. Because, exceeding the calculations of profit and loss, reciprocity, or fairness, objects can never be fully grasped even as they change hands. Most of all, they should never be ignored.

Notes

1. Jean Baudrillard, *Passwords* (London: Verso, 2003), 10

2. Similar notions have been explored by Michel Foucault, whose notion of governmentality can be formulated as the management of a population according to an economic logic. See Michel Foucault, *Security, Territory, and Population: Lectures at the Collège De France 1977–1978* (New York: Picador, 2007).

3. Arjun Appadurai, "Introduction: Commodities and the Politics of Value," in Arjun Appadurai, ed., *The Social Life of Things: Commodities in Cultural Perspective* (Cambridge: Cambridge University Press, 1986).

4. Appadurai, 4.

5. Nor can an object's exchange-value be seen simply as a mystification obscuring its actual utility or the amount of socially necessary labor that is required to produce it.

6. See, SOSka Group, *Barter* (2007). www.soskagroup.com/home/barter

7. In the case of the "contemporary art regime," they might refer to the relations that bring together super-wealthy members of the international jet-set and set them against each other in an elite game of consumption and one-upsmanship.

8. Graham Harman, *The Quadruple Object* (Alresford, UK: Zero Books, 2010), 47.

9. Graham Harman, "Asymmetrical Causation: Influence without Recompense," *Parallax* 16.1 (2010), 98.

10. Harman, *The Quadruple Object*, 47

11. Nor does it by any means suggest that acts of sexual abuse or human slavery can be justified because human beings are "mere" objects.

12. For more, see Isabelle Graw's essay "The Value of Painting: Notes on Unspecificity, Indexicality and Highly Valuable Quasi-Persons" in Isabelle Graw, Daniel Birnbaum, and Nikolaus Hirsch, eds., *Thinking Through Painting: Reflexivity and Agency Beyond the Canvas* (Berlin: Sternberg Press, 2012), 45–57, in which she discusses the concept of paintings as "quasi-persons" and stand-ins for the artist.

13. Graham Harman, "The Third Table/Der dritte Tisch," *dOCUMENTA 13 100 Notes—100 Thoughts No.085* (Berlin: Hatje Cantz, 2012).

14. For another perspective, see Donna Haraway, *The Companion Species Manifesto: Dogs, People, and Significant Otherness* (Chicago: Paradigm Press, 2003).

HOW FREE IS FREE?

PROPERTY, MARKETS, AND THE AESTHETIC(S) OF THE COMMON(S)

Ignacio Valero

They hang the man and flog the woman / That steal the goose from off
the common,
But let the greater villain loose / That steals the common from the goose.
The law demands that we atone / When we take things that we do not own
But leave the lords and ladies fine / Who take things that are yours and mine.
The poor and wretched don't escape / If they conspire the law to break:
This must be so but they endure / Those who conspire to make the law.
The law locks up the man or woman / Who steals the goose from off
the common,
And geese will still a common lack / Till they go and steal it back.

—Anonymous English poem ca. 1764[1]

Man being born, as has been proved, with a Title to perfect Freedom, and an uncontrolled enjoyment of all the Rights and Privileges of the Law of Nature, equally with any other Man, or number of Men in the World, hath by Nature a Power, not only to preserve his Property, that is, his Life, Liberty and Estate, against the Injuries and Attempts of other Men; but to judge of, and punish the breaches of that Law in others, as he is perswaded the Offence deserves, even with Death it self, in Crimes where the heinousness of the Fact, in his Opinion, requires it."

—John Locke, 1690[2]

The Capitalist form is not only a set of economic rules and functions, it is also the internalization of a certain set of limitations, of psychic automatisms, of rules for compliance.

—Franco Berardi, 2012[3]

Introduction

The 99 percent is no mere rhetorical device but the actual statistic of the new political economy of contemporary capitalism, what William L. Robinson calls the "epochal shift" of world capitalism,[4] a shift founded also on a particular hyperindividualist aesthetic, and automated, networked technological subjectivity,[5] facilitated by the relentless utilization and debasing of the idea of freedom and the free. "Free," whether it is the "free press" or a "free" sample, is a sound bite that is nothing but a nostalgic attempt to cynically mine the sediment of four centuries of Enlightenment philosophical, political, and economic ideals, ideas that initially attempted to make a dent on the suffocating and immiserating stranglehold of monarchy, aristocracy, and church, developed after the fall of the Roman Empire.

Along with the Enlightenment's laudable goals of liberation and critical modernity, there was always an ugly shadow side, namely colonialism and imperialism, and the violent appropriation and enclosure of the commonwealth (the modernity/coloniality rift).[6] It was precisely because of this "darker side of the Renaissance," as Walter Mignolo puts it, that the development of early capitalism became possible, and continues to be so to this day. There is no space here to detail these highly complex historical processes, but some highlights can be outlined. The reflection contextualizes aspects of our contemporary crisis, showing that this has been a constructed project, not an "act of God" or a purely natural happening, and as such it can be deconstructed, transformed, and rebuilt anew.

At the end of the European Middle Ages, three interrelated processes were set in motion, each of which has greatly impacted all subsequent world history: (1) the so-called Age of Discovery, with its symbolic start year of 1492, that in fact largely leads to a worldwide racist, patriarchal, genocidal, and ecologically destructive Eurocentric project of plunder colonialism and religious zealotry;[7] (2) the development around the same time of early capitalism in the English countryside and its derived social, technological, ecological, and market exchange imperatives; and (3) the profound modification of human subjectivity, especially as it relates to the common and commons of human-to-human and human-to-nature relations. When the first and second of these processes were conjoined, we have the basic ingredients for Western modernity. When the third of these processes is added, we witness the full project of freedom and enclosure, one that, Janus-faced, contains both the recipe for societal control and the dream of individual freedom.

The animus here is not to engage in a facile diatribe of all things "Western" and a corresponding idealization of all things "non-Western," for they are in themselves ambiguous dualistic epistemological and historical categories burdened with the unfortunate legacy of the colonial project. Powerful, destructive, and benevolent forces (and everything in between) have existed in the past and will in the future, but the "elephant in the room" of the global Eurocentric project of the last three hundred to five hundred years is impossible to ignore, if the "history of the present," as Michel Foucault suggests,[8] is to make sense, and, pragmatically, if we are to find new and/or hybrid alternatives. I feel these three dynamics, outlined above, best illuminate the opacity of the structural conditions and contradictions of the present, since they reinforce each other like intertwining coils around the central axis of "*possession by dispossession*," as David Harvey has put it.[9] The key arguments, thus, will revolve around: (1) property and production, (2) appropriation and enclosure, and (3) aesthetics.

Coloniality

Much has been written about the Columbian discovery and its ramifications, and about the "invention" and possession of the exotic other. It is a mixed dynamic that at one level may be said to be truly curious about difference and diversity, and thus animated by a certain capacity to acknowledge "an-other," cultural or biological, but, on the other hand, it is fully embedded in a discursive practice of dominion and ownership. Stephen Greenblat speaks of the enslavement of indigenous peoples: "the kidnapping and misunderstanding of their languages, and how the Europeans looked at the 'possession acts' as a form of ultimate gift-giving. After taking their land, the conquistadors forced Christianity upon the Indians and gave them salvation through a Lord they could not read about for themselves."[10] The concept of "ownership," a wholly alien idea in the Americas, is introduced to justify who is the legitimate owner of these "new" lands. Roman law and Christian theology are enlisted to discern whether the indigenous inhabitants have a soul, and thus are fully human or not. This is a key question, for if they are not, or if they are less than humans, they may not have a right to own, and in fact they may even be owned. As such, grabbing their lands is an act of mercy, a favor, extended to the "heathens" and "barbarians" in exchange for the protection of the Christian kings and queens and their God. They are like children, like "minors," who now have the lucky tutelage of said royals, popes, and their delegates, the colonial masters and clergy.[11]

The church, Catholic and Protestant alike, and the colonial administrations conspired systematically in low- to high-grade demographic and cultural genocide, one aspect of which was the destruction of native languages and beliefs.[12] Walter Mignolo's study of the obliteration of knowledge production in Spanish America maps colonial dominion there, but also in the rest of the colonized world, and is an excellent example of how lingering arrogant cultural and aesthetic attitudes have survived to the present.[13] Mignolo has recently published a complementary tome suggesting an end of "coloniality," thanks to two major global processes at work: "*dewesternization* . . . an irreversible shift to the East in struggles over knowledge, economics, and politics"; and "*decoloniality*, [which] requires delinking from the colonial matrix of power underlying Western modernity to imagine and build global futures in which human beings and the natural world are no longer exploited in the relentless quest for wealth accumulation."[14] Here the calling of *What We Want Is Free* could join forces with such decolonial projects. For the struggles of resistance cannot be simply divided between center and periphery, as we have both center and periphery in both the center and the periphery. An early example of internal colonialism, or periphery in the center, is the Holy Inquisition created by Pope Gregory IX ca. 1231, in collusion with the feudal powers, to violently eradicate Jews, Moors, and heretics of all stripes, but really devoted to stamp out any kind of resistance of peasants, town women, and other social groups challenging the status quo—an inquisition later reenacted in the colonial world. The merciless killing of emancipated women as witches, brutally thrown from their former lands. This institution and its history can only be understood in light of the absolute ideological and economic control the Church and its feudal allies wanted to exert. It shows also how the double process of colonialism and the "transition" to capitalism was strenuously resisted by the dispossessed. As Silvia Federici notes:

> Although influenced by Eastern religions brought to Europe by merchants and crusaders, popular heresy was less a deviation from the orthodox doctrine than a protest movement, aspiring to a radical democratization of social life. Heresy was the equivalent of "liberation theology" for the medieval proletariat. It gave a frame to peoples' demands for spiritual renewal and social justice, challenging both the church and secular authority by appeal to a higher truth. It denounced social hierarchies, private property and the accumulation of wealth, and it disseminated among the people a new, revolutionary conception of society that, for the first time in the Middle Ages, redefined every aspect of daily life (work, property, sexual reproduction, and the position of women), posing the question of emancipation in truly universal terms.[15]

These so-called heretics are heroic ancestors to the myriad contemporary decolonizing, *indignados*, and Occupy resistance movements throughout the world. Even today some of the main social and economic conflicts, both within nations and globally, are between national capitalisms and global capitalisms. Yet, as Ellen Meiksins Wood notes, we cannot "deny that much remains to be said about the connection between capitalism and imperialism. But to understand that connection—and to mount an effective challenge to Eurocentric neglect of Western imperialism—requires us to take into account the very specific conditions in which traditional forms of colonialism were transformed into capitalist types of imperialism. That means acknowledging *the very specific effects of capitalist social property relations*."[16]

The Origins of Capitalism and the Early Transition to Capitalist Subjectivity

The rise of early capitalism in the English countryside during the Renaissance was enabled by a series of political, institutional, and ideational changes, which together set in motion a new production of value. Of these changes, the shift from use value to exchange value and the reconceptualization of property are of special concern to this essay, as they construct the process through which traditional feudal property and the commons become mere commodities, real estate, along with the transformation of the peasantry into a "factor" of production, now "freed" from feudal obligations, through the violent process of the "*enclosure of the commons*."

The question of the "commons" and the "common" is a fertile area of study, struggle, and practice today, arguably sharing a similarly complex world ancestry. But, in this context, we refer to the land-use form that evolved in Europe over the course of hundreds of years after the collapse of the Western Roman Empire—specifically, the common-law land-use tradition arising from medieval England. During Feudalism there existed the manorial lands, the small subsistence plots of the peasant serfs bonded to a given manor or feud, and the lands beyond, "belonging" to all: the commons. They included "meadows, forests, lakes, wild pastures, that provided crucial resources for the peasant economy (wood for fuel, timber for building, fishponds, grazing grounds for animals) and fostered community cohesion and cooperation . . . So important were the 'commons' in the political economy and struggles of the medieval rural populations that their memory still excites our imagination, projecting the vision of a world where *goods can be shared* and *solidarity*, rather than desire for self-aggrandizement, can be the substance of social relations."[17]

The violent destruction and enclosure of these historical commons play a fundamental role in early capitalism: it is not possible to separate the actual enclosure of such common lands from the subjective rationalization and internalization of this process through moral, legal, and political strategies. It is a slow intertwined unfolding wherein, as E. P. Thompson writes, "Capitalist notations of property rights arose out of the long material processes of agrarian change, as land use became loosed from subsistence imperatives and the land was laid open to the market."[18] John Bellers, writing in the late 1600s, manages to be both colonialist, racist, as well insulting to the growing number of English landless peasants, but he is also mirroring a change of subjectivity: "Forests and great Commons make the Poor that are upon them too much like the *Indian*." Commons are "a hindrance to industry . . . Nurseries of idleness and insolence."[19]

This unfolding subjectivity is based on a particular interpretation of the European Enlightenment. John Locke's conception of private property is particularly relevant here. Locke, much influenced by Newton, is of course the canonical author that fought against monarchical tyranny and was notably influential on the English Glorious Revolution and the American Revolution, but his formalization of the then-unwinding ideas on property still has an oversized weight today.[20] "For Locke," Arturo Escobar argues, "politics was subordinated to morality and economics. A key notion in his political theory, which was going to gain crucial importance in economics, was that of *property*," . . . and "its introduction raised to a central position . . . the *individual* . . . From then on, happiness will be equated with human order but only as it appears to the individual who is bound to think of his/her own interest."[21] It no doubt helped justify the massive enclosures of the commons in England as well as the colonial dispossession of indigenous lands, directly connected as they were to the concept of *improvement*, the utilization of the land's productivity for profit, called "*mejoras*" in Spanish America.[22]

"In the early modern period," according to Wood, "productivity and profit were inextricably connected in the concept of *improvement*, and it nicely sums up the ideology of a rising agrarian capitalism."[23] Wood argues that it was not simply new techniques of cultivation but more importantly a new institutional subject formation:

> Improvement meant, even more fundamentally, new forms and conceptions of property. "Improved" farming, for the enterprising landlord and his prosperous capitalist tenant, ideally, although not necessarily, meant enlarged and concentrated landholdings. It certainly meant the elimination of old customs and practices that interfered with the most productive use of land . . . Peasants have since time immemorial employed various means of regulating land use in the interest of the village community . . . In England, there were many such practices and customs . . . *common lands* . . . various other kinds of use rights in private lands . . . land had to be *liberated* from any such obstruction to their productive and profitable use of property.[24]

This institution of *enclosure*, of "freeing" commons, comes into being to carry out the above program, and it is the embodiment of redefined property rights, which, as Thompson notes, is later conveniently brought into a false equivalence with the Enlightenment idea of liberty:

> It was always a problem to explain the commons within capitalist categories. There was something uncomfortable about them. Their very existence prompted questions about the origin of property and about historical title to land. In the sixteenth and seventeenth centuries landowners had asserted their titles in land against the prerogatives of the king, and copyholders had asserted their titles

> and customs against their lords. Yet if they fell back on Hobbesian violence or on the right of conquest, how could they reply to the telling counter-argument of the Norman Yoke? When Locke sat down to offer an answer, all this was stewing around in his mind. In his First Treatise he dismissed notions of the title by succession from Father Adam or from the donation of God. In the Second Treatise his chapter on property commences with an extended metaphor of common right usage. God granted the world to "mankind in common," and the fruits and beasts "are produced by the spontaneous hand of nature." *But the common was seen as a negative . . . : it belonged to nobody and was open to any taker.*"[25]

During the seventeenth century, property becomes more and more *salable*; by the eighteenth, it is the norm, enshrined as well in the new political economy of Adam Smith, whereby "property was either 'perfect' and absolute or it was meaningless," and "it was the function of government to protect property from the indignation of the poor."[26]

Social conditions are violently disrupted and suddenly and, increasingly, hordes of property-less peasants are spit out from the land. "*Dispossessed 'masterless men*' "[27] wander the countryside and slowly ring London in squalor. The Glorious Revolution and the subsequent "*inclosure acts*' of a Parliament wholly at the service of large landholders are the harsh context under which Locke writes about property.[28] As Wood writes:

> The theme running throughout his [Locke's] discussion is that the earth is there to be made productive and profitable, and that this is why private property, which emanates from labour, trumps common possession . . . Money and commerce are the motivation for improvement; and an acre of land in unimproved America, which may be as naturally fertile as an acre in England, is not worth 1/1000 of the English acre, if we calculate 'all the Profit an *Indian* received from it were it valued and sold here' (II. 43). Locke's point, which not coincidentally drips with colonialist contempt, is that unimproved land is *waste*, so that any man who takes it out of common ownership and appropriates it to himself—he who removes land from the common and encloses it—in order to improve it has *given* something to humanity, not taken it away . . . It appears that the issue for Locke has less to do with the activity of labour as such than with its profitable use . . . [I]n America, for instance, he talks not about the Indian's expenditure of labour, but about the Indian's failure to realize profit . . . This emphasis on *the creation of exchange value as the basis of property* is a *critical move in the theorization of capitalist property*.[29]

Here, too, the global conjunction of coloniality and capitalism is at work, as a practice of "dispossession," reinforced by "private property" both as a legal, concrete institution and as an internalized subjectivity. Again, we turn to Locke to find a direct reference to a precapitalist subjectivity of not "knowing" enclosure: "The wild *Indian* . . . who knows no Inclosure and is still a Tenant in common . . ."[30] Indeed, writes Thompson, "Locke decided that the American Indian was poor 'for want of improving' the land by labour. Since labour (and improvement) constituted the right to property, this made it the more easy for the Europeans to dispossess the Indians of their hunting grounds. The Puritans were ready to moralise their appropriation of Indian lands by reference to God's commands, in *Genesis* 1, 28, 'to replenish the earth, and subdue it.' "[31] However, Puritan "moralizing" is yet another instance of clashing subject formations: indigenous and agrarian colonial capitalist, built on arguments, like those of Locke, favoring a landed gentry, and mixing God and class, under the guise of land "improvement": "subduing or cultivating the Earth, and having Dominion, we see are joyned together. The one gave Title to the other. So that God by commanding to subdue, gave authority so far to *appropriate*. And the Condition of Human Life, which requires Labour and Materials to work on, necessarily introduces *private Possessions*."[32]

It is worth quoting these detailed arguments at length because of their direct contemporary ramifications to the question of what is *free*. Substitute removing "land from the common" for "removing information or cultural production from the common" and we are talking about cognitive capitalism: Facebook, Google, et cetera. It is crucial to foreground the implications of connecting labor with the creation of profit and exchange value, ignoring labor's use value, and then to derive "property from the creation of exchange value." The modern "derivatives," the ponzi-like financial "innovation" at the base of the 2008 Great Recession, are buried deep in the ideas of Locke et al. on property, as again these passages in the *Second Treatise* disclose:

> We see in *Commons*, which remain so by Compact, that 'tis the taking any part of what is common, and removing it out of the state Nature leaves it, which *begins the* Property; without which the common is of no use. And the taking of this or that part, does not depend on the express consent of all the Commoners. Thus the Grass my Horse has bit; the Turfs my Servant has cut; and the Ore I have digg'd in any place where I have a right to them in common with others, become my *Property*, without the assignation or consent of any body. The labour that was mine, removing them out of that common state they were in, hath *fixed* my *Property* in them . . . So that God, by commanding to subdue, gave Authority so far to *appropriate*. And the condition of Human Life, which requires Labour and Materials to work on, necessarily introduces *private Possessions*."[33]

These statements are truly revealing: not only do they contain the justification for appropriating the labour of one's servants (one's employees), they also put forward the intellectual foundation for considering that such labour *belongs to the master*, and is equivalent, or even the same, as any such labour that the master might undertake with their own body and time. It is God's "command," and thus the master has no need of the "consent of any body" to appropriate for himself what belongs to the commons—since the common is "of no use," unless it is privatized. By the late eighteenth century, this "master" becomes even more enlarged, as the legal foundations are set in England through which "corporations" (which has at its root the word corpus, or body) become like human beings, entitled to natural rights of ownership, inheritance, and legal recourse. The "producer" becomes the appropriator, what might be called today by some a "job creator," ignoring the key social dimension that is necessary for capital accumulation to occur. It shows, too, the radical influence of Locke's mentor, the big English landowner and "Chief Lord Proprietor of the Carolina Colony," the First Earl of Shaftesbury: "We owe *Two Treatises* to the wonderful knowledge of state affairs which Locke acquired from frequent discourse with the First Earl of Shaftesbury; indeed the evidence suggests . . . that he actually wrote the book *for Shaftesbury's purposes*."[34]

It is in this traditional refusal on the part of the few to acknowledge the contribution of the many that we find the roots of "*possession by dispossession*." Recall the heated discussions during the 2012 US election year on "makers" and "takers," the great bank and corporate bailout of 2008–2009, and the continuing income-tax cuts to the very rich. These represent a massive transfer of social wealth (dispossession), via unemployment, home foreclosures, huge government debt, and so forth, to the 1 percent, basically telling us that the "Turfs that my servant hast cut" belongs to me, the corporation-as-person or the wealthy beneficiary of big tax cuts—the very ghosts of Locke's "cuts" haunt the present.[35]

Aesthetic Alienation and Subjectivity

Now, then, how is the above history connected to the European development of the field of aesthetics in the eighteenth century, and how is this related to some of the ethical, political, and philosophical considerations behind the title of this book, *What We Want is Free*? Three concepts will be briefly utilized: *aesthetic alienation*, *commodity aesthetics*, and my own developing concept, *aesthetic(s) of the common(s)*.

The word *aestheticae* (of sense perception and the sensuous) appears for the first time in 1735 at the end of a small book, *Reflections on Poetry*, written in Latin by Alexander Gottlieb Baumgarten.[36] It is a forerunner of his 1750 *Asthetica* treatise, which launches the modern discussion on philosophical aesthetics. He recalls how the ancient Greek philosophers and the Church Fathers always distinguished between *aistheta* (objects of sense) and *noeta* (objects of thought), and gave them a clear separation and hierarchy. In his initial introduction of aesthetics he reflects how "Therefore, *things known* are to be known by the superior faculty as the object of logic; *things perceived* [are to be known by the inferior faculty as the object] of the science of perfection or aesthetic."[37] This abstract primacy over the material haunts the aesthetic since antiquity; it is the setting for the contradictory relation between the intelligible and the sensible, and the modern weaving of "aesthetic alienation" with "commodity aesthetics." Baumgarten writes a mere forty-five years after Locke's *Second Treatise on Government*, at the dawn of the capitalist Industrial Revolution, and as the European "Age of Reason" actively unfolds. As Terry Eaglteon notes:

> Anyone who inspects the theory of European philosophy since the Enlightenment must be struck by the curiously high priority assigned by it to aesthetic questions . . . Why, more particularly, should this *theoretical* persistence of the aesthetic typify an historical period when cultural *practice* might be claimed to have lost much of its traditional social relevance, debased as it is to a general branch of commodity production?[38]

Eagleton, a contemporary Marxist literary critic, further offers that, due to the "progressively abstract, technical nature of modern European thought, . . . art would still appear to speak of the human and the concrete, providing us with a welcome respite of the *alienating* rigours . . . and offering at the very heart of this great explosion and division of knowledges, a residually *common* world." Yet, he continues, "with the birth of the aesthetic, the sphere of art itself begins to suffer something of the abstraction and formalization of modern theory in general."[39] Art practice and aesthetic theory exist in paradoxical contradiction, concrete and conceptual, embedded in the world and struggling for autonomy.

Eagleton continues: "The *aesthetic* is at once . . . the very secret prototype of *human subjectivity* in *early capitalist* society, and *a vision* of human energies as radical ends in themselves which is the implacable enemy of all dominative or instrumentalist thought."[40] In this view, Eagleton puts forward the idea that the emergence of the *aesthetic* in this period is extremely significant, as it both confirms the rise of the subjective self that the Enlightenment is known for, while it is planting the seeds for a more utopian, or liberatory, promise of reconciliation that complexifies the relation of the individual to the emerging capitalist state.

This is the conundrum that J. M. Bernstein calls the "aesthetic alienation," which seems to be the *fate of art.* [41] It mirrors the "ancient quarrel" between poetry and philosophy, art and politics, inaugurated by Plato when he exiles (specific) arts and artists from his ideal-state *Republic* because they engage in the dangerous practice of *eikasia*, that "state of vague image-ridden illusion"[42] (making him, perhaps, the first systematic art and media critic), because image, icon, distort truth—the core of the community must not be affected by image ghosts, the *phantasma* of the slumber of truth. Baumgarten's aesthetics, then, reiterates Plato's formal hierarchical split between the "intelligible" and the "sensible." Such a break is at the edge of this *alienation* that constantly "swerves"[43] from one domain to the other, where the life of the mind is viewed as *superior* and dictating to the *inferior* changing affairs of humanity: "Henceforth," Bernstein writes, "politics (practice) was to be only the application of theory to the world." This new "knowing" was to be *autonomous*, limiting practice to the mere "application of theoretical understanding," in lieu of "a form of *worldly engagement* . . . The triumph of the life of contemplation in Plato—which would be continued in Christianity, in modern philosophy of history and the *economic* organization of mass societies—spelled the end of ethical life almost before it had begun."[44]

This opposing "foreignness" emerging from this oscillating identity with life reflects in fact the birth of a new subjectivity, one that is tied up with the enclosure of life by the commodity. Eagleton writes:

> The emergence of the aesthetic as a theoretical category is closely bound up with the material process by which cultural production, at an early stage of bourgeois society, becomes "autonomous"—autonomous, that is, of the various social functions which it has traditionally served. Once *artefacts* become *commodities in the marketplace*, they exist for nothing and nobody in particular, and can consequently be rationalized, ideologically speaking, as existing entirely and gloriously for themselves. It is this notion of *autonomy* or self-referentiality which the new discourse of aesthetics is centrally concerned to elaborate . . . [A]rt is . . . sequestered from all other social practices, to become an isolated enclave within which the dominant social order can find an idealized refuge from its own actual values of competitiveness, exploitation and material possessiveness.[45]

Commodity Aesthetics, Industrial Fordism, and Post-Fordism

And, it is this estrangement from the common and the commons that private property and the "new regime of accumulation" imposes on the social and the ecological, that will prepare the ground for a new and more radical round of alienation when art and aesthetics are "invited back" to the *Republic*, primarily as "commodity aesthetics," during Fordist industrial mass consumption and the "society of the spectacle," and the Post-Fordist "creative economy" of semiocapitalism.[46]

Henry Ford's assembly line organization, modeled after F. W. Taylor's "scientific management," along with his attempt to "regulate the private lives of his workers, including especially their domestic arrangements," is a condition already prefigured by Antonio Gramsci, namely, "a new model of relationship between the spheres of *economy* and *culture*." After the Great Depression of the 1920s, a "New Deal"—the truce between labor and capital—resulting eventually in the so-called "Affluent Society"[47] of affordable mass consumption, tranquilizing advertising and banal television, represents the mature phase of Fordism and peaks around the late 1960s, precisely, and not coincidentally, at the start of the mass popular movements of the 1960s.[48] Roughly corresponding to this Fordist phase, and becoming even more entrenched during the intensified phase of the "society of the spectacle" and the neoliberal post-Fordist "creative economy," commodity aesthetics, as defined by Wolfgang Fritz Haug,

> designates a complex which springs from the commodity form of the products and which is functionally determined by exchange-value—a complex of material phenomena and of the sensual subject-object relations conditioned by these phenomena. The analysis of these relations reveals the *subjective* element in the political economy of capitalism in so far as subjectivity is at once a result and a prerequisite of its functioning . . . The term "commodity aesthetics" narrows it [aesthetics] down to "beauty," i.e., an appearance that appeals to the senses; and, on the other hand, a beauty developed in the service of the realization of exchange value, whereby commodities are designed to stimulate in the onlooker the desire to possess and the impulse to buy . . . Commodity production has as its aim not the creation of certain use-values as such, but rather manufacture for sale. Use-value only figures in the calculations of the commodity producer in terms of buyer-expectation . . . In all commodity production a double reality is produced: first, the use-value; second, and more importantly, the *appearance* of use-value . . . The aesthetics of the commodity . . . the sensual appearance . . . its use-value become detached from the object itself.[49]

Such detachment is what links commodity aesthetics with aesthetic alienation, entering in a mimetic dynamic of mutually reflecting mirrors, whose *appearance* of use value is what Haug calls the "aesthetic illusion," which is eerily reminiscent of Plato's old idea of *eikasia*. It becomes an "instrument in accumulating money," and through a "technocracy of sensuality" promotes "an exaggeration of the apparent use-value of the commodity." In short, "sensuality in this context becomes the vehicle of an economic function," and "under the pressure of competition," it is "ultimately necessary to gain control over . . . this aesthetic process . . . Whoever controls the product's appearance can control the fascinated public by appealing to them sensually." And, in a prescient critique of the global role of branding, Haug affirms: "It would be particularly absurd in the case of commodity aesthetics to ignore the fact that its current dominant form is *the aesthetics of the monopoly-commodity*, i.e., the forms in which trans-nationals in particular intervene directly in the collective imagination of cultures."[50]

By the 1980s, the newly "emerging" *economies*, no longer deemed "underdeveloped" or "developing" or "Third World" *countries*, were now seen as mere *economies*, that is, entities that should be or should promptly become neoliberal free-markets. The cultural, geographic, and ecological context and meaning of what is to be a country and a nation, a community, and a citizen is relegated to an "externality"; that is, any and all things that cannot be reduced to the calculus of private property, utility, and price in the capitalist market are by definition *external* to the market.[51] It is also not a coincidence that these externalities pertain largely to the common and the commons or to third party gains or losses. This further means that for them to be considered they must be "internalized," or reduced to dollars and cents. This leads to the bizarre false equivalence of market internalization of, say, giving a money price to the Amazon, the Arctic, the health of your loved one, or the free exchanges of social media. It is a Catch-22 that absorbs the world under a planetary global "market," now become a giant closed system, showing once more capitalism's strong historical tendency to "free ride," to force everything, everyone, every common and commons, life itself, into a reductive straitjacket of capital accumulation that pays no attention to its true costs, hidden behind a radical individualistic subjectivity, onerous power and property relations, and a furious technological treadmill—a new radical round of "possession by dispossesion" or, precisely, post-Fordist neoliberalism.

David Harvey observes: "Future historians may well look upon the years 1978–1980 as a revolutionary turning point in the world's social and economic history." Deng Xiaoping in China, Margaret Thatcher in Great Britain, Ronald Reagan in the United States, and General Adolfo Pinochet in Chile, all launch within a few years apart a new radical breed of capitalism characterized by a global rapid and massive "deregulation, privatization, and withdrawal of the state from many areas of social provision," accompanied by "changes of ways of life and thought." It maintains that "the social good will be maximized by maximizing the reach and frequency of market transactions," bringing "all human action into the domain of the market."[52]

The Aesthetic(s) of the Common(s)

One hundred years earlier, Georg Simmel had noted already that one-sided tendency, warning, according to Donald Levine, that "when the last trace of reciprocity in a relationship has disappeared, it no longer exists as a social fact; society, in Simmel's sense has ceased to be."[53]

It is against this new "enclosure of the commons" and lack of reciprocity that the questions and examples this book addresses become even more fully relevant. It is not possible to speak of our "wanting the free" without interrogating aspects of this longing (and implied political call to action), and without revisiting how is it that we are becoming increasingly less free, in spite of all sound bites to the contrary. This has been the aim of this chapter, but I cannot close without making a brief reference to one suggested concept and practice I am studying: the aesthetic(s) of the common(s).[54] Confronted with the global and local paradox of hearing more and more about the "free" and the "common" (cognitive and affective sharing) and its "commons" (the constant material creations of this common), and by an aesthetic(s) that is multiple, global, and diverse, there is a renewed need to revisit these domains within the contemporary present.

This plurality of conditions is a mirror, too, of neoliberal globalization at the macro level and its localized market targeting at the micro level of post-Fordism. It is a mesh, a web, one that contains giant monopolies, but potentially also a liberating force at the interstices of the material geographies and cultures and the virtual networks of the WorldWideWeb. Anthropologist and Political Ecologist Arturo Escobar calls this potential force "territories of difference."[55] Political Philosopher John Holloway calls this threshold "the crack."[56] Artist, activist and academic Gregory Sholette depicts this invisible common(s) as "Dark Matter,"[57] Manuel Castells, an early theorist of the "network society," has called this interstitial resistance, "networks of outrage and hope,'[58] and locates its power within geopolitics and affect. Paul Hawken, environmentalist, writer, and tech entrepreneur, a few years earlier sounded a similar note with his *Blessed Unrest*,[59] documenting myriad divergent social and environmental justice movements coalescing into the "largest movement in the world." Once again, "social movements" dynamics as a global phenomenon have returned with force, albeit quite unevenly, since the late 1990s, as the deleterious effects of neoliberal "disaster capitalism" have become more widely felt.

In this context, I believe this collaborative book to be a good example of this impetus, which like these global movements may be viewed as an expression of the aesthetic(s) of the common(s). Others have called it "communities of sense," the idea that the "'science of the sensible' is not a depoliticized discourse or theory of art but a factor of a specific historical organization of social roles and communality." It is

> to open the possibility to a politics of collectivity beyond collectivism or identity politics . . . It is to recognize a contingent and non-essential manner of being-together in a community . . . Such a concept of *community* acknowledges politics to contain a *sensuous* or *aesthetic aspect* that is irreducible to ideology or idealization . . . being-together only through a considerable dismantling of any idealized common ground, form or figure . . . reemerged today, as contemporary artistic practices engage with the realities of globalization.[60]

This contingency of "being-together" is another way of "making sense" of the world by "coming to our senses," really, a *social practice* of aesthetics—an aesthetic(s) of the common(s), which seeks to avoid the dangers of "immunity," the ever-present tragedy of all fundamentalisms and jingoisms.[61] But besides the making sense of common(s) in social movements and aesthetic(s), there is a third angle of common(s) that complements the other two, one coming from the sciences: evolutionary biology and biopolitics, where a more literal "sociobiology" is giving way to a more empirical understanding of cooperation and competition and the production of the common(s) in "group selection," beyond crude versions of Darwinism like social Darwinism. Three recent examples are worth noting: *The Social Conquest of Earth*, from E. O. Wilson, the famous biologist, who, in a profound gesture of honesty, revisits the issue of "altruism" and his own earlier sociobiology and finds it to be more expansive and global—group dynamics, not the selfish gene, propel altruism: "Can true altruism ever exist? Is generosity a sustainable trait? Or are living things inherently selfish, our kindness nothing but a mask? This is science with existential stakes,"[62] comments Jonah Lehrer of the *New Yorker*. The second is from mathematical biologist Martin Nowak's *Supercooperators*,[63] no less controversial and a more autobiographical take on the matter, which views the Lockean-accented "tragedy of the commons" as a greedy, ultimately unsustainable paradigm. Thirdly, Melinda Cooper's *Life as Surplus* addresses some of the above but from the angle of biopower and biopolitics, which has the added advantage of an original integration of political economy with the life sciences that reveals how

> Just as complexity theorists are celebrating the new political economy of nature, a certain kind of vitalism is coming back into fashion in economics . . . It is because life is neguentropic, it seems, that economic growth is without end . . . because life is self-organizing that we should reject all state regulation of the market . . . a vitalism that comes dangerously close to equating the evolution of life with that of capital.[64]

Perhaps it is merely capital trying to naturalize itself, and to vaccinate and immunize itself from the common(s), branding the sensuous, the aesthetic, as a primary accumulation strategy, but there are also the empowering myriad movements and counterpoints of a social practice ever trying to jump the barbwires of enclosure and dispossession in search of the Free.

Notes

1. Anonymous English poem ca. 1764, in David Bollier, *Silent Theft: The Private Plunder of Our Common Wealth* (New York and London: Routledge, 2003), xi.

2. *Locke: Two Treatises of Government* (1690), ed. Peter Laslett, (Cambridge: Cambridge University Press, 2004), 323–324; emphasis added.

3. Franco "Bifo" Berardi, *The Uprising: On Poetry and Finance* (Los Angeles: Semiotext(e), 2012), 58.

4. William I. Robinson, *Latin America and Global Capitalism: A Critical Globalization Perspective* (Baltimore: Johns Hopkins University Press, 2008).

5. Gary Genosko, ed., *Felix Guattari in the Age of Semiocapitalism: Deleuze Studies* 6.2 (Edinburgh: Edinburgh University Press, 2012).

6. Cf. "The Latin American Modernity/ Coloniality/ Decoloniality" Research Project"; also the work of Arturo Escobar, Walter Mignolo, Rolando Vazquez, Anibal Quijano, Enrique Dussel, et al.

7. This process lingers today in the tenuous disguise of neoliberal globalization.

8. Cf. Michael S. Roth, 'Foucault's "History of the Present,"' *History and Theory* 20.1 (February 1981), 32–46, an informed early account on Foucault's historical method.

9. David Harvey, *The New Imperialism* (Oxford: Oxford University Press, 2005) and A *Brief History of Neoliberalism* (Oxford: Oxford University Press, 2007); see also Devi Dee Mucina, *Ubuntu: A Regenerative Philosophy for Rupturing Racist Colonial Stories of Dispossession* (Toronto: University of Toronto, PhD Thesis, 2011) http://www.academia.edu/1320525/Ubuntu_A_Regenerative_Philosophy_for_Rupturing_Racist_Colonial_Stories_of_Dispossession

10. Cf. Stephen Greenblatt, *Marvelous Possessions: The Wonder of the New World* (Chicago: Chicago University Press, 1992).

11. To be sure there were efforts by some enlightened clergy to mediate in this despicable act of dispossession, though time and again trumped up by the geopolitics of plunder and greed. In 1550 Bartolomé de Las Casas, a conquistador turned Dominican friar, first notable defender of the rights of the native peoples, engaged in a famous debate in Valladolid with Juan Ginés de Sepúlveda, who advocated against indigenous rights, seeing aboriginals as less than human and therefore subject to dispossession and enslavement.

12. *The Mission*, a poignant 1986 film, depicts the tribulations of a eighteenth-century Jesuit mission as it faces the injustice and cynicism of the Spanish and Portuguese colonial enterprise.

13. Walter Mignolo, *The Darker Side of the Renaissance: Literacy, Territoriality, and Colonization*, 2nd ed. (Ann Arbor: University of Michigan Press, 2003).

14. Walter Mignolo, *The Darker Side of Western Modernity: Global Futures, Decolonial Options* (Durham, NC: Duke University Press, 2011); emphasis added.

15. Silvia Federici, *Caliban and the Witch: Women, The Body and Primitive Accumulation* (New York: Autonomedia, 2004), 33.

16. Ellen Meiksins Wood, *The Origin of Capitalism: A Longer View* (London: Verso 2002), 33; emphasis added.

17. Federici, op. cit., 24; emphasis added.

18. E. P. Thompson, *Customs in Common* (Pontypool, Wales: Merlin, 1991; 2010), 164.

19. Quoted in Thompson, 165.

20. John Locke, *Two Treatises on Government and a Letter Concerning Toleration* (New Haven: Yale University Press, 2003), 111 ff.

21. Arturo Escobar, "Economics and the Space of Modernity: Tales of Market, Production and Labor," *Cultural Studies* 19.2 (March 2005), 155; emphasis added.

22. "mid-15c., *enprowment* 'management of something for profit,' from Anglo-French *emprowment*, from *emprouwer* 'turn to profit' (see *improve*). Meaning

'betterment; amelioration' is from 1640s. Meaning 'building, etc. on a piece of property' is from 1773" (Online Etymology Dictionary, http://www.etymonline.com/index.php?term=improvement). *Mejora* in Spanish literally means 'improvement.'

23. Wood, op. cit., 106; emphasis added.

24. Ibid., 107–8; emphasis added.

25. Thompson, op. cit., 159–60; emphasis added.

26. Referring to *The Wealth of Nations*, in ibid., 162.

27. Wood, op. cit., 108.

28. Neal Wood, *John Locke and Agrarian Capitalism* (Berkeley and Los Angeles: University of California Press, 1984). Also, Thompson, op. cit., III–IV.

29. Wood, op. cit., 110–11; emphasis added.

30. *Locke: Two Treatises of Government*, op. cit., Ch.5, § 26, 287; emphasis in original.

31. Locke on "Property," as cited by Thompson, op. cit., 164–65.

32. *Locke: Two Treatises of Government*, op. cit., Ch.5, § 35, 292; emphasis in original.

33.Ibid., Ch. 5, § 28, 288–89, 292; emphasis in original.

34. Ibid., 27;; emphasis added.

35. "While the top 1 percent of income earners took home 93 percent of the growth in incomes in 2010, the households in the middle—who are most likely to spend their incomes rather than save them and who are, in a sense, *the true job creators*—have lower household incomes, adjusted for inflation, than they did in 1996. The growth in the decade before the crisis was unsustainable—it was reliant on the bottom 80 percent consuming about 110 percent of their income" (Joseph Stiglitz, "Inequality is Holding Back the Recovery," *The Opinionator* (blog), *The New York Times*, January 19, 2013, http://opinionator.blogs.nytimes.com/2013/01/19/inequality-is-holding-back-the-recovery/?src=recg; emphasis added).

36. Alexander Gottlieb (Berlin, 1714–1762) retrieves *aisthesis* and *aesthetica* (aesthetics) from the ancient Greek and Latin philosophical lexicon, crucially intensifying the discussion between "the traditional theory of aesthetic experience as a special form of the cognition of truth, and the newer theory of aesthetic experience as a free play of cognitive (and sometimes other) mental powers in eighteenth-century Germany" (http://plato.stanford.edu/entries/aesthetics-18th-german/#Bau). This retrieval was to largely inaugurate the modern field of philosophical aesthetics, later refined by Kant, Schiller, Hegel, and by the numerous schools of thought that reach to the present.

37. A. G. Baumgarten, *Reflections on Poetry* (1735; repr. Berkeley: University of California, 1954), 78.

38. Terry Eagleton, *The Ideology of the Aesthetic* (Oxford: Blackwell, 1990), 1–2; emphasis in original.

39. Ibid.; emphasis added.

40. Ibid., 9; emphasis added.

41. Cf. J.M. Bernstein, *The Fate of Art: Aesthetic Alienation from Kant to Derrida and Adorno* (University Park: Penn State University Press, 1992).

42. Iris Murdoch, *The Fire and the Sun: Why Plato Banished the Artists* (Oxford University Press, 1977), 5. *Eikasia* relates to *Eikon*, or icon.

43. Cf. Stepen Greenblatt, *The Swerve: How The World Became Modern* (New York: Norton, 2012).

44. Bernstein, op. cit., 12.

45. Eagleton, op. cit., 8–9; emphasis added.

46. Pamela M. Lee, *Forgetting the Art World* (Cambridge, MA: MIT Press, 2012), 22ff. See also Genosko, op. cit., 149ff.

47. Cf. J. K Galbraith, *The Affluent Society* (New York: Houghton, 1958). It's an early warning of a debasing public sector and an increasingly rich and powerful corporate sector.

48. Cf. *Teorema*, Pier Paolo Pasolini's enigmatic film, which is a profoundly lyrical, melancholic, yet hopeful rendering of the looming demise of industrial Fordism and the deep crisis of European bourgeois subjectivity.

49. W. F. Haug, *Critique of Commodity Aesthetics: Appearance, Sexuality and Advertising in Capitalist Society* (Minneapolis: University of Minnesota Press, 1971), 7–8 and 16–17; emphasis in original.

50. Ibid., 11; emphasis added.

51. Cf. Yann Moulier Boutang, *Cognitive Capitalism* (Cambridge, UK: Polity, 2011).

52. David Harvey, *A Brief History of Neoliberalism* (Oxford: Oxford University Press, 2005), 1–3. Paul Treanor further states that: "Neoliberalism is not just economics: it is a social and moral philosophy, in some aspects qualitatively different from liberalism" (http://web.inter.nl.net/users/Paul.Treanor/neoliberalism.html).

53. Georg Simmel, *On Individuality and Social Forms*, ed. Donald N. Levine (Chicago: University of Chicago, 1971), xxxiv.

54. Initially inspired by an Aristotelian psychology of perception concept, *Aisthesis Koine* or *Sensus Communis* ('common sense[s]')—the ability to perceive more holistically when we employ all our senses at once—has slowly developed into an aesthetics, biopolitics, and social practice reflection.

55. Arturo Escobar, *Territories of Difference: Place,Mmovements, Life*, Redes (Durham, NC: Duke University Press, 2008): "Any territory is a territory of difference in that it entails unique place making and region making, ecologically, culturally and socially . . . is the understanding and defense of life itself" (25).

56. John Holloway, *Crack Capitalism* (London: Pluto Press, 2010): "Break. We want to break. We want to create a different world . . . Our method is the method of the crack. It is time to learn the new language of the struggle," pp. 3–13.

57. Gregory Sholette, *Dark Matter: Art and Politics in the Age of Enterprise Culture* ((London: Pluto Press, 2011). "Art is big business," for a privileged few, the rest is invisible—the "dark matter" of the art world . . . essential to the survival of the elite and they frequently organize in opposition to them," Introduction, pp. 1–7.

58. Cf. Manuel Castells, *Networks of Outrage and Hope: Social Movements in the Internet Age* (Cambridge, UK: Polity Press, 2012): "No one expected it. In a world darkened by economic distress, political cynicism, cultural emptiness, and personal hopelessness, it just happened" (1).

59. Cf. Paul Hawken, *Blessed Unrest: How the Largest Social Movement in History Is Restoring Grace, Justice, and Beauty in the World* (London: Penguin, 2008): "If you look at the science that describes what is happening on earth and aren't pessimistic, you don't have the current data. If you meet the people in this unnamed movement and aren't optimistic, you haven't got a heart" (4).

60. Beth Hinderliter et al., *Communities of Sense: Rethinking Aesthetics and Politics* (Durham, NC: Duke University Press, 2009), 1–2

61. Cf. Roberto Esposito, *Communitas: The Origin and Destiny of Community* (Stanford, CA: Stanford University Press, 2010); see also his *Immunitas: The Protection and Negation of Life* (Cambridge, UK: Polity Press, 2011).

62. Cf. E. O. Wilson, *The Social Conquest of Earth* (New York: Norton/Liveright, 2012).

63. Cf. Martin Nowak, *Supercooperators: Altruism, Evolution, and Why We Need Each Other to Succeed* (New York: Free Press, 2011).

64. Melinda Cooper, *Life as Surplus: Biotechnology and Capitalism in the Neoliberal Era* (Seattle: University of Washington Press, 2008), 42–43.

II

THE HANDBOOK FOR CRITICAL EXCHANGES IN RECENT ART

edited by Ted Purves and
Shane Aslan Selzer, with Jacob Wick

Part One
ARTISTS' PROJECTS

INTRODUCTORY REMARKS

Ted Purves

Editors' Note: The projects section for the Handbook for Critical Exchange builds on a body of research that was originally undertaken in 2002 and was completed for the first edition of this book in early 2003. When we began the task of revising the book for the current edition, one of the central questions was how to update the handbook not just to reflect newer projects, but also how to realign the prior material to reflect the newly expanded lens for the book, which grew from initial ideas of *generosity* and *gift economies* (which were very much "in the air" at the time) to our current concept of *critical exchanges*. As such, it seems necessary to use the space of this introduction to not simply give an overview of what follows, but to also account for what has been removed and how certain entries may have been reframed.

At this point, it is important to mention what might have been one of the more difficult decisions in revising this handbook. When it was first written, the decision was made to include a handful of what could be termed "historical" projects; at the time, these were included to give a larger context for the exploration of gift economies and exchange within the first edition. Projects such as Franz Erhart Walthers's *1st Werkset*, Mierle Ukeles Laderman's *Maintenance Art*, and Palle Nielsens' *Model for a Qualitative Society* stood out as true bellweathers for a consideration of the projects that the book sought to understand. When we set up the parameters for this new edition, we fully intended to keep them in place, but as the framework of critical exchange grew, it became more difficult to justify doing so. To make a history of art projects that leverage critical exchange would be a vast project, one that would include far more than a handful of art projects. In the end, it seemed wiser to simply present projects from recent art. The construction of their histories will come in time, and it is hoped that the following handbook will serve as an ongoing resource for such an undertaking.

The first edition of this book began with two basic questions: Why are artists giving things away, and what happens when this gesture is embedded in an art project? The primary goal of the first edition was to somehow make sense of a phenomenon through an act of pulling material together. What emerged from this was not something that could be thought of as an art movement, style, or a medium. Rather, what was revealed was a constellation of projects that were each investigating, quite literally, the possibilities of exchange and the limits and boundaries of what value might mean. Each of these projects examined the inherent exchanges that occur between artist and audience, and gave the possibility of understanding what "art" might actually give to its audience, if even in a simple way. The result of this research was presented in the first edition as "The Handbook for Gift and Exchange-Based Art," and it contained a survey of over fifty projects produced between 1991 and 2003, with some historical entries added in to provide a larger context.

Returning to the book in 2011, and considering projects that have been created since 2003, we found, after an extensive survey of artists' works, that while these original questions had not entirely faded away, the ways to think about such inquiries had shifted significantly. In the intervening years, years that saw unprecedented changes in global economics, Internet communications, and technology (as well as widespread recession, automated warfare, and climate change), not only had the nature of artists' work changed, so had the context of abstract concepts of *generosity* and *gifts*, or even what was meant by the word *free*. While these more recent projects still gave some attention to freeness, gift economies, generosity, *detournement*, and human intimacy, much of their focus had shifted. Thus, it became necessary to consider how all of the projects in the new edition of the handbook, both recent and carried over, might be linked under the much broader notion of what could be termed the *politics* (or *landscape*) of exchange. Given this, the questions for this edition might be: What has shifted in the ways that we exchange goods, services, and information, and what can projects by artists do to somehow insert themselves into these changes?

Following on this, our intention with the handbook for this second edition was to focus on a range of works, created within the context of contemporary art, each of which contained some intervention or reflection of this landscape of exchange, with an eye to towards understanding how they might be "read" for critical insights into this landscape. The projects entries are created to present, as much as possible, a straightforward description of the project, followed by some observations about the particular project's context, social form, production, and/or the actual circumstances through which it became "public." The editors were interested in also understanding, from an artists' perspective (if available), what interested them about the project, and in many cases, the entries were enhanced by correspondence and conversation between the artists and the editors.

As such, our considerations of the projects were written to somewhat deemphasize what the project might "mean," and instead to try to describe them somewhat as they were during their moment when they were public. This includes a consideration of context and, new to this edition, an interest in form (social or otherwise). As the new project entries were written, it became apparent that this shift in methodology was significant enough to necessitate a substantial re-writing of the project entries from the first edition, and readers familiar with the earlier edition will notice the change of emphasis and tone.[1]

One significant fact that emerged during the research for this edition was that there was a marked increase in the institutional sponsorship and commissioning of these sorts of projects, made visible by the fact that many of them either were produced as museum exhibitions or were commissions for festivals or biennials.[2] While this was certainly present in the projects of the prior edition, a much larger percentage of the earlier projects either were made in collaboration with a commercial gallery or were simply done as DIY style endeavors. Alternatively, some were made as local public art commissions; not so today. With this shift, there has not simply been a rise in the amount of writing (or content) that one can find about these works, but the nature of that writing has also changed. In most cases, we can find a curatorial statement or e-flux announcement as well as entries on artists' websites, and this information is also "reblogged" and reposted across any number of online platforms that digest and promote contemporary art. While this sort of information is certainly of interest, there is a growing tendency within these texts to attempt to frame the works, to construct a set of meanings for them.

While this is not necessarily a bad thing, it seems somewhat problematic as a way to contemplate works, which, more often than not, are encountered by publics outside of the ready confines of the "art world." When an artwork is encountered in a storefront on a shopping street, such as *Money Watching* by Cesare Pietroiusti; as a light switch in front of a famous church in a public square, as in the project *Everything is Contestable* by Ashok Sukumaran; or even by a judge in a US District Court, a potential "public" for a project such as *This Is The Public Domain* by Amy Balkin, how is it even possible to know what the work might "mean"? Beyond the improbable possibility that we could even determine a particular meaning for these works, such an interest ultimately seems to run against the interest in making these works in the first place. They enter the public realms in sites that are not necessarily associated with either artwork or the art world (a realm that one might term the "world at large"), and manifest in social forms that are continuously at play with the forms around them.

Given this, our research, and the following presentation of it, was written to give an informed "reading" of each work. When possible, we both solicited information from the artists about their thoughts behind each project's creation as well as requested something of an assessment: What did the project end up exchanging? Did it work as anticipated? How did audiences respond? How did the exchanges within the work change it? It is worth stating that such questions are not put forward to focus entirely on materialist notions. As most of these were also created as artworks, there is an abiding interest in subjectivity in their creation, and their ends are not simply to distribute things, but to manifest a more idiosyncratic vision of exchange.

Notes

1. Beyond the shift in tone, there were some projects that were taken out, due to both space considerations and the shift in the book's emphasis. In some cases, this was done to address issues of internal redundancy, for example, projects by Jorgen Svensson and Ben Kinmont were removed largely because they were discussed much more thoroughly in texts that the artists had, themselves, written earlier in the book.

2. This period also saw the marked rise of a tendency in museums and arts centers to also escalate their educational programming, and participatory, temporary projects that directly engaged the public were increasingly commissioned as a part of an institutions' educational programming as well as in the exhibitions department. To account for this shift in the currents of the art world is beyond the scope of this short essay, however, interested readers are directed to books such as *Art Incoporated* by Julian Stallabrass (New York: Oxford University Press, 2004) or *Social Works* by Shannon Jackson (New York: Routledge, 2011).

1 EURO BLINKY MARKET (2006) SURASI KUSOLWONG

1 Euro Blinky Market existed as a project contained within the "Einmal Empire und zurück" ("Empire and Back Again") exhibition at Westfälischer Kunstverein, Münster, Germany, in 2006. One of an ongoing series of markets produced by Bangkok-based artist Surasi Kusolwong, the *1 Euro Blinky Market* sold items, originally bought for negligible prices in Bangkok street markets, for one euro each. The items were presented in a garish display that evoked the mind-numbing display of a street—or retail—variety market. Most of Kusolwong's *Markets* appear in galleries and museums in similarly garish fashion, selling items collected by the artist in Bangkok for whatever national variety market chains sell items for: €1, $1, £1, etc. These *Markets* generally open with an event wherein the artist, often absurdly attired, goads his audience into purchasing as many items as possible.

Kusolwong's *Markets* aim to make apparent a series of uneven or arbitrary exchanges that occur often unacknowledged within participatory art. There is, at the outset, Kusolwong's status in the international art market, which confers on him the authority with which to saddle international institutions with the cost of shipping large amounts of cheap items from Bangkok to Germany, Sweden, the United States, et cetera. At the openings, and to a lesser extent throughout the duration of the *Market* installations, Kusolwong uses his status as a recognized artist to goad museum- or gallery-goers into taking part in a frenzied spectacle that mirrors commodity exchange markets.[1] Upon purchasing an item, the museum- or gallery-goer not only becomes complicit in a confusion between *participant* and *consumer*, but also participates in a doubly uneven currency exchange, purchasing an item likely bought for less than €1—which might be sold at the next *Market* for $1—for €1.

ANY WEDNESDAY (1993–PRESENT) DIANA MARS

In her ongoing project *Any Wednesday*, San Francisco artist Diana Mars has made dinner available, free and without strings attached, every Wednesday evening at her apartment since 1993. She advertises discreetly, by word of mouth, through the distribution of handmade calling cards.

Mars's calling cards, which serve as invitations, plainly state: "At home, Making Good Food, Wednesdays 7:00–10:00." There is no requirement for people to bring food, though Mars notes that most often people do anyway. As she observed in a July 2002 conversation, it is an interesting quality of this work that even when something is known to be free, like a free meal, people will very often bring food to share even though it isn't asked of them.

---

1. "Surasi Kusolwong," Polly Staple, accessed December 29, 2012, http://www.frieze.com/issue/review/surasi_kusolwong/

The Art and Cold Cash collective conducted a variety of investigations related to the introduction of capitalist exchange in the Baker Lake, Nunavut, community and its relation to art production across Canada. The group was motivated by a perceived discrepancy in treatment by the Canadian government of northern and southern Canadian artists. In their analysis, northern aboriginal artists were encouraged by the government to make art in return for readily available grant money, whereas government funding was less readily available to southern artists, generally of Western descent. This situation generated a number of questions when considered alongside traditional aboriginal attitudes towards art, which did not associate art production with individual value, and traditional Western attitudes towards art, which did. The Art and Cold Cash collective included Patrick Mahon, Sheila Butler, and Jack Butler, all of southern Canada, as well as William Noah and Ruby Arngna'qaaq, both of Baker Lake. The collective was active from 2004–2007 and produced a book, *Art and Cold Cash*, published in English and Inuktitut, and a website, artcoldcash.ca.

The collective undertook a variety of approaches in order to address the ironic predicament they had identified. These approaches included a drawing series wherein members of the collective, along with artists from Baker Lake, utilize drawing as a means to transform "emotional and psychic realities into material being."[2] The collective also organized an event wherein Baker Lake artists bartered for photographs taken by Jack Butler with their own artwork, conducted interviews with Baker Lake residents about the introduction of capitalism to their community (published in *Art and Cold Cash*), and held group exhibitions.

BARTER (2007) SOSKA GROUP

Barter was an auction, with photographic and video documentation, held in 2007 by the Ukrainian artist collective SOSka group. The SOSka group, based in Kharkiv, in the northeast of Ukraine, drove to a nearby village in a van full of famous artist prints—of a Cindy Sherman photo, of Chuck Close's self-portrait, of a Warhol soup can, and so on—and set these prints up against the corrugated tin wall of a local shack. Once they had set up their wares, the group attempted to trade the prints for local goods, such as chickens, potatoes, and eggs. A Cindy Sherman print sells for a chicken, a Chuck Close print and a Roy Lichtenstein print sell for three dozen eggs, and a Neo Rauch print sells for a jar of pickles. During each exchange, the villagers are asked why they like the print and where they will hang it. Following this action, the group produced a six-minute video and a photographic series, which have been shown in gallery settings in the United States and Europe.

---

2. "Drawing as a component of 'Art and Cold Cash,'" http://www.artcoldcash.ca/

BARTER (2007) SOSKA GROUP

Barter yielded different results in different contexts. The event itself yielded 40 kilos of potatoes, a chicken, a jar of pickles, several dozen eggs, and other local goods. The series of photographs—which consists of portraits of the farmers with their prints, the prints inside the farmer's homes, and screenshots from the video—belies, among other things, a confusion of cultures, with the Chuck Close portrait placed over an ornamental rug on a bedroom wall. The video, meanwhile, expresses not only a whimsical exchange in regards to the arbitrary nature of the art market, but also underscores a colossal gap between the gallery setting, in which it is shown, and living conditions in rural villages in the Ukraine. This is particularly apparent in a scene, towards the end of the video, in which a woman feeds her chickens in the lot where the prints hang, gallery-style, on corrugated tin.

BEAUTIFUL CITY (2007) MARIA PASK

For skulptur project 7 münster, Welsh-born and Amsterdam-based artist Maria Pask erected *Beautiful City* in a park north of the city's iconic castle. Pask invited the public to camp in the meadow and partake in a series of presentations programmed to occur in a large white tent at the center of the meadow, essentially attempting to create a temporary living commons (in a location that was not normally available for public camping). The presentations revolved around a set of questions that addressed faith, religion, and politics, with the goal of imagining "not of walls and towers, but of visionary ideas, ethics and mutual trust."[3] The presenters were a diverse group of theologians, philosophers, artists, and activists. The grounds of *Beautiful City* were maintained by groups of students, who camped at the site on a weekly basis. Pask would meet each student group at the beginning of their week at *Beautiful City*, show them around, and hand them a set of detailed instructions. These occasionally beatific instructions included practical instructions, hypothetical day plans, stretches, and so on.

Beautiful City existed for fifteen weeks and is documented extensively—including audio recordings of lectures in German and English—on a website, beautifulcity.de. The website's "PhotoBlog" section depicts students barbequing, attending lectures in the tent, reading, and frolicking. Photographed presentations appear to be well-attended. While it is unclear to what extent an ongoing dialogue developed between the various student groups that lived at the site, the presenters and the general public, it does appear that *Beautiful City* succeeded in providing a relaxing and idealistic space for its participants to inhabit, while at the same time offering the possibility of residence to anyone interested, modeling an alternate notion of what set of constructions (physical or philosophical) would bring a "beautiful city" into being.

3. "About," http://www.beautifulcity.de/about%20us.htm

William Pope.L's production *The Black Factory* began yearly tours across the United States in 2004, but the larger project began in 2003. The specifics of the *Factory* changed, sometimes drastically, depending on the town and context in which it stopped, but it generally included *The Black Factory* truck, a modified shipping van painted white with the *The Black Factory* logo, a team of young assistants who operated the truck and organized the various events, installations, and interventions that occurred at each stop, and a call to the public to bring objects to *The Black Factory* that somehow referenced blackness to them.[4] According to Pope.L.

> The BF gathers, shapes and repackages feelings, ideas, absence and experiences and makes products of them, e.g., a tour, a participatory-community artwork, an art experience as ramshackle noble mobile economy . . . at each stop on its journey, the Factory welcomes visitors to bring the cultural material that references blackness for them (which is usually them).[5]

The assistants who operated *The Black Factory* had a set of routines—questions, speeches, actions—devised by Pope.L and rehearsed before the truck left for each tour. A version of *The Black Factory* was commissioned by MASS MoCA as part of "The Interventionists: Art in the Social Sphere," a 2004 exhibition, curated by Nato Thompson. MASS MoCA partly subsidized the 2004 tour of *The Black Factory*.[6]

At many stops, the items brought in by the truck would be unloaded and displayed alongside items brought in by the local public. Assistants would display the items in a variety of fashions and ask a series of semi-scripted questions about how the objects connected with a host of subjects such as gender, unemployment, and morality. At some stops, items were displayed in museum galleries; at others, they were displayed in the street. In some cases, items brought in by the public were repackaged and reproduced, and were made available for sale as Black Factory souvenirs or went to support local organizations.

The truck itself played a role in many installations: at the 2009 Art Basel Miami, for instance, the truck appeared on a platform in the Miami Botanic Gardens half-buried in black silica; in 2005, in Chelsea, it appeared trailing a giant inflatable igloo with the *The Black Factory* logo. However, according to

4. A very partial list of collaborators: Josh Atlas, Pasqualina Azzarello, Jeff Barnum, Mark, H. C. Bessire, David Charron, Ryan Conrad, Nathaniel Edmunds, Darby English, Shaun Fogerty, Lydia Grey, Julie Hammond, Rufat (Ru) Hasanov, Justin Lander, Jamie Lynch, Christina Marsh, Patrick Mills.R, Justin Moriarty, Nikki Pike, Michael Reidy, Craig Saddlemire, Nato Thompson, Renu and Shannon, and the San Fran BF Crew.

5. William Pope.L, email correspondence with the editors, 2012.

6. http://theblackfactory.com

the artist, the truck itself "is the most tangible but mistaken matrix for the bf."[7] In 2007, The Black Factory, sans truck, was the subject of a monograph exhibition at Yerba Buena Center for the Arts, San Francisco.

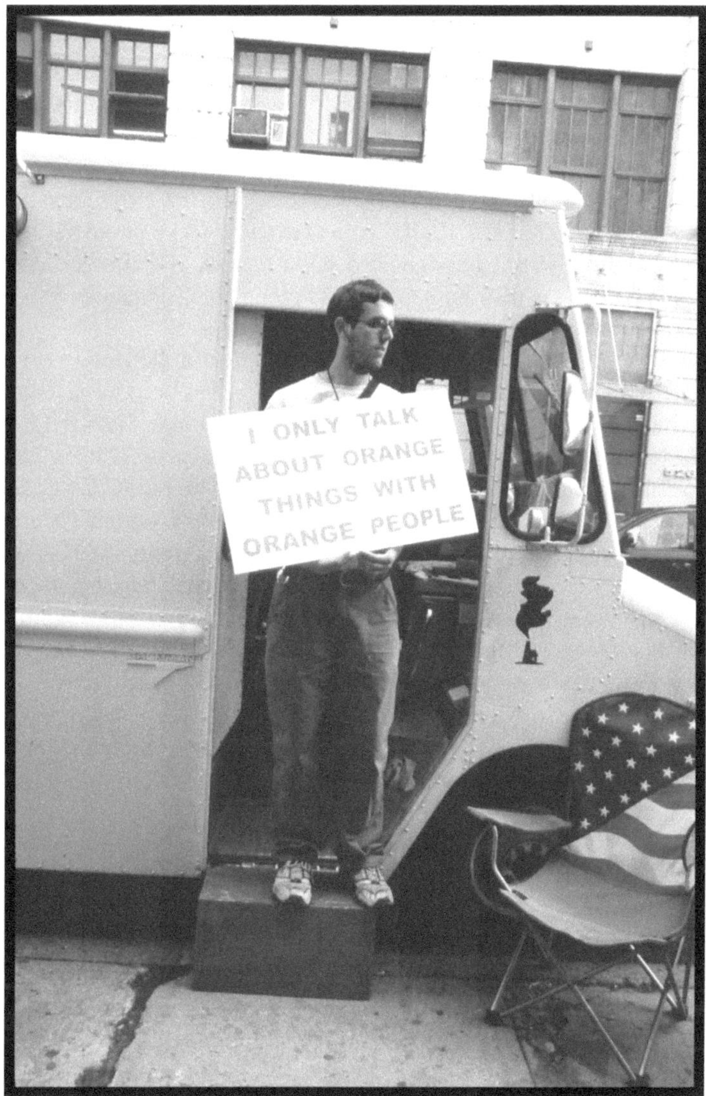

William Pope.L *The Black Factory* 2004–present

7. William Pope.L, ibid.

Border Farm (2011) is a film written, performed, and partially crewed by the Dulibadzimu Theatre Group. South African artist Thenjiwe Nkosi and Zimbabwean writer, farmworker, and community organizer Meza Weza sought to create a framework for intensive dialogue between individuals of different circumstances that might result in a collaborative project. To attempt to accomplish this feat, Nkosi organized a group of artists from Johannesburg to travel to a farm on the border of South Africa and Zimbabwe, where Weza, in turn, organized migrant farmworkers and other interested local individuals. A series of weekly conversations resulted in the decision to focus on border jumping—common practice among asylum seekers and day laborers seeking entry to South Africa unable to obtain a visa—as the focus of production. Over the course of seven months between 2009 and 2010, the group created a set of photographs relating to border jumping, which has travelled domestically, and the docudrama film *Border Farm*, which is distributed on DVD along the Zimbabwe–South Africa border and shown at select festivals and conferences.

Nkosi and Weza's idea did indeed result in a collaborative project; in fact, it resulted in two separate projects assembled and produced by a collaborative theater company. This company, the Dulibadzimu Theatre Group, was comprised of artists from Johannesburg and migrant laborers from Zimbabwe, two populations that traditionally do not interact. The result of this successful collaboration, however, had its own intentions. The Dulibadzimu Theatre Group hoped that the film and photographs would address the xenophobia prevalent in South African society. It is difficult, however, to estimate the impact of either, especially given the informal distribution of the DVD. Within the group itself, however, Nkosi reports that the intensive dialogues that drove the project did result in participants establishing commonalities that might have otherwise gone unrecognized.[8]

8. E-mail from Thenjiwe Nkosi.

BORDER FARM (2011) THENJIWE NKOSI, MEZA WEZA, AND THE DULIBADZIMU THEATRE GROUP

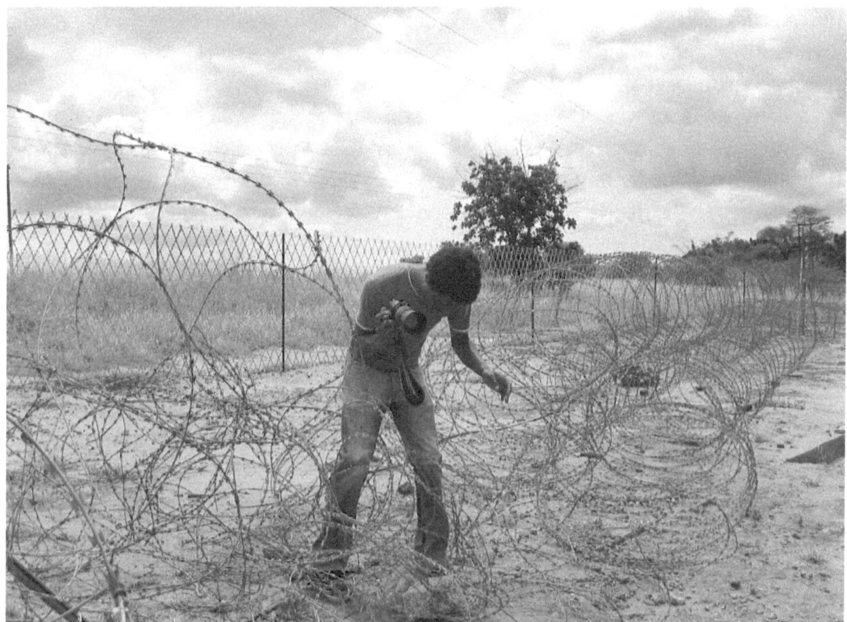

Thenjiwe Nkosi, Meza Weza, and the Dulibadzimu Theatre Group *Border Farm* 2011

BREMEN POSTCARDS (2005) ALEKSANDRA MIR

For the 2005 exhibition "A Lucky Strike: Kunst findet Stadt" at Gesellschaft für Aktuelle Kunst (GAK) in Bremen, Germany, artist Aleksandra Mir produced *Bremen Postcards*, a series of eight postcards, printed in an edition of 300,000. The images on the postcards were culled from royalty-free stock postcard photos from across the world. None of the images were of Bremen. Mir hired a designer in Bremen to design a typeface, slogans, and insignia that mimicked existing local postcards. The designed type, slogans, and insignia were overlaid on the stock photos, creating a series of postcards that picture non-Bremen cities that claim to be of Bremen. GAK Bremen financed the production of the postcards. The postcards were displayed in the museum, in boxes fresh from the printers; curators then distributed the postcards throughout Bremen, through formal and informal networks. The project was meant to highlight the insidious nature of tourism, which the artist suggests may be "the defining industry of our times," by pointing out that a postcard becomes "the very instrument for the transformation of the place it depicts," despite its claims to authenticity.[9]

9. Aleksandra Mir, e-mail message to editors.

There is no way to measure the effect of the postcards. Their distribution—displayed alongside standard tourist postcards in the sort of tour-centered knick-knack shops that litter the commercial centers of cities worldwide—made it so that the unsuspecting tourist would presumably have no idea that the postcard they were sending was false, unless they had an adequate knowledge of Bremen to recognize the inconsistency. Perhaps for this reason, the artist asks that if the reader encounters or receives a *Bremen Postcard*, and recognizes it as such, that the reader scan the back of the card and e-mail it to her. The artist writes: "maybe one day, there'll be a book."[10]

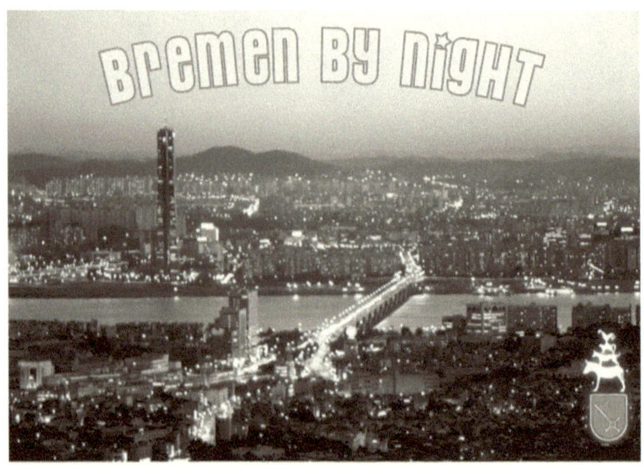

Aleksandra Mir *Bremen Postcards* 2005

CITY COUNCIL MEETING (2012–PRESENT) AARON LANDSMAN

City Council Meeting is a participatory theater piece written by writer Aaron Landsman, with dramaturgy by Mallory Catlett and design by Jim Findlay. The set for the piece is modeled after standard city council meeting setup: a table, or tables, for councillors, a screen for presentations, and chairs for the audience. When the performance begins, *City Council* "staff"—actors and other performers trained by Landsman and his collaborators—asks for volunteers from the paying audience to "play" the part of mayor, council member, people to give testimony, and so on. Participants then perform *City Council Meeting*, a multipart play in which each part is derived from minutes from actual city council meetings across the United States. Landsman and his collaborators visited city council

10. Ibid.

meetings in California, Oregon, Texas, New York, North Dakota, and other states, taking notes and conducting interviews with staff and councillors, to develop the text for the piece. The project has a website, citycouncilmeeting.org, a Facebook page, and a Twitter handle, @citycouncilmtg.

City Council Meeting was commissioned by DiverseWorks, a nonprofit art center in New York City, and was developed through the HERE Artist Residency Program. The piece premiered in Houston on November 1, 2012; future premiers are planned in Tempe, New York City, and San Francisco. A Houston critic who attended a performance of *City Council Meeting* noted that, while compelling, the piece resulted in some "awkward" moments as a result of its participants being mostly white males, particularly as they read testimonies given by young black males at a city council meeting in San Antonio.[11] However awkward, the ongoing performances are designed to create this sort of confusion, wherein spectatorship is turned upon itself, as it channeled into a reenactment of the local dialogues of decision-making and power.

CLOTHING PROJECT (2003) IT CAN CHANGE

> The Clothing Project is an ongoing interactive public exhibition. Participating artists are requested to create wearable artworks, which will be given away by It Can Change to anyone who is interested in wearing them. Every artwork has a label sewn into it describing the project, containing the name of the artist, contact information for It Can Change, and directions for each recipient to pass the artwork along to the first person to show interest in it. The selection of the artists in the exhibition, like that of the participants, is determined only by an interest in the project. Anyone who is interested in making a wearable artwork is included in the show.[12]

It Can Change's *Clothing Project* typified an approach to aesthetic practices that were rooted in ad hoc community construction and an expansive definition of both "art" and "art shows." In the initial manifestation of the project, It Can Change showed all of the clothes they received (over fifty people from around the world sent in articles of clothing to be distributed) at the Kunsthalle Fridericianum in Kassel, Germany, at the exhibition's opening, and subsequently took them to the city streets and cafes, where they gave them away to people

11. John Pluecker, "City Council Mayhem: El Desmadre De La Política Local," *Houston Free Press*, November 2, 2012, http://www.freepresshouston.com/art/city-council-mayhem-el-desmadre-de-la-politica-local/

12. It Can Change, website statement, www.itcanchange.com, 2003.

they encountered. By distributing the clothing outside of an "art" context, the aesthetic status of the clothes became less predetermined and more open to individual systems of value. Because of this, the recipients could take an active role in accepting clothes either as "artworks" or as clothing that they simply would like to wear (or both).

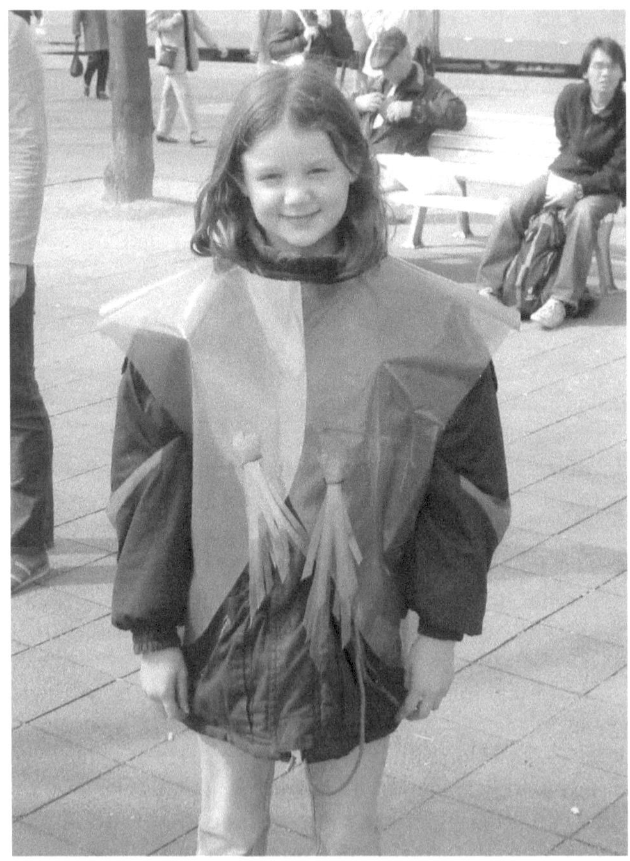

It Can Change Clothing Project (poncho by Hanna Bayer) 2003

Alicia Framis, a Spanish-born artist currently residing in the Netherlands, has focused her work on the contemporary condition of "loneliness in the city." Her contribution to an art festival in Utrecht consisted of the work *Compagnie de Compagnie*. This piece created an escort bureau in Utrecht Central Station where lonely travelers could acquire a companion and have their company for a short while. The escorts were all identical twins, which the artist considered to be experts at togetherness.

The work existed for the duration of the festival and was not documented in any way. The only tangible item left at the end was the poster for *Compagnie de Compagnie*, which was displayed as a functional advertisement for the work while it was occurring and serves as its only documentation beyond the memories of those who participated.

DAY TO DAY (2002) CAROLINA CAYCEDO

During the month of June, Carolina Caycedo occupied the Secession Gallery in Vienna, Austria, and negotiated such daily needs as food, shelter, and

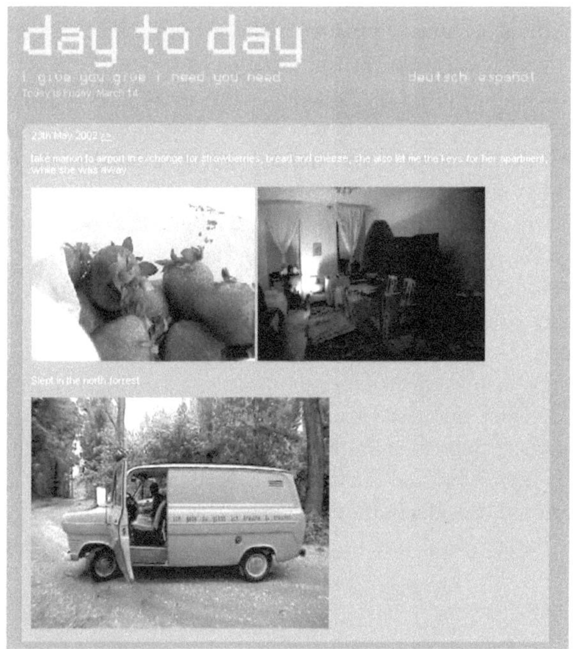

Carolina Caycedo *Day to Day* 2002

transportation by bartering with both gallery visitors and people she met in her daily life. Caycedo envisioned the project as a social performance/installation that would facilitate both an investigation and daily enactment of the use of barter, exchange, and gifts as an alternative method of negotiating business and personal transactions. The project, which is ongoing and will continue indefinitely after the gallery show ends, acts as a lens and laboratory for the explorations of different economies that can exist on an interpersonal scale.

During the project's initial month at the gallery, Caycedo bartered conversations, document typing, massages, and other services to obtain transportation, meals, and other necessities. Her transactions were posted to a website in the form of an exchange diary. The website also contains an interactive form for conducting transactions over the Internet. Through the Internet site, the needs of the artist and the items and services she offers are updated on a continuous basis, determined by her physical situation and current circumstances.

EDIBLE ESTATES (2005–PRESENT) FRITZ HAEG

Edible Estates is an ongoing garden initiative by Los Angeles–based artist Fritz Haeg. The gardens are planted, as the title of the project suggests, in formerly unused or underutilized areas on the grounds of estates large and small—from suburban homes (Salinas, Los Angeles, New Jersey, Budapest) to museums (Aldritch Musem) to apartment blocks (New York City) to community centers (Rome). Generally commissioned and/or funded by horticultural or agriculture nonprofits and/or arts institutions, the *Estates* are intended to be "regional prototype gardens,"[13] examples of alternate uses for the spaces they occupy, established in the hope that their example will be repeated.

As a regional prototype, each garden reflects the specific growing capabilities of its location and generates public programming, including—depending on the site, its financial resources, and its apparent social needs—videos and photographs displayed on Haeg's website, and agricultural or horticultural workshops. The first eight gardens are anthologized in *Edible Estates: Attack on the Front Lawn*, published by Metropolis Books (second edition, 2010). It remains to be seen whether *Edible Estates* will inspire owners of arable land to plant functional, nondecorative gardens. Further, the Baltimore instance of *Edible Estates* has resulted not in neighboring suburban homes planting their

13. E-mail from Fritz Haeg.

own gardens, but instead in neighbors using portions of the *Edible Estates* garden to grow their own crops, a development Haeg's website describes as "a casual community garden."[14]

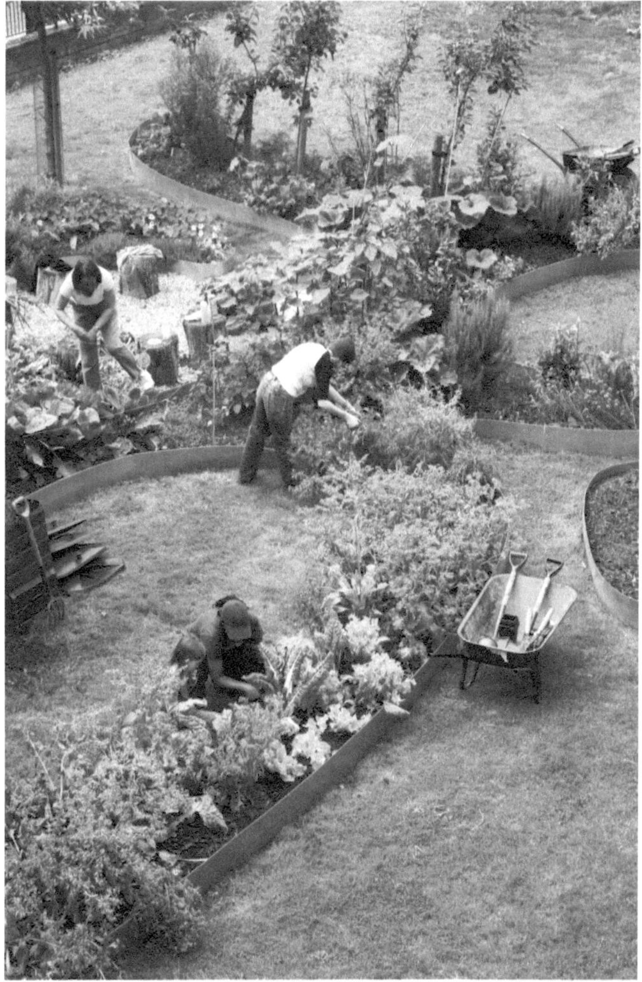

Fritz Haeg *Edible Estates* 2005–present

14. "EDIBLE ESTATES regional prototype garden #6: BALTIMORE, maryland," http://www.fritzhaeg.com/garden/initiatives/edibleestates/baltimore.html

Enlarged Clothing is a set of enormous clothing commissioned by Romanian artist Matei Bejenaru and produced by textile factories in his hometown of Iasi, Romania. Bejenaru researched cut, make, and trim (CMT) prices in Romanian textile factories in the early 2000s. CMT essentially bundles together various aspects of textile production enabled by computer-assisted design; it is widely utilized by clothing companies that outsource their production. He then researched the profit margins of Western companies selling Romanian-made clothing in Romania during the same time period, shortly after the collapse of the totalitarian regime in 1990 and the introduction of a Western-style free-market economy. The difference between Romanian CMT and Western profit margin became a percentage increase in scale for common clothing items—sweaters, track pants,

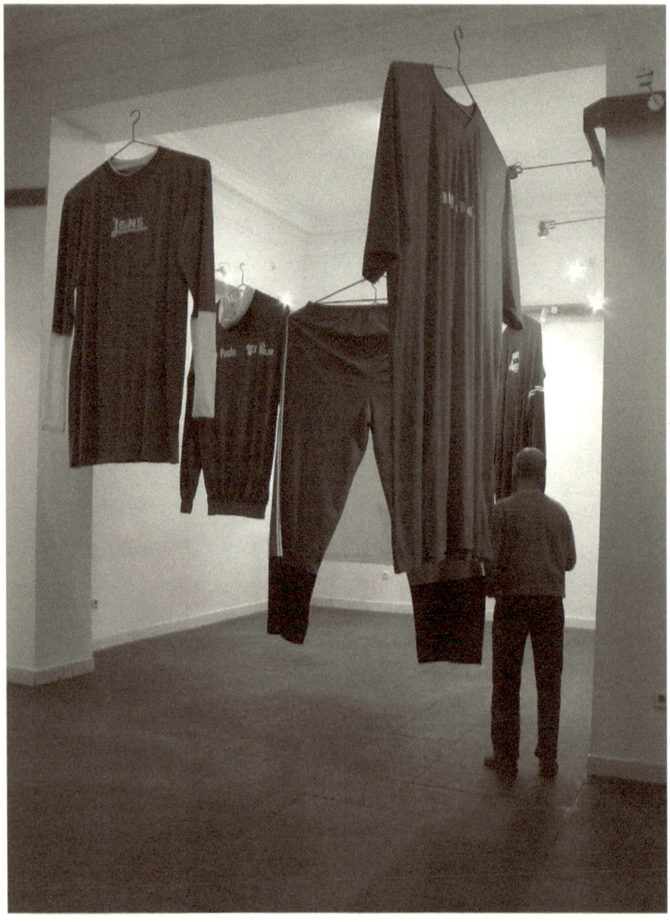

Matei Bejenaru *Enlarged Clothing* 2005

and so on—that Bejenaru commissioned from local textile factories. The resulting *Englarged Clothing* was displayed hanging on giant hangers, suspending from the ceilings of galleries in Eastern and Western Europe.

The huge clothes, some of which appear to be at least eight feet high, certainly lead to a sense of wonder. This sense of wonder might lead to an inquiry into their enlargement, which would in turn lead to Bejenaru's calculations, which in turn highlight the exploitation of post-Communist Eastern European laborers—especially in Romania—by Western economies under the guise of the free market in the late twentieth and early twenty-first centuries. Rather than labor conditions disappearing in the final product, aside from perhaps a small "Made in Romania" tag, in *Enlarged Clothing* they are made glaringly obvious.

EVERYTHING IS CONTESTABLE (2006) ASHOK SUKUMARAN

For *Everything is Contestable*, Bombay-based artist Ashok Sukumaran installed a pair of switches outside the Church of Gregory the Illuminated in Singapore. The Church of Gregory the Illuminated, an Armenian church, was the first building in Singapore to have electricity. Sukumaran installed two switches outside the church, one next to the entrance gate, one across the street in a less apparent location. Both switches controlled the series of lights that illuminate the church at night. The switch nearest to the gate had a 24 percent chance of working; the switch across the street had a 76 percent chance of working. These percentages match, respectively, the percentage of the electricity market in Singapore owned directly by the government and the percentage of the electricity market that is contestable, or open to purchase by various small firms. A sign next to each switch explained what percentage chance the switch had to work and why. *Everything is Contestable* took place as part of the 2006 Singapore Biennale, which happened to overlap with the annual meeting of the boards of governors of the IMF, taking place in Singapore that year.

The signs explaining each switches' respective chance of working listed additional information related to the unequal distribution of power—electrical and otherwise—embedded in these statistics. Although 76 percent of the market is technically contestable, Sukumaran—and, one assumes, the sign—notes that nearly half of this market is contested by firms that are owned by the government, resulting in extremely limited options for lower-income consumers. This information, displayed in a city/state that tightly controls dissent, may have been previously unknown to those who were turning the switch. A brief video of the piece, as well as the code for the program that ran *Everything is Contestable*, is available on Sukumaran's website.

Founded in 1988, Haha was a Chicago-based, collaborative group comprised of Richard House, Wendy Jacobs, Laurie Palmer, and John Ploof. In 1992, as part of "Culture in Action" (a public art program in Chicago curated by Mary Jane Jacob), Haha opened a storefront in the north side neighborhood of Rogers Park, where they established a hydroponic garden (a system of growing plants without soil). This garden produced vegetables low in bacteria and high in nutrition, creating an ideal food source for people with the HIV virus and AIDS. The bulk of the vegetables were then distributed to Chicago House, a group residence for AIDS patients.

Supported by the local community, *Flood* became a horticultural laboratory that produced medicinal herbs and vegetables and provided a gathering place for classes and informal discussions about AIDS, alternative medicines, herbal remedies, and community resources. The project transformed an "art space" into a place of action and education. The garden itself functioned practically for the community and metaphorically as a center for growth, interdependency, and the cycle of life.

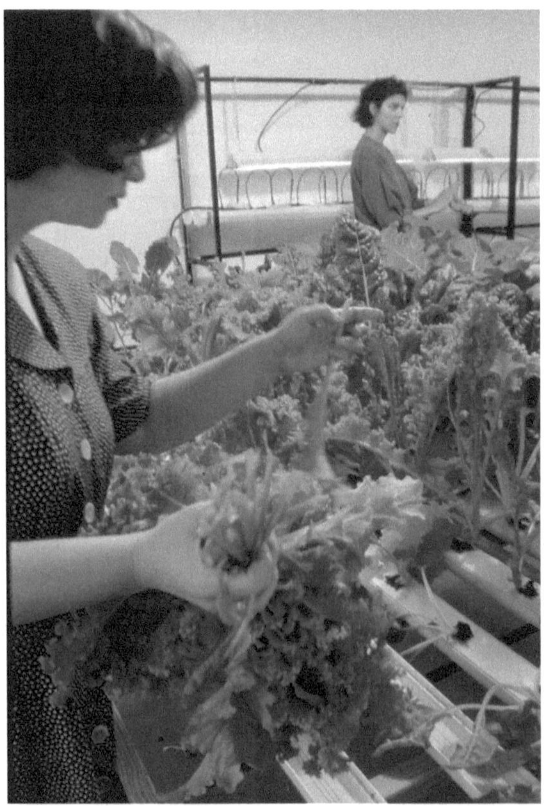

HaHa *Flood* 1992

> "I will [*sic*] like to participate in the show with a piece called 'Foreigners Free,' which is a change in the entrance tariffs of the museum that makes it possible for everybody who is not Korean to enter the exhibition for free."[15]

Through the simple gesture of eliminating the entrance fee to an art institution for a selected group, Danish artist Jens Haaning effectively crafted a work that directly reconfigured issues of race, immigration, and cultural tourism within the spaces of contemporary art. The piece has been "exhibited" as Haaning's contribution to various group exhibitions in seven different countries. In each case, for the duration of the exhibition, anyone who is a foreigner to the country in which the exhibition takes place is admitted to the museum for free.

While the work could simply be seen as a pluralistic gesture to open up the space of the museum to groups that might not otherwise be able to afford it, *Foreigners Free* actually invites multiple interpretations. On one level, the piece brings up the idea of who is normally allowed into museums for free (donors, members, etc.), while on another level it plays with the ideas and expectations one might have of exactly who a foreigner is in the context of visiting an art museum. Does one think of immigrants who live in the city? Foreign tourists? The various layers of meaning that attend this work underscore the idea that works that intervene in and attempt to reorganize an economic system do not necessarily have any fixed meaning; they only contain questions. As Lars Bang Larsen notes, "To Haaning, it is a question of a mixture between opportunism and radicalism, where the activities of the entrepreneur and of the activist merge into a higher unity. Here art as institution provides an opportunity for exploring how significations and economies may be given new directions, stressed, or dissolved by an artistic counter-power."[16]

FREE BASIN (2000) SIMPARCH

Free Basin was designed as a functional sculpture by the collaborative team SIMPARCH (Steve Badgett and Matt Lynch) for the Hyde Park Art Center, in Chicago. The sculpture combined a gallery installation project with a temporary, functioning structure for local skateboarders. Entering from below, visitors saw the underside of a kidney shaped, wooden bowl, which vibrated with sound above the viewer's head. Stairs at the far end led the viewer up to

15. Jens Haaning, artist's statement for an exhibition at Rodin Gallery Korea, http://www.rodingallery.org/rodingallery/rodin/ehibition/myhome/e_intro/03_b.html, 2000.

16. Lars Bang Larsen, "Manifestoes of Renunciation: On the Metaphysics of Jens Haaning," in *Hello, My Name Is Jens Haaning* (Dijon: Les Presses du Réel / Xavier Douroux and Franck Gautherot, 2003), 129.

an observation deck where the bowl dipped down, reminiscent of the perfect pools that West Coast skateboarders were known to ride in the early days of the sport. This large-scale, abstract sculpture completely filled out the exhibition space of the Hyde Park Art Center and transformed it into a skate park for the duration of the exhibition.

While anyone could skate on the structure for free during the day, in the evenings dozens gathered to watch a program of professional skaters ride *Free Basin*, the motion of speed itself activating the static sculpture beyond its own inert potential as an aesthetic object. Free Basin has been reconstructed in other exhibition contexts, including the "Beautiful Losers" exhibition at San Francisco's Yerba Buena Center for the Arts in 2004. In each venue, a crucial part of the display of the work is the proviso that gallery visitors who arrive with skateboards in hand cannot be charged admission and must be allowed access to the bowl during open hours.

FREE BEER (1999) GUY OVERFELT

Guy Overfelt's *Free Beer* was installed at Refusalon Gallery in San Francisco as a "solo show" in the main gallery space. Overfelt secured a donation of several kegs of beer from the Lagunitas Brewing company and made a large promotional poster which was prominently wheat-pasted throughout downtown San Francisco. The gallery was left empty except for a makeshift bar that facilitated the serving of free beer to anyone who came to the gallery and requested it.

Made in part as a response to—or a "new skool version"[17] of—the 1970s social/concept work *Free Beer* by West Coast conceptual artist Tom Marioni (who incidentally maintained a studio in the same building), Overfelt's situational work also played off a long-standing rock-concert promotional tradition of free beer at summer concerts. The tenor of the work was also influenced by the surveillance cameras hidden by Overfelt in the space and by the fact that the gallery's business neighbors were outraged by the show, due to the accumulation of drunken crowds around the gallery on a daily basis. Following an attempt to close the show by the California Alcohol Beverage Control agency, Overfelt shifted strategies and turned the gallery into a club with a nominal membership fee. With said membership one received a free 16 oz plastic cup. It just so happened that there were 5 kegs on tap available in the gallery. Overfelt had initially negotiated a sponsorship deal of 10 Kegs from local brewer by Lagunitas Brewing Co. but by the end of the exhibition it turned out that the actual amount of beer consumed was closer to 35 kegs, due to the overwhelming interest in the art exhibition.[18]

17. Guy Overfelt, email correspondence with Ted Purves, 2002.
18. Ibid.

FREE BEER (1999) GUY OVERFELT

Guy Overfelt *Free Beer* 1999

FREE FOR ALL (2000) TEMPORARY SERVICES

"With *Free For All,* Temporary Services is giving away over 9,000 items! These items cover an immense range of practices from art making to religious pamphleteering."[19]

With this declaration, the Chicago-based collaborative group Temporary Services opened a gallery exhibition of vast amounts of printed and produced media-works, such as artists' 'zines, corporate promotions, mass-produced art works, and religious pamphlets, all of which were free for the taking by the gallery visitors. This material was collected by direct solicitation from their friends and artists' contacts, as well as by members of the collective who signed up or requested information by phone or mail from companies and organizations.

Presented nonhierarchically (one could find a religious tract next to an underground comic book), the contents of the exhibition took on dimensions of cultural documentation as well as describing the vast amount of sheer surplus that American culture generates. To augment the viewers' collection of the material and to "frame" the event within their own efforts, Temporary Services printed special containers for people to collect the material in. In effect, this allowed them to establish a small library and created a system where the materials gathered would become a continuing document of just how much "free stuff" there is in the world.

---

19. Temporary Services, *Free For All* brochure, self-published, Chicago, 2000.

FREE FOR ALL (2000) TEMPORARY SERVICES

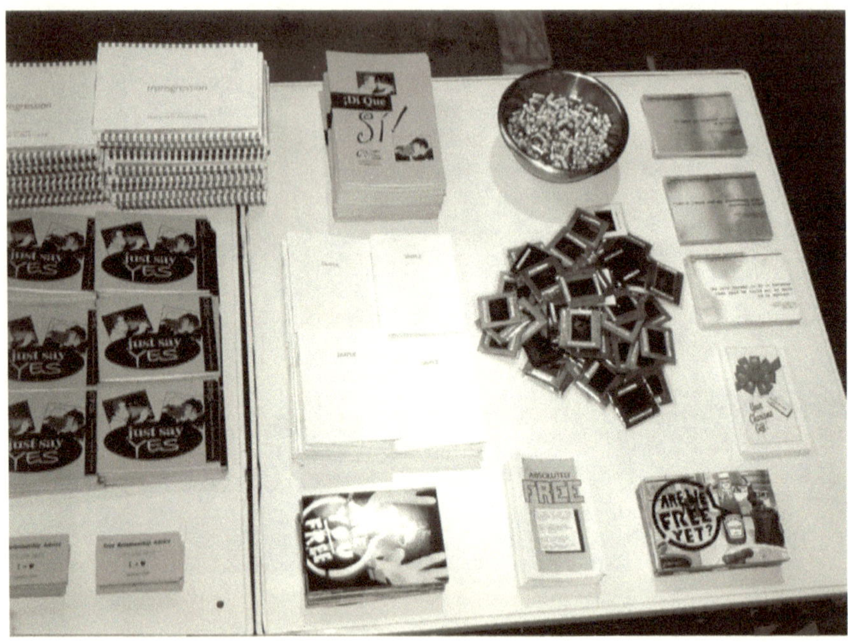

Temporary Services *Free For All* 2000

FREE FRUIT/FRUTA GRATIS (2001–2006) PAMELA BOLTON AND CINDY CLEARY

Free Fruit/Fruta Gratis was a series of actions initiated in the fall of 2000 by the artists Pam Bolton and Cindy Cleary as a collaborative response to a rapidly unfolding shift in the agricultural economy of Sonoma County, California, where the artists lived. Central to this shift was the fact that increasing property prices, driven up exponentially by the rush in exurban housing development, had created a situation wherein owning and maintaining a fruit orchard was untenable; there was no possibility of profit. Fruit orchards were being uprooted and sold for housing development, or were being converted to wine-grapes (the only crop that remained profitable), or were left fallow and unpicked.

The actions were performed in the towns of Healdsburg, Graton, and Santa Rosa, as well as in nearby San Francisco. The details of each action varied. The first consisted solely of mailing fruit seeds to a random selection of thirty three county residents, each of whom lived at an address whose name referenced the county's agricultural history, such as Forestville or Orchard Lane.[20] For subsequent actions, the artists variably distributed citrus, gleaned

---

20. Give and Take: Fruta Gratis and the transient art of fruit, Sara Bir, Metroactive Newspaper, July 17, 2003. Archived online at http://www.metroactive.com/papers/sonoma/07.17.03/fruta-0329.html.

Pamela Bolton and Cindy Cleary Free Fruit/Fruta Gratis 2001–2006

from unpicked yard fruit, or "starts" for apple trees, ready to be planted, along with poems and leaflets. The sites were chosen because of proximity to foot traffic, or populations of day laborers waiting for work, or social services offering free meal programs.

Initially, the works were meant to remain uncontextualized as art and did not seek to appear within the art world. The fruit itself, as well as paper bags to carry it away, were stamped with the words Free Fruit/Fruta Gratis. Beyond that there was no contact information or indication of authorship provided. As the project continued, however, the artists produced versions of the action for museum and gallery exhibitions, including the group show "Hybrid Fields," which opened at the Sonoma County Museum in 2006.

IVE MORE THAN YOU TAKE (2010) PRATCHAYA PRINTHONG

give more than you take is the title of an exhibition by Thai artist Pratchaya Printhong, developed and presented at CAC Brétigny, near Paris, and GAMeC Bergamo, near Milan. In 2010, Printhong was invited to a residency at CAC Brétigny. Instead of staying in Brétigny, Printhong travelled to northern Sweden and joined migrant Thai workers as they picked berries. Throughout the duration of his two-month residency with the migrant workers, Printhong picked 549 kilos of berries, for which he was paid 8000 Swedish krona; however, after travel expenses were deducted, Printhong made only 2153 krona, or the equivalent of US$389, for his labor.[21] From this experience, Printhong derived two works: "tod tee sweden mend thung mor-chit," which consists of instructions, information, and a website; and "allemansrätten," a dismantled watchtower and a set of instructions. In both pieces, the curator—or collector, or whoever—is instructed to display the materials of the piece as they wish. In "tod tee sweden mend thung mor-chit," these materials are a volume of refuse equal to the volume of berries picked; in "allemansråtten," the material is the dismantled watchtower. The website portion of "tod tee sweden mend thung mor-chit," which included photo and video documentation of the labor conditions of the migrant workers Printhong worked alongside, was only online for the duration of the two exhibitions.

The exhibition has not been restaged since closing in Bergamo in 2011. Owing to the structure of the two pieces, however, the shows at CAC Brétigny and GAMeC Bergamo were quite different. In Brétigny, for instance, the 549 kilos of refuse consisted of assemblages of dismantled shelving units, useless electronics, a disco ball, and so on; in Bergamo, however, the refuse was 549 kilos of earth taken from an active construction site on the museum grounds. In Brétigny, the watchtower was assembled; in Bersamo, it hung from the ceiling, bound with plastic.

21. Barbara Cassavecchia, "Focus: Pratchaya Printhong," *frieze* Nov/Dec 2011, http://www.frieze.com/issue/article/focus-pratchaya-phinthong/

THE GREAT CLEANSING OF THE RIO GRANDE (1987–1994) DOMINIQUE MAZEAUD

The Great Cleansing of the Rio Grande was begun in 1987 by the New Mexico–based artist Dominique Mazeaud. The original intent of the piece was to visit the Rio Grande River once a month on the same date, and to take garbage from the river and the banks surrounding it. During some months, this activity was carried out solely by Mazeaud and witnessed only by the river. During other months, friends assisted her. Over the work's duration, the actual action of the artist expanded to include writing and listening, as well as simply removing garbage and waste. Over the seven years in which the piece unfolded, countless bags of garbage were removed and hundreds of passersby witnessed the removal, many of whom talked with Mazeaud about the project and its implications. Along with the removal of trash from the river, which is most likely the most visible documentation of the project, Mazeaud kept a journal of these activities, which, alongside the occasional displays of material objects she has collected, forms the primary public presentation for the project.

HAIRCUTS BY CHILDREN (2006–PRESENT) MAMMALIAN DIVING REFLEX

Haircuts By Children is a workshop and event conceived by Canadian "research-art atelier" Mammalian Diving Reflex.[22] Children aged 8 to 12 train with professional beauticians for a period of time, at the end of which they give free haircuts to members of the public. Cutting an adult's hair, the group writes, demonstrates children as competent individuals whose aesthetic choices should be trusted and respected. For Mammalian Diving Reflex, this aesthetic competency points to a larger civic competency, intentionally confronting the contemporary construction of childhood as a time set apart from both the realm of politics as well as the world of creative industry. Fliers for *Haircuts By Children* make the case that if adults can trust children to cut their hair, they should also trust children to vote.

The project shifts roles across the socially constructed lines of "adult" and "child" and highlights the various exchanges that occur within the performance. "Professional" training for adults is given to a group of children who are, under normal circumstances, legally prohibited from applying it. At the same time, the product of the performance, a haircut, is shifted from its everyday form of a professional service transaction into something unfamiliar and potentially creative. *Haircuts By Children* has occurred in Toronto, Cork, and New York City, under the auspices of civic or art fairs.

22. Website text, www.mammalian.ca, 2013

HAIRCUTS BY CHILDREN (2006–PRESENT) MAMMALIAN DIVING REFLEX

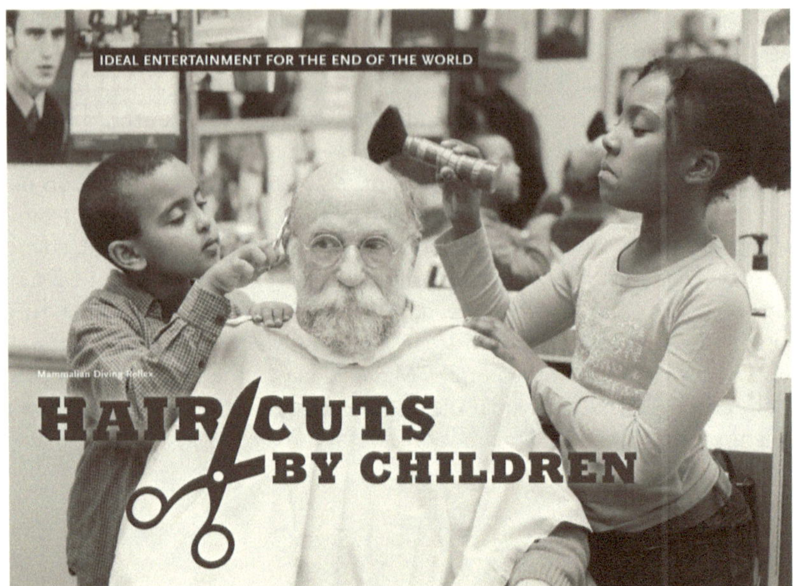

Mammalian Diving Reflex *Haircuts By Children* 2006–Present

HAMDALLAYE PROJECT (1998–2002) HUIT FACETTES

The Hamdallaye Project was an initiative begun by the Dakar-based collaborative group Huit Facettes. Centered in the village of Hamdallaye (located in southern Senegal), the project brought international artists into contact with local artists and craft producers through the creation of a series of workshops and exhibitions. These are constructed as dialectical situations, where both the visiting and local artists are learning from each other, through the simple structure of having both groups of people active as both leaders and participants. One of the aspects of this project that is inherent in its structure is the move to invite the "global" art world, represented by the participating international artists, into an extremely local art world and to stage the exchange there. This structure reverses the more common trajectory where peripheral, local artworks are exported to the global system of museums, galleries, and art-fairs, a decontextualizing process that frequently alters or deprives the work of its inherent social meaning.

The members of Huit Facettes serve as organizers and planners of these projects and use their position as known international artists to broker this exchange. "What Huit Facettes has been doing is rather to 'go the other way'—that is, to use their international network to open up or internationalize the local art world. Again this is done in an unconventional way in the name of decentralization by bringing participants of the western art world not to the capital Dakar as might be expected, but to places quite off the art track like Hamdallaye, Joal, and Mbour."[23] The use of their own status to put pressure on a system and reverse the typical flow of cultural capital aligns Huit Facettes with the concept of the artist as a leveraging agent, where the conferred privilege they have been given by the "art world" is redistributed to those the "system" has overlooked.

THE HILLMAN CITY FREEMOBILE (2003) JON RUBIN

The Hillman City FREEmobile wound its way through the streets of Hillman City, a residential neighborhood of Seattle, over the course of a summer, distributing free homemade products and personal services supplied by the neighborhoods residents. The FREEmobile, a modified maintenance step van conceptually based on a traditional ice cream truck, was created by San Francisco artist Jon Rubin to "create a system that publicly celebrates the hidden talents and resources of the neighborhood."[24] The FREEmobile was made available to residents on a "signup" basis, and each participating resident or family was given access to the van for an entire day. The FREEmobile drove through the entire neighborhood, stopping on request whenever it was flagged down. Serving both as a roving museum of local interests and folk culture and as a distribution system for homemade goods, the FREEmobile also functioned as a mechanism for the residents of the neighborhood to know and understand one another through the lens of their hobbies, passions, and personal industry.

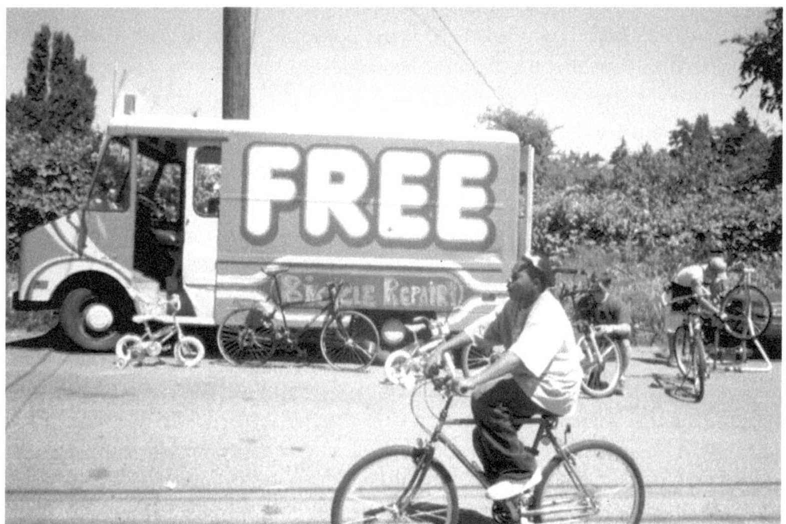

Jon Rubin The Hillman City FREEmobile *(incense trees)* 2003

23. Mariann Komissar, *Dakar Visions of Art,* The University Museum of Cultural Heritage, University of Oslo, 2000 (unpublished paper).

24. Jon Rubin, excerpt from a letter/statement sent to Ted Purves, May 2002.

ICE: CENTRAL CHINA (1996) WANG JIN

Wang Jin's *Ice: Central China* was a massive temporary sculpture commissioned by the city of Zhengzhou (the capital of Henan province in central China) as a part of the opening ceremonies for a large shopping mall. This mall was the first "Western-style" shopping mall to be opened in the city, and represented a milestone, both for the residents, in regards to their own access to luxury goods, as well as for the city's image as a globally "connected" locale. The wall itself was over thirty meters long and several meters thick. Inside this translucent wall, the artist had frozen over one thousand luxury items, including jewelry, cosmetics, toys, electronics, cell phones, and pharmaceuticals, creating something of a monument to the products that would soon be available within the shopping mall. The "original goal of the project," according to Wang, "was to cool down and purify the public with the ice, with reason."[25] As designed, the piece would allow for the gods to slowly melt out from the ice, where they could be taken in a gradual fashion, as they emerged. However, the wall was destroyed almost immediately when the crowds attending the opening ceremonies attempted to dig out the frozen objects.

INTERVENTION IN A SCHOOL (1996–1997) WOCHENKLAUSUR

In 1996, at the request of the Vienna University of Applied Art, the group WochenKlausur was given the opportunity to work with a group of schoolchildren to help them redesign their own environment, as the standardized forms of the typical Austrian school were functional but stifling and uncomfortable. The standardization of the seats and room design served very few of the diverse students' physical needs and generally created an atmosphere of tension and discomfort. Using a program of consensus-based decision making and design experience, the members of WochenKlausur worked with groups of students from two grade levels and redesigned their classrooms to better suit the students and their daily needs.

> The precisely elaborated standards contained in a booklet that normally provides guidelines for school interior designers were simply ignored. Instead the pupils were asked to make design proposals and voice their needs. Pets, retractable TV sets, and jungle plants were among the wishes expressed by the twelve-year-olds of the second class: Getting them to express their less fantastic desires took quite some patience. Finally, WochenKlausur discovered that the seating arrangement was unbearable and discouraged group work. In response, the group built rounded desks in four concentric rows. The radial

---

25. Inside Out: New Chinese Art, Minglu Gao and Norman Bryson, University of California Press, 1998, 164.

organization of the desks improves communication and provides a better view of the blackboard. Coat racks that had long been in the way were transferred to the corridor, and the space thus saved was turned into a cushioned sitting corner. The lighting system was improved and adapted to the new situation.[26]

IT'S NOT ABOUT THE NEIGHBORS (2011) WANG GONGXIN

It's Not About the Neighbors was an architectural intervention by Chinese artist Wang Gongxin at the Arrow Factory in Beijing. Wang drew on the Arrow Factory's location, in an alley next to a popular northern Chinese-style bakery, a location similar to where he grew up. In alleyways such as these, Wang writes, "neighbors are considered as part of the family"—as such, developments in the neighborhood are treated with great interest.[27] For *It's Not About the Neighbors*, Wang and Arrow Factory constructed a façade identical to the bakery next door. At night, when the bakery was open, a video Wang made of the front of the bakery next door was projected at the modified Arrow Factory, resulting in two bakeries: one real, one a projection. The projection would end at daybreak, when the bakery closed.

The construction of the façade, the existing façade, and the projection led to confusion and exasperation among the residents of the neighborhood that frequented the bakery. While the piece was under construction, residents wondered if the popularity of their bakery was resulting in a competitor being constructed directly next door, an unwelcome development; when it was completed, and when the projection shone at night, residents wondered if it was an advertisement for the bakery next door. When they realized that it was not an advertisement, and was instead an installation of contemporary art, they wondered why it existed and if it were for sale.[28] A brief video of the installation at night is available on Wang's website.

26. WochenKlausur, project description, http://wochenklausur.t0.or.at/05p_lang_e.htm.
27. Wang Gongxing and Pauline Yao, e-mail message to the editors, 2012.
28. Wang Gongxing and Pauline Yao, ibid.

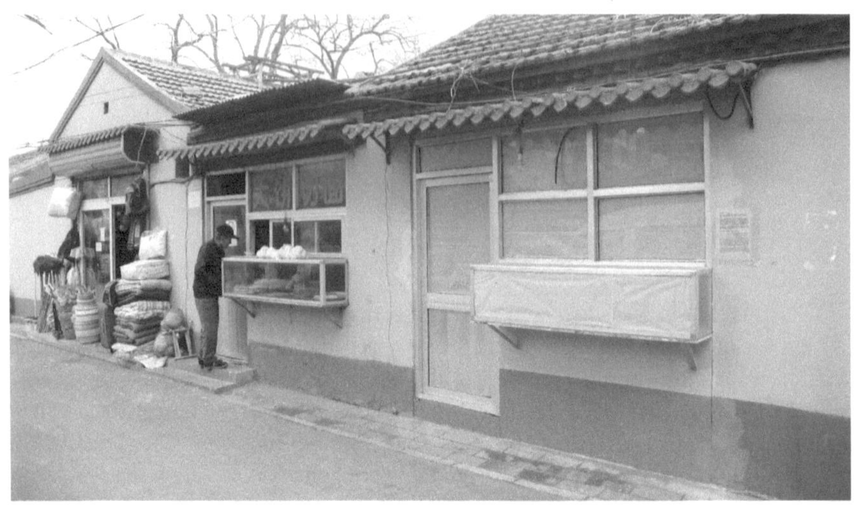

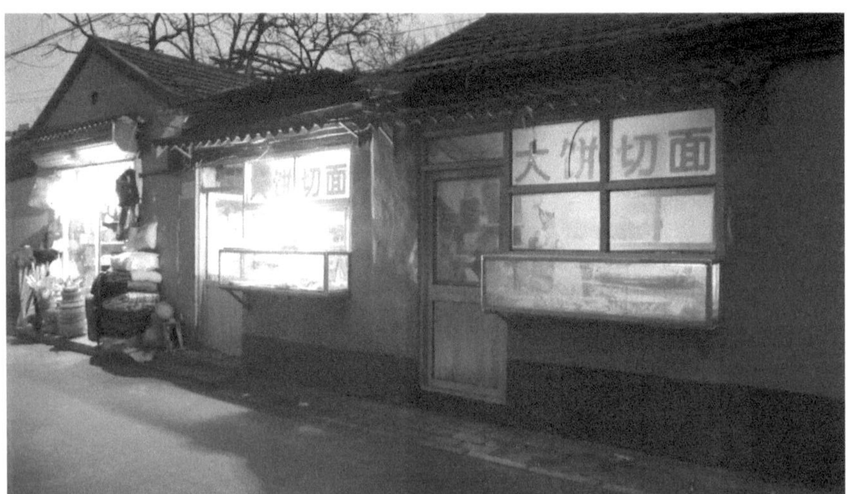

Wang Gongxin *It's Not About the Neighbors* 2011

In *Learning Thai: A Writing Reform*, the members of Nuts Society redesigned a basic, traditional Thai alphabet learning/coloring book to create a poster and CD-ROM-based computer program that teaches the Thai alphabet using associations between letters and words that promote social values, democratic thought, and compassion to others. The various letters of the Thai alphabet are each linked to words, with the underlying intent of creating lifelong associations between letters and concepts that are activated in the daily process of writing and spelling. The writing reform was designed to be useful to children and adults, as well as to nonnative Thai speakers who might begin a study of the language.

Nuts Society has exhibited and demonstrated Writing Reform in both gallery and community settings and has sought to adapt and integrate it into existing structures such as gallery exhibitions, community gatherings, and home learning. As the project evolved, the members of the Nuts Society, have devised alternate modes through which to implement the basic pedagogy of the Writing Reform. This has included a t-shirt production studio and shop at the Cincinnati Arts Association in 2001, and a series of exercise classes conducted during an exhibition at the Museum Fredericianum in Kassel in 2003.

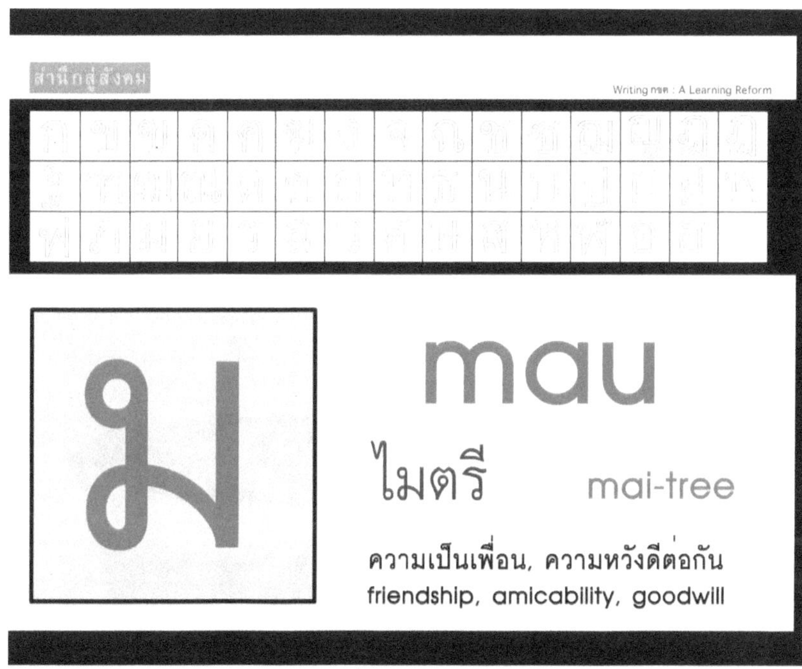

Nuts Society Learning Thai: A Writing Reform 1998–ongoing

Over the course of five years, California-based artist W. A. Ehren Tool mailed gifts of handcrafted ceramic bowls and cups decorated with military insignia, toy soldiers cast in clay, and various weapons to people in power, as well as those connected to the military. These ceramics were accompanied by personal letters that connected the artist's earlier experiences as a marine in the First Gulf War with his political and social concerns about the (then) escalating wars in both

W. A. Ehren Tool
2810 Ellendale Place
Los Angeles, CA 90007

Kent Kresa, CEO
Northrop Grumman
1840 Century Park E.
Los Angeles, CA 90067

26 June 2002

Dear Sir,

My name is W. A. Ehren Tool. During operations Desert Shield and Desert Storm I was a Marine with the 1st Marine Division. I am now an artist living in Los Angeles.

I am writing because I would like for you to have this bowl that I have made. It is food safe

I have met a few people since I have been out of the Marines that have worked for defense contractors who quit because they thought it was wrong to work there. I feel like I cannot throw stones because, I remember the feeling of relief when our bombs started exploding in Iraq and Kuwait. Other feelings came later. I thought that the more bombs that fell over there, the better the chance my friends and I would come home alive.

I am in awe of the things that the defense industry has created.

Sincerely,

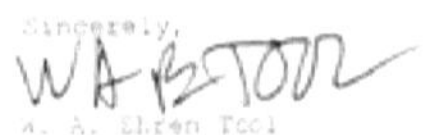

W. A. Ehren Tool

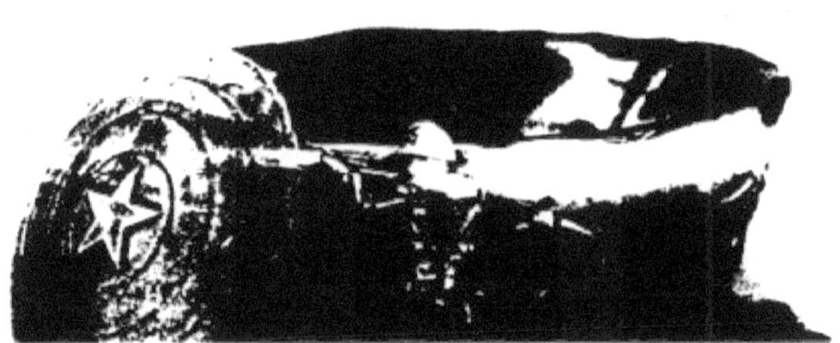

W. A. Ehren Tool Letters ca 2001–2005

Iraq and Afghanistan. When the project is exhibited in an art context, it includes pictures of the gift ceramic, combined with framed copies of Tool's letters, as well as any of the correspondence that might have been received from the recipients.

The artist mailed these cups and letters to a wide variety of public figures, including the top chamber of command for the US Military, defense contractors, oil company CEOs, NGOs such as Human Rights Watch, and celebrities (including Martha Stewart). Tool abandoned this project sometime after 2005, noting that the growing attention that he received from having the works discussed and shown within the art world was impacting the recipients' decisions to both keep the cups and write him back.[29]

MOBILE PORCH (2000) KATHRIN BOEHM AND STEFAN SAFFER (ARTISTS) AND ANDREAS LANG (ARCHITECT)

Mobile Porch was created in response to a public commission offered by the North Kensington Amenity Trust for the creation of community-based artworks in the North Kensington area of London. Boehm, Saffer, and Lang chose to locate their project in an interstitial area of the neighborhood—a strip of land located below a motorway overpass—which was being used by the local residents as the site for a public market and gathering place. The physical realization of their project was a mobile kiosk called the "Mobile Porch": a long oblong trolley that could be unfolded in various configurations, facilitating its use as a shop stall, a stage, or a platform for dancing or gathering. It was made available to area residents through a simple registration process, and became an integrated piece of communal property, identified with both the neighborhood and the market zone where it was used most prominently.

The designers' comment on the structure underscores the relation between the flexibility of its use and the fluid nature of the public space for which it was created: "*Mobile Porch* is an Urban Toy—a multifunctional mobile space, designed for roaming the public sphere, to engage with the users and the governing bodies of public spaces. *Mobile Porch* is a tool for exploring and activating public space and for getting in contact with local users and residents."[30]

29. "Spirit & Place: Reclaiming Armistice Day." Scott Shoger, *NUVO: Indy's Alternative Voice*, Nov. 11, 2012, www.nuvo.net. It is worth noting that the artist still is producing and giving away cups, though he has shifted his focus towards distributing them directly, through events, private meetings, or galleries.

30. Kathrin Boehm, email correspondence with Ted Purves, 2002.

MOBILE PORCH (2000) KATHRIN BOEHM AND STEFAN SAFFER (ARTISTS) AND ANDREAS LANG (ARCHITECT)

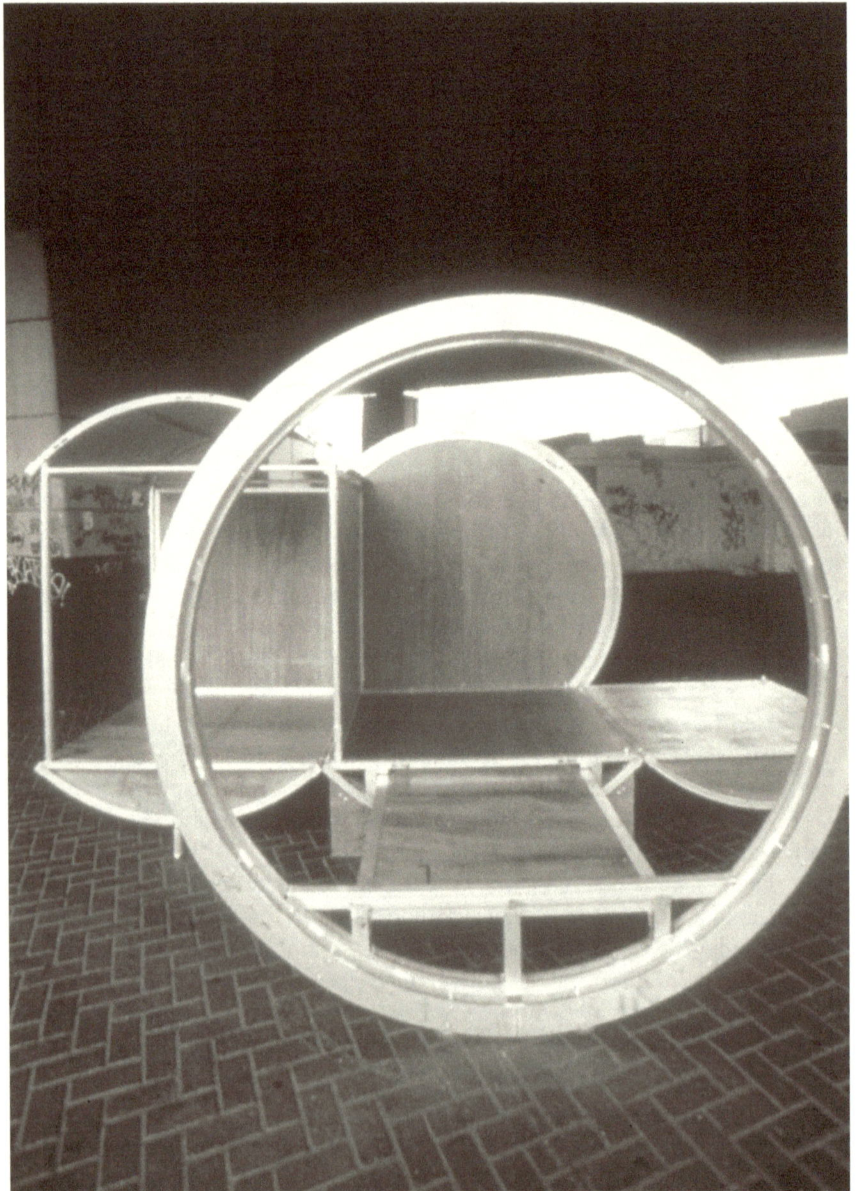

Kathrin Boehm, Stefan Saffer, and Andreas Lang *Mobile Porch* 2000

In his project *Money for Art*, Lee Ming Wei constructed nine individual origami sculptures, each made with a United States ten dollar note, while sitting in a café. The production of the sculptures attracted the attention of other patrons and spurred conversation, as people came to sit with him while the sculptures were being made. From these conversations the artist arranged for nine people to take one of each of the sculptures, in exchange for a commitment to keep in touch for the period of a year, during which time they would report whether they had unfolded the sculpture and used it for currency, or whether they had left it folded and retained it as an artwork. The nine participants also agreed that if they decided to transfer the sculpture into currency that they would inform him of what they bought.

The project has been documented through a series of photographs that chronicle the nine sculptures. These images serve as both a record of the project, and, in a small way, as something of a catalogue raisonné of the sculptures themselves. After one year, five were still folded, three had been used to purchase goods (including a pair of moccasins, a CD, and some groceries), and one had been stolen. The artist has reflected in later interviews that the various participants all were quite candid about their decisions to "use" the sculpture as either money or art. One woman spent it almost immediately on groceries, as having a work of art was not as important as buying food that she needed. One man, who described himself as homeless, kept the work in his wallet, preserved in its original, folded state.[31]

MONEY WATCHING (2007–ONGOING) CESARE PIETROIUSTI

In *Money Watching*, a single participant is asked to watch a banknote, housed in a vitrine, until a predetermined "quantity" of attention has been given to the banknote. If adequate attention is given, the participant receives the banknote. Petroiusti displays more than one banknote (in separate vitrines), meaning the participant may have to make a choice based on the value of the banknote. Participants may only look at one banknote at a time. *Money Watching* first occurred in a vacant storefront in Birmingham, England, one of a series of performances titled "Paradoxical Economies," made for the 2007 Fierce! festival organized by Birmingham's Ikon Gallery. The storefront was open from 10am to 6pm for one day; participants would receive a £10 note if they watched it for 15 minutes or a £20 note if they watched it for 25 minutes. The banknote would be flipped over halfway through the watching. *Money Watching* has since occurred, in similar formats, in Johannesburg, Paris, and Costenza (Italy).

---

31. Lee Ming Wei, "Eat, Sleep, and Pray: Everyday Rituals and Contemporary Art," with Tino Sehgal, audio interview archived on the New York Museum of Modern Art website, http://www.moma.org/explore/multimedia/audios/156/1668.

While the artist conceived of the work as a way to demonstrate the arbitrary nature of the art market, and valuation more generally, and dislodge currency from fetish status, its location in a storefront, set between other shops, also served created to generate a basic reversal of roles.[32] Perhaps unsurprisingly, given its humor, its gamelike quality, and the novelty of participants receiving money, *Money Watching* has generated media interest: YouTube videos exist of *Money Watching* in Birmingham, Costenza, and Johannesburg. Although no record of the total funding distributed exists, many participants have received banknotes. Because of this, *Money Watching* has recently been listed in a database of "Arte Utíl," or useful art, hosted by the Queens Museum of Art.

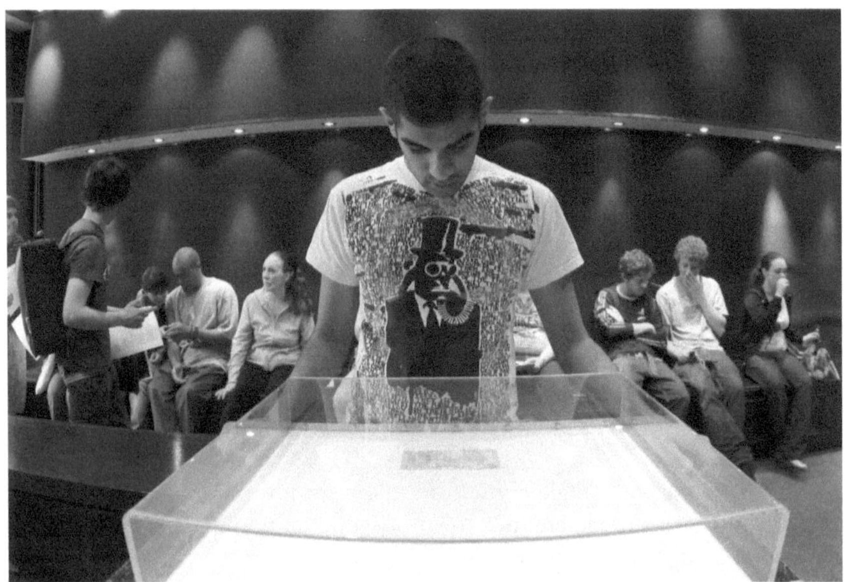

Cesare Pietroiusti *Money Watching* 2007–ongoing

MUSEO DE LA CALLE (1999–2002) COLECTIVO CAMBALACHE

The collaborative group Colectivo Cambalache was founded in Bogota, Colombia, in 1999 with a specific interest in exploring direct exchange and cultural recycling as an artistic strategy. Though it has no set members, it has primarily been the co-creation of Carolina Caycedo, Adriana García, Alonso Gil, and Federico Guzmán. Their project, *Museo de la Calle*, began in the streets of Bogota, where the collective members made a street cart, modeled on the

32. Cesar Petroiusti, e-mail message to editors.

types of carts used by street recyclers or peddlers, which functioned as an open space for bartering. Goods held within the cart could be freely traded between the collective members, the audience, with the only prohibition being that money was not to be used.

> We organized a big barter and giveaway, bringing out all kinds of things and artifacts we don't use anymore but can be useful to others. We collected from our family and friends and a lot of things were brought in. Clothing, toys and home appliances were given away for anything useful or useless that people wanted to give in exchange . . . We are talking about an open museum without categories nor walls to recycle and give new use to all kinds of objects obtained through barter.[33]

This project continued intermittently in Bogota and has since been staged in other cities around the world (Istanbul, Venice, and Seville) by various members of the collective, often in response to invitations from art festivals and exhibitions. Over time, the collective has also began to explore other forms of cultural bartering and exchange through the use of mobile sound stages and DJ stations, where people on the street can also exchange their favorite music and add their own voices to a live street mix. This interest in on-the-spot[34] exchange has been the primary impetus for the development of their work, which has consistently sought to place itself in the public sphere, rather than within such set cultural containers as art galleries and museums.

LOS MUTANTES (2000) CARLOS AMORALES

Working in conjunction with the social service program El Caracol, which functions as a halfway house and support service for former street kids, Carlos Amorales began the *Los Mutantes* project with the idea of creating a series of artistic encounters by bringing former street kids from Mexico City's poorest neighborhoods into contact with international artists. The purpose of the meetings and collaborations were for the two parties to work together to generate a collaborative art project using the artists' germinal concepts and the kids' daily lives and perspectives as a catalyst for combined work. Amorales chose to call

33. Cambalache Collective in conversation with Carlos Basualdo. *Flash Art* 214 (October 2000).

34. "We always thought that our activity should be about giving or constructing something; not tourism but exchange; exchanging is a direct way to approaching people in the street, an ephemeral contact where we propose a quick exercise of rethinking our values in a non monetary transaction." Cambalache Collective, unpublished artists' statement, 2003.

the former street children "Mutant Units" out of respect for the fact that they are, by choice, no longer "street kids" and are in the midst of transformation (i.e., mutation) into another social role.

As an example of one of the *Los Mutantes* projects, the artist Michael Blum developed *Los Mutantes Trans-Class Dinner,* in which groups of three to five "mutant-units" were invited to dinner in a family home. The artist's project description provides detail about the selection of the hosts and the intended results:

> . . . the selection of hosts should reflect an unusual cut into the Mexican Society. . . . an old, established bourgeois family, with high-level education with at least one child of the same age range as *los mutantes*, a storyteller, a foreigner working for a transnational corporation, a political activist, a popular film-maker, somebody active in a very specialized/rare field (e.g., an astronomer, a cook, an architect) . . . or an immigrant family from an unknown/remote country. The core of the dinner is the encounter itself, provoked as an opening to forms of life that *los mutantes* have probably never experienced before but also as a confrontation to their beliefs and feelings . . . Nonetheless, there is a utopian part of this project: the simple act of providing one single table around which such different beings will sit goes along with a search of a lost community."[35]

NOVA POPULARNA (2003) LUCY MCKENZIE AND PAULINA OLOWSKA

In May 2003, artists Lucy McKenzie and Paulina Olowska ran *Nova Popularna*, a "temporary illegal speakeasy/artist salon" in the gallery of the Society for the Friends of Fine Arts in Warsaw, Poland. The artists sought to inhabit a trope of European 1920s avant-garde, the underground artist salon, to see what relevance it retained, while at the same time reflecting the location of the project's location in a rapidly changing country. While the salon was in fact an illegal business, due to the untaxed sales of primarily homemade alcohol at the bar, it was able to remain open because it existed as a "legal" art exhibition, due to the fact that the artists' had rented the gallery from the Society of the Friends of Fine Arts, for the purpose of staging an art exhibition. This legal status as an art exhibition allowed a certain margin of tolerance to be maintained. In the artists' words: "When we bothered the neighbors with late sounds, which was most nights, we could announce that evening as simply another vernissage."[36]

---

35. Michael Blum, excerpt from an unpublished report on the *Los Mutantes* project submitted to the Rijksakademie von Beeldende Kunst Library, Amsterdam, 2001.

36. Paulina Orlowska, in Lucy McKenzie and Paulina Olowska, *Nova Popularna*, (Warsaw/Frankfurt: Galerie Foksal/Revolver Books, 2003).

The salon was designed to consciously evoke an earlier moment, one located well before the idealism of modernist production was sundered in half by the advent of the Cold War. At the same time it played upon the divergent histories that followed as modernist design was adopted by both the West and the East. The room was adorned with references to early twentieth-century British design, with curtains modeled after Scottish designer Charles Rennie Mackintosh and wallpaper that evoked the Vorticists, a short-lived British art movement modeled partially on Cubism. The barmaids (who were usually the two artists) wore costumes designed in "cool 1920s Functionalist style" by Edinburgh-based designer Beca Lipscombe.[37] The bar, however, "related to the consumer reality of Poland's recent past . . . To actually get a drink, the customer had to purchase with hard cash a small card with a reproduction of the mural on the opposite wall at a separate counter and then take it to the bar, and exchange it for alcohol."[38] The bar served primarily local, homemade (and thus illegal) alcohol, along with a single brand of beer and one type of cigarette.

Over the course of the month, *Nova Popularna* hosted exhibitions, live music, performances, and informal gatherings in their highly stylized space. It was supported by the Foksal Gallery Foundation and Warsaw-based curator and critic Lukasz Gorczyca and was documented in a print anthology, printed by Frankfurt-based press Revolver, and an LP, printed by Los Angeles–based collective Ooga Booga.[39]

NUNAVUT (1983) IGLOOLIK ISUMA PRODUCTIONS

Nunavut (which translates as "Our Land") is a thirteen-part television series produced by Isuma Productions, a video production cooperative that is located in Igloolik, a small Inuit village on the remote northern edge of Baffin Island. It is owned and operated by members of the village, who are also its writers, camera operators, editors and actors. It was incorporated in 1990, and at the time, was Canada's first Inuit independent production company. The company is 75 percent Inuit-owned and was founded by Zacharias Kunuk, Paul Apak Angilirq, Pauloosie Qulitalik, and Norman Cohn; all but Cohn were born in Igloolik.

---

37. Jan Verwoert, "World in Motion," *Frieze* 84 (June/August 2004, http://www.frieze.com/issue/article/world_in_motion.

38. Lucy McKenzie, in *Nova Popularna*, op cit.

39. The print anthology includes artists' texts, interviews, collaged photographs, and reproductions of event posters. The LP contains recordings of performances at the salon by various bands; the sleeve and jacket depict collaged photographs, with a pop-up version of the bar.

The scripts for the *Nunavut* series were drawn from interviews with the elders of the community, who recount what life was like when they were growing up, or things that they were told by their parents and relatives when they were young. Younger members of the community, who have to literally relearn the traditional parts of their culture to inhabit the roles, then act out these scripts for the actual video production. As such, the video is actually showing people in the very act of *re-learning* how to do something like build an igloo and a sod house.

While Nunavut's production is located in this transfer of information from one generation to another, it builds upon a tradition of oral history and storytelling that was always present in the community. For us, as outsiders, viewers sharing in the intensive process of the video's creation, there is a different but equally important transmission—instead of watching something produced simply for our own learning or "interest," we are watching others in the process of their own learning, which is then given to us to make meaning from.

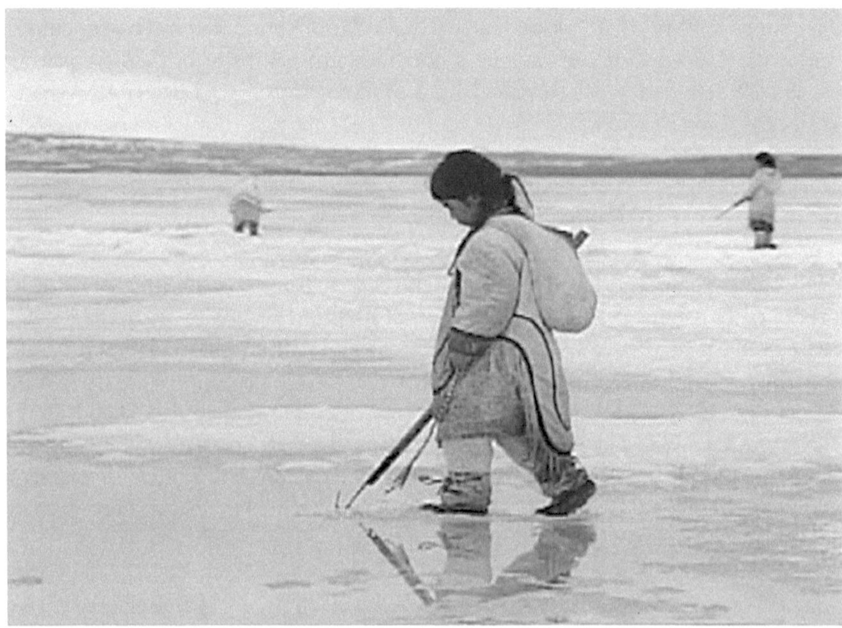

Igloolik Isuma Productions *Nunavut* 1983

For the *$100 Project*, artist Elisabeth Smolarz travelled, over a period of six years, to all of the G8+5 member countries: Canada, France, Germany, Italy, Japan, Russia, the United Kingdom, the United States, Brazil, China, India, and South Africa. At each location, Smolarz calculated how many people in that nation's working class she could hire, assumedly at minimum or average wage, for the local equivalent of US$100 for one hour. In most European countries, she was able to hire three people; in India, she was able to hire thirty-six. The hired laborers would sit in room, generally with a table, chairs, and light refreshments, for an hour, and do whatever they wanted. These activities included talking, playing games, singing, and so on. A stationary camera recorded their activity for the hour. Before filming began, Smolarz would have a conversation, usually through an interpreter, with the laborers about the meaning of "free time," whether "free time" should be compensated, the "situation of the working class in each culture, capitalism," her reasons for the project, and related issues.[40] Smolarz intended "the gesture of compensating the participants for their 'free time'" to point towards global socioeconomic inequality.[41]

When presented in institutional contexts, the *$100 Project* appears as a 33-minute, 13-channel video. The structure of the installation, writes the artist, reflects "global socioeconomic inequality"—the sample video on the Smolarz's website includes a 14-minute sample version of clips in the following order: Germany, China, England, Brazil, France, Mexico, Italy, South Africa, Japan, the United States, India, Canada, and Russia.[42] Smolarz also notes that the notion that they might be paid for "free time" was a novel concept to many of the participants.

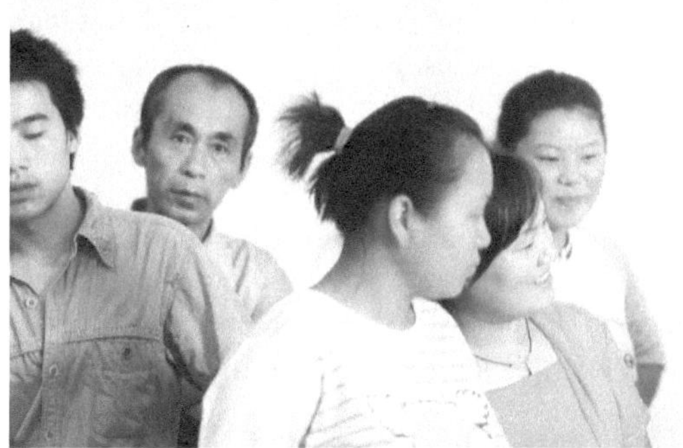

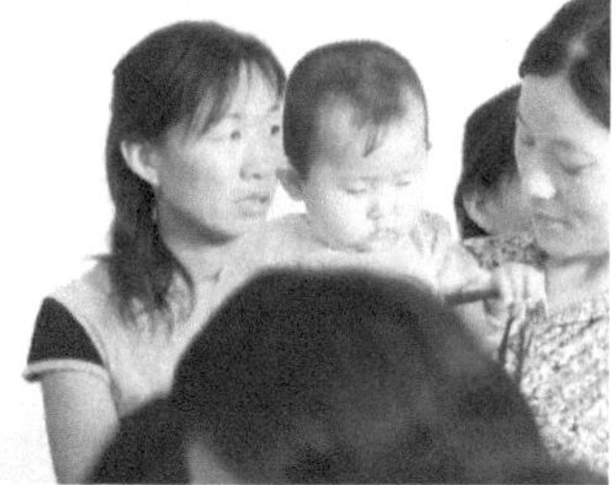

Elisabeth Smolarz *The $100 Project* 2006–2012

40. Elizabeth M. Grady, Jan Wilker, Elisabeth Smolarz, e-mail message to editors.
41. Ibid.
42. "The $100 Project," http://www.smolarz.com/the-one-hundred-dollar-project.html.

Una Tonelada de Libros Tirada sobre la Avenida de la Reforma (*One Ton of Books Dumped on Reforma Avenue*) was an action conceived by Anibal López, an artist who lives and works in Guatemala City. In this action, produced by Prometeo Associazione per l'Arte Contemporanea Luca (IT) and carried out in 2003, a dump truck dumped "exactly one ton" of books in the middle of Reforma Avenue, a busy thoroughfare in Guatemala City.[43] The form of the action was intended to evoke Robert Smithson's *Rundown* and *Pour* works, while the content pointed to what the artist viewed as soaring illiteracy and unequal access to culture in his home country of Guatemala. By placing the pile of books in the middle of the street, López, who uses his government ID code A-1 53167 to sign his public actions, intended to make the books available to passersby regardless of social standing—although literacy would likely still be a requirement for enjoying the books.

The pile of books caused a traffic jam as Guatemalans, who as a nation have a 74 percent total adult literacy rate,[44] rushed into the street to peruse the selection. A video, available on art-bus.com, shows a ring of city residents leafing through the selection as bewildered motorists crawl by and police assess the situation. A later shot shows three young men walking proudly away with their spoils. The video, available on the Internet and distributed in art and university contexts, is the sole record of the action.

OTIUM LEINEWIJK (2002) THE OBSERVATORIUM

Otium Leinewijk is a small, self-contained structure situated on the public easement along a dike outside of the village of Hoogezand-Sappemmeer, near to the the city of Groningen, The Netherlands. Designed as a public structure that provides private space, the Observatorium group conceived that *Otium Leinewijk* would be a permanent site for seclusion and retreat available to residents of the village and the general public. Though the project was generated through a publicly funded commission, the Observatorium group decided that an important aspect of the *Otium* was that its ultimate management and ownership would rest with a single individual, rather than being maintained by the municipality and/or the artists. This decision created a symmetry between the physical intent and the management of the structure, where a public space, owned by a single individual, was made available for private use as the resolution of a public commission.

43. "One Ton of Books Dumped on Reforma Avenue, 2003," art-bus.com, http://www.art-bus.com/A153167TONELADA.html.

44. "At a glance: Guatemala," UNICEF, http://www.unicef.org/infobycountry/guatemala_statistics.html.

After soliciting applications for consideration from interested citizens of Leinewijk, the artists selected a single individual, Linda Schregardus, a resident of Hoogezand-Sappemmeer, who seemed most suitable for the task. *Otium Leinewijk* is currently available for use by any interested party and is managed by a foundation that M. Schregardus created to oversee the *Otium*. Located alongside a canal, the structure has two spaces, one suitable for sleeping and sitting and the other designed for cooking and other domestic activities.

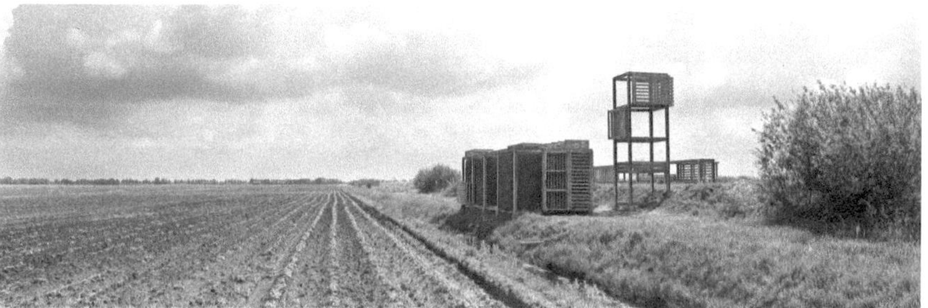

The Observatorium *Otium Leinewijk* 2002

PARASITE (2000) MICHAEL RAKOWITZ

The *paraSITE*s were a series of inflatable structures built by artist Michael Rakowitz specifically for the purpose of creating warm, portable spaces for homeless persons to use as ongoing personal shelters. Designed to take advantage of the surplus warm air flow that can be found throughout most urban areas as a byproduct of a given building's heating and ventilation system, each shelter was made from readily available material (mostly plastic bags and tape), and could be inflated by attaching a part of the structure to the exterior vent of a building.

In a process that somewhat resembled the dialogue between an architect and a client in the construction of a house, each Parasite was created in dialogue with eventual users, and took into account their needs, means of mobility, and the areas they frequented. The artist's website details many of these consultations, and provides a context for each design decision. For example in Bill S.'s *paraSITE* shelter. "He requested as many windows as possible, because 'homeless people don't have privacy issues, but they do have security issues. We want to see potential attackers, we want to be visible to the public.' Six windows are placed at eye level for when Bill is seated and six smaller windows for when Bill is reclining"[45]

45. Michael Rakowitz, from http://michaelrakowitz.com/projects/parasite/

paraSITE (2000) MICHAEL RAKOWITZ

One of the critical aspects of the shelters is their dependence on the airflow and space around buildings; they, quite literally, are parasitic, recuperating a common surplus and structuring it into a usable form. As such, each *paraSITE* operates on two levels, providing an economical means of providing warm shelter and visibly using a formerly unexploited byproduct of contemporary building engineering.

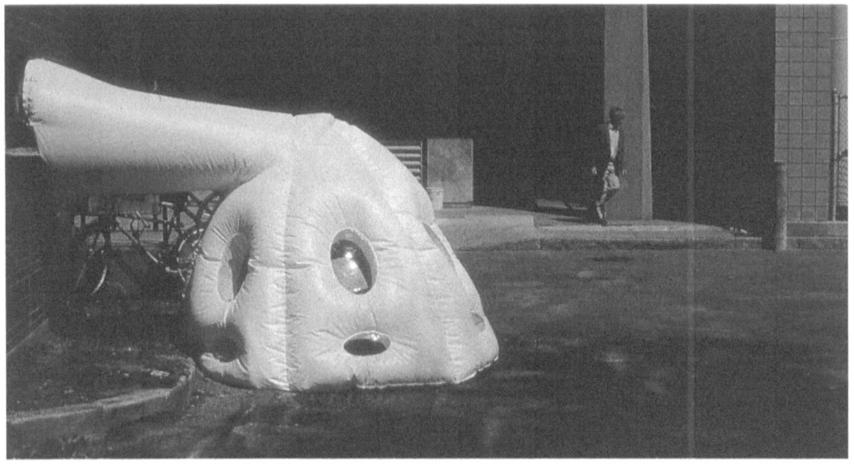

Michael Rakowitz *paraSITE* 2000

LE PONT DES REGARD (2003) KAN-SI

Le Pont Des Regards was a photographic intervention by Senegalese artist Kan-si between the inhabitants of the island of Fadiouth, on the southern coast of Senegal, and tourists to the island. Constructed on bed of clamshells, the island is popular with tourists, as are its inhabitants, who maintain some traditional Serer customs. Fascinated by the nonchalance with which tourists photographed the island's inhabitants and the process of "othering" that such actions signaled, the artist provided cameras to participating community members with express instructions to only photograph tourists. Kan-si then installed the resulting photographs along one side the 800-meter footbridge connecting Fadiouth with the town of Joal. On the other side of the bridge, the artist installed photographs of the community participants; at either end of the bridge was a text explaining the project. The intervention occurred as part of "Universalism at stake: Dialogues with Senghor," a five-month workshop and exhibition, curated by Marie-Thérèse Champesme, wherein international artists were invited to Joal-Fadiouth to develop work in dialogue with the community.

For its duration, the project allowed the community in Fadiouth to claim some agency in regard to their photographic representation, causing occasionally uncomfortable interactions with the tourists who frequent the island. The tourists apparently were often taken aback by being photographed. The German online arts journal *Nafas* relates one such encounter wherein a tourist angrily confronted the artist about not having consented to being photographed; in response, Kan-si—who apparently also participated in his project—pointed out that the tourist had not asked consent of a local community member he had apparently just photographed.[46] This was apparently just one of many such instances.

PUBLIC FRUIT MAPS (2004–ONGOING) FALLEN FRUIT (DAVID BURNS, MATIAS VIEGENER, AND AUSTIN YOUNG)

Fallen Fruit's *Public Fruit Maps* are a series of maps of fruit trees that grow in areas accessible to the public. Partially hand-drawn, partially computer-illustrated, the maps are intentionally inexact: whereas each map does list street names, and although each map does indicate which direction is north, no map includes specific addresses and no map includes a scale. Each map does, however, include instructions to "take only what you need/say 'hi' to strangers/ share your food/take a friend/go by foot."[47] When maps are drawn for areas in non-English-speaking areas, the directions appear in the local language. Different types of fruit trees are represented by way of a simple legend ("Ap" for apple, "Bb" for blackberry, etc). Fallen Fruit has produced dozens of maps for neighborhoods across the United States and Europe, in addition for a series of maps for neighborhoods in Calí, Colombia, and Guadalajara, Mexico. When printed, the maps range from 8" × 10" to 40" × 60".

The *Public Fruit Maps* are intended to be more than simply utilitarian documents by which to locate fruit. In their inexactness, they encourage wandering, exploring, and collaboration, with the aim of creating a sense of community and agency around public resources that may have previously gone unnoticed. The maps are distributed at the galleries, museums, or other institutions that commission them; they are also available in PDF format for free download on Fallen Fruit's website, fallenfruit.org. At time of writing, Fallen Fruit anticipates further maps of neighborhoods in Atlanta, Honolulu, London, New York, Paris, and further locales.[48]

46. "Kan-si, Le Pont des Regards," Maria Thereza Alves, http://universes-in-universe.org/eng/nafas/articles/2004/kan_si

47. Fallen Fruit, "Fallen Fruit of Virginia City," PDF file. http://www.fallenfruit.org/wp-content/uploads/FallenFruitofVirginiaCity.pdf

48. Fallen Fruit, e-mail message to editors.

PUBLIC FRUIT MAPS (2004–ONGOING) FALLEN FRUIT (DAVID BURNS, MATIAS VIEGENER, AND AUSTIN YOUNG)

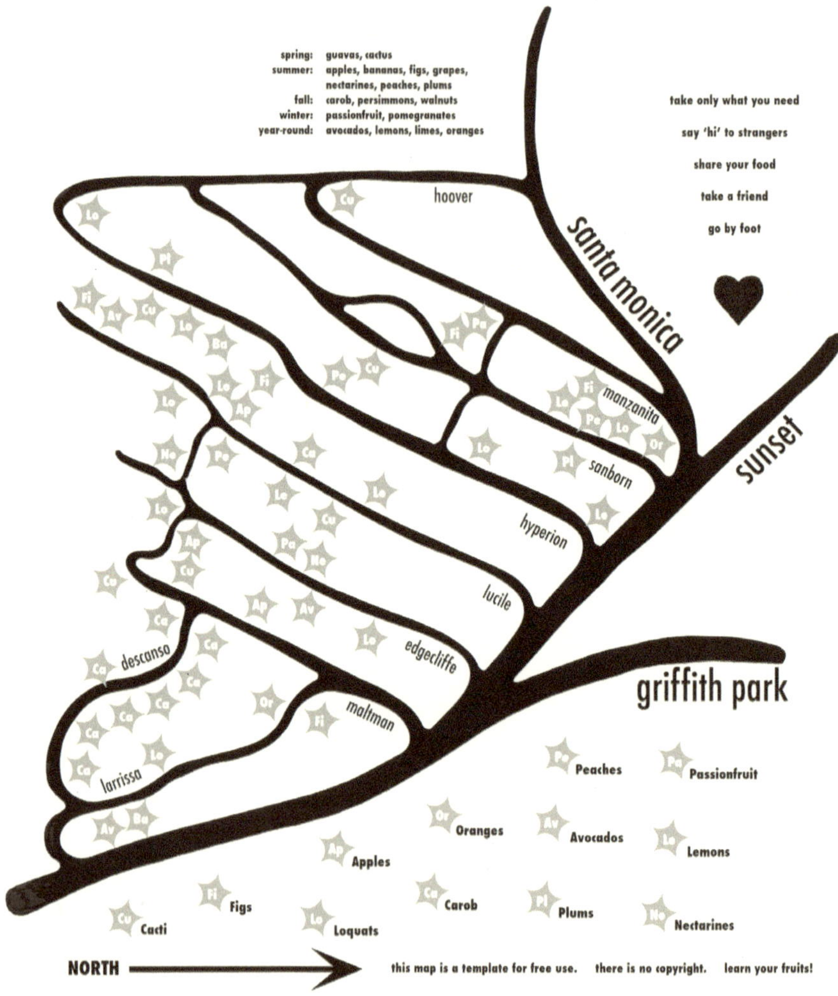

FALLEN FRUIT OF SILVER LAKE

more information at http://www.fallenfruit.org

David Burns, Matias Viegener, and Austin Young *Public Fruit Maps* Fallen Fruit 2004–ongoing

Question Bridge: Black Males is a transmedia art project by Chris Johnson, Hank Willis Thomas, Bayeté Ross Smith, and Kamal Sinclair. Black males across the United States—from New York City to New Orleans to Chicago to the San Francisco County Jail in San Bruno, CA—were filmed asking questions they had for other black males they felt different or estranged from; black males in other locales were filmed responding to those questions. The project is meant to bridge, through video-mediated question-and-answer exchanges, geographic, generational, and socioeconomic divisions within the community of black males throughout the United States, while simultaneously elaborating and complicating what "black male" might mean.[49] The artists involved in *Question Bridge: Black Males* see *Question Bridge* as a flexible module that could be extended to other communities or groups. The videos produced through the mediated question-and-answer process have been displayed as a five-channel video installation at museums across the country, including the Brooklyn Museum, the Oakland Museum of California, and the New Frontier program at the 2012 Sundance Film Festival, as well as other festivals within and outside the United States. A single channel version of the project has travelled to smaller venues such as galleries, universities, and YMCAs across the country. The artists are developing an interactive website to document the project (questionbridge.com), where viewers will be able to trace topical threads of the narrative and upload their own questions and answers.

Question Bridge is a multiple-platform project. In addition to its well-received installation and film versions, the project has extended to panel discussions held in Brooklyn and Oakland, including a repeating model, *Question Bridge Blueprint Roundtable*, inspired by a question asked of the civil rights generation by younger man during filming. A curriculum has been developed around the project, which has been piloted at high schools, community centers, and arts organizations in New York City and London.

49. Bayeté Ross Smith, e-mail message to editors.

QUESTION BRIDGE: BLACK MALES (2012) CHRIS JOHNSON, HANK WILLIS THOMAS, BAYETÉ ROSS SMITH, AND KAMAL SINCLAIR

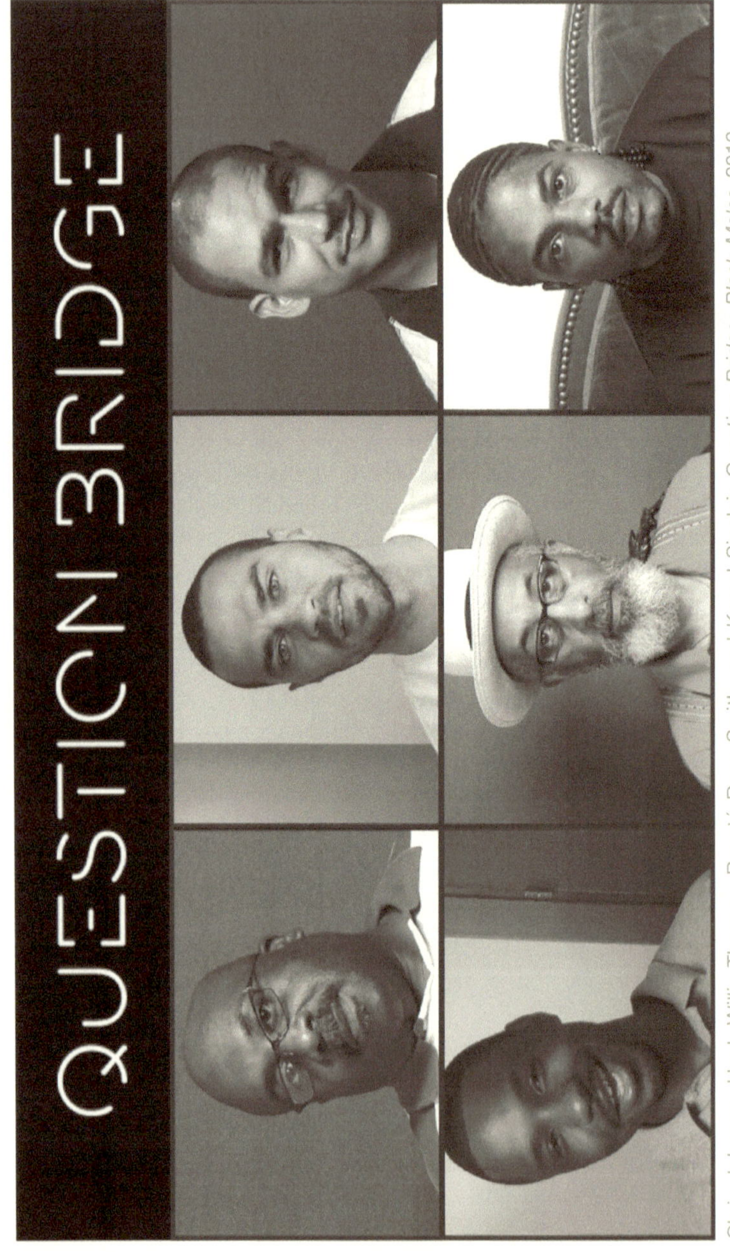

Chris Johnson, Hank Willis Thomas, Bayeté Ross Smith, and Kamal Sinclair *Question Bridge: Black Males* 2012

In the late 1980s, Colorado-based artist Lynne Hull began constructing a series of large, outdoor sculptures that were also designed to function as roosts and nesting platforms for predatory birds. These sculptures, collectively titled *Raptor Roosts*, initially were sited in areas of Colorado and Wyoming that had been deforested. As such, the roosts, which are installed in a similar fashion to telephone poles, and are constructed with branches and limbs at their tops, provide habitat where there was none, and attempt to preserve some viable margin for these birds to continue living within their original ecosystem. Hull terms her work "trans-species art," and her raptor roosts (and subsequent projects)[50] navigate the relationship between the opportunity for the installation and funding of outdoor sculpture and the larger eco-systemic needs of the environments that such sculptures will occupy.

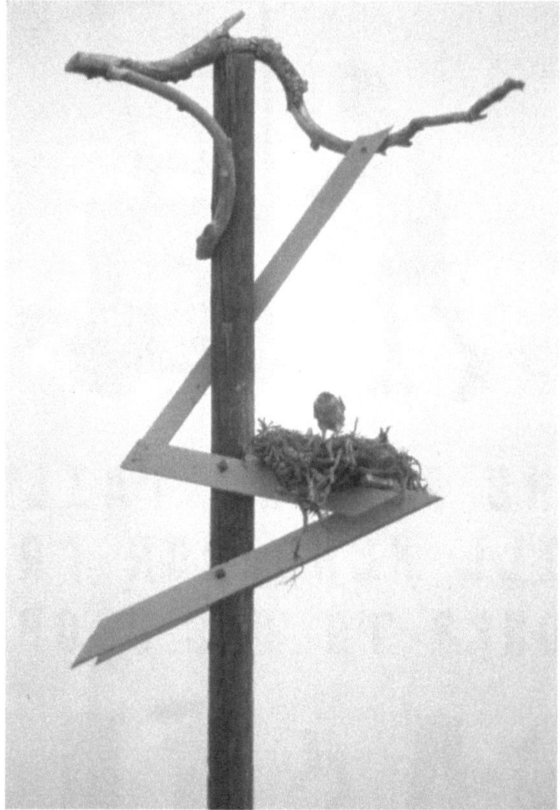

Lynne Hull *Raptor Roosts* 1988–1990

50. An example of a related projects would be Hull's "hydroglyphs" series, which are engraved designs in desert boulders that also serve to collect and preserve water for local reptiles, further extending the margins of their environment. For more on Hull's work, readers are invited to visit her website: http://eco-art.org/.

For a period of one week, San Francisco–based artist Michael Swaine wheeled a handmade cart through the city on a prescribed route. The cart contained an antique, treadle-powered sewing machine and various materials for patching and repairing clothing; Swaine's services as a tailor were offered to anyone who

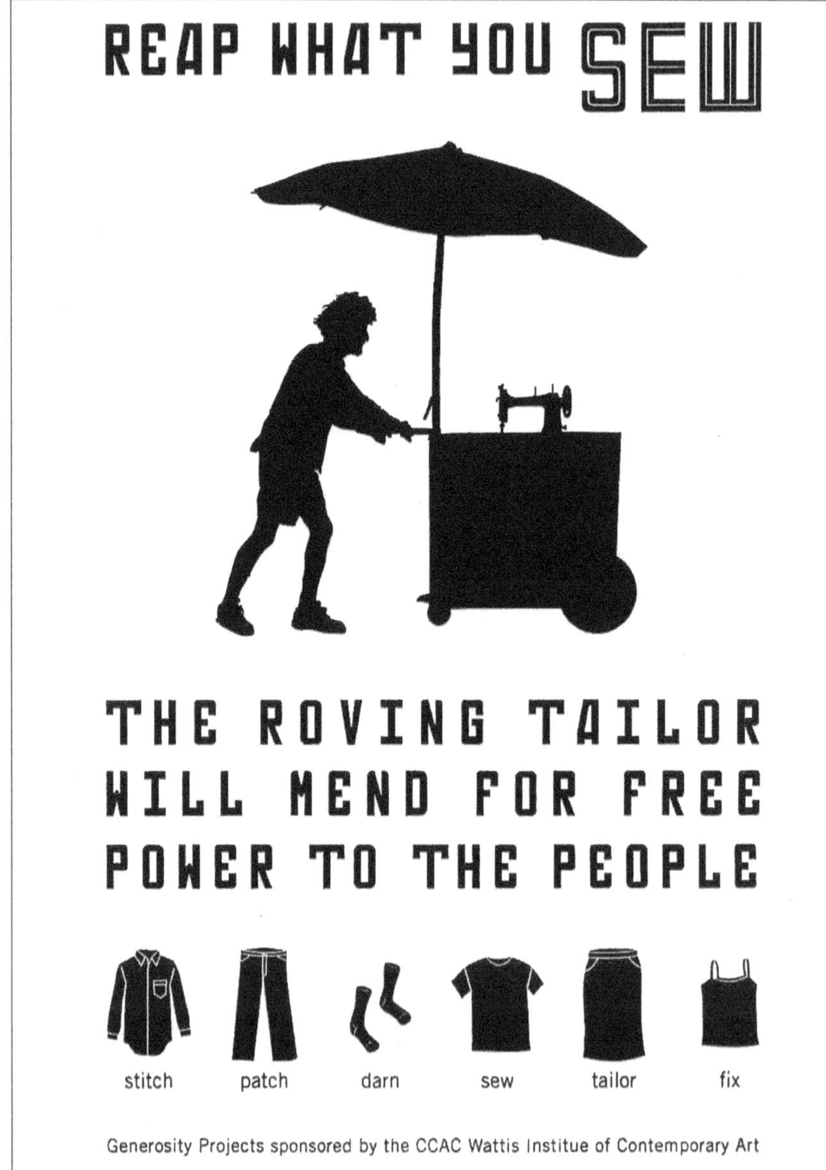

Michael Swaine *Reap What You Sew* 2002

asked. Since the project continued over the course of a week and the cart's route remained the same, people who were simply curious on one day got an opportunity to bring something to repair the next.

Swaine's daily route through the city began and ended at the front doors of the California College of Arts and Crafts (which sponsored the work) and took him through the warehouse district—where clothing was made by garment workers—to the downtown financial districts. It also went through the city's civic center, where the municipal government offices are located, and doubled back through the Mission district, home to (at that time—the area has since been heavily gentrified) day laborers, immigrants, and artists. While most of the public's interaction with the cart was discrete, in that each person's encounter with the project took place at a single point in the city, one of the project's other layers was the "invisible" map that was traced through the city each day. The movement of the clothing repair cart linked sites of production, profit, policy, and domestic space, all moored to the endpoint of a college that, not coincidentally, has one of the largest fashion design degree programs in the area.

REBECKA IS WAITING FOR ANNA, ANNA IS WAITING FOR CECILIA, CECILIA IS WAITING FOR MARIE . . . (1994) ELIN WIKSTROM

Rebecka is waiting for Anna, Anna is waiting for Cecilia, Cecilia is waiting for Marie . . . was a gallery-based situation constructed by Elin Wikström in 1994. In the piece, a woman waits for another woman to arrive for fifteen minutes. Once the woman arrives, the woman who was waiting leaves, and she—the woman who has just arrived—waits for fifteen minutes, until another woman arrives. Performed over the course of a day, the piece results in a stream of lone women arriving, waiting for another woman, and leaving. Performed over the course of a day or several days, the piece aims for its participants to "become a part of the chain of trust."[51] Wikström has released detailed instructions for the re-performance of the piece, including that documentation of the piece should not be exhibited.[52] The Moderna Museet in Stockholm purchased the piece, including its attendant archive of documentation, in 2000. It has been performed in Stockholm, Baltimore, London, and other locations.

Wikström intends for the piece to highlight the typical cinematic image of the lone woman, waiting, and turns it on its head. The women who participate in the piece, in her view, do not simply repeat the image of the waiting woman

51. "Looking for women to participate in an artwork!" Elina Suoryö, http://www.modernamuseet.se/en/Stockholm/Newslist/Looking-for-women-to-take-part-in-an-artwork/

52. "Re-doing Kaprow," *Metropolis* M, http://metropolism.com/magazine/2006-no6/re-doing-kaprow/english

that is often presented in cinema and television, wherein a woman passively waits (for a man, for a family, for domestic bliss) to resolve her situation. Rather, participants in *Rebecka is waiting for Anna, Anna is waiting for Cecilia, Cecilia is waiting for Marie . . .* actively wait for another woman, who actively waits for another woman, and so on, trusting that the woman they waited for would arrive. Trust, in this case, is generated by the participants' fidelity to the artwork, as the participating women arrive and depart according to a schedule set between the piece, the presenting institution, and the participants, rather than schedules set between each other.

rEpL1CA [SP4M] (2007) CONRAD BAKKER

In 2007, Conrad Bakker initiated *Untitled Project: rEpL1CA [SP4M]*. *rEpL1CA [SP4M]* utilized, first, a set of replica Rolex watches that sat in custom display boxes; second, an e-commerce website that sold the watches; and third, a set of ten spam messages from which readers could access the e-commerce site. These three aspects of the piece each mimicked a common trope of e-commerce, but each replica had a catch: the watches, a common item on eBay and other e-commerce sites, were actually carved and painted, not real watches; the e-commerce site was only online for a limited time, and only accessible through the spam e-mails; the spam e-mails were embedded with quotes from Volume 1 of Marx's *Capital*. The *Untitled Project: STORE*, the e-commerce site on which the replicas were temporarily available, closed on November 18, 2007. *Untitled Project: rEpL1CA [SP4M]* was included in the 2007 exhibition "Transactions," at the Blanton Museum of Art in Austin, TX.

rEpL1CA [SP4M] confused a series of tangentially related consumer systems and markets: the replica market, the art market, the spam market, e-commerce, and so on, exemplifying the project's mission to utilize "a variety of social, consumer, and institutional contexts" using "humor, contextual awareness, formal play, interventionist strategies, and imperfect carving and painting techniques."[53] In this piece, for instance, Bakker marketed imperfectly carved and painted replicas of real luxury watches using the vocabulary and syntax of spam e-mails, confounded with Marx, which were then sold through a "store" that adopted the form and syntax of an e-commerce site, referencing not only the art market but also the replica market and, more specifically, the Rolex replica spam market, which was booming at the time.[54]

53. "About," Untitled Projects, http://www.untitledprojects.com/index3.php

54. Will Russell, "Replica spam, Where do you send it?" posted on Spamcop.net, March 2007, http://forum.spamcop.net/forums/index.php?showtopic=7989

From: Untitled Projects
Subject: [SPAM] REPL1CA W4TCHES
Date: September 7, 2007 12:39:15 AM CDT

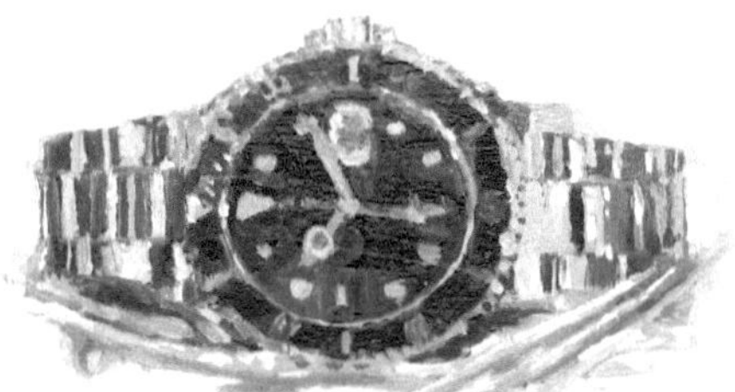

A commodity appears, at first sight, a very trivial thing, and easily understood. Its analysis shows that it is, in reality, a very queer thing, abounding in metaphysical subtleties and theological niceties. So far as it is a value in use, there is nothing mysterious about it, whether we consider it from the point of view that by its properties it is capable of satisfying human wants, or from the point that those properties are the product of human labour.
It is as clear as noon-day, that man, by his industry, changes the forms of the materials furnished by Nature, in such a way as to make them useful to him. The form of wood, for instance, is altered, by making a table out of it. Yet, for all that, the table continues to be that common, every-day thing, wood.
But, so soon as it steps forth as a commodity, it is changed into something transcendent. It not only stands with its feet on the ground, but, in relation to all other commodities, it stands on its head, and evolves out of its wooden brain grotesque ideas, far more wonderful than "table-turning" ever was.

Karl Marx: Capital Volume 1, Section 4, Paragraph 1

Conrad Bakker *rEpL1CA [SP4M]* 2007

London-based artists David Brazier and Kelda Free inaugurated the *Satpula Super Series* in 2009. Faced with the problem of describing a historical area of New Delhi—Satpula is a stone dam constructed in the fourteenth century—whilst somehow avoiding the "uneven balance of power found in traditional ethnographic documentary formats," the artists became interested in the daily cricket matches that occurred in a vacant area behind the Satpula dam, between teams of local, primarily lower-income, youth. Brazier and Free decided to create a (seemingly) simple frame around these ongoing matches, and worked with the youth to create the "Satpula Super Series." For the series, the artists produced a set of printed posters for the neighborhood featuring the local players, and hired a professional commentator for official cricket games to call the match.[55] The commentator, Saleem Zaidi, wore a suit and sat at a table with a white tablecloth. He called the game in Hindi and was broadcast via a PA system, which attracted a small crowd. His commentary was recorded, but not translated, and is now available on the artists' website. A second *Satpula Super Series* was

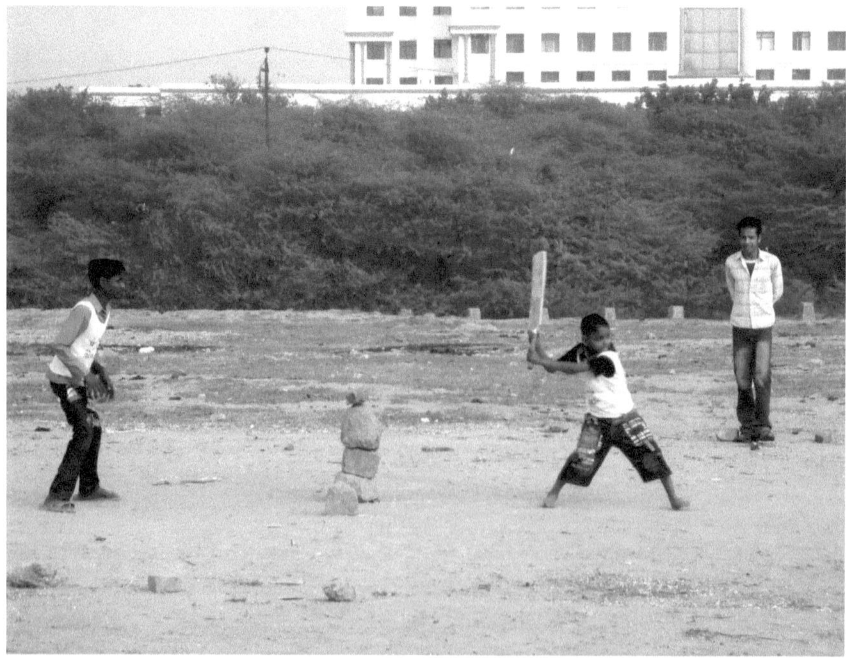

David Brazier and Kelda Free Satpula Super Series 2009

55. David Brazier and Kelda Free, e-mail message to editors, 2012.

facilitated in 2010 by Khoj International Artists' Association, who provided extensive assistance to the artists during their 2009 project.[56]

Cricket may seem a strange choice for two London-based artists attempting to avoid "colonial connotations" while doing a project in/around a New Delhi slum.[57] However, the artists maintain that the subsumption of the sport into Indian culture marks it not as a symbol of the lingering effect of British colonialism, but rather a symbol of postcolonial evolution; indeed, Cricket is more widely played, watched, and discussed in India than any other sport. Further, the artists chose to severely limit access both to the event and its document. In the case of the event, the commentary was broadcast on a PA system, a system capable of broadcasting a limited physical distance. The document, a recording of the broadcast, has not been translated. Thus, although it is accessible to Western—or, more broadly, global—audiences on the artists' website, comprehending the document requires not only an understanding of Hindi, but also an understanding of national and local variations of the formerly British game of cricket in India.

THE SCHOOL OF PANAMERICAN UNREST (2006) PABLO HELGUERA

From May to September 2006, *The School of Panamerican Unrest* travelled the Pan-American Highway, from Anchorage, Alaska, to Ushuaia, Argentina. The *School* was spearheaded by New York City–based artist Pablo Helguera and supported by more than forty partner organizations and over a hundred collaborators along its thirty stops from the northwest of North America to the southeastern terminus of South America. At each stop, Helguera's "nomadic think-tank" conducted a variety of activities, including panel discussions, workshops, meetings with speakers of endangered or nearly-extinct languages, film screenings, and so on, each addressing the relation of art-making in relation to local and international histories, sociopolitical issues, and the utopian dream of Pan-Americanism.[58] Meetings, as well as film screenings, were in the "schoolhouse," a portable yellow tent. The schoolhouse opened at each location with the ringing of a "Panamerican Bell," and closed with the signing of a declaration written with and read by local participants, as well as a performance of the "Panamerican Anthem," composed by Helguera. The *School* also maintained an active online presence, with a discussion forum and a website, panamericanismo.org (no longer extant).

56. Brazier and Free, e-mail.

57. Brazier and Free, e-mail.

58. Julie Rodrigues Widholm, "Pablo Helguera," in Julie Widholm, ed., *Escultura Social: A New Generation of Art from Mexico City*, (Chicago: Museum of Contemporary Art, in association with Yale University Press, 2007), 144.

The School of Panamerican Unrest had a variety of goals, not the least of which was resuscitating a notion of Pan-Americanism, an idea barely present in the present-day US cultural imaginary, despite its importance in the mid-nineteenth-century. Helguera's Panamerica dreamed of a new cultural paradigm, turning on a north-south, rather than east-west, axis, open to intercultural and multilingual dialogue. As Helguera's van travelled through the Americas, when the Panamerican Bell rang, this Panamerica existed; now it is kept alive by extensive documentation across a range of media: photographs, videos, transcripts of interviews, and so on. With the support of a Creative Capital grant, a bilingual *School of Panamerican Unrest Anthology* was published in 2011 by Jorge Pinto. A three-part documentary of the project appears on Helguera's YouTube channel.[59]

SERVICE-WORKS (2005–2010) JOSH GREENE

In *2010*, Bay Area conceptual artist Josh Greene conducted *Service-Works*, a micro-grant series that funded a variety of artist projects. Once a month, Greene retained tips from his job as a waiter at a high-end restaurant in San Francisco; he then granted this money to an artist project chosen from a pool of monthly applicants. The projects, titled with the artist's name and the amount granted (*Helena Keefe's $256 Project* or *Kara Hearn's $231 Project*, for instance), continue to be displayed on a website that documents the project. As part of each entry, Greene would provide a narrative description of the night during which he collected the tips that funded the project. Over the course of its existence, *Service-Works* funded seventeen projects, granting a total of $4,328.00.[60]

Service-Works deftly combined and/or conflated a variety of patronage systems and hierarchical roles. Greene pooled money gained through the convention of tipping servers, and then re-purposed the income by not keeping the tips for himself, transforming taxable wages into tax-reducing art expenses. By placing himself instead in an administrative role and re-distributing the funds to an artist or collaborative effort, Greene subjectively inserted himself into the role that purportedly objective "panels" play in the granting of artist's projects. He then subsumed these efforts into his own practice, using his own particular brand of frank language and dry humor in the naming of the projects and the descriptions provided of his nights collecting tips.[61] The piece, now an

59. http://www.youtube.com/user/Racatepupup

60. http://www.service-works.us

61. Scott Oliver, "Josh Greene's Service-Works," *Art Practical* Shotgun Review Archive, accessed 2/24/13, http://www.artpractical.com/shotgun_review_past/josh_greenes_service-works/

art project, continues to have the potential for a final economic shift, whereby Greene could potentially be compensated several times over what he paid in tips, were it somehow to be sold or acquisitioned by a museum. At the same time, the project gains a level of irony when it is considered that the patrons of the high-end restaurant he worked at were likely of the same class as those who found or donate to philanthropic foundations for art.

THE SCULPTED BASKET PROJECT (2007–ONGOING) AMUCHE NGWU-NNABUEZE

The Sculpted Basket Project is an ongoing effort by Nigerian artist Amuche Ngwu-Nnabueze to encourage a return to traditional basket weaving in Nsukka, Enugu State, Nigeria. The introduction of disposable materials and the popularity and convenience of Western throwaway culture has mixed toxically with Nigeria's infrastructural shortcomings. The lack of adequate garbage service and the absence of a recycling program have resulted in a proliferation of open waste dumps full of useless unsorted throwaway materials, some degradable and some not.

Dismayed by this situation and the disappearance of traditional basket weaving from popular culture and curricula, Ngwu-Nnabueze began *The Sculpted Basket Project*, an attempt to address Nsukka's waste problem through a series of public programs focusing on waste separation, composting, and basket weaving. The project presents baskets as traditional, sustainable, functional replacements for plastic bags, plastic seats, and other items generally made from imported or unsustainable materials.

In 2007, *The Sculpted Basket Project* received a grant from TerraKulture Lagos in 2007 for a basket weaving residency program. However, the funds were not enough to continue the residency past 2007 and the program was disbanded. Despite this, Ngwu-Nnabueze continues the project, teaching workshops, and organizing meetings with government and civilian ministers, educators, and church leaders. *The Sculpted Basket Project* functions as a springboard for awareness about these issues, utilizing radio stations, bulletins, church meetings, and mourning houses to circulate its message.

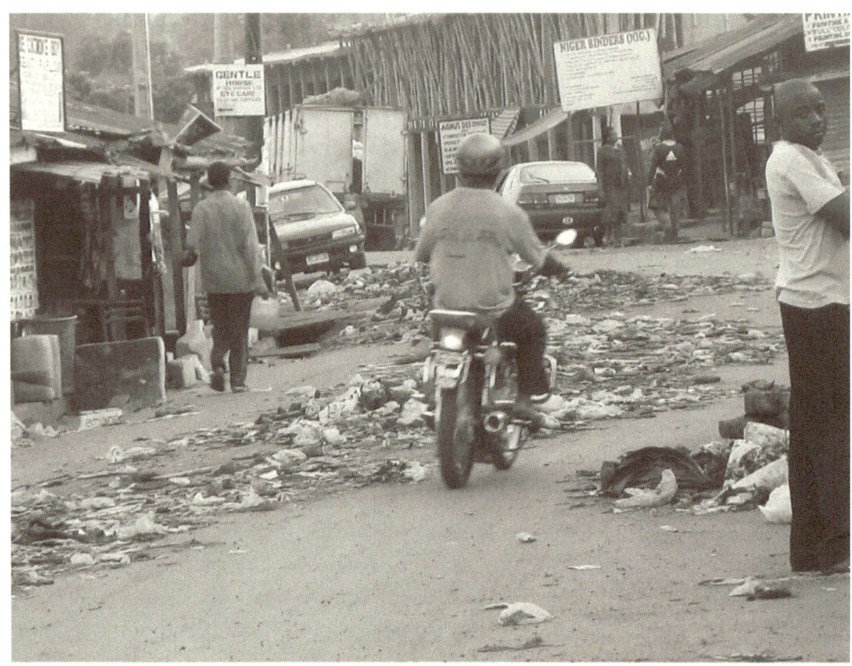

Amuche Ngwu-Nnabueze *The Sculpted Basket Project* 2007–ongoing

SEEDING THE CITY (2009–2011) EVE MOSHER

From 2009 to 2011, artist Eve Mosher's *Seeding the City* project sought to introduce green roof remediation, a process by which pollutants and rainwater run-off are mitigated by plants on roofs of urban buildings, throughout New York City, where she lives and works. Mosher distributed fifty 2' × 1' × 4' plastic trays filled with growing medium—a mix of soil, sand, gravel, and hydroponic grow rocks—and sedum, a hardy, low-maintenance succulent. Participants also received a flag, to mark their inclusion in the *Seeding the City* community, and an invitation to upload geotagged photographs to a *Seeding the City* Flickr group. To help promote the project, Mosher constructed a website, seedingthecity.org. The planters were distributed through workshops with schools and art organizations throughout New York City and in Washington, DC. *Seeding the City* also participated in the 2011 "Festival of Ideas for a New City StreetFest," constructing and distributing an additional fifty modules.[62]

62. Email from Eve Mosher to editors.

The project sought to highlight New York City's density as an opportunity for wide-scale green roof remediation. The *Seeding the City* website's network map shows the green roof locations throughout New York. However, with around seventy modules distributed over the duration of the project, there are now many more locations, in New York City and in Washington, DC. The *Seeding the City* website remains online, with detailed instructions on how to build, plant, and manage Mosher's Green Roof Modules. Additionally, the artist is currently working with a number of institutional partners to incorporate the construction of modules into such ongoing endeavors such as school curriculum and community projects.[63]

SOME PEOPLE FROM AROUND HERE (1997) HARRELL FLETCHER AND JON RUBIN

Developed as a side project during their tenure as artists-in-residence for the city of Fairfield, California, *Some People from Around Here* soon became the most visible work that Harrell Fletcher and Jon Rubin made for the city. Based completely around their accumulated encounters with a variety of the residents of the city, Fletcher and Rubin constructed and painted a series of six large (eight-foot square) portraits of Fairfield residents. These portraits were installed on the side of the I-80 highway, near the Fairfield exit. Put simply by Rubin: "After several months spent in the town as artists-in-residence, we developed this project to highlight some of the folks we had met during our stay. In some ways it was an attempt to look at how towns are experienced through the seemingly random people you meet there."[64] Over the course of the three months that the project was installed, the portraits were seen by an estimated five million passing motorists. Ultimately, *Some People from Around Here* served both to present a unique spectacle amidst the generic billboards and ubiquitous architecture of freeway exits and to foreground the very thing that makes any given place different.

63. One such partner is Covenant House (http://covenanthouseny.org), a New York–based adolescent care agency serving homeless youth. Seeding the City worked with Covenant House in 2012. http://www.seedingthecity.org/an-exciting-new-development-or-growth-really

64. Jon Rubin, excerpt from a letter/statement sent to Ted Purves, May 2002.

SOME PEOPLE FROM AROUND HERE (1997) HARRELL FLETCHER AND JON RUBIN

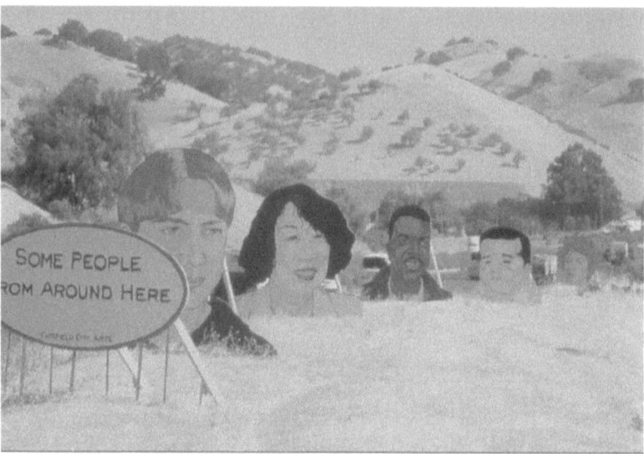

Harrell Fletcher and Jon Rubin *Some People from Around Here* 1997

SOUND MASKING FOR ROAD AND EXPRESSWAY: FM 89.5 (1999) BRENNAN MCGAFFEY

In this project, Chicago-based artist Brennan McGaffey utilized the science of sound masking (literally the use of one noise to prevent the audibility of another) to create a radio station that sought to remove noise from its listeners' lives. Working with a professional sound masking firm that makes audio tracks for industrial and office locations, McGaffey recorded common sounds on freeways and streets throughout Chicago and created soundtracks of modulated tones that "cancelled" out the dominant automobile noises. The continuous program was designed to cancel out an entire day's worth of urban automobile noise and contained provisions for rainy days. As McGaffey stated in a press release:

> Considering that automobiles dominate a city's acoustical environment, custom sound masking tracks have been created to match and blanket these tonal and noise levels. These tracks are being broadcast 24 hours a day over FM 89.5 for the month of June. There are six different masking tracks, each one responding to common conditions encountered during the time of transmission. For example, early morning (2am–6am) is less dense and quieter than rush hour (6am–9am, 3pm–6pm). An interval signal will be broadcast at the beginning of every hour. In addition to this broadcast schedule, a special masking track for weather will be transmitted during rainstorms.[65]

65. Gallery Statement/Press Release, Brennan McGaffey, TBA Exhibition Space, Chicago, 1999.

The radio station itself was an automated unit that was installed in the gallery space for the duration of the exhibition. It did not broadcast any sound into the space itself, and apart from the occasional sight of a gallery worker changing the programming during a rainstorm, there was little to "see" in the exhibition. This presentational minimalism was fully intended, as the actual work was designed to be encountered by people outside of the gallery who were driving through the city. This audience was intended to simply "find" the station while driving, whereupon the sound sculpture would manifest within their car, experienced as a (possibly) profound reduction of urban white noise.

THE SQUARE CIRCLE (2005) AMY PLANT

The Square Circle is a website and a potential collaborative project initiated by Amy Plant and developed by Plant and a group of local community leaders in Farnborough, Hampshire, UK, between 2003 and 2007. The Square Circle arose out of a commission from the UK Public Art Commission for a public square that was to be at the center of a private business park slated for construction on a piece of land formerly used as a military aviation test site. Plant, wishing to create something beyond "a set of sculptures," invited a group of community leaders to collaborate with her on a participatory project that aimed to restore the square to its pre-military use: a commons, available for recreational use by anyone in the Farnborough community.[66] This collaborative group was the Circle, who would facilitate the Square, the commons. This Square Circle proposed a plan to the business park developers wherein the funds from the commission would be used to support the infrastructure of the Circle and maintain the newly-restored commons. The only physical marker of the Square Circle would be a stone inscribed with the name, mission statement, and contact information for the Circle.

The Square Circle, however, manifested only as a series of extensive negotiations with developers and a prototype website, thesquarecircle.net, which remains online. The negotiations, while ultimately fruitless, provided impetus for the community leaders, the developers, and Plant to jointly research and discuss topics that might not have otherwise come up, such as land use, land art, and corporate responsibility. The website projects a potential existence for the Square Circle wherein it functions as a sort of outdoor community center, with workshops, presentations, performances, and so on. At the time of writing, the business park is again for sale, jeopardizing the project's continued existence as "as a possible project for community members to take on."[67]

---

66. Amy Plant, e-mail message to editors, October 20, 2012.
67. Ibid.

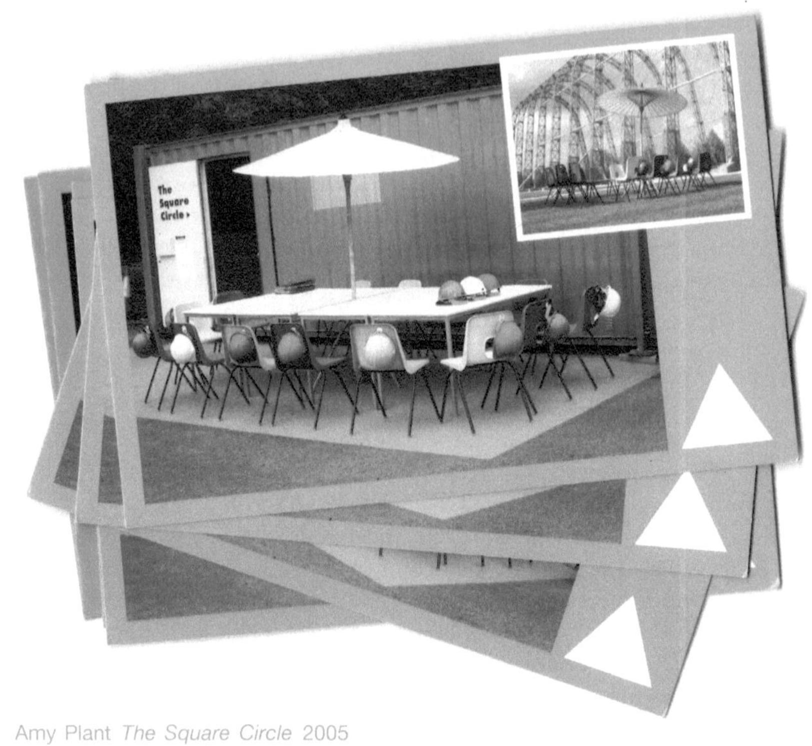

Amy Plant *The Square Circle* 2005

STUDENT IDENTIFICATION CARDS (1999–PRESENT) MEJOR VIDA CORPORATION

With the help of a sympathetic official in a Mexico City University, the Mejor Vida Corporation, directed by the Mexican artist Minerva Cuevas, has made available, free of charge, student identification cards for anyone who applies for one. The applicant sends in a photograph and some personal information and receives a valid student identification card for his or her own use. This process is facilitated through the artist's website, and has been made available through a series of exhibitions. The idea of the project is to make available to anyone the widespread discounts on cultural events, food, and other sundry items that are given to students around the world.

By taking advantage of systems already set in place, Mejor Vida Corporation crafts a symbiotic set of relations based around opening up a closed system of privilege to a larger population, while passing on the actual costs to merchants and cultural institutions who must honor its bearer with reductions and savings. The eventual outcome of this project, a world where many costs would be reduced by 10 to 15 percent for the entire population, contains elements of utopian thought, social democracy, and economic critique.

In a project commissioned for the River Hull Commission in Yorkshire, Simon Grennan and Christopher Sperandio, working in collaboration with the *Hull Daily Mail* (a local newspaper), invited readers of the paper to submit personal stories about the River Hull. The artists chose ten stories to make into comic strips and worked with the individual storytellers to develop a cartoon likeness that was both recognizable and stylistically rendered. Looking much like the "normal" fare of serial comics, while actually revealing a highly local and unique set of stories and revelations, each of these comic strips ran in the Hull Daily Mail over the course of six months.

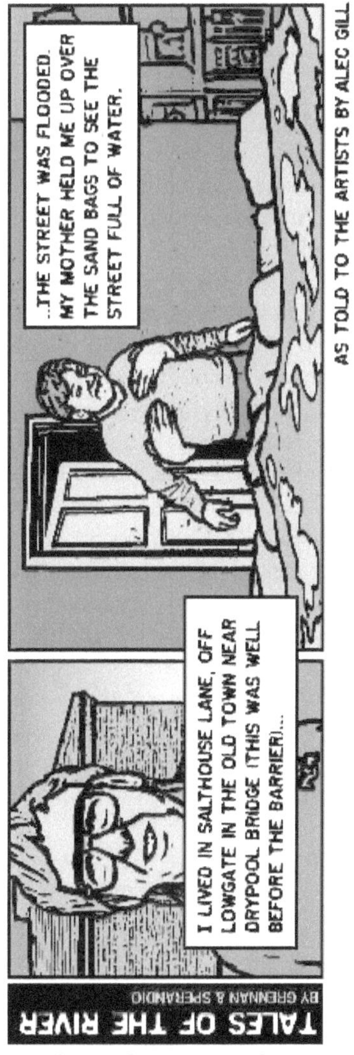

Tales of the River (2001–2002) Simon Grennan and Christopher Sperandio

The artists have consistently implemented this working method of illustrating people's lives and stories around social themes. *Tales of the River*, like many of Grennan and Sperandio's projects, sought to make a coauthored artwork through a direct collaboration with people and their stories. By allowing the residents of Hull to act as their own "art directors" while they talked about their relationship to the river, the artists opened up the authorship of the project and thus the public art campaign itself to the very people who were meant to "receive" it.

T A X I (2007) JAIME GILI

For the 6th annual Mercosur Biennial, in Mercosur, Brazil, Venezuelan-born, London-based artist Jaime Gili created *T A X I*, a three-part project derived from a residency, sponsored by the biennial, in the Mercosur Triple Frontier Zone, which lies at the intersection of Brazil, Paraguay, and Argentina. Gili focused on the Ponte de Amizade, which connects the Brazilian town of Foz do Iguaçu with the Ciudad del Este in Paraguay.

For the project, the artist first designed a custom font, called "Fuente Triple," based on writing styles he encountered on hand-painted signs around the tri-border region. Gili then designed and distributed posters advertising the font. Next, Gili designed a set of stickers, sized to fit on the helmets and motorcycles of motorcycle taxis, the dominant mode of transport in the area. The stickers, utilizing the font alongside designs typical of Gili's work, were distributed to the motorcycle taxi drivers, who then showed Gili how they had placed the stickers. Gili then purchased and distributed new helmets with the designs and font on them. Finally, Gili hired a sign painter in Paraguay, who painted giant metal sign versions of the stickers' designs, with the intent of eventually using the signs to advertise a particular motorcycle taxi company.

The stickers and redesigned helmets were distributed to motorcycle taxi drivers at no cost; the font was also available as a free download, and remains so on Gili's website.[68] For his exhibit in the Biennial hall, Gili displayed examples of helmets, the metal signs of stickers painted by the sign painter in Paraguay, photographs of motorcycle taxi drivers using or posing with their adorned helmets, and posters advertising the Triple Fuente font.

68. "6o Bienal do Mercosur," jaimegili.org, http://www.jaimegili.org/mercosur.htm

Conceived as a "social sculpture" by artists Susanne Cockrell and Ted Purves, who at the time were residents of the neighborhood, Temescal Amity Works utilized two resources that exist in abundance in Oakland: empty storefronts and yard fruit, primarily citrus.[69] The project, which was funded by several artists' grants, consisted of two main programmatic components, "The Big Back Yard" and "Reading Room." The Big Back Yard was based around a steel pushcart, which the artists' designed and built as a highly visible (and somewhat unwieldy) vehicle to harvest unwanted or underutilized fruit from trees growing in local yards. Meanwhile, the Reading Room, located in a storefront just off the neighborhood's main thoroughfare, served as a public space to redistribute the fruit that they harvested. It also housed a small resource library and hosted public events, including film screenings and projects initiated by other interested individuals or collectives. *Temescal Amity Works* also produced, by way of documenting itself and the neighborhood, a series of postcards, broadsides, and a neighborhood map, which were also distributed free of charge.

Temescal Amity Works was modeled after agrarian and urban collaborative actions, and consciously intended to extend a punk, DIY ethos into a more communitarian sphere. Through providing space and frameworks through which the neighborhood might locate itself in relation to its resources, the artists hoped to generate an active spirit of mutuality, rather than provide a service that could set up more hierarchical relations of cliency. However, after three years and 750 open hours, the artists closed the storefront. The project, they write on their website, had been intended to function as an ongoing social sculpture, one which might inspire citizen networks of sharing throughout the neighborhood. However, it was increasingly under pressure to transform into a formalized nonprofit, which would function as a service organization.[70]

69. "Ted Purves, Susanne Cockrell: Temescal Amity Works," http://creative capital.org/projects/view/112

70. "Temescal Amity Works," fieldfaring, http://fieldfaring.wordpress.com/temescal-amity-works/

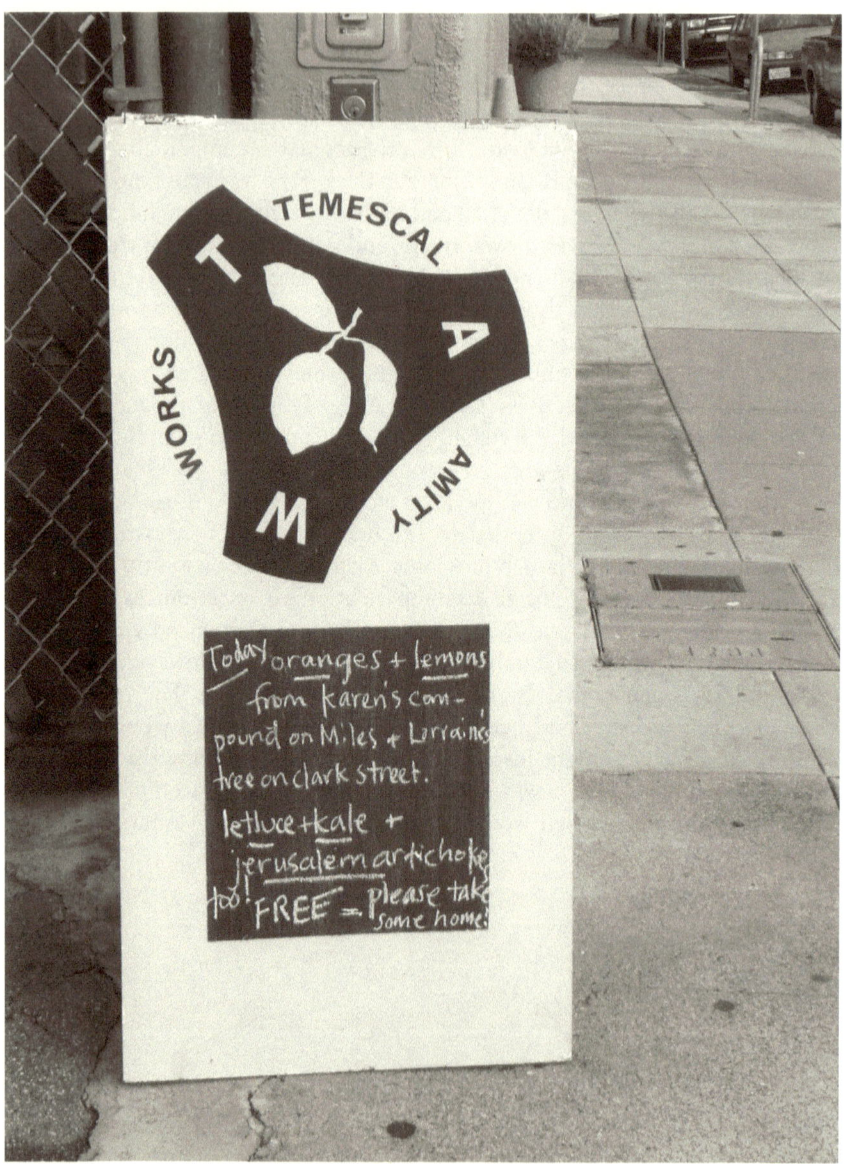

Susanne Cockrell and Ted Purves *Temescal Amity Works* 2004–2007

This is the Public Domain is an ongoing project by San Francisco Bay Area artist Amy Balkin involving the legal transformation of a small plot of land in California by shifting its current status as an individually owned piece of real estate into a piece of land that legally has no owner whatsoever (i.e., a legal commons). The project has consisted thus far in the purchase of a 2.64-acre parcel of land in Tehachapi, California, paying property taxes on this land, researching legal mechanisms to make a permanent handover to the global public possible, and the creation of a website, thisisthepublicdomain.org. The website includes a brief description of the project, a list of possible legal strategies of the project, directions on how to arrive at the current location of *This is the Public Domain*, a suggested reading list, and contact information. Physical documentation of the project has been shown in traditional art spaces where land disputes are ongoing: in Derry/Londonderry in Northern Ireland and in Vitoria-Gasteiz in the autonomous Basque Country.

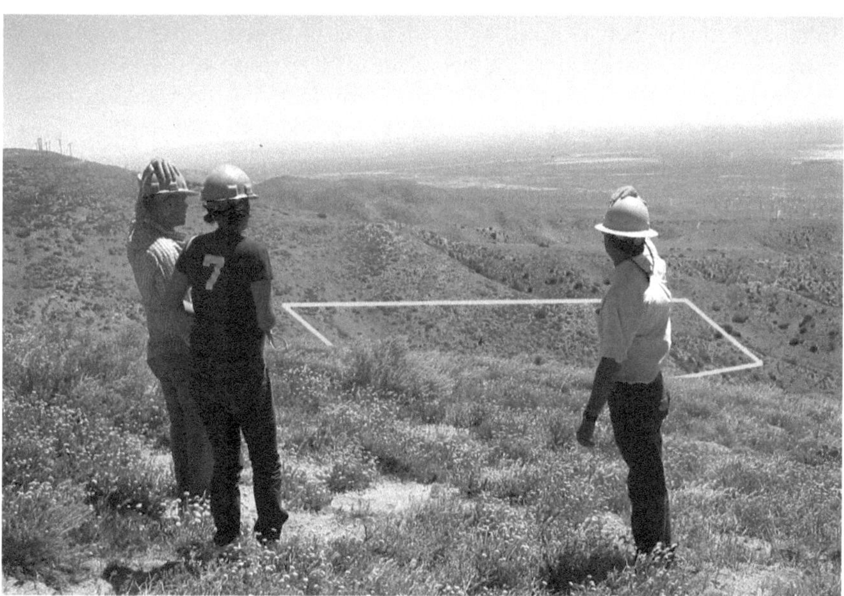

Amy Balkin *This is the Public Domain* 2003–ongoing

The project's current location has recently come under pressure from both the state of California and the Terra-Gen Alta Wind Energy Center, a wind farm. The former could invoke eminent domain, from which *This is the Public Domain* is not yet protected, to acquire the land for the California High Speed Rail project, which, according to its current plan, would exit a tunnel nearby. The latter, already one of the largest wind farms in the world,[71] seeks to purchase wind rights to the current location of *This is the Public Domain* as part of a $650 million expansion plan backed by Google, Citibank, and others. These demands on the land may lead to drastic changes in the nature of the project. Regardless of its location, however, *This is the Public Domain* will continue to engage, by its very nature, with a complex set of economic, legal, and social frameworks around land use, the commons, and notions of the public.

THIS PROGRESS (2010) TINO SEGHAL

For his solo show at the Guggenheim in New York City, Berlin-based artist Tino Sehgal developed *This Progress.* Taking advantage of the museum's iconic spiraling rotunda, Sehgal asked a diverse group of "interpreters"[72] to engage in conversations with museumgoers about ideas of progress as they walked from the entrance of the museum down to the sixth floor. Visitors would be greeted by a child at the beginning of the ramp, who would inform them that "This is a work by Tino Sehgal" and ask "What is progress?" The visitor, guided by the child, would continue up the ramp. As they ascended towards the top floor, visitors would be met by a teenage interpreter, an adult interpreter, and finally an older adult interpreter. Each interpreter would continue to ask questions related to the idea of progress. At the top floor, the piece would end and the visitor would be left alone.

For *This Progress*, Sehgal recruited nearly three hundred interpreters. Adult interpreters were paid $18.75/hr, while teenage interpreters received $7.25/hr; child interpreters were unpaid, but received complimentary museum membership, a Guggenheim bag, and a Guggenheim hat.[73] The piece received extensive written documentation in the form of blog posts, reviews, and even Craigslist missed connections. These reactions tended to focus on Sehgal's anti-photography policy, interest in or curiosity about Sehgal's troupe of interpreters,

71. "Allco Finance Group (AFG) Announces the Sale of the Tehachapi, US Wind Development Project," Terra-Gen Power, LLC, accessed December 27, 2012, http://www.terra-genpower.com/News/Allco-Finance-Group-(AFG)-Announces-the-Sale-of-th.aspx

72. "In the Naked Museum: Thinking, Talking, Encountering," Holland Cotter, http://www.nytimes.com/2010/02/01/arts/design/01tino.html

73. At the Guggenheim, the Art Walked Beside You, Asking Questions," Alicia Desantis, http://www.nytimes.com/2010/03/13/arts/design/13progress.html

and the shock of encountering the bare walls of the museum, rather than on the content or quality of the questions and conversations that constituted the piece or on further notions of progress. Indeed, it would appear that for many of the over 100,000 paying visitors to the museum during the run of *This Progress*, Sehgal's work was the first experience of an artwork that consisted not of something looked at, but rather of something participated in.

TIME DIVISA (2006–2010) JOSE ANTONIO VEGA MACOTELA

From 2006–2010, Mexico City-based artist Jose Antonio Vega Macotela conducted *Time Divisa*, 365 time-based exchanges with male inmates at the Santa Marta Acatitlan penitentiary in Mexico City. In meetings with inmates, Vega would ask if they wished him to perform an action outside of the penitentiary; the artist would agree if the inmate performed, in exchange, a task that Vega wished him to perform. The resulting efforts by the inmates, *Intercambio/Time Exchange 1–365*, are displayed together, with the inmates listed as coauthors. Documents of actions performed by Vega at the behest of inmates, if they exist, remain in the penitentiary. Vega does relate narrative accounts of these actions, however, and it may be assumed that inmates relate narrative accounts of actions they performed for Vega. Steve Turner Contemporary, the gallery that represents Vega, notes that *Time Divisa* is not for sale, as Vega is not the sole author.[74]

Time Divisa, because of the nature of the project, had a number of real-world effects. The piece consisted of, and aspired to be, a series of exchanges. Each exchange would result in an action, which would have a more or less palpable effect. The actions that inmates asked Vega to perform included spying on ex-lovers, filming children's first steps, getting drunk at baptisms, and so on. Inmates, in exchange, made board games out of lovers' hair, shredded contemporary art books and made them into bags, or carved phrases across bricks and installed heating elements in the grooves. *Time Divisa* has been shown in a number of institutions, including the 2012 Triennial at the New Museum in New York City.

74. Chin-Chin Yap, "Prison Breaks," *Art Asia Pacific*, June/July 2012, http://artasiapacific.com/Magazine/79/PrisonBreaks

In 1996, herman de vries created a public commission in the neighborhood of Tuindorp (which is literally translated as "Garden Village"), which was, at the time, a newly constructed housing development on the outskirts of Tilburg, The Netherlands. The *tuindorp collection* manifested as a public garden of culinary, medicinal, and decorative plants, laid out along the streets and in the parks of the area. These plants ranged in size from herbs to trees and were organized by street.

In addition, de vries published a small book with the commission, which detailed each plant's history and use as well as a map for locating the specific plants in the neighborhood. The book was published and distributed free to each of the area's residents. In this way, the *tuindorp collection* became an attempt to insert a "botanica" into the daily lives of a neighborhood and also, through the agency of the guidebook, to create a body of common knowledge between citizens about their surrounding garden and its potential usefulness.

UNTITLED (BEAUTY) (1994) RIRKRIT TIRAVANIJA

For his solo exhibition at the Jack Hanley Gallery, Rirkrit Tiravanija staged a project wherein gallery visitors were served Thai-style curry free of charge to anyone who wanted it, during all gallery hours, for a month.[75] The artist derived the name of the work, *Beauty*, from the brand label on the face of the stove, as the stove was, in many ways, the central feature in the gallery space. Tiravanija also installed works by various artists from the gallery's back room around the space, salon-style, which created a more "home-like" atmosphere.

While the artist cooked the food for the first few days, he then gave the recipe to the gallery workers, so that they could continue the project. Over the course of the month, local business people and workers would meet at the gallery during lunch breaks.[76] At the exhibition's close, a San Francisco collector purchased the stove, pots, and pans, still dirty from the last meal. This collection of objects served as both the documentation for the project, as well as a discrete artwork that functioned as something of an icon or relic through which the project became "preserved."

---

75. While Tiravanija created many versions of this work in a variety of galleries, the editors chose to focus on this specific example mainly for its location, as it was possible to interview the gallery owner and original participants to get more specific information about what the actual work was like as it unfolded.

76. Jack Hanley, personal conversation with Carolyn Mackin, 2002.

Working in conjunction with both the Amsterdam Fund for the Arts and the Woningbedrijf Housing Corporation, Franck Bragigand made contact with all of the residents of a single housing district in Tuinwijk (seventy-six houses in total, spanning over five different streets), asking them questions about the potential for color on the exterior of their houses. The districts' houses, an array of uniformly designed modernist row-houses, were originally planned to have simple brick exteriors with white geometric wooden panels around the window and doors. After making contact with the residents, a process that included over six hundred personal appointments,[77] Bragigand devised a palette of seventy-two different colors, which was circulated though a questionnaire sent to all of the residents. Following up on the residents' responses, and meeting each one in turn, the artists proceeded to paint all of their houses over a period of a year.

In the artists' words, "I asked to live in the area, learned Dutch, to be close to the reality that I had to deal with. I painted (it) all myself so that every new idea or color could change at any time."[78] What resulted was a neighborhood where each row-house had a distinctly colored exterior, while the streets of the district took on the overall character of Bragigands palette. After the residents reported high satisfaction with the project, the artist was able to convince the city to change the colors of the streetlights (using a range of seven different colors) in the district so that the houses' palette would have a contrasting element within the street.

VALLEY VIBES (1998–2002) JEANNE VAN HEESWIJK WITH AMY PLANT

Valley Vibes was a public project made for the Leigh Valley district of London, created by Jeanne Van Heeswijk, in collaboration with (then) curator Amy Plant and London's CHORA Institute for Architecture and Urbanism. *Valley Vibes* was constructed around a device called the Vibe Detector, which "was not devised as a work of art but as an instrument, designed to investigate different kind of lives connected to the area. It was a cross between a big ghetto-blaster and an ice cream trolley, of simple design, made of gleaming aluminium, small enough to fit in a domestic doorway, tall enough to stand or sit behind."[79]

---

77. Nov Amenomori, "Long Interview vol. 03: Franck Bragigand," http://www.log-osaka.jp/movement/vol.32/amenomori/ame_eng.html, No Date.

78. Franck Bragigand, Bragigand 2002–2004, PDF text, download from http://franckbragigand.weebly.com/

79. Jeanne Van Heeswijk, website, http://www.jeanneworks.net/#/projects/valley_vibes._the_vibe-detector/

Inside the mobile unit was a full sound system with a PA, mixing consoles, media ports, and recording equipment. Residents of the neighborhood were able to use the Vibe Detector free of charge for any function they wished that might need a professional sound system, such as weddings, dances, poetry readings, political meetings, and so forth. This service was advertised through a series of handbills (and later simply through reputation and word of mouth). The Vibe Detector was rotated through a sequence of community centers and halls to widen its accessibility. The *Valley Vibes* project was funded for a three-year period and concluded its service to the neighborhood in 2002.

Though the use of the detector was free, there was one stipulation or condition of use: any sound that went through its system was automatically recorded. This resulted in a cross-sectional archive of the neighborhood's sonic culture, which could be used to map the shifting social spaces of the area. To use the Vibe Detector, one had to consent to being included in the collective history that it was constructing. This consent and archive formed the "edge" of the project, creating a mirror between the service performed by the Vibe Detector (and thus the artist) for the user and the service provided by the user to the larger idea of creating a community document: to have access to a louder "voice" required one to take on the responsibility of that voice becoming a part of a shared history.

WORK ON PROGRESS (1998) JEREMY DELLER

As a response to a public commission for local arts initiatives and a group exhibition, Jeremy Deller set up a digital recording studio in The De La Warr Pavilion in Bexhill-on-the-Sea, at which local seniors could record their own music. The De La Warr Pavilion is a utopian structure built as a grand community center with free access to local residents. Deller turned the education room into a place to introduce new utopian technology to an older generation. Using a sampler and sequencer, the retirees enjoyed themselves, activated the center, and interacted with tools normally utilized by younger artists.

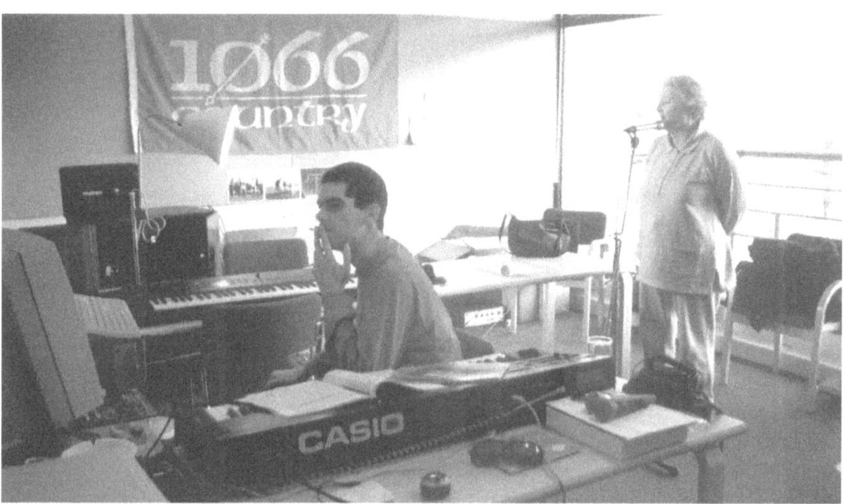

Jeremy Deller *Work on Progress* 1998

Part Two
STRUCTURES AND INSTITUTIONS

INTRODUCTORY REMARKS

Shane Aslan Selzer

In 2007 a group of art-administration students at The School of The Art Institute in Chicago (SAIC) decided to form an arts research initiative that outwardly functions like an arts organization while expressly challenging the infrastructure associated with the dominant institutional models populating the global art world: the commercial gallery and the nonprofit space/museum. Although they were eager to participate in programming and producing art projects, they wanted to push against the limits of current models for arts organizations. The result was an called the Institute for Community Understanding Between Art and the Everyday (InCUBATE), which continues to this day to set the parameters for traveling exhibitions, a residency program,[1] and a micro-grant program called Sunday Soup. While InCUBATE began in a storefront, it has carried on as a roving structure, putting little emphasis on infrastructure, in favor of a site-responsive adaptability.

InCUBATE's programming is entirely funded by strategies that could be deemed "post-capitalist." These include member-ownership, service-subscriptions, shareholding, and bartering within a local network. They expressly do not compete for grants, nor do they desire nonprofit status; rather, they are interested in exploring a space for arts institutions beyond the simple distinction of for-profit galleries vs. not-for-profit. By setting these parameters, InCUBATE is utilizing the umbrella of arts administration as a project model for how any *arts worker* (a term that might eventually demand to sit parallel to *artist*) can construct critical structures for production. At the same time, they are putting forward their institutional structure as an example of creative structure-building.

This move towards alternative structures for institutions can be seen as a reaction to a succession of governmental shifts, which can be traced from the election of President George H. W. Bush in 1989 to the global financial crisis in 2007, which left artists facing major changes to domestic and international funding strategies. These shifts are sometimes drastic, like the closing of so many long-running nonprofit organizations that supported socially engaged, difficult projects such as Exit Art in New York City[2] and New Langton Arts in San Francisco,[3] each of which had produced nearly thirty years of alternative programming.

That said, if one only see these shifts as adaptations to a funding crisis, there is a risk of missing a second, more emergent idea that institutions such as InCUBATE demonstrate. Alongside a willingness to embrace new models for funding, administration, and constituency, they have a DIY attitude toward social engagement that has the ability to react in real time to the needs and concerns of very specific localities.

The real-time relevancy of long-term programming is a major factor in the changes witnessed during the nineties and the early part of the new millennium. The notion of nonprofits working on 2–3 year grant cycles became a less functional model for producing socially engaged projects that confronted everyday realities. Nonprofits, once associated with risk-taking, found themselves struggling to fund artists that didn't have established track records, or projects that didn't have predetermined outcomes.

We have seen a number of artist-led initiatives confront the old models for what an art space can mean in real time. These activities are similar in spirit to the artist projects we explore in the project handbook, in that they hold critical exchange at the core of their output and productivity. Many in fact, begin as artist projects without a long term plan for development or sustainability. But these initiatives have achieved a longevity (through stakeholders) or scope (through programming) that asks the work to evolve beyond the boundaries of a singular artwork. Some fill a temporary need, produce a frenzied amount of programming and then disappear. Often these structures aren't ever looking for longevity or stability, they are responding to a circumstance that requires a short burst of intense energy and administration in order to be most effective. This temporality can also be attributed to the lack of long term funding, which would normally create stable administrative positions to oversee operations. Instead, these structures survive only if their organizational strategy isn't dependent on single individuals or events, but rather a system that cycles people into it, bringing renewed energy and effort.

In cases like Sunday Soup, a program initiated by InCUBATE, a replicable model is put into motion and adapted by local communities that choose to engage and adapt the structure. Sunday Soup provides an artist project grant by inviting people to pay for and join in a community meal where they will consider pre-solicited project proposals. Diners are invited to vote on which proposal to fund, using the direct profits from the meal itself as the grant funds to be distributed. Since its start in Chicago, Sunday Soup has been adapted by over sixty cities around the world.

If we break down Sunday Soup into its major components, we have a group meal (an exchange ritual rooted in a social/traditional economic system), a crowdsource-funded grant (direct democracy at work), and a community action (a new definition of community through the collective act of funding an art project together). These components are both indebted to and independent from their historical precedents. The physical location of the dinner is roving, and yet the concept is highly dependent on new articulations of locality and local issues.

In this case, the insistence on local (and locality) is an excellent way to understand the gravity of the shift this represents. The meal is prepared by a respected, local chef, while the traditional gatekeepers in the arts (grant jurors) are replaced by the diners at the meal. The consumers become the producers as well. Contrast this to what might be considered a typical scenario from a more traditional arts institution. A panel of jurors is selected from a list of regionally or nationally recognized arts professionals. They are flown to the location for a weekend of jurying, at the conclusion of which they redistribute funds that the hosting institution has collected from private foundations, individual donors, or various levels of government.

The emergence of new institutional structures that are constructed with notions of critical exchange highlights a larger paradigm that we inhabit. It engages the world at an extremely local level while simultaneously tapping into a wide-reaching global network. This is the major shift in how we navigate exchange today. Over the past five years, while the presence of social media has become integrated with how we receive news, communicate with friends, track celebrities, extend our communities, and share information, the market forces behind these new resources have also been working to capitalize on our new accessibility to personal information. Social media thrives by siphoning personal information, particularly in the form of the preferences of its users. It has become the ultimate polling zone, a place where data can be collected, analyzed, and ultimately targeted back towards the user who serves as both producer and consumer. The artist-led institutions we are exploring in this handbook are grappling with these same tensions. They are questioning how we fund what we want to fund and for whom we fund it. They are rethinking our relationship to locality, network, and individualism. This critical engagement works in response to the development of web-based social media platforms such as YouTube, Facebook, Instagram, Tumblr, and crowdsource funding sites like Kickstarter and USA Projects, all of which produce continuous content, alerting us to updates by the second.

Through self-reflectivity and criticality, contemporary artists engaged in critical exchanges have largely renegotiated the terms of their participation. The perceived failures of many nonprofits are not just economic, they are the failure to adapt and change quickly enough to accommodate fleeting communities of people and ideas. In this section, on Artists' Structures and Organizations, we find Tradeschool.coop using barter networks to fuel its learning service organization. Through database logs, we witness Feral Trade relying on informal couriers to move food-based products between nation states. We generate new values for discarded drawings when The Play Generated Map and

Document Archive (PlaGMaDA) collects ephemera created as a bi-product of game playing. And we question the objectness of damaged works that have been deemed "a total loss" as valued artworks by insurance claims, when collected by Salvage Art Institute.

When artists leave the protective cloak of academia today, they often carry with them newly acquired MFAs in Social Practice and $50,000 to $100,000 in student loan debt.[4] Steeped in the language of institutional critique and relational aesthetics, these practitioners aren't content to tear at the old models, they want to build new ones with their own friends, working at a scale that encourages more vulnerability and more temporality than larger institutions. These parallel institutions don't replace nonprofit art spaces or museums, but they stand alongside them, borrowing their language and forms, while casting a critical eye at themselves all the while; the view of the consumer turned producer, turned consumer again.

Notes

1. At the time of writing, the residency program was not active.

2. Exit Art was cofounded in New York City in 1982 by Papo Colo and Jeanette Ingberman and is one of New York's oldest nonprofit galleries.

3. Founded in 1975, New Langton Arts was one of the first alternative art spaces in the United States.

4. Portland State University, California College of the Arts, Otis College of Art and Design, Queens College CUNY, and the Maryland Institute College of Art all offer degrees in social practice at the time of publication.

The Chiapas Photography Project, based in San Cristóbal de Las Casas, Chiapas State, Mexico, seeks to provide the local indigenous Mayan community the tools with which to represent and express themselves through photography. The CPP was founded in 1992 by Carlota Duarte, a Mexican-American artist and nun, upon her graduation from the Rhode Island School of Design. The CPP has been supported by the Ford Foundation since 1995.

The CPP provides classes, workshops, and individual instruction for members of the local community, ranging from basic instruction on how to operate a camera to more specialized sessions focused on realizing a personal voice and other creative concerns. For its advanced students, the CPP recommends and helps facilitate opportunities outsides Chiapas, travel grants, residencies, and exhibitions. The CPP has published eight books of photography from its members and is at work on a photography primer in two Mayan languages, Tseltal and Tsotsil.

In addition to assisting the local community with creative development, the Chiapas Photography Project also maintains the Archivo Fotográfico Indígena, an archive of images created by CPP participants, housed at the Center for Research and Higher Studies in Social Anthropology Southeast in San Cristóbal. The AFI is staffed by volunteer interns, and provides a darkroom for its volunteers, as well as for CPP participants.

> AFI serves as a meeting place for over two hundred affiliated photographers from ten ethnic groups, a place where they can pick up film, discuss work, or review the ever-expanding photography collection. Six staff photographers and a director teach basic camera skills, maintain the archive, and work on developing new projects, shows, and publications. The project has three main areas of focus: *education*, which involves teaching basic camera skills and improving literacy; *collection*, which involves archival maintenance of approximately seventy-five thousand images; and *outreach*, which pursues exhibitions and publications and disseminates knowledge about the project.[1]

1. Jessica Ingram, quoted in Ted Purves (ed.), *What We Want Is Free: Generosity and Exchange in Recent Art* (Albany: State University of New York Press, 2005), 111–12.

Dorchester Projects was founded by Theaster Gates and is based on the format of a house museum, comprised of three newly renovated buildings on South Dorchester Avenue in Chicago, each serving specific community functions. The Black Cinema House is a film screening site dedicated to showing videos and films about and by people of color, as well as running youth workshops on film production and video editing. The Archive House is the new home to local archives from sources that are relocating their holdings or selling off the collection. At the time of writing, this included an Architecture and Design Library from Prairie Avenue Bookstore, the Listening Room, which houses over eight thousand LPs from Dr. Wax Records (a closed record store in Hyde Park), and a glass lantern slide collection donated from the University of Chicago. This two-story vacant house was redesigned to be a community hub, with the intention of drawing local interest towards the revitalization of cultural legacies and creative commons. Archives are donated from local sources such as neighborhood businesses that have closed down. Another building will become the Johnson Library Staging House, home to a special collection of *Ebony* and *Jet* magazines, and other periodicals, journals and books focusing on the Black experience in America (donated by the Johnson Publishing Company).[2]

Dorchester Projects led Theaster Gates to establish Rebuild Foundation, a nonprofit, design-build firm that specializes in affordable creative space development within low income areas. Rebuild is currently managing projects in Chicago, Detroit, St. Louis, and Omaha, including Bemis Art Center in Omaha and all of the Dorchester Projects' buildings in Chicago. Each project uses local artists, architects, and educators to form a team that is specific to the locale, with the idea that creative cultural hubs will transform neighborhoods.[3]

Example of programming posted on the Dorchester Projects Tumblr site:[4]

> Posted on April 29, 2011
>
> Last night, April 28th, we all gathered at Dorchester Projects to celebrate programming and the Dorchester residency program. Erika Dudley, our old friend and phenomenal chef, made us one of her increasingly famous Japanese Soul Food spreads.
>
> Thanks so much to Erika, David, Ayana, Nancy and Avery for all coming and sharing their warmth, ideas, and laughter with us all last night!

2. Gathered from website http://theastergates.com/section/117693_Dorchester_Projects.html
3. http://rebuild-foundation.org/the-art-of-placemaking/projects/dorchester-projects/
4. http://dorchesterprojects.tumblr.com

The menu:

Satsumaino No Aka Dashi, Dark Miso with Sweet Potatoes

White Miso with Potlikker and Soul Food Style Tempura (fried skins and bbq sauce)

Su Meshi, Black-Eyed Pea Rice Balls with Louisiana Hot Sauce

Su Meshi, Rib Tip Rice Flowers with "Sauce"

Neckbones in Gravy

Black Rice Pudding

Mississippi Mud Bricks with White Cream

Accompanied by: Kuro Goma, Matcha Salt, Katsuo Fumi Furikake

Global Crit Clinic (GCC) was born as a ten-day pilot program at Centre for Contemporary Art (CCA), Lagos, in the summer of 2011. Founded by Kianga Ford and Shane Aslan Selzer, GCC provides intensive professional practice workshops grounded in the fine arts model of studio critique for artists located in regions where there is limited access to rigorous idea-based discussions about art practice.[5]

The workshops are structured around a curriculum of group critique, professional development, peer networking, and one-one-one mentorship. GCC is a mobile platform, which shifts and adapts to the needs of its local participants. GCC operates through a local host organization, which provides basic infrastructure (a room with seating, a generator, and a digital projector) and cultivates the participants for their clinic. A peer network is fueled as past participants invite GCC to their home towns and become facilitators in future clinics.

To date, GCC has held two clinics in Lagos, Nigeria, at CCA, Lagos, and one in Accra, Ghana, at the Foundation for Contemporary Art. New clinics are being planned for Ghana, India, Vietnam, Cambodia, the Dominican Republic, Senegal, Mozambique, Kenya, Zimbabwe, and South Africa.

As an example, see the call for participants from Centre for Contemporary Art, Lagos, for their residency program in Accra 2013, which holds a Global Crit Clinic as a core module within its program:

> In 2010 Centre for Contemporary Art, Lagos began an innovative programme with the aims of filling a gap in the educational system in Nigeria and many African countries, which tend to ignore the critical methodologies and histories that underpin artistic practice. The programme comes out of the need to build local support structures for art production, critical thought and to provide a conducive framework that encourages and advances the individual research and production of participants.
>
> Using the format of part art laboratory, part residency and part informal art academy, over the course of 35 intensive days "The Archive: Static, Embodied, Practiced" will focus partially on technique and primarily on methodology, critical thinking, and the implementation of conceptual ideas. The programme will be of benefit to people interested in thinking through the conception and execution of work, artists and curators who are curious and interested in experimenting with modes of practice and thought outside of the traditional modes of working but not to its total exclusion.
>
> After two very successful programmes which took place in Lagos, *On Independence and The Ambivalence of Promise 2010* and

5. http://globalcritclinic.wordpress.com

History/Materiality in 2012 for the first time the initiative will move to another West African country Accra, Ghana. The international art programme will take on an itinerant characteristic that intends to see it take place in Dakar in 2014 and in Mozambique in 2015 as a way of engaging the rest of the continent.[6]

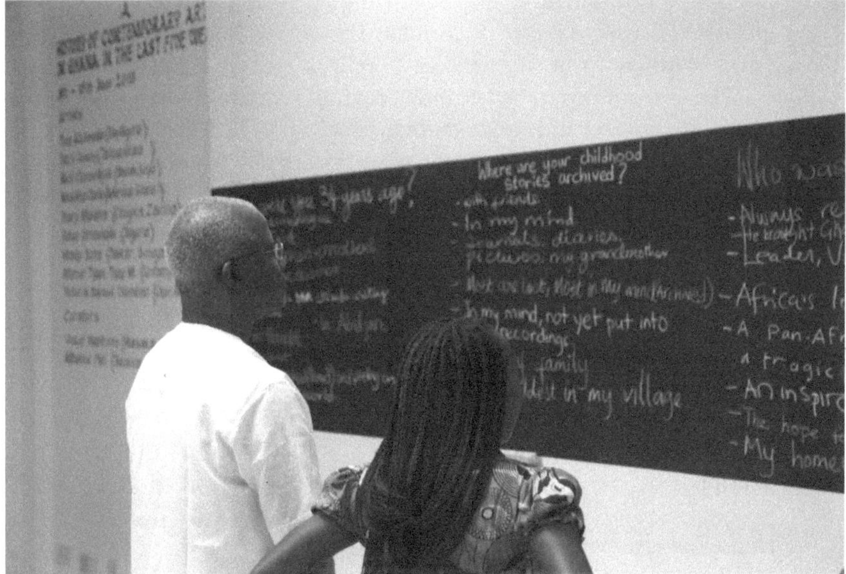

Global Crit Clinic 2011–present

6. Written by Bisi Silva on the Centre for Contemporary Art, Lagos, website, http://www.ccalagos.org/open-call-2013

InCUBATE was started in 2007 by a group of arts administration students at the School of the Art Institute in Chicago as a research group exploring and challenging current arts funding and organizational strategies. The activities of this research group have taken the form of a residency program, travelling exhibitions, and alternative project grants. The group is committed to approaching arts administration as a creative practice, which has the potential to create innovative solutions to some of the problems of hierarchy, and access to resources that are shared by artists globally.

InCUBATE is co-directed by Roman Petruniak, Abigail Satinsky, Bryce Dwyer, and Matthew Joynt. It began in storefront space adjacent to Chicago's Congress Theater, but has since become a roving structure that comes together around specific projects and programming.[7] InCUBATE deliberately does not have nonprofit status, nor does it apply to traditional granting foundations, choosing instead to generate a self-sustainable model for arts production in the public sphere:

> We started InCUBATE with a few simple ideas and questions about money. How could we better understand the lack of funding for alternative and innovative cultural work? Is it possible to develop new infrastructures to qualitatively affect artists' lives?[8]

Here is an example of an InCUBATE initiated program described on their website:

> Hello friends, Between 2007 and 2009, InCUBATE ran a meal-based micro-grant called Sunday Soup out of our shared storefront space in Logan Square. Over the past few years, an incredible worldwide network of organizers have taken the basic premise of Sunday Soup—collect grant proposals, cook a meal, invite people to pay and eat, and have the diners democratically allocate the meal's profits—and adapted it to their own local purposes. Sister projects have now taken place in over 60 cities around the world. More about the global network can be found at sundaysoup.org . . .
>
> For each event, the organizers of Sunday Soup choose five projects to put to the vote. We're interested in funding all kinds of cultural projects from community arts, to organizing from all disciplines, to grassroots efforts. We'll be choosing projects that represent a diversity of approaches, mediums, and creative communities. Projects with limited funding options elsewhere are particularly

---

7. http://incubate-chicago.org/about/

8. Quote from "InCUBATE 2nd Year Report: The Slow Build—March 2009," http://incubate-chicago.org/about/

interesting to us. Anyone from the Chicagoland area is welcome to apply. You do not have to be present at the meal to submit an application. However, the grant winner of each cycle will be invited to return at a future Sunday Soup to present their project. Your submitted proposal will be made available to each diner in the form of a printed pamphlet.[9]

9. http://incubate-chicago.org/sunday-soup-chicago-returns/2012/

The International Village Shop is an ongoing organizational project organized by Kathrin Böhm, Wapke Feenstra, and Antje Schiffers. The International Village Shop is a sister project of the artists' effort myvillages.org, a registered International Stichtig (cultural organization) in the Netherlands, a multi-scalar project that imagines "the rural as space for and of cultural production."[10] The International Village Shop works with local arts organizations, artisans, farmers, and others in order to produce goods that are inspired by the location and produced nearby. These goods then enter the International Village Shop trade network, and are available for sale, on a limited scale, at future International Village Shops. In 2007, for instance, the International Village Shop worked with local farmers and in Neuenkirchen, Germany, to produce, with the support of the local arts association, the "Potato Sleeper." The Potato Sleeper was made from felt from a nearby town and sewn by a local tailor. The product premiered at the annual Neuenkirchen Potato Festival.

The International Village Shop is documented extensively—in English, Dutch, German, and Spanish—on its website, internationalvillageshop.net. The website includes descriptions of the project, an index of shops, and an index of products available at International Village Shops. Each shop page includes a variety of information, including, but not limited to, the date(s) the shop was open, a brief narrative summary of the shop, the forms of exchange utilized at the shop, what currency (if any) was used, the host institution, the participants, and costs associated with the shop. Each product page includes a brief summary of the product's production, a map telling where it was made, and pictures from the shop(s) at which it was sold. At time of writing, International Village Shops have been opened in the United Kingdom, Switzerland, Germany, the Netherlands, and Sweden.

10. Myvillages.org, "About Us: General Info," http://myvillages.org/index.php?a=about

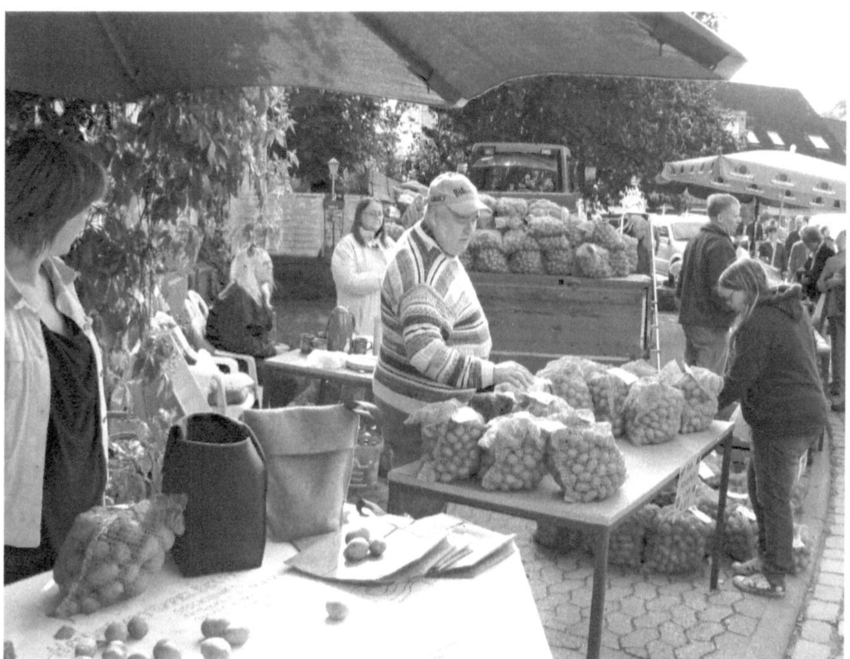

International Village Shop 2007–present

In 1996, artist and now filmmaker and writer Miranda July—with the assistance of Julia Bryan-Wilson and others—began the project *Big Miss Movieola*. Looking to create a distribution network of movies made for women, by women, July posted, mailed, and handed out flyers and pamphlets asking women to send her a movie. The pamphlet explained that if a woman was to send *Big Miss Movieola* a movie, that movie would be placed on a VHS with nine other movies by nine other women, and the final VHS—now with ten films by ten women—would be sent back to all the contributors, as well as all subscribers to the *Big Miss Movieola* chainletter. *Big Miss Movieola*'s name was changed to *Joanie4Jackie* under legal threat from the owners of the word "movieola."[11]

As its popularity grew, *Joanie4Jackie* expanded into other areas beyond just the mix-VHS tapes. *J4J* started a series of tapes called *Co-Star Compilations*, in which women could apply to curate a tape according to a theme they suggested. These tapes were distributed along the same DIY network that the *Joanie4Jackie* tapes circulated along. Once July acquired funds for a projector, she also organized public screenings, which would introduce more women to *Joanie4Jackie*, growing her network of contributors/receivers. July also would create a new movie with the audience at screenings.

The *Joanie4Jackie* project grew too large for July to manage in 2002, after releasing thirteen chainletter tapes, three *Co-Star* tapes, and numerous screenings, mailings, and more. The *J4J* archive is currently housed at the Bard College Film Department in Annandale-on-Hudson, New York.

Participants were solicited as follows:[12]

How To:

The Chainletter Tapes:

1. Send send me a high quality copy of your film or video on regular (1/2 inch SP) VHS video tape, miniDV or DVD. The tape should begin with 30 seconds of black. If your movie is longer than 20 minutes I may only be able to include an excerpt. It is best if you pick the excerpt or make a short version/trailer. Put your name/address/phone #/email address on the tape, as well as the length of your movie. Do not send your original movie; you will not get your tape back.

2. Write one letter to the nine other lady-moviemakers who you will be sharing the tape with. You can do no wrong: advice, questions, schemes, scams, confessions. The chances are very

11. "Joanie4Jackie," ZineWiki, http://www.zinewiki.com/Joanie4Jackie

12. "So you wanna be a star," Joanie4Jackie (archived), http://archive.joanie4jackie.com/chainletter/star.php

high that at least one of these ladies will know what you're talking about. You also might want to mention what you shot/edited with, how you gained access to this equipment, and how you found out about Joanie 4 Jackie. The dimensions of your letter should be within 5.5inches x 4.25 inches (1/4 a piece of standard paper). Your letter will be reproduced exactly as it is received, so make sure it's readable and that your pictures and decorations will xerox well. Don't forget to include your mailing address and or email address. Email these things to us at joanie–at–bard–dot–edu. And let me know how you found out about Joanie 4 Jackie.

3. Now sit on the curb and wait 1–6 months for your Joanie 4 Jackie Tape to arrive. The Chainletter tapes are an ongoing project, so you can send your movie at any time, or keep sending your movies as you make them.

Director, performance artist, and activist John Malpede founded the Los Angeles Poverty Department (LAPD) in the Skid Row neighborhood of downtown Los Angeles in 1985. The LAPD is dedicated to connecting "the experience of people living in poverty to the social forces that shape their lives and communities."[13] In order to do this, LAPD draws on the history of social theater, involving Skid Row residents in productions that make visible the often dire circumstances of living in poverty. The LAPD's board of directors includes Malpede, the attorney Laurence M. Lavin, the arts producer Julia Carnahan, and historian Catherine Gudis; they have a staff of six writers/directors/organizers and a team of performers, who are all residents of the Skid Row neighborhood. The LAPD is a nonprofit organization supported by a variety of city- and state-level arts organizations, in addition to individual contributions through platforms like PayPal and USA Projects.

LAPD has toured productions or hosted residencies in the United States, the Netherlands, Belgium, France, Bolivia, and the United Kingdom. Their productions are co-created with the performers; when productions tour, residents of the host community are often invited to become involved in the production. LAPD productions tend to highlight issues of concern to skid row communities in the United States and internationally: the so-called war on drugs, mass incarceration, a lack of public services, and so on. These productions are often multifaceted, spinning off into papers, curricula, and videos.

Here is a sample invitation to participate in an LAPD performance:

> BIGGEST RECOVERY COMMUNITY ANYWHERE: LAPD has started a new performance project that highlights the fact that Skid Row is one of the most significant recovery neighborhoods in the country. Performance of finished work: May 2013. Open rehearsals every Tuesday and Thursday evening from 7 till 9 pm and Saturday 2 till 5pm at UCEPP, at the corner of 6th and Stanford street.

---

13. "LAPD Mission," Los Angeles Poverty Department, http://www.lapovertydept.org/about-lapd/index.php

The Māhākād, or "Epic Arts in the Market," was a temporary arts festival organized around the centennial of the Warorot market in Chiang Mai, Thailand, by Navin Production, a collaborative effort headed by Bangkok- and Fukuoaka-based artist Navin Rawanchaikul, in 2010. The festival operated in four venues throughout the market and aimed to highlight the "epic" nature of the diverse market vendors, who hail from Northern Thailand, China, India, and elsewhere throughout the region, as well as the market's history. The Māhākād, whose title references another epic, the Indian Mahābhārata, opened on December 25, 2010, and continued through February 6, 2011.

The Māhākād featured work by a variety of artists across its four venues. Embedded within Warorot market itself was a group portrait of more than two hundred vendors significant to the history of the market, produced by Navin Production, and a group of photographs compiled by Assada Porananond. In the historic residence of Thai photographer and philanthropist Luang Anusarnsunthorn, previously unseen photographs by Anusarnsunthorn were displayed alongside historical photographs of Chiang Mai, videos by Navin Production documenting Warorot, and works by area architectural students that came out of workshops on the history and future of the market. The third location, the Chiang Mai Philatelic (postal history) Museum, featured a variety of work from Thai conceptual and performance artists and photographers; while the fourth, the Chansom Anusan Bridge, hosted a series of historic photographs of Chiang Mai that focused on environmental issues.

The spirit of the Māhākād may best be expressed in this detailed description of the Anusarnsunthorn location:

> Formerly the Mae Ping Post Office, this attractive well preserved colonial style building is celebrating its 100th anniversary jointly with Kad Luang market. The Philatelic Museum is located on the banks of the Ping River near Ton Lumyai market. The Māhākād exhibition is on display on the 2nd floor. Creating an interesting dialogue with the museum's collection of old equipment and photographs, Dow Wasiksiri's conceptual photography links the past to the present with his superb snapshots taken around the market place. Situated in an a joining room, a grand mural depicts the Kad Luang community from the past by well known Lanna painter Pornchai Jaima whose concept of the lost beautiful temple at this market place was based on images inspired from a dream. The work is being displayed in dialogue with documentation by Chakkrit Chimnok, a performance artist whom recently traveled the Ping River and recorded his journey. This exhibition includes unique handmade postcards created by students from Kamthieng Primary School which is located next to the museum. Visitors are invited to write postcards in exchange for a donation towards the school's art activities fund.[14]

14. http://www.navinproduction.com/achives_detail.php?id=305

Makan Art Space began as a convivial space for the discussion and production of artwork, and remains committed to gathering around the tenants of domestic existence; the organizers write: "the table goes wherever Makan goes."[15] Makan Art Collective/Art Space was founded in 2003 by Ola El-Khalidi in Amman, Jordan. Makan has operated, in the past, as an independent nonprofit space in Amman, occupying an uneasy relationship with the Jordanian government around issues of culture critique and lifestyle. At the time of writing, Makan is transitioning to a less location-dependent format, as El-Khalidi and other members of the Makan collective travel or relocate across the globe, and reassess the funding policies of Makan's structure.[16]

In the nearly ten years since its existence, Makan has supported, hosted, and organized numerous programs for the local and international arts community, including skillshares, studio space, group exhibitions, and innovative artist

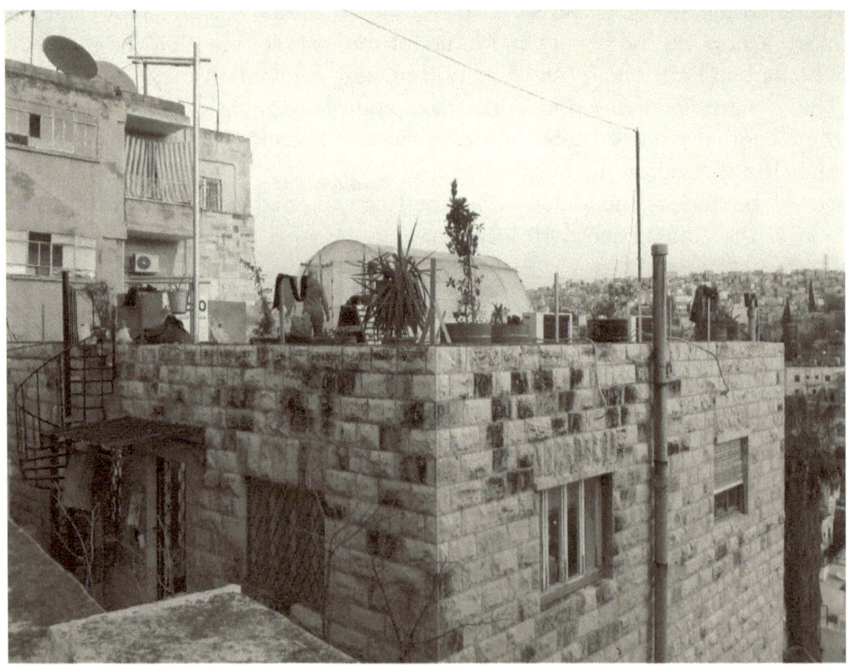

Makan Art Space/Collective 2003–present

15. Makan Collective, e-mail message to editors.

16. The Makan Collective consists of Diala Khasawnih, Ola l-Khalidi, and Samah Hijawi

residency programs. These programs included a residency in a bedroom within the Makan Art Space; an Arab artist exchange, sponsored by the Arab Fund for Art and Culture, whereby artists from other Arab cities travelled throughout the region, staying at centers like Makan; and the Shatana International Artist Workshop, which, from 2007 to 2010, invited international mid-career artists to live and work in the village of Shatana in northern Jordan. Artists who participated in the workshop would spend two weeks living in accommodations secured through Makan and its local collaborators; at the end of the two weeks, the work would be presented to the villagers and the wider Jordanian arts public in a daylong exhibition that resulted in sometimes awkward encounters between artists, the arts public, and the rural inhabitants of Shatana.[17]

The majority of Makan's programming is on hold at time of writing, as they strategize new modes for operation in the future. The Makan Collective holds community rituals at its core logic, such as sharing food at a common table, sleeping under the same roof, and bartering with friends. family, and volunteers. Currently, the Jordanian nonprofit Meezan operates a rooftop garden on the roof of the Makan Art space in Amman.

---

17. Ola El-Khalidi, presentation at the California College of the Arts, April 2012.

Megafone.net is an online platform for the webcast of mobile phone content produced by marginalized groups worldwide. The project was created by Spanish artist Antoni Abad, who continues to serve as its director, working in collaboration with a range of software designers. Since its inception in 2004, Megafone.net has assisted thirteen communities in Europe, South America, Africa, and North America, ranging from sex workers in Madrid (2005), to refugees from the partially recognized Sahrawi Arab Democratic Republic (Western Sahara) in Algeria (2009), to persons with limited mobility in Montréal (2012–2013). Megafone.net programs are supported by grants from local and national arts organizations, universities, and other arts funding structures.

Megafone.net is organized around the notion of the "communal mobile phone," a GPS-enabled camera phone installed with Megafone software. At weekly programming meetings, the community Megafone is working with decides who will carry the phone that week and what content will be webcast. This framework allows for a variety of content, enabling, on the one hand, ignored or ill-regarded communities to claim agency over their own representation; and on the other hand, providing the tools necessary for disabled communities to map obstacles or other dangers in their respective cities. The disabled community in Barcelona, for instance, geotagged 3593 obstacles in their city using the tools provided by Megafone.net. Meanwhile, communities such the Sahrawi refugees are finally able to make their worlds visible on their own terms, posting dozens of pictures, videos, and captions describing their experiences.

Videos, photos, geotagged maps, and other entries are available through the interactive map on Megafone.net's front page. Interviews with and essays by Megafone.net organizers and contributors are available on their "Info" page in English, Spanish, Portugese, and Catalan, along with a tutorial on how to use Megafone.net communal phones. In an essay available for free download as a PDF on the website, Eugenio Tisselli and Luc Steels describe their experience working with the disabled community in Barcelona:

> The project canal*ACCESSIBLE was initiated in 2005, with the aim of enabling people on wheelchairs in Barcelona to defend their access to the commons of public spaces and streets, a.o. by classifying the physical barriers that they encounter and locating them on a map . . . Each week, the 40 participants got together in a meeting space which was especially set up for them at the Centre d'Art Santa Mnica [*sic*], an arts centre located in the heart of Barcelona and discussed different strategies for finding and publishing their images. On some occasions, they used the digitized map as a reference, and organized special trips to cover unexplored areas of the city. Thus, the map became both a record that reflected their activity and also a live Community Memory interface, which they used to decide on future actions. The discussions at the meetings also

resulted in a basic classification of urban barriers. The participants categorized them as "stairs," "steps," ephemeral barriers caused by "inconsiderate" citizens (such as a parked car blocking a sidewalk), "badly adapted" infrastructures (for example, ramps steeper than the accepted maximum of 12 degrees), "transportation," "sidewalks," and "public toilets." This minimal taxonomy emerged through group discussion, and was used throughout the project to categorize the incoming images. The project was widely disseminated through all types of media ranging from press to TV, and of course the Internet itself. This maximized the communicative potential of canal*ACCESSIBLE, and gave it widespread attention. At the end of the project, several thousands of maps of Barcelona with colored markers that corresponded to the architectural barriers were printed and handed out to the public and the city's authorities, which felt the need to respond [*sic*] their own map.[18]

18. Luc Steels and Eugenio Tisselli, "Social Tagging in Community Memories," October 5, 2007, http://www.megafone.net/INFO/files/pdf/2007steels-tisselli.pdf

For nearly ten years, Mess Hall operated in the Rogers Park neighborhood of Chicago, Illinois. Describing itself as an "experimental cultural center," Mess Hall provided space for a wide range of cultural and political activities, including exhibitions, discussion groups, screenings, meals, public and private meetings, and more.[19] Due to unsustainable rent hikes in the neighborhood, however, Mess Hall has closed on March 31, 2013.

The events coordinated and supported by Mess Hall centered on Mess Hall's rejection of the scarcity theory that, in the organizers' view, drives capitalist production, instead focusing on "redistributing surplus at every level of production and consumption."[20] Such events included a poetry workshop that invited participants to leave their expertise at the door, hosting weekly meetings of Occupy Rogers Park, gift circles, and seminars organized around investigating or rejecting neoliberal capitalist structures.

Throughout its existence, Mess Hall avoided incorporation into a framework that extended beyond its rotating group of organizers and contributors, referred to as "keyholders." Mess Hall was never a nonprofit and never sought legal status as such, evading the entanglement with bureaucracy that such a move would necessitate. Instead, Mess Hall operated through monetary and material donations by individuals and organizations interested in supporting Mess Hall. Events were proposed and coordinated by both Mess Hall keyholders and outside contributors, who were able to propose ideas to Mess Hall through their website.

A typical Mess Hall event might be their seminar "Three Crises," described briefly in the excerpt below:

> Welcome to the self-organized seminar "THREE CRISES: 30s—70s—Today."
>
> In this seminar we take a closer look at two turning points of economic and social history, to find out where we've been and what we have become as the United States and the world traverse a third major crisis. The aim is to grasp what's happening before our eyes, and to gain some influence over the new forms of society that will emerge over the next decade.
>
> Each session includes a lecture by Brian Holmes as well as presentations by members of the Slow-Motion Action/Research Collective and invited guests.

---

19. "About," Mess Hall, http://messhall.org/?page_id=467
20. "Mess Hall will close March 31," Mess Hall, http://messhall.org/?p=1359

Open engagement is an ongoing conversation about the social potentials of political and public art that is facilitated through the structure of an open-source, free-to-attend academic conference. Initiated in 2007 in Regina, Saskatchewan, and later expanded in Portland, Oregon, it was initiated by Jen Delos Reyes for the purpose of her own MFA degree and then used as pedagogical structure for her students at the Portland State University Art and Social Practice MFA Program.

The conference themes shift annually according to current research and inquiry within the field. Speakers are selected by students and faculty with the aim of fostering a local and international dialogue which results in shared knowledge, resources and partnerships.

The focus of Open Engagement is to provide a forum for like-minded practitioners to ask questions and engage in rigorous discussion around their research. The format of the conference has shifted from single speakers to three-person panels in order to reflect the diversity of voices active within this collective event. During the course of the conference there are many off-site projects, breakout workshops, and informal discussions taking place in real time.

The following is an excerpt of an assessment of the Open Engagement 2012 conference, as reflected by founder Jen Delos Reyes:

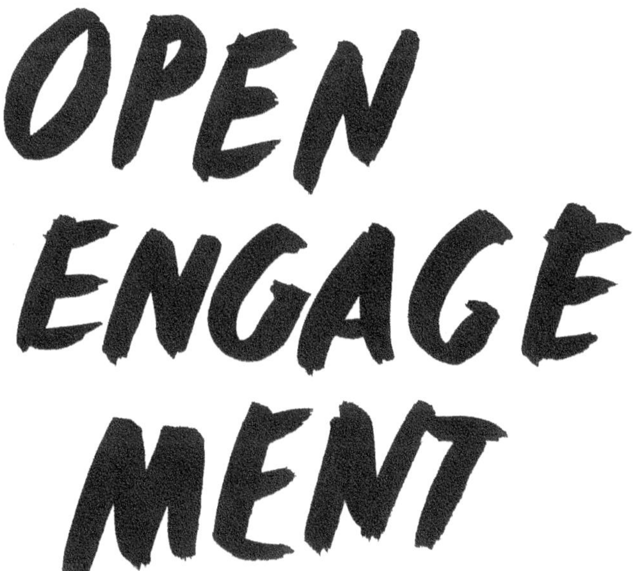

Open Engagement 2007–Present

During this year I reflected a lot on the past conferences and was reviewing a lot of old related materials. In a letter from Darren O'Donnell from 2007 where he discusses his experience that year. In the letter he writes: "I'm feeling confident that there are brilliant people chiseling away at this, and that the annoying but interesting question of 'is it art' won't be interesting to us for long." In the closing event for Open Engagement 2011 in the conversation between Rick Lowe, Pablo Helguera, Julie Ault, and Fritz Haeg, they tackled that very question: "But is it art?" This repetition made me wonder if there is a muscle memory for inquiry and if so, what are the questions that we can begin to ask that can disrupt this pattern and move us beyond.[21]

21. Email from Jen Delos Reyes.

New York City–based artist Timothy Hutchings began the Play-Generated Map and Document Archive (PlaGMaDA) around 2007. PlaGMaDA solicits donations from players of tabletop role-playing games (RPGs), such as Dungeons and Dragons, that often involve extensive player-generated, often hand-drawn, content—maps, records, portraits of characters, fan art, even wholesale reinventions of popular games. Such content may have been generated when players were quite young or may be the product of an adult hand, by dabblers or enthusiasts. PlaGMaDA generates new value for largely discarded ephemera, by recontextualizing these works as autonomous drawings.

The PlaGMaDA archive contains both digital scans and physical editions of RPG ephemera. Digital scans are available for public perusal through an online gallery, easily accessible from the PlaGMaDA website, plagmada.org. Physical ephemera has been displayed, through the archive, at the Cranbrook Academy of Art in Detroit; the Foundation for Art and Creative Technology, in Liverpool; and the Nikolaj Kunsthall in Copenhagen, among others. These exhibitions are coordinated by Hutchings or by contributors. Contributors to the archive are solicited online and through a network of gamers, conventions, and game stores that Hutchings and other contributors to PlaGMaDA have access to. Nonexclusive rights are ceded to the archive upon donation in return for safekeeping by the archive "for perpetuity."[22]

A typical donation to PlaGMaDA might be the album "Luke Crane," accessible on the archive's website.[23] The album includes several scans of detailed hand-drawn maps of cities or towns, complete with detailed keys describing the contents and/or inhabitants of buildings, and a sheet that seems to sketch out the outline of a character and a scene that character may have been part of.

22. "Participate," PlaGMaDA, http://www.plagmada.org/Participate.html

23. "Album: Luke Crane," PlaGMaDA, http://plagmada.org/gallery/main.php?g2_itemId=709

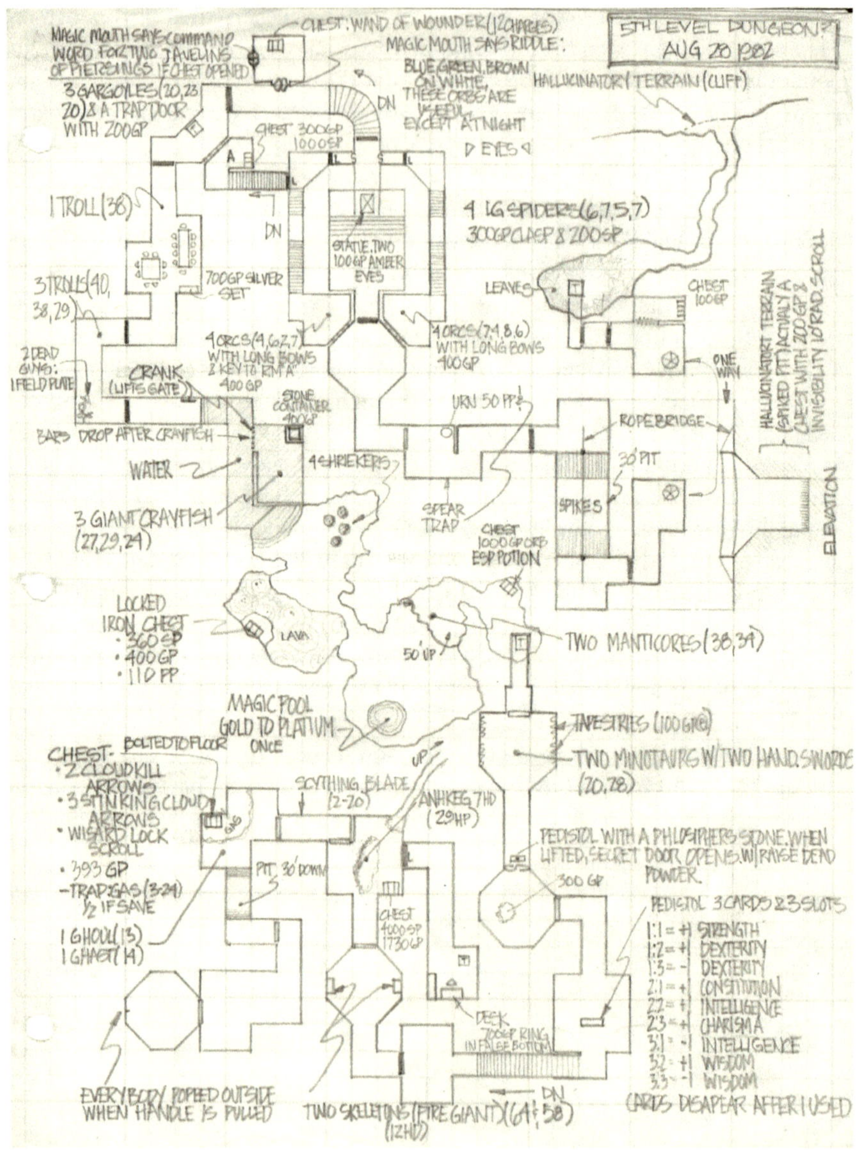

Play-Generated Map and Document Archive 2007–present

Artist and community activist Rick Lowe began Project Row Houses in 1993, in the Third Ward, a then-blighted neighborhood of Houston, Texas. Lowe acquired twenty-two abandoned shotgun-style houses, all within a 1.5-block radius, and set about turning them, and their community, into a Beuysian "social sculpture." This sculpture was to be a community, created through "the celebration of art, African American history and culture."[24] The Project Row House neighborhood has since expanded to six blocks and spawned numerous programs that integrate and support the community with art and artists from around the world. In 2003, the Row House Community Development Corporation (RHCDC) was founded. RHCDC is a nonprofit affiliate corporation that seeks fair material development of the area and manages the properties within it; it is funded by, among others, the Bank of America, Houston Oil Producing Enterprises Inc, and Project Row Houses. Project Row Houses itself is also a nonprofit organization, funded by, amongst others, the Warhol Foundation, Chevron, and the RHCDC.

Project Row Houses, with the assistance of the RHCDC, currently supports programming in four main areas: public art, arts education, a young mothers program, and a pair of community development programs devoted to the social and physical architecture of the community. The "public art" program affirms a broad definition of public art as anything that responds to, involves, or reflects the community.[25] This includes a residency program for visiting artists and curators, exhibition-style programming that fills six of the original twenty-two row houses, artist studios available to artists willing to work in/with the community, a summer studio program, and an artist incubation program. The arts education program focuses on after-school programming for local youth; the young mothers program offers low-rent accommodation and basic support services for young, low-income mothers in the area. The RHCDC manages the community development aspect of the neighborhood, focusing on architectural inquiries and pursuing the establishment of a laundromat and food co-op for the neighborhood.

An idea of what life is like in the Project Row Houses neighborhood is expressed in the following paragraph, available on the Project Row Houses website:

> A stroll through the campus of Project Row Houses is a stroll into a world where passion for art collides with compassion for people. Walking down Holman Street, one is surprised to find this world and its inhabitants, moving with excited energy, each step intentional with purpose. A noisy, giggling group of uniformed students

24. "Our History," Project Row Houses, http://projectrowhouses.org/about/

25. "Public Art at Project Row Houses," Project Row Houses, http://projectrowhouses.org/public-art/

race each other toward the open doors of the after-school program. A single young mother waves to her child among the group as she heads to her weekly Young Mothers Residency Program workshop. An artist greets her by name as he steps out onto the porch of a row house, reflecting on his work and its relationship to the world around him. The sun sets on another day at PRH, another day where community is created as it meets art.[26]

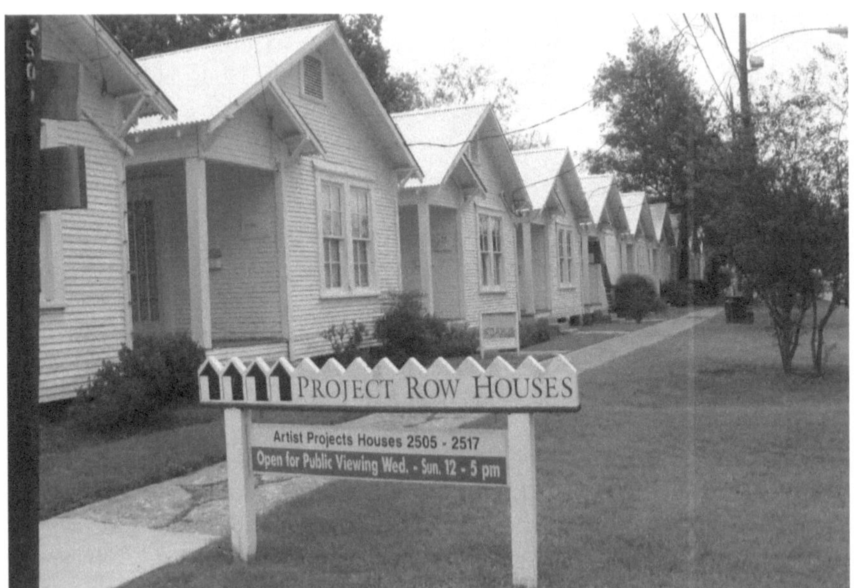

Project Row Houses 1993–present

26. "Community," Project Row Houses, http://projectrowhouses.org/community/

Salvage Art Institute (SAI) is focused on physical material that has been deemed "no-longer-art" as the result of damages determined by an art-insurance company to be "beyond repair." Founded by Elka Krajewska as a research institute with the assistance of a Rockefeller grant, SAI concerns itself with the objectness of materials that find themselves in a "total-loss" state, thereby existing outside of the circulation and valuation within the art market.[27]

In 2010, SAI began a relationship with AXA Art Insurance Corporation (a global art insurance company) in order to gain access to the materials they had archived in storage. While developing this relationship, Krajewska ran two studios at Columbia University focusing on the issues of "home" with regards to the inventory of SAI. In April 2012 SAI signed "the Deed of Gift of AXA Art's total loss inventory" and subsequently moved the inventory to Morgan Manhattan Storage.[28] In November 2012, SAI teamed with the Columbia University Graduate School of Architecture Planning and Preservation to present the exhibition *No Longer Art: Salvage Art Insittute* at the Arthur Ross Architecture Gallery.[29]

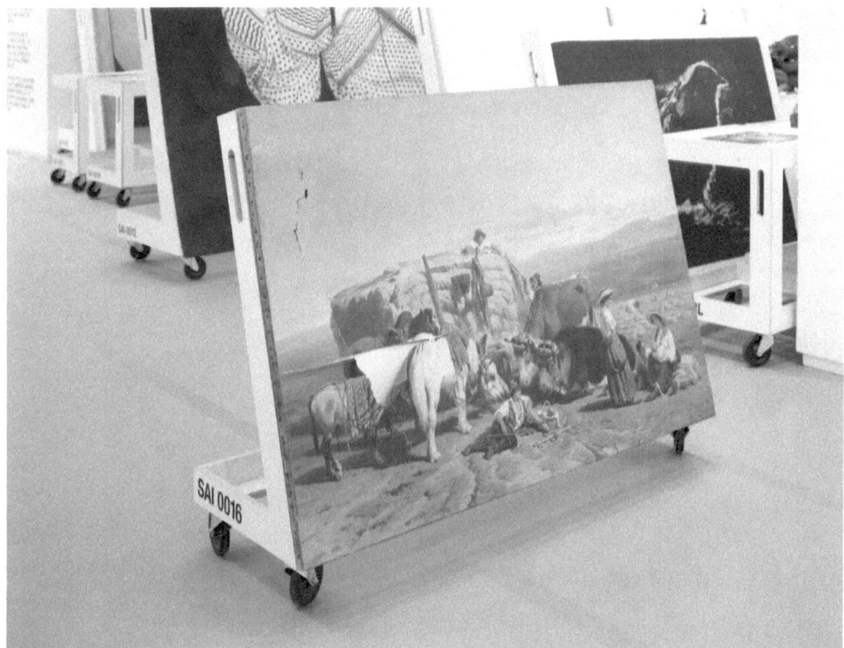

Salvage Art Institute 2010–present

27. "Short History by Elka Krajewska—SAI President and Founder," http://salvageartinstitute.org

28. "SAI Timeline," http://salvageartinstitute.org

29. http://events.gsapp.org/event/damage-no-longer-art-salvage-art-institute

Below is a selection from the policies listed on The SAI website:

1. SAI is a haven for all art officially declared as total loss, removed from art market circulation and liberated from the obligation of perpetual valuation and exchangeability.
2. SAI claims stewardship over all total loss inventories as they are declared, wherever and whenever, with or without physical transfer.
4. SAI seeks to maintain the zero-value of No Longer Art and recognizes its right to remain independent and divorced from the demands of future marketability.
6. SAI approaches the No Longer Art inventory through a non-hierarchical system and aims at democratic principles. Each item of SAI inventory can potentially deliver equally valid revelations.
9. SAI is centered on the tactile objecthood of No Longer Art, on its obdurate survival, and on its transformed physicality. SAI confronts viewers with the material signs of alteration and the legible traces of each piece's history.

Superchannel was a project by Danish collaborative group Superflex. Active from 1999–2005, Superchannel anticipated the popularity of the sort of DIY broadcasting now ubiquitous on YouTube, Vimeo, and so on. Each *Superchannel* studio provided easily accessible space, open to the public, for the discussion, production, and presentation of Internet TV content. This relatively minimal model was easily adaptable to a variety of contexts; by the time the Superchannel project "went to sleep," between 2005 and 2007, over thirty studios were in operation throughout Europe, Asia, and northern Africa.[30] Some spinoffs of Superchannel studios continue to operate, however. Tenantspin, for instance, located in a housing block in Liverpool, continues to produce content as its own separate nonprofit Internet TV channel. Superflex saw itself as a tool for the communities in which it was located, rather than as a discrete artwork or series of artworks.

A typical Superchannel studio included a computer, video, and audio recording hardware and software, a backdrop, space in which to meet, and some variety of publicly accessible sign-up form. This setup allowed for the community in which the studio was based to determine, on their own terms, the programming that the station would broadcast. The studios were set up in galleries, apartment blocks, and community centers, and were supported by funding from arts organizations, community organizations, or arts festivals, including several biennials. A Superchannel studio was set up, for instance, at the Chiang Mai Social Installation, an early project of Navin Production, the "company" that also set up the Mākāhād Festival, discussed elsewhere in this book.

A typical Superchannel set-up might have looked like this:

> SuperTeens: The Trapholt SuperTeens studio was setup during the exhibition "Pyramids of Mars" the 10th of May to the 5th of August 2001 at the Trapholt Museum of Modern Art, Applied Art, Design and Furniture Design in Kolding, Denmark. During this period Trapholt invited teenagers and children who live in Kolding or were on visit at the museum, to make their own Internet tv-programmes. During the exhibition 56 programmes were produced, all very different. The first show on this channel was "Tøzeznak—Tøzens krop" followed by "Tøzeznak og Teenagetalk." These two shows give a good picture of the profile of this channel—they can be found in the archive. This was made as a part of the exhibition Pyramids of Mars organised by Lars Bang Larsen and The Modern Institute, Glasgow, in collaboration with Karen Groen curator at the Trapholt museum in Kolding, Denmark.[31]

---

30. "Superchannel—not dead, just sleeping!" http://www.superchannel.org/ The *Superchannel* page on the Superflex website claims that Superchannel ended in 2005; the Superchannel website claims that Superchannel stopped in 2007, but will return.

31. "Superchannel," Superflex Tools, http://superflex.net/tools/superchannel/

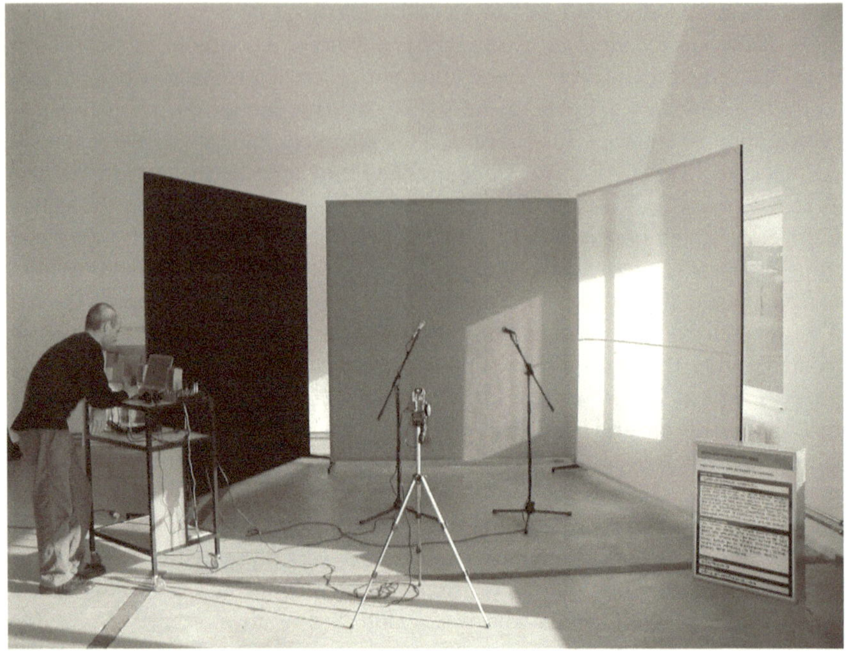

Superchannel 1999–2005

Begun in New York in 2010, TradeSchool.coop is continuously being built by an expanding group of people around the world. The organization is founded and maintained by Or Zubalsky, Caroline Woolard, Louise Ma, and Rich Watts.

TradeSchool.coop is an alternative learning service organization that runs on a barter economy established between participants. People sign up to teach a self-proposed class. These classes vary widely, from "Speaking With Confidence" to "Singing for Pleasure" to "Equality and Diversity in Mental Health." Teachers are compensated by student–participants, through the barter items (such as food or services) that they decide to accept for their class.

TradeSchool.coop functions as a template, which can be reproduced anywhere in the world. The website provides technical and structural assistance for individuals to initiate new Trade Schools. The organization is focused on examining and shifting the format and system of higher education through mutual aid and self-organized learning structures. TradeSchool.coop holds cooperation and shared resources at the core of its education mission, by focusing on hands-on service learning.

TradeSchool.coop has run programs in countries around the world, including the United States, Canada, the United Kingdom, France, Spain, Italy, Germany, Ecuador, Brazil, Thailand, Singapore, the Phillippines, and Mexico (a complete list of cities with TradeSchool programs can be found at tradeschool.coop). It continues to expand horizontally with new locations around the world.

The following is an example of classes that have been taught at the Charlottesville, Virginia, Trade School:

> *The Resilient Pantry*: Whether you are stocking up for the winter or for an emergency, learn some of the basics for building your resilient pantry.
> WHEN: Monday, November 12, 2012
>
> WHERE: The Bridge PAI, 7–8:30 PM
>
> TEACHER: Lorrie Delehanty from Transition Charlottesville/Albemarle
>
> TRADE: Bring one can of food that can be collected up and donated to the Blue Ridge Food Bank.
>
> *Bicycle Maintenance*: In partnership with the Charlottesville Trade School, Transition Charlottesville-Albemarle Presents:
>
> WHEN: Monday July 9, 2012
>
> WHERE: The Bridge PAI, 7–8pm

TEACHER: Scott Paisley of Blue Wheel Bicycles

CLASS DESCRIPTION: Whether you're a routine bike commuter or a veteran of cross-country tours, your bike needs regular love and attention to keep you riding safely. Join us for a hands-on workshop with Blue Wheel Bicycles owner Scott Paisley on the basics of bike maintenance.

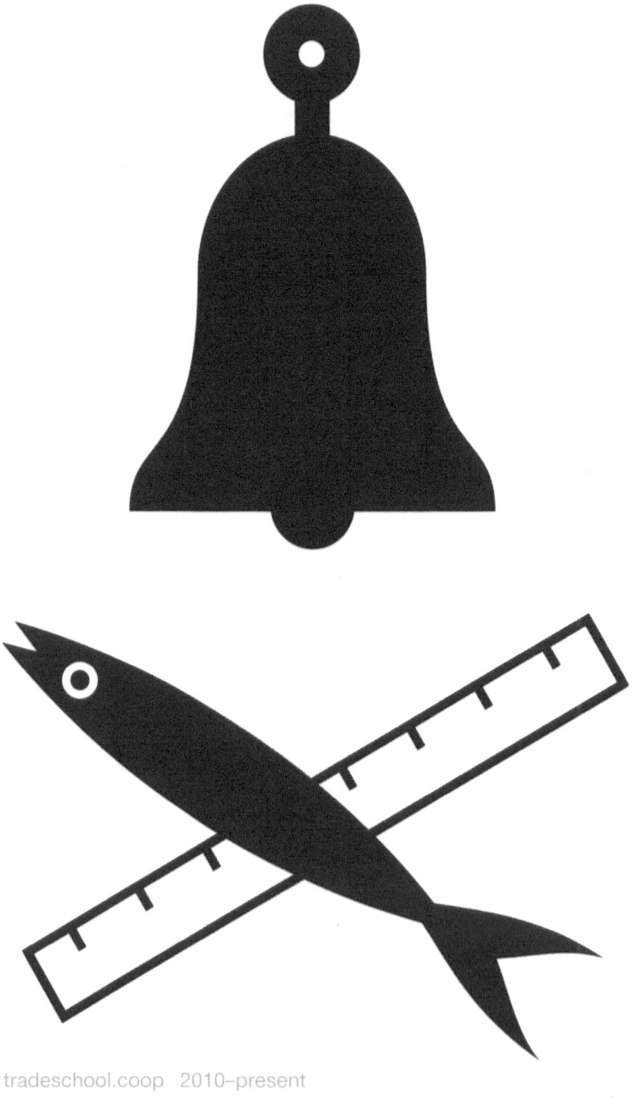

tradeschool.coop 2010–present

WHAT TO BRING: Yourself—and your bike, if you like.

BARTER REQUESTS: Give up fossil-fueled transportation for a day (or a week or a month) and ride your bike instead! Volunteer at Community Bikes. Homemade baked goods, homegrown veggies, etc. . . .

Part Three

CODA, OR WHAT REMAINS

THING—CITY—STORY: TRAJECTORIES OF URBAN EPHEMERA

Elyse Mallouk

Leftover objects do not explain themselves. Unlike other forms of documentation, the power of ephemera lies in their unabashed inability to depict past events. It's this failure that enables things originally intended to serve a distinct purpose to retain an unruly sort of narrative potential, a kind of flexible agency that otherwise erodes in direct proportion to a document's illustrative success. Even the most commonplace things, from park benches to paint on pavement, help to define a set of potential exchanges that can occur in their orbit.

The following materials were generated during a range of projects that altered sclerotic, urban infrastructures, from a city's concrete to its economic silos and social conventions. Initially, these things authorized actions and enabled collective behaviors. Now, they reanimate the proposals put forth by past projects, though the tenor, force, and direction of their influence are mercurial. These photographic representations mimic the ability of the objects themselves to move ideas, shape-shifting along with their contexts: from street, to archive, to page.

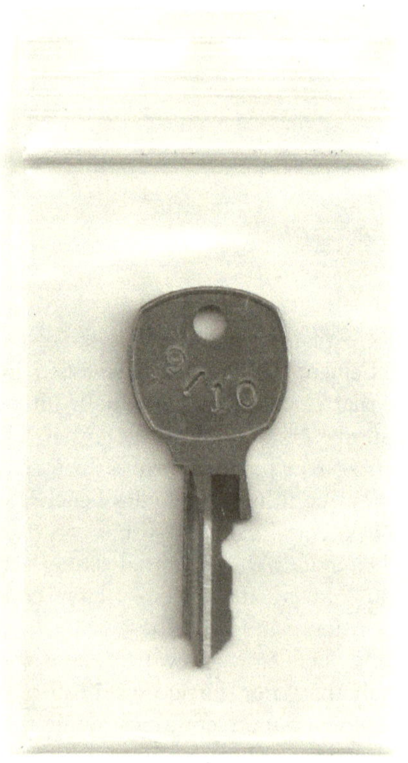

a.

AREA
LEGAL DE
ESPERA

USTED TIENE DERECHO
A ESPERAR AQUI A UN AMIGO,
A SU MAMA
O SIMPLEMENTE PORQUE ESTA
DEMASIADO CALIENTE EN SU
APARTAMENTO

Casale v. Kelly, 2009 WL 1159187 (S.D.N.Y., April 28, 2009).

b.

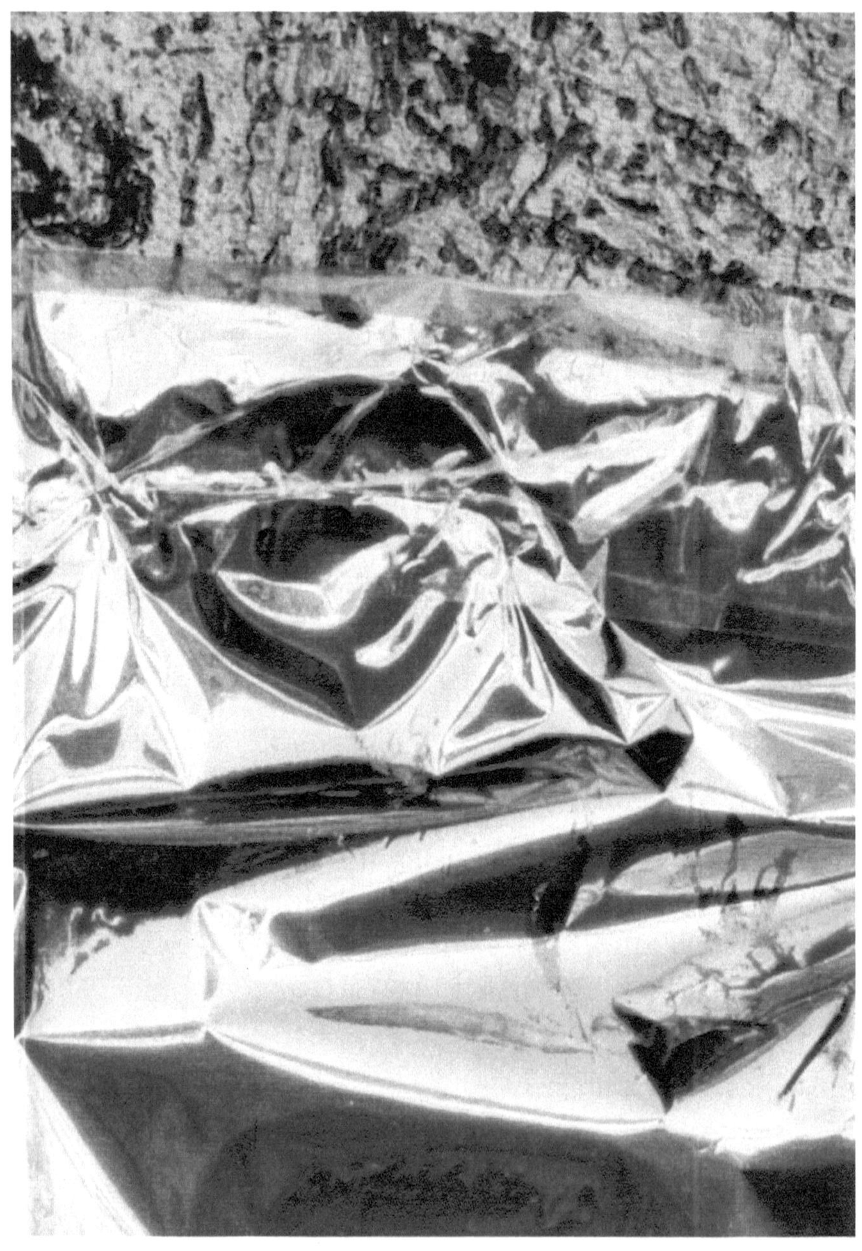

c.

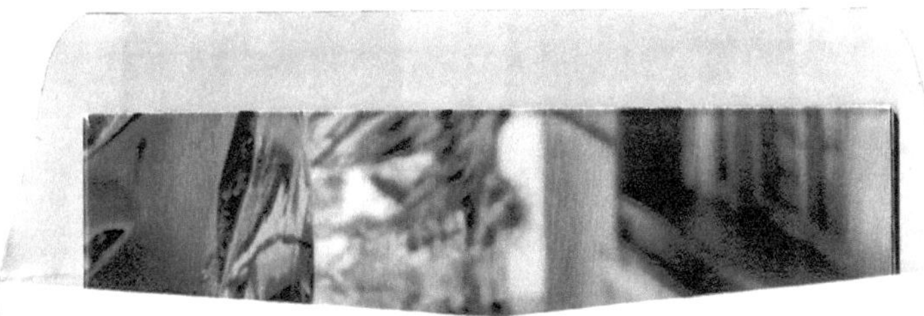

G
pe
tea

AUI
it tog
to pre:
about da.
took it off, the tree sweated underneath and then this insulation tried to preserve the tree from severe cold and the condensation from the moisture. I'm not, you understand, an agricultural person. But the thing was not to deface the trees, but to do the art.

GREGORY: Also you don't want to be put on a podium. You don't want to be crowned king, God.

AUDRAE: I can't do it all. Maybe next year. It's not like this crazy lady who has a place to live is coming down. It's only by God's grace I'm not down here smoking crack, selling my ass sucking dick in a Porta-Potty. Okay, I'm spared. It's not about Skid Row. I believe Skid Row is in your mind.

...

AUDRAE: Who gives a damn? Who do I have to impress? They think bad of me anyway. You know, what is normal? I don't know. Who is normal? If I decide to wash my car at three o'clock in the morning, is that normal? For who is it normal? Because I am the only one in about a block of a hundred families doing it.

GREGORY: You can be abnormal. You can be accepted. This is the place where you can be yourself.

AUDRAE: You can act out your psychotic fantasy within reason, in a spiritual helping sense. So this is the place. This is a hidden secret. I mean if you are seeing a nice psychiatrist, and you say to a psychiatrist, "I feel like doing something healthy and loving and giving to get out of myself or I will kill myself this weekend." Just come incognito and make little things that say "I love you" without anybody knowing. This is the place it doesn't cost much, just a little time and money.

...

MICHAEL: How do you think it strengthened your community then?

AUDRAE: Back to the hope! I believe, hmm. I didn't really ask anybody.

GREGORY: You asked me. I'm in the community. It had a calming and soothing affect.

AUDRAE: [To Gregory] Honey, Honey. [To Michael] I believe it had a therapeutic effect, though people wouldn't actually acknowledge that. If you had a survey and asked people if there was something different down here— I'll show them one of these pictures, give them

MICHAEL: Do you think your guerilla style sculpture made people who live in the neighborhood look more deeply into themselves? Or their neighbors? Or their world?

AUDRAE: Their life. I would hope it did that. I don't know. [To Gregory] What did you do different after observing the trees? Did you drink less that week? Did you go to sleep early, get some exercise?

GREGORY: I reminisced a whole lot, so I probably did all of the above. It gave me some hope.

MICHAEL: What about those who work in the neighborhood?

AUDRAE: When I was out early in the morning, I was seeing the police going to the station and the bus drivers coming through. They do this route for their daily work-week. Those trees caught them, put them in a different mindset. See, behind your job you are a person. Maybe after seeing that tree they went home and had their kid decorate a tree wherever they live in suburbia. You never can tell what effect it had.

MICHAEL: Are you trying to activate change in the larger society? Do you think this is an activist gesture?

AUDRAE: An activist gesture of willingness. Come down, come down. Wherever society level you think you're at in life: middle class, upper class, low class, no class, okay. I'm no different from you and you're no different from me. If there was a nuclear bomb on Beverly Hills, you won't be safe there or here; everybody is exposed. So, yes, it's an activist— a subtle activist gesture. You know, right now, I am sitting in this red, white, blue, patriotic-flag-fold-up chair from Kmart and this is America. You see, Skid Row increased my level of acceptance.

...

MICHAEL: Do you think this flipped power relationships?

AUDRAE: It did.

GREGORY: It transformed Skid Row to Rodeo Drive.

AUDRAE: I don't know whether we went to that level. But it—

GREGORY: It went to that level.

s

GREGORY: He didn't know, he didn't know.

AUDRAE: You live in the community, sir? Where?

CESAR: Right here on Ohio, on the corner hotel. I used to be out here too.

AUDRAE: Oh did you? Good, a constituent of the community. You file taxes this year?

CESAR: Yeah.

AUDRAE: Did you see the trees up a few weeks ago?

CESAR: The what?

AUDRAE: The trees.

GREGORY: I told you, I told you! He didn't pay no attention.

AUDRAE: These trees. [She rattles bag full of purple plastic wrapping scraps. Everyone chimes in to describe Audrae's project.]

CESAR: Oh yeah, I saw them trees! Yeah, they were on the trunks. They were wonderful.

AUDRAE: How did it affect your day?

CESAR: It didn't affect it, but it made me feel like it's good for everyone, you know making it look nice and all that. It was good. We gotta' do stuff like that. [Everyone starts talking.]

GREGORY: Okay, Cesar, see you. There's one person whose day it brightened. [Cesar continues past us sweeping the gutter.] The man didn't know. The man had no idea you done this.

AUDRAE: I don't need to be acknowledged, okay?

...

ALYSE: How long did the wrappings stay up for?

AUDRAE: Probably about two weeks.

[Contents: envelope ed. 100; poster ed. 250]

d.

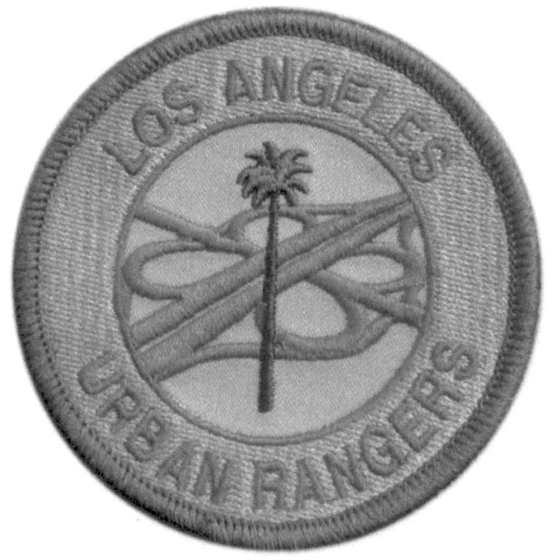

e.

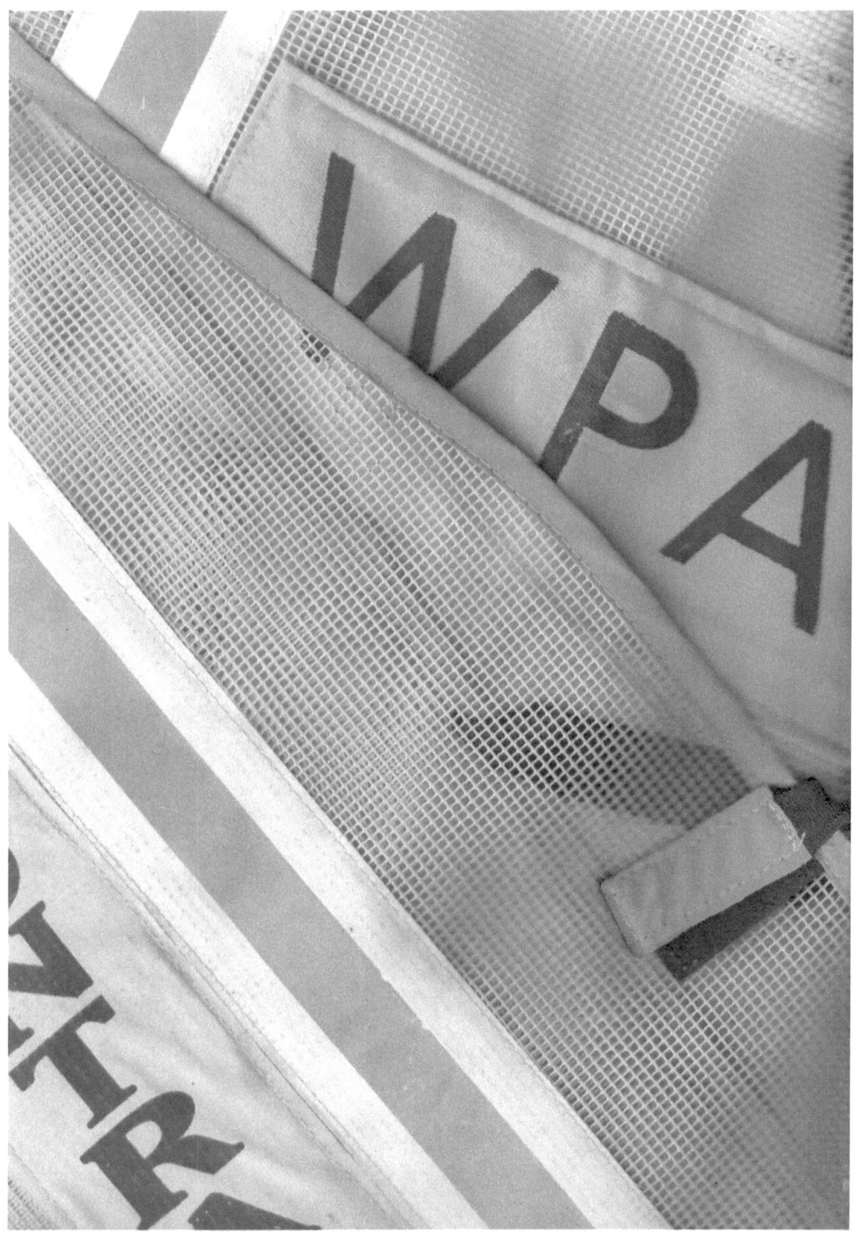

f.

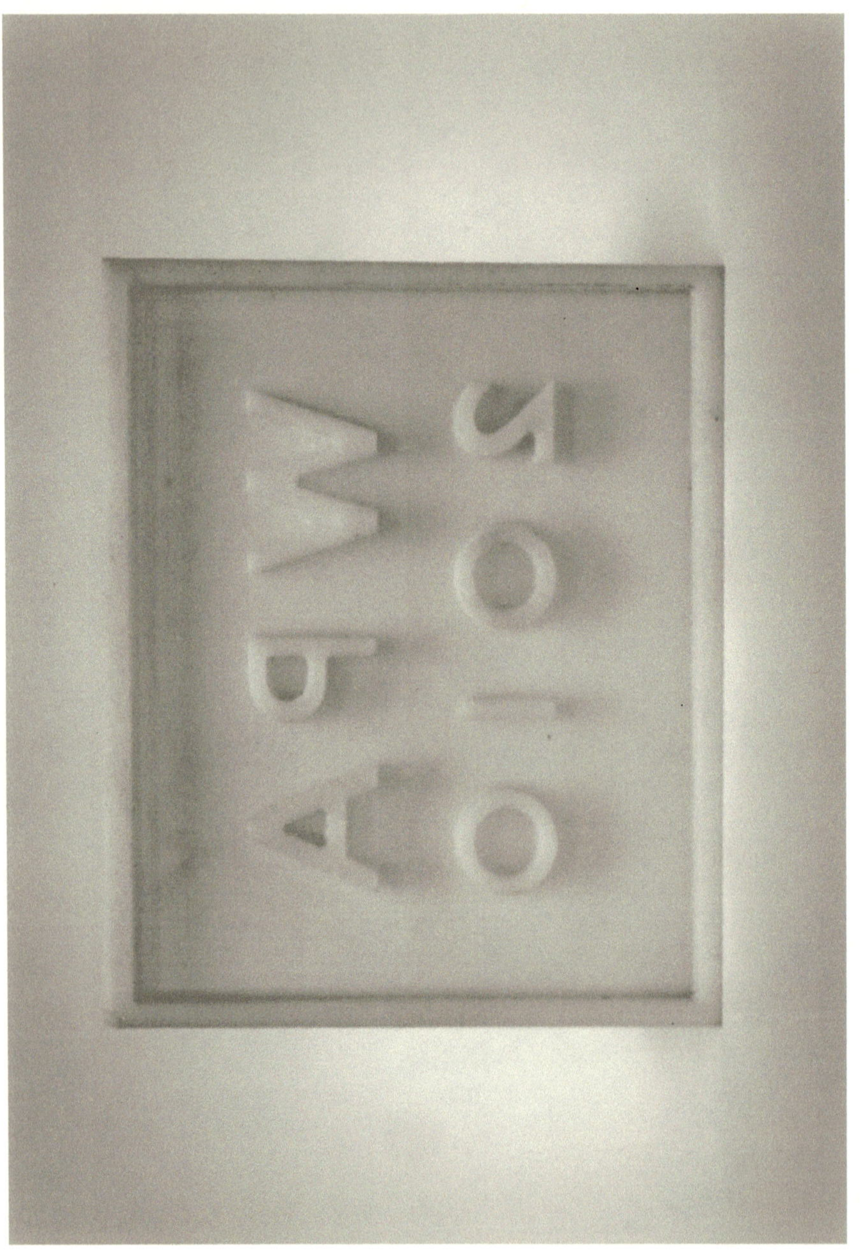

g.

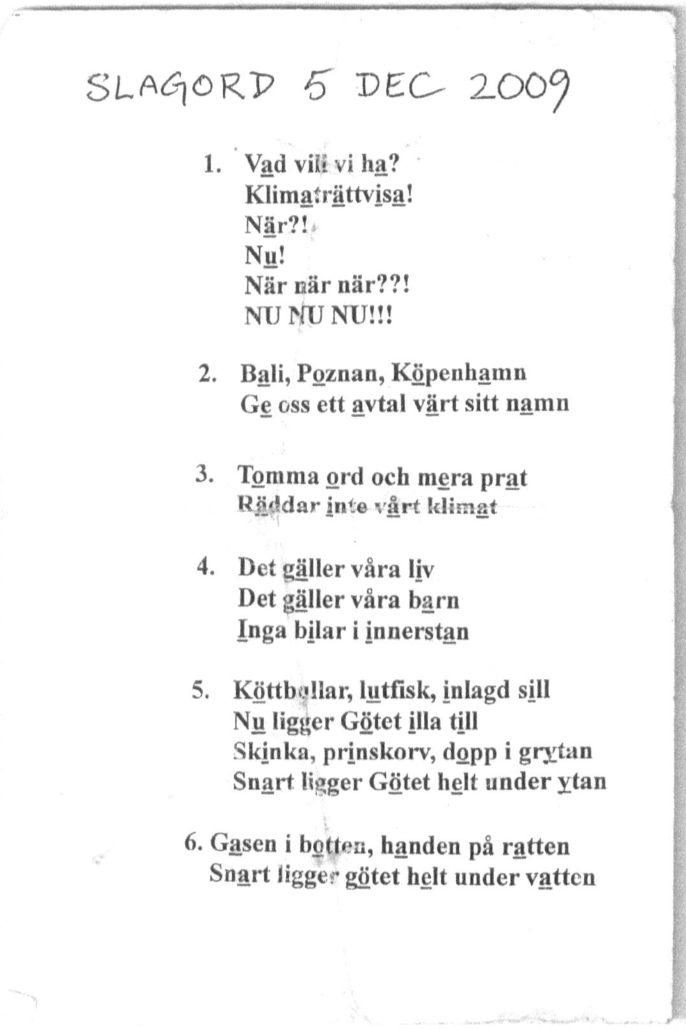

SLAGORD 5 DEC 2009

1. Vad vill vi ha?
   Klimaträttvisa!
   När?!
   Nu!
   När när när??!
   NU NU NU!!!

2. Bali, Poznan, Köpenhamn
   Ge oss ett avtal värt sitt namn

3. Tomma ord och mera prat
   Räddar inte vårt klimat

4. Det gäller våra liv
   Det gäller våra barn
   Inga bilar i innerstan

5. Köttbullar, lutfisk, inlagd sill
   Nu ligger Götet illa till
   Skinka, prinskorv, dopp i grytan
   Snart ligger Götet helt under ytan

6. Gasen i botten, handen på ratten
   Snart ligger götet helt under vatten

h.

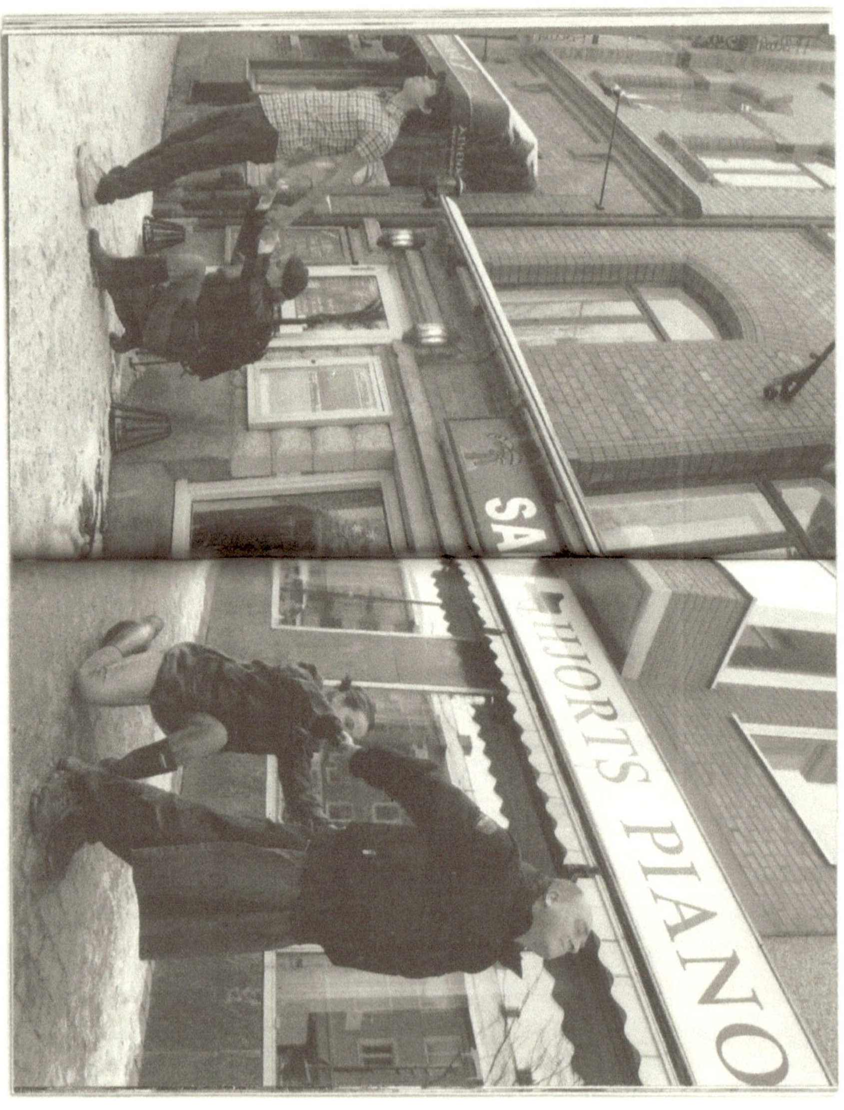

i.

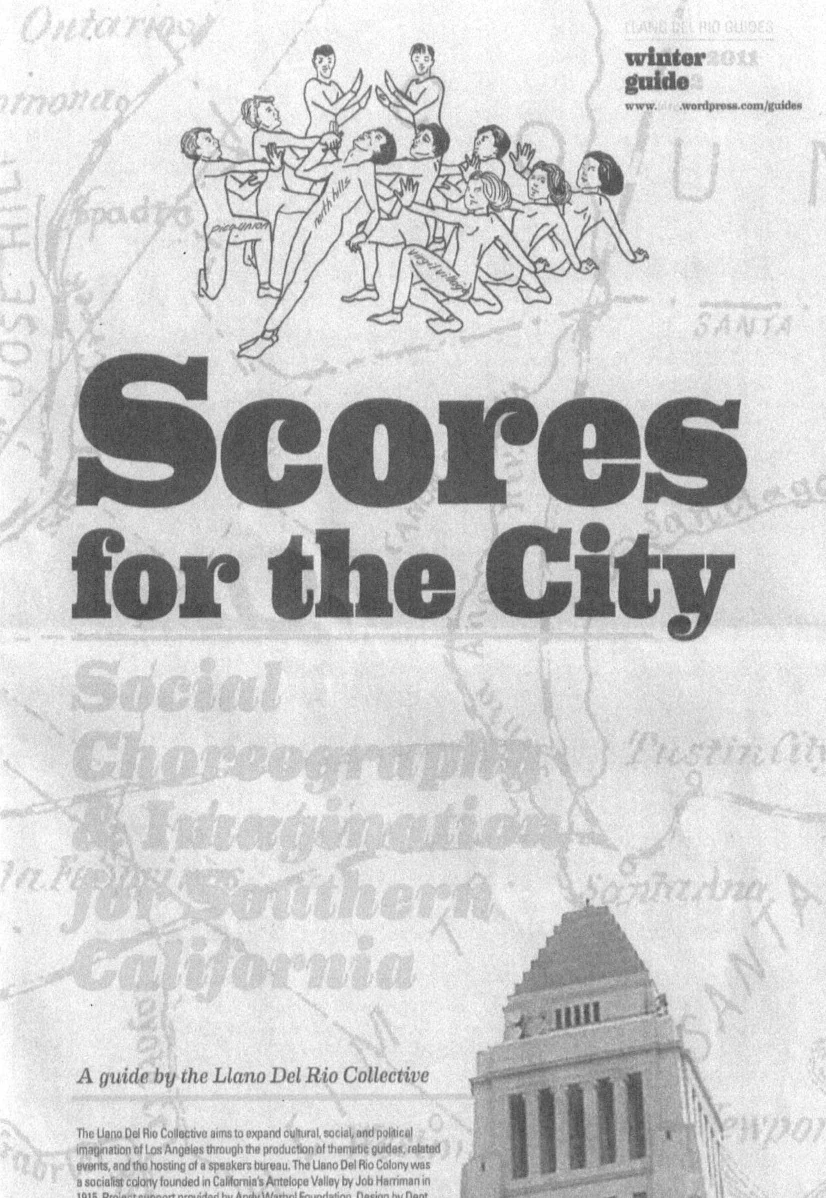
winter
guide
Scores
for the City
Social
Choreography
& Imagination
for Southern
California
A guide by the Llano Del Rio Collective
The Llano Del Rio Collective aims to expand cultural, social, and political imagination of Los Angeles through the production of thematic guides, related events, and the hosting of a speakers bureau. The Llano Del Rio Colony was a socialist colony founded in California's Antelope Valley by Job Harriman in 1915. Project support provided by Andy Warhol Foundation. Design by Dept of Graphic Sciences. llanodelrio@gmail.com

j.

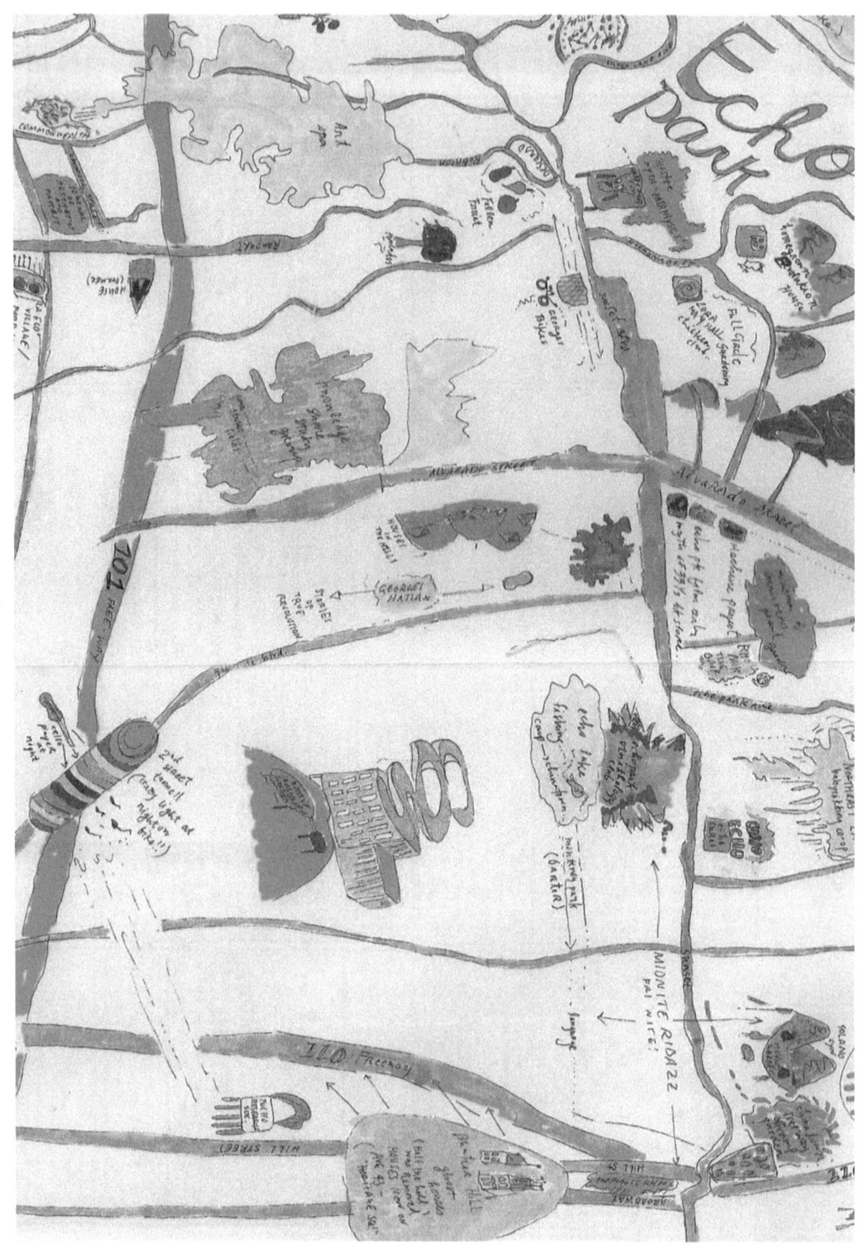

k.

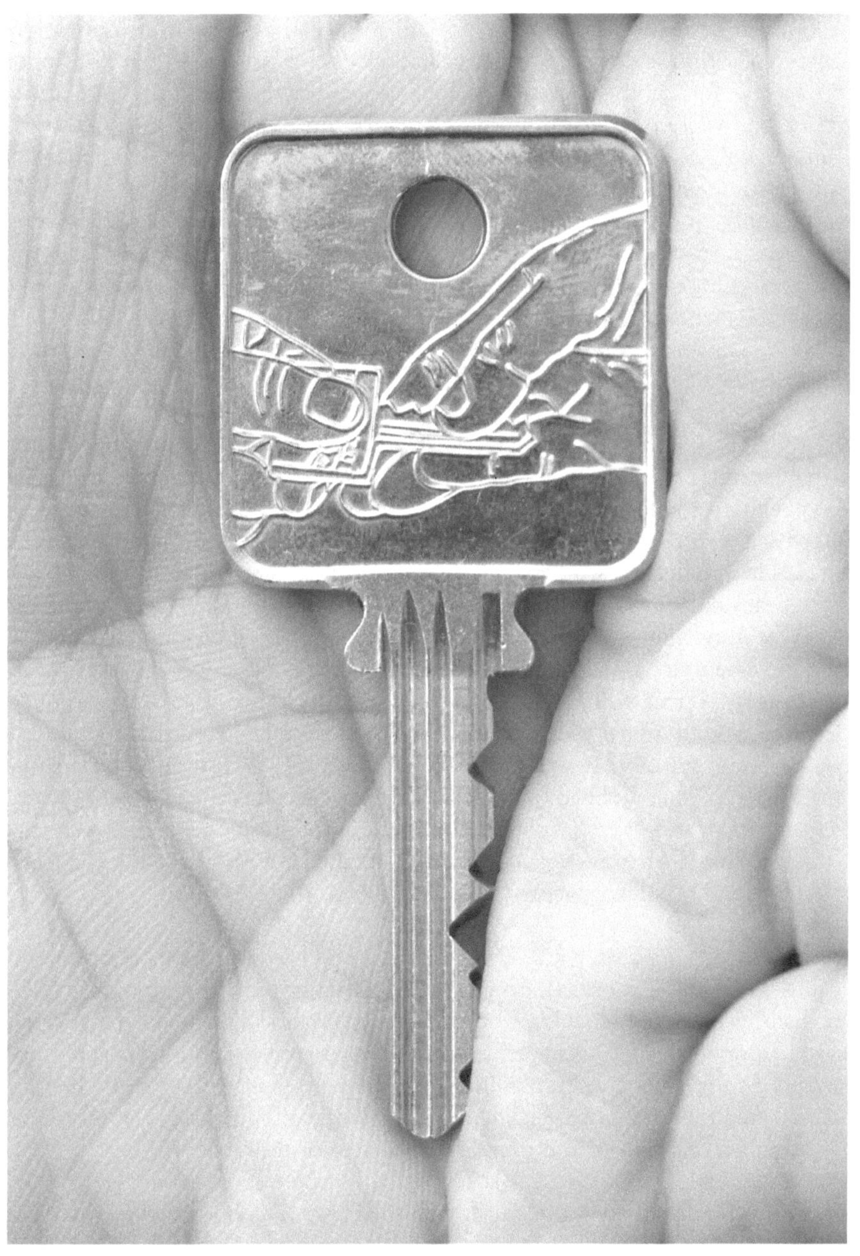

I.

a. This key was obscured in the pocket of Lucas Murgida, who himself was obscured within a six-foot-long credenza which he built and then positioned on a New York City sidewalk. On two September days in 2008, he climbed inside and waited. When an unsuspecting trio found and decided to keep the cabinet despite its locked drawers and remarkable heaviness, they rolled it into a commercial kitchen, where the jostled artist finally emerged. Having successfully transgressed the threshold between city street and locked interior, Murgida left the key for the cabinet's new owners. It opens the exterior locks, turning a Trojan horse into a functional piece of private property, and implementing a final twist in the project's dialectic between public and private. The fraction etched on the key alludes to the truism, "possession is nine tenths of the law."

b. While *9/10* made use of the sidewalk's capacity to turn private property into a public offering, *Legal Waiting Zones* revealed the public nature of the space between street and storefront to be contested. Ghana ThinkTank created these green flyers in response to a problem the group identified in Corona, Queens, in 2011: Immigrant workers felt harassed by police, who questioned and sometimes detained them for lingering on the sidewalk. The signs announced "legal waiting zones," which the group delineated by applying green tape to the pavement in already-public spaces including a subway platform and an extensively policed section of Roosevelt Avenue. With words excerpted directly from conversations with immigrants, the flyers counter unconstitutional "loitering laws," stating: "It is OK for you to wait here, and in all public places, for a friend, your mom, or simply because it is too hot in your apartment." Though the flyers were prototypes for more authoritative-looking street signs which followed, they provoked impassioned conversation about the right of a public to use a public space.

c. In Central City East, a fifty-five–block swath of Los Angeles more commonly called Skid Row, city ordinances prohibiting sleeping outdoors during nighttime hours are suspended, enabling the nation's largest homeless population to live there, contained. In 2009, a resident of the neighborhood, Audrae Rena Jones, wrapped fifty of its tree trunks in purple metallic plastic. The trees, in turn, punctuated the dimly lit streets with bright flashes of reflective, magenta light, creating a disruption in the normal appearance of those blocks.

d. When Michael Parker saw the embellished trees, he photographed them and sought out the person who had wrapped them. *I Am a Citizen* is his response, which documents and memorializes Jones's project. A poster depicts one foil-wrapped tree in full color; on the back, images of the others are arrayed in a two-toned grid. The poster is packaged in an envelope, which is printed with a conversation involving Parker, artist Alyse Emdur, Jones, and other Skid Row residents. The sleeve effectively wraps Jones's gesture in a discourse about art, intention, speech, agency, and imagination. In the interview, Jones describes her project as hope-giving. She asserts: "It's not about Skid Row. I believe Skid Row is in your mind."

e. As part of a one-night event, the Los Angeles Urban Rangers and members of the Los Angeles Poverty Department (LAPD) led museumgoers on a tour of Skid Row. The looped trail began at the Museum of Contemporary Art and progressed from the city's affluent Historic Core across Main Street, easily perceptible as the effective perimeter, as attendees took note of changes to their surroundings. Uniforms and patches worn by guides from both groups leant the tours an air of legitimacy, as they have to numerous other Los Angeles Urban Ranger interventions. The crowd drew interest from some residents and challenge from others—"You're taking a tour? I'm proud of your bravery! Welcome to poverty!"

f. This safety vest similarly legitimated a feigned public bureau: an ad hoc Works Progress Administration, originated in 2010 by Christopher Robbins. The vest enabled its wearer to patch sidewalks, repair curbs, and complete other public works in Queens and Wassaic, New York. The project began in 2010, in response to widespread layoffs in the wake of the 2008 financial crisis. The new *WPA* paid wages using funds acquired through crowdsourced donations, and determined which projects to undertake by collecting requests at its field offices. Though the project failed to spur the government to reinstate the program, it united its workers—libertarians and liberals, old and young—with a uniform, a paycheck, and a common purpose.

g. Signs of Robbins's *WPA* can still be detected in the sidewalks of Queens. This stamp displaced the wet cement left by fresh repairs, producing impressions in the pavement. While similar marks left by the FDR-era WPA publicized government support in times of hardship, the 2010 *WPA* stamp speaks of federal inaction, and constitutes a series of almost-imperceptible public sculptures.

h. In December 2009, citizens of Gothenburg, Sweden, took a different approach to decry top-level lethargy. *Göteborg Under Vatten* (Gothenburg Under Water), a demonstration that took place during the December 2009 UN Climate Change Conference, demanded meaningful action against rising tides that continue to threaten the city with submersion. Broken into numbered stanzas, the anonymous protest slogans read like a poem: "Meatballs, lutefisk, pickled herring / Now Göteborg is bad / Ham, mini sausages, farmer dip the pot / Soon Göteborg is completely submerged."

i. *Skidbladnir's Figurehead*, a pocket-sized book by Brindalyn Webster, takes the urgent temporality of that demonstration and folds it into ancient legend. In Norse mythology, Skidbladnir is a mythical ship that can hold all the gods of Asgard, and collapse so small it can be carried over land in one's palm. Along with a reproduction of the protest sheet, Webster's book contains nineteenth-century photographs of Gothenburg's canals, and an imaginative proposal for a contemporary reconstruction of Skidbladnir. It also documents a series of performances in which the city's shop owners posed as figureheads using Webster as a counterweight, arching their backs with their feet planted on the ground. The gestures invoke the myth in order to assert a pressing need: a ship of state that can safely hold all of the city's people.

j. *Scores for the City* scripts such ephemeral performances for the streets of Los Angeles. Produced by the Llano Del Rio Collective, the poster provides historical performative precedents ranging from seasonal rituals once performed by the Wilshire Witches at the city's La Brea Tar Pits, to rioting. Among the proposed actions is *the subtle body series*, an open set of muted movements to be carried out in public places, altering the environment—even if they go unseen.

k. *Map for An Other LA* divulges the locations of collectivist and utopian spaces that point "elsewhere" within Los Angeles, and offers up little-known treasures in a city whose niches are deep but can be difficult to find. A loosely sketched marker-drawing overlaid with a lettered, numbered grid indicates the relative locations of community gardens and bike kitchens, a former tent city, and a tunnel off the 101 where a cello player performs at night.

l. Paul Ramirez Jonas's *Key to the City* cultivated a similar sense of discovery by generating a new set of New York City secrets. The project turned a rare municipal honor into a mutual contract; both the medieval custom and its contemporary, democratized adaptation use the key as a symbol of free, unimpeded entry. In a short ceremony repeated hundreds of times over the project's duration, New Yorkers bestowed copies of the key upon one another, citing reasons large and small. The key unlocked twenty-four sites around the five boroughs, and can still be used in ten locations. In the artist's words, "Not only does the key open up specific sites, but it can also make us aware that the city is a series of spaces that are locked or unlocked."

a. Lucas Murgida. Key for *9/10*, 2008. Courtesy of the artist.

b. Ghana ThinkTank in Corona (Christopher Robbins, John Ewing, and Maria Del Carmen Montoya). Flyer for *Legal Waiting Zone* in Corona, Queens, 2009. Courtesy of the Queens Museum of Art and Creative Time.

c. Michael Parker, with Audrae Rena Jones, Gregory Gibson, and Alyse Emdur in conversation. *I Am A Citizen*, 2009–10, detail; custom envelope and poster, edition of 100.

d. Michael Parker, with Audrae Rena Jones, Gregory Gibson, and Alyse Emdur in conversation. *I Am A Citizen*, 2009–10, detail; custom envelope and poster, edition of 100.

e. Los Angeles Urban Rangers. *Los Angeles Urban Rangers Official Patch*, 2004. © Los Angeles Urban Rangers, 2004

f. Christopher Robbins. Contractor's vest from *WPA*, 2010.

g. Christopher Robbins. Pavement stamp from *WPA*, 2010.

h. Anonymous. Protest slogan for United Nations Climate Change Conference, 2009.

i. Brindalyn Webster. *Skidbladnir's Figurehead*, 2009–10; book of photographs, an interview, protest slogans, a prediction, and a proposal.

j. Llano Del Rio Collective. *Scores for the City*, 2011; two-sided poster. Courtesy Llano Del Rio Collective.

k. Llano Del Rio Collective. *Map for An Other LA*, 2010; two-sided poster. Courtesy Llano Del Rio Collective.

l. Paul Ramirez Jonas. Key for *Key to the City*, 2010. Paul Ramírez Jonas' Key to the City project, presented by Creative Time in cooperation with the City of New York. Image by Paul Ramírez Jonas, courtesy Creative Time.

III

ACTORS AND AUDIENCES

GENEROSITY AND SOCIAL AESTHETICS IN PRAXIS

THE ARTS, GENEROSITY, AND POLITICS

Peter Coyote

Authors note: this text is adapted from a speech given at a public symposium for the arts at the California College of Arts and Crafts.

I'd like to thank Ted Purves and the California College of Arts and Crafts for inviting me to speak today, and also my old friend and mentor Stephen Goldstine for suggesting me. Before directly addressing a subject of such complexity as generosity, I'd like to frame things with a story told to me by film director Martin Ritt, as we were about to begin a film twenty years ago. Marty was a tirelessly political man and the creator of such wonderful films as *Hud* and *Norma Rae*. He was, to say the least, often cranky and pessimistic, and he told this story traditionally at the first read-through of each of his films. After hearing it, perhaps you'll understand how I feel today.

Once, in the town square of a small Russian village, a sign appeared on the street proclaiming: "World's Oldest Living Jewish Acrobat—The Mosque—9 PM Tonight." That night the local people assembled, and they saw the same sign, established at stage left: "World's Oldest Living Jewish Acrobat." At stage right was a cannon with a man-sized bore, pointing towards the rear of the mosque, where a trampoline had been angled next to the wall in such a fashion as to receive a body fired from the cannon and deflect it towards a tight-rope stretched across the center of the hall. There was no safety net. An extremely old and fragile-looking man was hobbling back and forth across the stage, looking at the cannon, looking at the trampoline and then at the rope, shaking his head from side to side. He paced, shook his head and paced some more. Nine o'clock came and went. At 9:15, a rustling was audible in the house. At 9:30, loud muttering could be heard, and by 9:45 the crowd was stamping its feet and clapping in unison, shouting for the show to begin. The old man walked to center-stage, looked at the crowd dyspeptically, and held his hands aloft for silence. In the ensuing quiet, he shrugged fatefully and, addressing the audience, said, "All right. You vant to kill an old Jew? I'll *do* it!"

This story feels appropriate today, for several reasons. The obvious one is the personal risk inherent in undertaking a subject as vast and profound as generosity. However, buried within the joke, there is, in the image of the man's body itself being the offering, something extremely germane to our topic.

I would like to consider generosity, which originally referred to courage as well as munificence, in the larger context of the Buddhist assertion that nothing on earth, including one's self, stands independent of the rest of creation, with an isolated existence. Trees cannot be *independent* of sunshine, rain, and microbes in the soil any more than people can be independent of sunshine, water, microbes in the soil, and the flora and fauna of their own intestinal tracts. Only a very small enlargement of our frame is required to observe that this interdependence *is* generosity; an offering of mutual, interpenetrating support which is a fundamental characteristic of all existence. The "courage" implicit in the archaic definition of generosity is involved in the coming forward to participate fully, without shirking.

It has been my long-standing belief that artists of every discipline have an intuitive understanding of this reciprocity. Beginning with a field of perception that includes foreground and background simultaneously, the artist's understanding is fostered and forged by intimacy with his or her materials—whether words, the body, color, or sound. The creative process itself demands that artists apply their intuition and intention without overpowering or otherwise disrespecting the forms with which they work. The willingness to accept such a limit is also a kind of generosity to the material world on the part of the artist.

Furthermore, all artists require—or their work at least implies—an audience, with whom they are interdependent and upon whom they are to some degree dependent, for the meaning of what they do. For these reasons, the arts are particularly appropriate for exploring and expressing relationships, interdependence, and mutuality, and it is for this reason too that there is often such an intimate relationship between artists and the political issues of their times.

Having said this, I'd like to recall a time nearly thirty-five years ago when this explicit relationship between art and politics seemed more pervasive and generally more apparent than it does today. I'd like to review the ways in which some artists with whom I was familiar regarded their world then and what ramifications their history (which is also my own) might have for us here today.

I emigrated to California in 1964 to pursue a master's degree in creative writing at San Francisco State University. I had done a great deal of acting (or "ecting" as the old acrobat would say) in college in the midwest, and I joined a rather traditional rep company here while I attended school. One afternoon when my own theater was dark, I happened to attend an outdoor performance of the San Francisco Mime Troupe, an event that changed my life.

I was lolling around in Golden Gate Park when a small flatbed truck arrived and a ragged crew of people began assembling a small stage—really not much more than interlocking wooden platforms on top of overturned wine-barrel halves. A gaily painted rear curtain hung from a simple frame at the back of the stage, and that was the entirety of the performance space. Wicker trunks were dispersed about the grass and quasi-Elizabethan costumes made of rag-ends and flotsam appeared from them in staggering profusion, followed by tambourines, drums, whistles, and recorders. While some actors dressed and applied make-up, others played music and danced about, exhorting the growing audience to be seated. A theater company had materialized out of the fog.

For the next two hours, they sang, joked, and transfixed their audience with hilarious satire based on issues of the day. They lampooned politicians, warmongers, capitalists, pomposity, hypocrisy, and sexual up-tightness with flair and verve. It was not at all inconsequential to me that two of the actresses were breathtakingly beautiful and all but bursting out of their décolletage. Consistent with my life-long predilection for impulsive behavior, I changed theatrical and political allegiances on the spot and joined the San Francisco Mime Troupe.

For the next several years, almost without interruption, we rehearsed, argued, laughed, performed, laughed, toured, fought, and laughed some more without pause. Under the direction of R.G. Davis, the Troupe had an avowed Socialistic-sort-of perspective. Its multiracial membership included college graduates, cab drivers, labor organizers, realtors, and ghetto refugees, bound together by a common dedication to left-of-center politics and wacky humor. This tiny company, housed on the second floor of a warehouse at the intersection of San Francisco's Fifth and Harrison Streets (in days when young artists could afford to live in San Francisco) mounted two national tours and several mini-tours during my tenure there. Our provocative minstrel show—a blackface review which stole the stage from the white interlocutor and presented American history from the minstrel's perspective—garnered us an invitation to perform in New York City from two civil-rights champions, the comedian Dick Gregory and the singer Harry Belafonte, who sponsored our performances there. Following a triumphant tour of the East Coast, the Troupe garnered rave reviews for its work and was recognized with an OBIE award from New York's *Village Voice* newspaper.

In the face of such approbation, troupe members could hardly be blamed for feeling as if we had our fingers on the national pulse. In the whirl of the moment, the underlying principles of generosity inherent in the troupe's work evaded me, and I was more than satisfied with novelty and political satire. In retrospect, however, it is much easier to see that there were profound, non-ideological aspects of generosity underpinning everything we did.

First of and foremost, sharing and organizing information in a useful form is an essentially a generous act. *Real* information—data that makes a *difference*—is like oxygen to the bloodstream of clear thought. I am as convinced today as I was in 1966 that the primary social function of the major media is to obfuscate and confuse historical context. By burying valuable information in blood-drama or trivia, a much more effective form of censorship than repression is created, more effective because it calls no attention to itself. The more one reads and attends major media sources, the less one actually comprehends political events, and this state of affairs has been empirically verified by a media watchdog group called Fairness and Accuracy in Reporting (FAIR). FAIR created a series of scientific surveys and polls to determine the relationship between hours of media exposure and objective knowledge of current events, and the conclusions were precisely what you might expect: the more exposure to media they had, the less people understood the events being reported.

The troupe's antidote to this situation was obsessive study and discussion to refine and clarify issues until they could be dramatized in incisive forms. Characters in our dramas were rude cartoons, bold, iconographic *arguments*, that stripped away distractions and simplified relationships to encourage decisive action. As such, these characters were a *service* to the community, a gift quite different from the "he-said, she-said" reporting of the corporate media that makes judgement and decision all but impossible.

(*A digression about the relationship of the artist and audience is in order here*: Troupe members sometimes took Ezra Pound's dictum to be the "antenna of the race" perhaps too literally. The notion of being the vanguard, the first perceiver, is a seductive delusion that can lead artists into an arrogance implying that "we" know and our job is to "transmit our knowledge" to a passive audience. This is overly flattering to the artist and demeaning to the audience. Furthermore, it generates a style of self-importance that is the opposite of generosity.

Today, after having had much of my arrogance bludgeoned out of me by time, I would suggest that it's more accurate to describe the *audience* and the *artist* as the left and right hands clapping. The artist has the capacity to *articulate* and *express* novel perception and unexpressed thoughts and conditions for the delight and edification of others. The audience's *recognition* and *appreciation* of the articulation is proof that the artist's translation has succeeded. If the audience does *not* recognize the artist's expression, the relationship between them is severed and the artist is, at best, "misunderstood" or ignored. This even-handed relationship between artist and audience mimics the mutual coming-forward that creates our common world. It is for this reason that the arts are especially capable of the expressing complexity and contradiction beyond the logic of grammar and syntax that normally rule perception. For those of you still with me, the digression is officially over.)

The Mime Troupe might have continued like this indefinitely (and in fact the troupe continues to thrive here today) had not the success of our work in the early sixties led a number of us to consider whether we were rigorous enough in fulfilling the implications of our work.

Let me explain how we framed the problem for ourselves. Imagistically, a pedestal, a frame around a picture, or a stage can be regarded as the epitome of private property—space owned and controlled by the artist for his or her own purposes. A number of us became troubled by the tensions between our democratic intentions and our autocratic monopolization of the stage. A dissident movement evolved within the Mime Troupe, which sought to erase the imbalance of power between actor and audience and elicit creative participation from *everyone* to create what we hoped might be newly liberated public space and social forms. This internal subset of the Mime Troupe evolved into a loose gang of friends who called ourselves "The Diggers" and led to an eventual fissure in the company.

The original Diggers evolved during the early days of the Industrial Revolution in seventeenth-century England, when the king, needing more sheep to service his new woolen mills, violated ancient traditions by fencing public pastures for his own use. A man named Gerard Winstanley responded to this violation of custom with a number of pamphlets on the damnable attributes of private property. Influenced by his writing, the local peasantry marched to reclaim their land from the king, who responded by sending his Puritanical general, Oliver Cromwell, to meet them. (Imagining Cromwell, I envision a cross between the Tin Man in the *Wizard of Oz* and John Ashcroft). This dissident group was named the Diggers because each dawn they were observed burying their dead from the previous day's battles.

In 1967, a displaced Brooklyn visionary named Billy Murcott and his charismatic friend Emmett Grogan began to preach a digger-like ethos in San Francisco. They papered the Haight-Ashbury neighborhood with cryptic handouts proclaiming "It's Free because it's yours" and criticizing city officials and "hippie" merchants for capitalizing on the new phenomena of the counterculture without giving anything back. The two soon gravitated into the orbit of the Mime Troupe.

Under their influence, the dissidents in the Mime Troupe advanced their ideas until a spot in Golden Gate Park was established where free, hot food was delivered daily to the hordes of kids scrabbling to live on the streets. This was a direct-action intervention intended as a rebuke to the public hand-wringing of the city fathers, who were threatening the hordes of young visitors from around the nation with arrest. The Diggers visited the farmer's market for donations of day-old vegetables and cooked them in friend's kitchens to produce a hearty stew, which they delivered in steel milk containers, accompanied by small loaves of bread shaped like mushrooms (because of the way they rose over the old one-pound coffee cans in which they were baked).

At the food site, a yellow wooden frame, six feet by six feet, was assembled. One stepped through this "Free Frame of Reference" and, on the other side, was handed a smaller version (about an inch by an inch) attached to a cord for wearing. Then you were given food. The extent of the coercion was the *invitation* to look at the world from another perspective—a *free* perspective, a point-of-view one could assemble oneself, without the intervention of ideologues, scribes, pundits, or coercive behavior. It was, after all, a free exchange. This free-food program was a great success, not because it was "charity," but because by participating one created a world in which free food was "a fact."

The food was soon augmented by "free" crash-pads, free medical clinics, and free stores. In the Digger Free Store, not only were the *goods* free, but so were the *roles* of the customers and "employees." If someone entered the store, which looked just like any other Goodwill filled to overflowing with mid-twentieth-century detritus, and asked, "Who's in charge?" the answer was always, "You are." If the person rose to the occasion and assumed their authority, they might say, "Well, let's clean this place up, it's filthy." If the person dumbed out or failed to understand the invitation, there was no sense blaming "the man" or "the pigs" or "the system" for what was essentially a personal failure. That was an inherent part of the transaction.

The Digger Free Store, though unworkable as a permanent social model, called into question the relationships between people and property: Who "owns" it? What value systems and relationships are implied by the acceptance of terms such as "consumer" and "producer"? The Diggers sought artistic forms to articulate that which was unexpressed in our society. We believed that if someone did not have a commodity because they did not have the money, it was the *money* that was scarce, not the commodity. The Digger Free Store was an artistic solution for highlighting and creating dialogue about this state of affairs. The fiction of scarcity was exposed by direct action extending knowledge as a gesture of generosity.

All social and political forces are balanced by opposition, and the experimentation of the sixties could not continue indefinitely. The watershed event that began the dissolution of the decade's experiments was, for me, the oil crisis of 1973. A major hiccup in global distribution systems of petroleum was manipulated into a general anxiety about "scarcity," frightening people and leading them to doubt whether or not there was "enough to go around." The question of conservation was never raised in a serious manner, but conveniently undercut by the sudden absence of plenty (or at least the *perception* of absence), the revolutionary public experiments of the sixties were starved to death. Long lines at the gas pumps deflected the focus from generic social ills to personal loss. Scarcity became the environment in which social advances could be questioned and rolled back.

President Carter was politically emasculated for attempting to protect the citizenry from the gouging they were receiving from the nation's oil-companies under the pretext of crisis. The next president, Ronald Reagan, projected a cozy, avuncular camouflage for the corporate machinery that had placed him in office, thanking them by returning their tax monies and justifying it with a weird, later discredited, economic theory called "supply side economics." Reagan-era media concentrated on discrediting the recent political turmoil, condemning social activists as self-indulgent romantics and spreading the message that selflessness had been a failure and that material acquisition was a social good. Promoted by naked appeals to self-interest, the stock market rose to unparalleled heights, fueled by the tax monies extracted from the fiscal commons and returned to investors who dedicated them to personal speculation rather than rebuilding the nation's aging industrial sector. The lure of instant riches reoriented the majority of a decade's imagination towards personal gain. Social protest virtually disappeared, and "blink" . . . the sixties were over.

There is a synchronicity between the oil crisis and the tragedy of September 11th. Both events offered the authorities a *two-fer*—an objective situation requiring a political response, while simultaneously providing an opportunity to camouflage a political agenda that could never have passed public scrutiny without the hysteria of a crisis. This last point seems worth noting because it illustrates the manner in which political responses are often simplified and less appropriately complex than artistic ones. For that reason it's useful to compare some differences between the two.

Whether or not our response to the 9/11 terrorist attacks should have been orchestrated by the United States or the United Nations is debatable, but while I disagree with the Bush administration's position, I cannot fault them for not addressing the problem. However, the two-fer principle is also operative here. Administration proposals to retroactively return fifteen years of income taxes to the nation's largest corporations is an opportunistic fraud orchestrated under the cover of a national tragedy. Adding insult to injury, such legislation also exempts corporations from alternative minimum taxes, transferring that burden to individual taxpayers. This is the same order of thought that argues that giving your food to the neighbor's pit bulls will insure that your children get to live in a community of robust animals.

More of the nation's resources are being dedicated to weaponry and conventional weapons systems today than at any time since the Reagan years, and there appears to be little chance that the situation will improve now that we are on a continual war footing against yet-to-be-declared enemies in yet-to-be-declared countries.

These examples of simplistic political responses lead directly to the subject of the political class, the group least intimate with the creative process and most ignorant of interdependence and the innate generosity of the universe. A few random reminders of who is representing may clarify my position. The political class *twice* buried airline safety proposals recommended by congressional hearings, proposals that could have protected us against the September 11th attacks. The first was after Pan Am 103 was blown out of the sky by a bomb in 1988, killing 259 people; the second after TWA flight 800 exploded in 1996, killing 229. Magically, months of investigation, millions of tax dollars, and the recommendations themselves all disappeared as certainly as the airliners themselves, leaving no trace of censure or blame for the representatives who stage-managed this sleight of hand.

During the most prosperous decade in our nation's history, this same political class liberated forty *million* working poor people from the supposed indignity of paying for food with food-stamps with virtually no debate examining an economy where workers could be legally compensated with wages too meager to buy food! The same folks stifled *all* debate on a single-payer health plan used by many of our European allies and 12–15 percent cheaper than the current system, thereby fattening the bottom line of insurance companies.

They have determined that we the people agree to execute the mentally handicapped and that the "American life-style" is not up for review no matter how egregious its environmental consequences may be. The Democratic "opposition" has totally ceded the declaration of global war and the creation of an expanded National Security State to the president because they are afraid of his popularity and their corporate masters are getting rich off the war anyway.

These critiques of our political leadership are germane to my subject of generosity and the arts in several ways. Besides highlighting the one-sided and rudimentary nature of most political responses, they require at least posing if not answering the question, "What damage does such mean-spirited selfishness do to the individual and national spirit?" Interdependence implies that we cannot shelter ourselves from the implications and repurcussions of horrors perpetuated in our name.

Secondly, we must ask, what *physical* harm is being done to us, to our heirs, to others, and to our common environment by those who simulate concern for us while actually serving the interests of a corporate sector whose interests are inimical to those of the average citizen? If, for example, the seventy-seven senators who took money from Enron recuse themselves from the investigation, who will defend the tens of thousands of ruined employees and investors? Who but the Senate and House passed the laws making such a debacle possible, only a decade after the multibillion dollar collapse of the savings-and-loan industry and only shortly before the collapse of today's mortgage markets and hedge funds, which used shoddy properties as collateral.

Professional political behavior stems from one-sided, self-interested thinking. It is the common predilection of artists, however, to perceive "in the round" and interdependently. They are an available antidote to the fearful, one-sided thinking dominating public discourse today. Ralph Nader made a valiant try to impact this conversation and succeeded to a degree, but never approached the cultural effect of a Bob Dylan or Bruce Springsteen. This was not because he was not charismatic, but because the nature of the analysis he employed was essentially one-sided and linear thought, which is never complex and contradictory enough to express a true picture of events. He happens to express a point of view I agree with, but still it embraces only one half of a contradiction, instead of marrying both in a new, higher level of organization. What might "coming forward" with the mind of an artist contribute to the current malaise, I wonder?

Here's a clue. My wife told a friend, a sculptress, that I was coming to speak here tonight, and the friend commented on the number of homeless people she had recently seen surrounding the CCAC campus. Then she said, "Now *there's* an idea for an art installation—a soup kitchen!" Regardless of one's political persuasion, it is the nature of the creative process to perceive foreground and background simultaneously. As such, my friend could not choose *not* to see the homeless simply by switching her focus and imitating the mode of perception the average politician employs hourly to survive.

The self-serving conceit of the political class is that the public cannot follow the intricacy of the problems they deal with, and sometimes they may be right. Listening to even ten minutes of AM talk radio will deliver a shocking insight into the extent of bigotry, resentment, and rage coursing through public consciousness. Having admitted that, however, my rage is still expressly reserved for the political class, *because they have the information to know better.* They understand the ramifications of legislation that protect accountants and CEOs from being liable for improper decisions. (Watch this one resurface during the Enron investigations. It was passed during the Contract with America.) The politicians understand what deregulation of the banking and electricity markets implies, or that tax refunds are a back-handed way of limiting the government's ability to protect and serve the public. They are paid to consider these issues in the public interest and have access and reach that ordinary citizens do not.

Despite the omnipresence of vitriolic radio, my deep instinct remains that, on some level, the people, regardless of political persuasion, even the angry and bewildered, know that their interests are not being represented by Washington. They are deprived of a voice by the corporate media and in dire need of allies who can express their intuitions and speak plainly and pungently on their behalf. I believe that the times require artists to speak for those voiceless citizens, and by so doing restore a vital social balance.

The question for each of us here today is: To what purposes shall we raise our voices, unlimber our bodies, sharpen our pencils, and mix our colors? Will we choose the route of a personal salvation, seeking refuge in the fiction that we exist independently, or will we honor the mutually supportive processes of our own creativity by becoming expressions of generosity and interdependence? Some always have, and there are examples of good works available, but they are isolated instances that are not capable of rectifying the enormity of the problems before us today.

Troubled times offer all of us unparalleled opportunities for significance. I anticipate, with whatever optimism I can still muster, the responses of creative minds to the current maelstrom of our historical moment. Having declared that, it's time for me to abandon the rostrum and climb down into the mouth of the cannon along side the old Jewish acrobat. There's room in there for all who would join us in offering themselves to the present, and it certainly seems we're overdue to start the show. There is always risk. Even at this moment of commitment, while the fuse of the cannon is being lit and I am shoulder to shoulder with the old acrobat, I know that we are still mutually dependent on others. Consequently, in closing, I have to hope that the assistants who prepared the cannon have aimed it at the trampoline and not the wall. But that is where trust enters the picture.

FOUR PROJECTS

Jörgen Svensson

In this text I intend to discuss the term *generosity,* principally in relation to four of my projects, which characterize my overall work and also seem suitable in this context. I would like to start by saying that I find the concept of "generosity" problematic in that it assumes a hierarchical structure between a giver and a recipient. I think there are very few artists interested in such a structure, especially if they are working in a social context. In my opinion, the title of the symposium out of which this book grew, "Generosity Projects," aims at generally defining a phenomenon noticeable in contemporary art practice in the past ten to twelve years, namely, art projects that in a variety of ways contain an actual offer. To avoid potential misconception of this title, I have chosen to use quotation marks for the word "generosity."

I am, of course, discussing the material from a Scandinavian perspective. I am pointing this out since "Generosity Projects" might be said to embody a phenomenon of an international character, which does not fully take into account national and local differences. What I mean is that this type of art (social sculpture) is formed by a social context in a higher degree than most other art expressions and that the social context, in its turn, is the result of politics, economy, history, and so forth, factors creating great differences internationally, nationally, and locally. Most of my projects would probably have been impossible to carry out in the United States, as well as in several other countries.

In 1989 I graduated from the Valand Art Academy, which is part of the University of Gothenburg and one of five fine arts schools at university level in Sweden. During my five years there, I worked mainly with painting, and I considered myself a painter. By the time of my graduation exhibition, however, I had also started working with photography. I perceived my education at the Art Academy as very isolated. There were artists discussing art, art critics discussing art, art historians discussing art, and art scholars discussing art. The isolation of this education became even more evident when I graduated and entered a society where I needed both to work and to make a living as an artist. Through friends in other professions I became acquainted with other areas of society. In this context, I would like to point out that I completed a degree in sociology before entering art school. Thus, I already had a profound interest in society. Another very important aspect was the fact I had a very hard time identifying myself with the more traditional artist's role. I found myself wanting a social context for my work. I realized that in order to work as an artist, I would have to create a role that would also fulfill other important needs in my life.

The economic situation was another factor that influenced my direction. I graduated just before the recession of the early nineties hit, totally changing the flourishing economy that had characterized the art scene since the early eighties. By the time I was ready to exhibit my work, there were hardly any galleries left. They had disappeared due to the economic downturn. The surviving galleries concentrated on exhibiting established and traditional painters. Hence, very few galleries were interested in a recent graduate working with other expressions than pure painting. Public museums and art galleries seemed to operate in a similar fashion and were equally uninterested. Even their interest in art, considered narrow and unapproachable, decreased significantly with the budget cuts. A group of young artists realized that in order to work as artists and have their work be part of public discussions, they would need to find their own solutions and create new arenas for their art. Their thinking coincided with my own ideas, which I had started to formulate for completely other reasons.

Many critics and art historians, in their analysis of the art that can be placed within the frame of social sculptures, have seen this art more as a revolt against and a discontentment with institutional art. This analysis may be right for certain artists but not for all and absolutely not for me. I never looked upon it that way. I consider the gallery space to be a fantastic opportunity. To be able to enter a room for art directly off the street is truly a phenomenon, which is also true for all the beautiful spaces for art in museums and galleries. The change that took place was the realization that art could be so much more than it had been to date. Art can work in many contexts, and different artistic concepts require different spaces. I am also convinced that art created outside traditional institutions can influence them in a positive way. In many respects these institutions have also constituted an important counterpart to art created outside their framework.

The fact that I am lucky enough to live and work in a country that has a liberal policy towards financing the arts and culture has been another important factor in my development as an artist. The following is a good example of the cultural policy of that time. During the recession in the early nineties, the prime minister of our country declared that in difficult economic times it is more important than ever to support culture and the arts. Due to the fact that a number of commercial galleries disappeared and artists began to focus on project work, some state art funds reevaluated how their assets were spent, and more money was allotted to project-based art initiatives. In response, the government allotted more money to these funds. As a result of these initiatives, an increasing number of artists were able to realize their projects. At around the same time, the government created yet another fund to finance several large art projects, managed by artists working outside the confines of traditional institutions during the past few years. From an international perspective, the economic circumstances for Swedish artists have, without a doubt, been exceptional, favorably influencing both the number of projects and their content.

While describing the factors that have shaped the direction of my work, I would like to mention another that is as important when we discuss projects based around the concept of generosity. I firmly believe that what took place in the eighties and the discussion created by postmodernism are of major importance. The word *generosity* is rich in meanings that interest me, such as indulgence, forgiveness, tolerance—all concepts (with the exception of charity) that I connected with the situation and discussion that postmodernism created. This discussion had also bad effects, as, for instance, an absurd theoretical bias.

One may criticize a lot of what took place during the time, but for me personally, as a young artist educated in the modern tradition, it was immensely liberating to feel that everything was possible and allowed. I didn't have to be in opposition to anything, nor did I have to be angry. This feeling of openness was in itself generosity on a large scale. In this I found possibilities for a different artistic role, one with room for increased participation and one that would make me feel less of an outsider. I recommend that you keep this description of the political and economic climate in Sweden and the factors that influenced my direction as an artist in mind, as I move on to describe four of my projects.

Bus 993

In September 1993, a couple of artists living and working in Stockholm, the capital of Sweden, initiated an art project called *The Rules of the Game*. The number of invited artists equaled the number of balls in a billiard game. Every artist was asked to choose a number, which corresponded to one on the billiard balls. The balls were broken on a billiard table. After the break, the balls were placed on a city map of Stockholm. The position of the balls on the map determined the location where each artist would create his or her project. Thus the most important parameter for this project—the place—was determined by chance.

My billiard ball stopped next to a busy avenue in the city center. On this location were a couple of bus stops for local buses. There was also a statue of a famous Swedish poet who came from the same province as I do. The location also had another connection to my life and myself. I live and work in Gothenburg, which is a city on the Swedish west coast. The largest newspaper in the city is the *Gothenburg Post*, which happened to have its Stockholm office right where my billiard ball had stopped.

These three components—the bus stops, the statue, and the newspaper office—made me think about a journey, my own geographical journey. I had once left the same province as the poet. He moved to Stockholm, I moved to Gothenburg, which was also represented at this location in Stockholm where we now had all united.

Quite a few factors influenced the design of my project. One of the most important concerned the intention of *The Rules of the Game*, namely to comment on the big city. An effective way to comment on something would be to place it in relation to its opposite, I thought. Pondering this and a few other ideas eventually led me to the conclusion that I wanted to create my own bus line between my allotted location in Stockholm and a small community nearby. The little paper-mill community of Skoghall, which happens to be the place where I was born and raised, came to represent that small community.

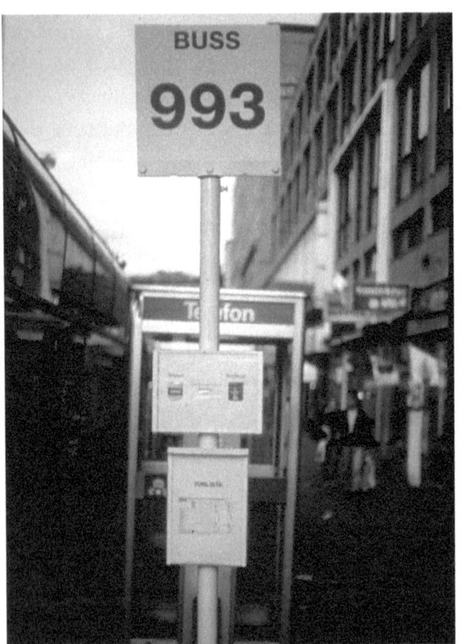

Jörgen Svensson *Bus 993* 1993

It was my intention to offer people the opportunity to travel to Stockholm, especially those people who, for whatever reason, had hardly ever traveled to or visited Stockholm previously. During the project, a total of approximately four hundred people traveled on the bus, which was called "993" and was completely free of charge. Travelers from Skoghall had a six-hour stay in Stockholm, to be spent any way they liked. Travelers from Stockholm, on the other hand, got a week's stay in Skoghall, since the bus only shuttled back and forth once a week.

In order to publicize the bus line, I placed ads in the local papers. I had scheduled office hours between eight and ten every morning so that people could call and book a seat. But in order to avoid giving away all the seats to the more proactive prospective travelers, I contacted the unions at the paper mill and asked them to inquire whether any of their unemployed or disabled workers would like to travel to Stockholm. The ministers in a small community also usually have a good knowledge of parishioners in need, and of those who might benefit from getting away from the everyday grind. Hence, I asked the ministers to help, and after a few days they produced a list of people who were interested. With such methods, a diverse crowd of people came together and traveled once a week, over a five-week period, between Skoghall and Stockholm.

There were variations both in age and in social status. And they sat together on the bus for nearly eight hours.

Since this was the first project of its kind in Sweden, discussions naturally arose about whether this project could be considered art or not. However, for me as an artist it was a milestone. I had never before, in any of the exhibitions I had participated in at museums or galleries, experienced so many interesting levels, touched so many people in so many different ways, and got officials to act upon the same idea. It was bewildering and very inspiring. Then there were the letters and postcards I received on an almost daily basis. For example, there was the family with six children who wrote to thank me for the bus ride, which had enabled them to go on an outing for the first time in many years. In the pile of letters there was also one from a grandfather, who thanked the bus project for making it possible for him to show Stockholm to his grandchildren.

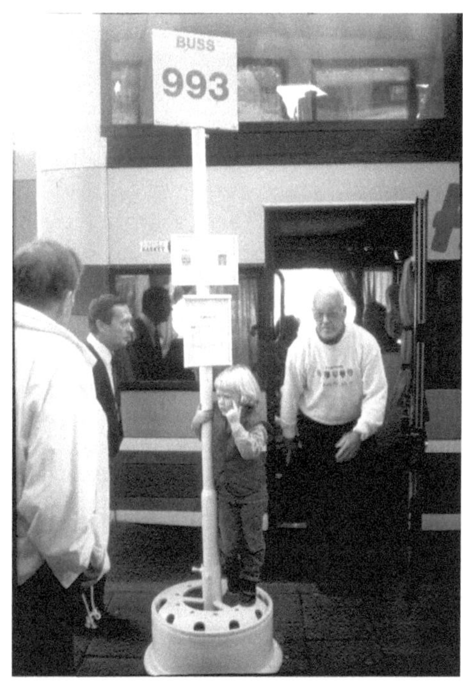

Jörgen Svensson *Bus 993* 1993

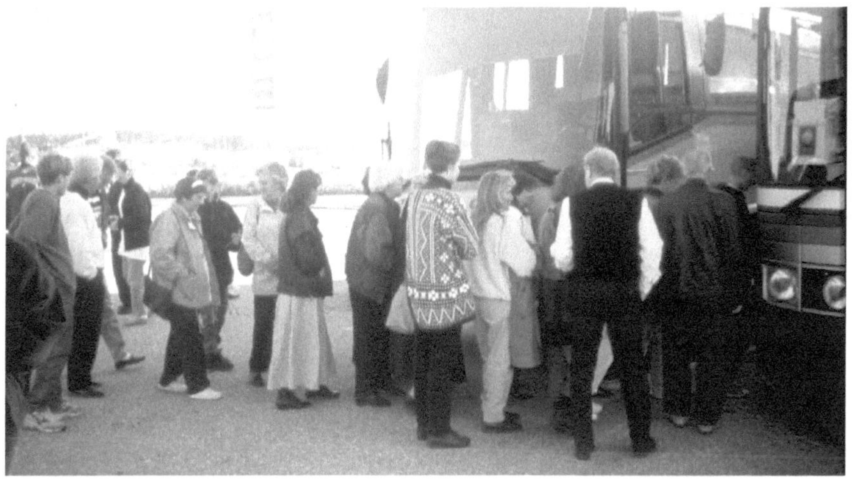

Jörgen Svensson *Bus 993* 1993

There were also the two teenage girls who traveled without their parents for the first time.

The time of the first bus departure remains one of my most vivid memories of *Bus 993*. It's early morning, just around sunrise, when the bus driver and I turn onto the main street of the little community. There they are, lining both sides of the street, people of all ages, dressed in their best clothes. They are quiet, but one can sense that they are full of anticipation. The tension in air is probably due to the fact that several people are still unsure what it is all about, and if they really will arrive in Stockholm.

F.ART

In 1994 a Swedish curator collaborated with a restaurateur in Stockholm on a project called *F.ART* (well aware of the English connotation of the word). It took the form of inviting one artist, one evening a week, to the restaurant and asking them to intervene. One artist made changes to the menu, another to the interior, a third staged a performance. At the time that I was asked to participate, Sweden had recently held elections and a new government had been formed. Technically, the formation of a government is called a "government installation" in Sweden. As most people are aware, there is also the concept of installation art. I told the curator that I intended to make a government installation. Subsequently, I was busy lobbying and convincing the prime min-

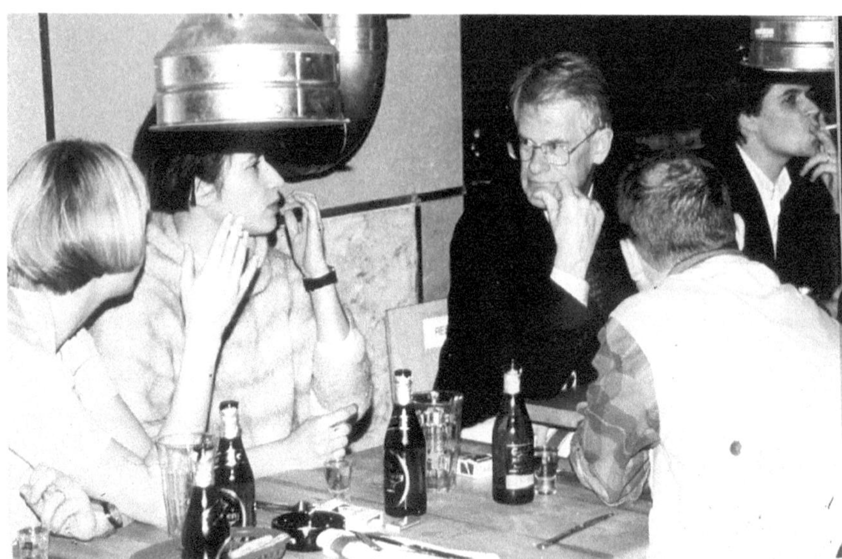

Jörgen Svensson *Government Dinner* 1994

ister and his cabinet to participate. After a couple of weeks, we were informed that there was a possibility the prime minister and some of the other ministers would participate. They even let us know what date and evening would work for them. We adjusted our schedule to theirs and arranged a government installation at the restaurant. Two days prior to the event, security police went through the whole building in which the restaurant was located. They even rented an apartment across the street, where they could observe who entered the restaurant. There were two plainclothes bodyguards in the restaurant. The tables were not reserved; anyone could come to the restaurant and have dinner with the government. The dinner was even subsidized. A threecourse dinner, including coffee and brandy, was offered at the equivalent price of four dollars. According to my arrangement, one minister was placed at each table. After each course, they would have to change tables, in order to avoid the same minister talking to the same people all evening.

Of course, the media showed huge interest in the event. However, I refused all inquiries from journalists and tried to keep the event a secret as long as possible. There were several reasons for this strategy. At that phase in my career, I was not quite sure how the media really worked, and with all the interest in the government dinner, I was afraid I wouldn't be able to handle the situation. It was important to me that the event would not turn into a stunt. I also wanted it to be possible for "ordinary people" to come to the restaurant. Their chances would definitely decrease if the event received too much media attention.

The discussion that followed *Government Dinner* was mostly about how I managed to get the government to participate in this art project. People seemed more interested in celebrity issues than in asking interesting questions about the relationship between artists and politicians, or what the dinner meant from an artistic perspective. This really surprised me, since it seemed that there was, after all, a very marked boundary between politicians and artists. They inhabited two separate worlds that, according to many, should not mix if art was to avoid being tainted and losing its value.

Later, when I worked as an advisor for the Swedish Minister for Culture, an assignment I also turned into an art project, I experienced these opinions even stronger. At the time, I thought, as I still do today, that such a view of the arts is completely outdated. I was surprised how strongly the romantic ideal about artists was still held in Sweden. Many held the view that an artist should not get involved with or be too close to the establishment or circles of power, but should instead stay out on the fringes of society. They meant that the risk of being "corrupted" was too big. It is this view of art that I mean is outdated. The risk of being corrupted is present in all contexts/situations, and it's therefore up to every individual artist to be aware of what situations/relations/contexts can influence his or her artisanship. In relation to the discussion of the extended concept of art, the "outsider position" is impossible, and not least when it comes to expressions of art such as "social sculpture" or art where the artist is an instigator in relation to the art that integrates into the environment. It's impossible to participate and stand outside at the same time.

Four Lectures

Six months later, I was asked to participate in another project. A curator had opened up his home, where he lived with his wife and three children, to artists who wanted to mount an exhibition or devise a project. The experiences of *Government Dinner* and the subsequent discussions around celebrity issues, together with the fact that I still had not completed my work with the politicians, made me come up with a proposal for a project I called *Four Lectures*.

I sent out a simple mailing, informing people that there would be four lectures held in the apartment, one every Saturday. In the mailing, one could, among other things, read the following:

> Saturday, February 18, 2pm
> DAMIEN HIRST
> Art process? Life process
>
> Saturday, February 25, 2pm
> CINDY SHERMAN
> What's the meaning of results?
>
> Saturday, March 4, 2pm
> BILL WOODROW
> Awareness of the expression in the material
>
> Saturday, March 11, 2pm
> MIKE KELLEY
> Art, art, art, bloody art

The content of the mailed piece was deliberately vaguely formulated. It was nowhere stated that the artists mentioned would actually attend. Hence, one had no idea if these artists would give a lecture, or if the lectures would be about them. The outcome, however, was that many people thought that Mike Kelley, Cindy Sherman, and the others would come to the little apartment in Gothenburg. If I was able to get the Swedish government to come to a restaurant and participate in an art project, people were convinced that I would be able to arrange for Cindy, Mike, and the other artists to come to Gothenburg. Hence, an earlier event had created so much confidence in me that even my fellow artist friends thought it was for real. I was at the time also working as an advisor to the Swedish Minister for Culture (a dinner invitation

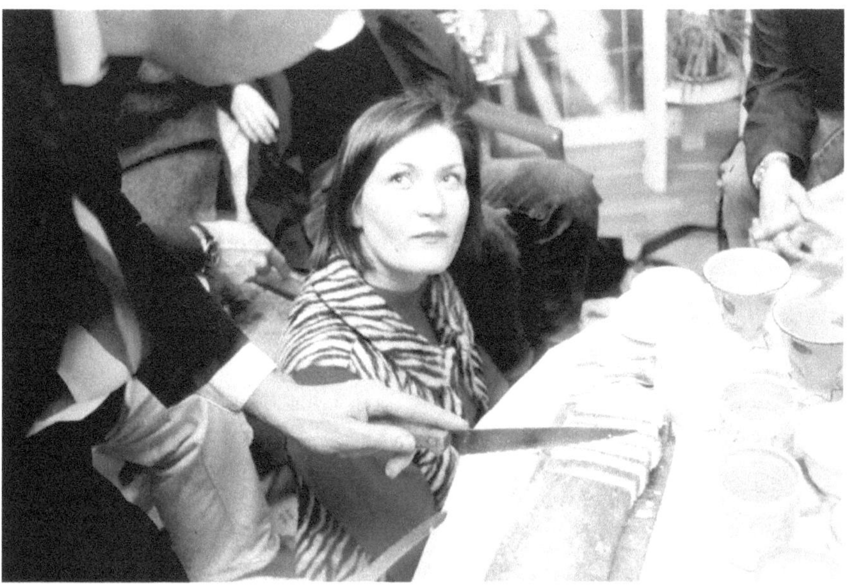

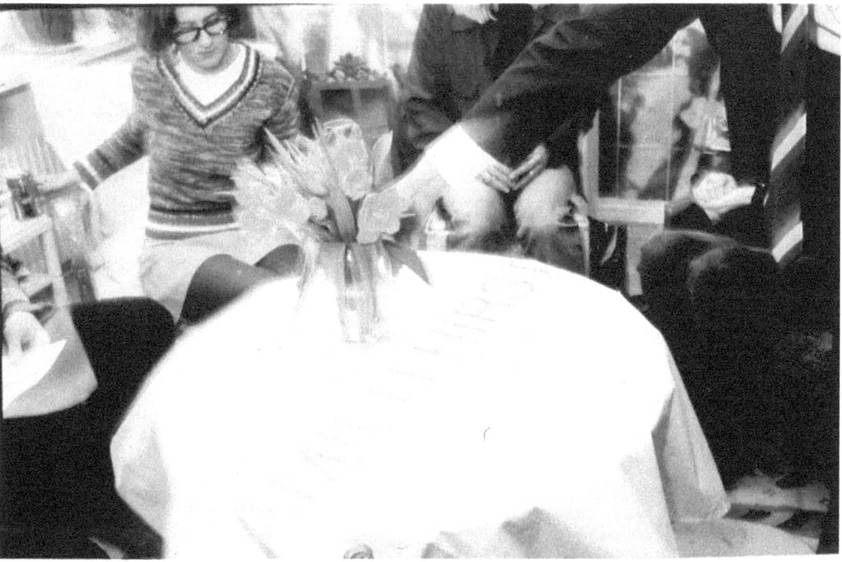

Jörgen Svensson *Four Lectures (Damien Hirst)* 1995

can lead to a lot!), which of course strengthened the trust in my being able to attract such artists. For example, it was thought I had received generous funding from the Ministry of Culture for this purpose.

The rumor of Cindy's, Bill's, Damien's, and Mike's eminent arrival in Gothenburg spread quickly. Journalists called, curators called, everyone wanted to meet the artists and interview them. I went underground and was unavailable. In my stead, the curator who owned the apartment took care of all external contacts. People were desperate to have an opportunity to meet the international art celebrities. At this point, I will not tell you the whole story about the project. I have only chosen the first two lectures, which concerned Damien Hirst and Cindy Sherman.

The Damien Hirst lecture was the first event and, of course, expectations were enormous. The line outside the apartment was long. I arrived fifteen minutes late. Later I was told that people in line had thought I might have been late due to traffic on the way back from the airport where I had, of course, been picking up Damien Hirst. I walked by the line that stretched all the way from the courtyard, up the stairwell, and into the apartment on the third floor. It was totally quiet. No one said a word. When I arrived in the apartment, I told the assembled that Damien Hirst had sent me a fax that morning excusing himself from coming to Gothenburg, due to personal reasons, but also, that he had faxed the script he had intended to read, asking me to read in his stead. The script, which I had written, was a text starting out with art theory but slowly going on to something resembling a cake recipe. Measure a cup of understanding, three tablespoons of love, half a cup of understanding, and so on. It then turned into a real cake recipe and I went into the kitchen and baked the cake. Oddly enough, people stayed in the apartment. Either they were in shock or possibly unable to act out of pure disappointment. I set a table with a tablecloth on which Damien Hirst's name had been embroidered and we shared the cake. It all ended in a very good discussion. We discussed the art scene, our views on artists as megastars, on a level with rock stars, but also our ability to handle disappointment. Some people were very upset; a few teachers and students from the Department of Art Theory at the University of Gothenburg felt especially cheated. Anyway, I had designed this Hirst lecture wholly with the help of the Bible. Everyone is waiting for the mighty god, who does not come, but sends his messenger instead. A lot of people are not pleased by this message. There was also strong biblical symbolism in the tablecloth/shroud and the shared cake/bread.

The following Saturday was not as crowded, for obvious reasons, but attendance was still unexpectedly high. I am told that people were under the impression that the lectures might have been planned on a Russian roulette principle, with one lecture being the real thing. No one wanted to miss it. Many who attended out of pure curiosity were interested to see how I would solve the assignment this time.

The following happened: I had already installed a speakerphone in the apartment. Right before the lecture, when everyone was gathered in the apartment, I called to say that I was at the airport waiting for Cindy Sherman, but she was not on the flight. I also mentioned that I just passed the café and had happened to see someone who looked like Cindy. This person was in fact the minister for culture (who does actually look a little like Cindy). I asked her if she would consider being Cindy's stand-in and she said "yes." So there we were in a room at the airport, planning to have a phone conference with those gathered in the apartment.

Most of this was true. I was in fact sitting in a room with the minister for culture, but far from the airport, in a totally different part of Sweden. When people in the apartment realized they had been given an opportunity to speak freely to the minister for culture, a discussion started and continued for almost two hours. Many topics were covered: the relationship between art and politics, politicians' incompetence when it comes to art issues, the economic situation of artists, and so on. I think everyone in the apartment realized that in being offered direct contact with the country's minister for culture, they were participating in a unique event.

Public Safety/Two American Policemen

In the summer of 2000 I returned to the little paper mill community of Skoghall with three other artists, each of us with a site-specific project in mind. The other artists were Alfredo Jaar from New York, Esther Shalev-Gerz from Paris, and Paco Cao, originally from Madrid, Spain, but now living and working mainly in New York. The name of the project was *Public Safety* and it touched upon many issues simultaneously. For a long time I had wanted to work with a whole community and Skoghall was perfect for this purpose. It had a full range of public institutions: church, police department, fire department, community hall, ball park, and so on, all located within a small radius and easy to oversee. I also had all the necessary local contacts to make this project happen. In this case, I do not want to describe the project in its entirety, but rather to focus on a few things that I find relevant in this context. I would like to mention though, that the project as a whole took three years to plan and execute. Within the framework of the project, an art conference with international speakers was arranged in Skoghall as well. A documentary was also filmed and a book documenting the event is currently being written.

For my project I brought two policemen from Phoenix to Skoghall. Neither of them had ever left the United States before, but for ten days they patrolled the town in their uniforms. Sweden is one of the most Americanized countries in Europe, and American cops are well known to the Swedish people, especially from movies and from other media, but more as fictitious characters than as real people. Hence, my idea of wanting to relocate these well known,

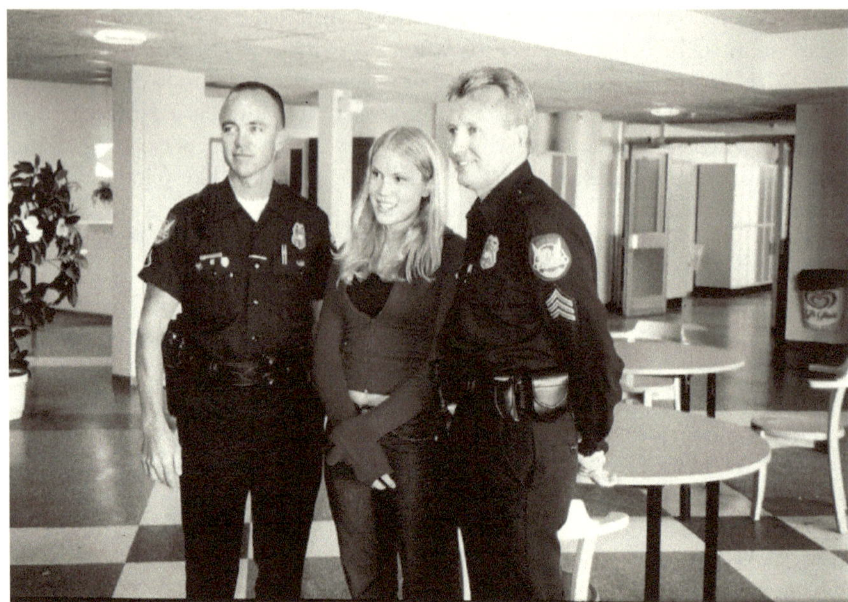

Jörgen Svensson *PUBLIC SAFETY* 2000

clearly American symbols in the little community and making them real to the residents in their own environment. In the movies, actors play the cops. In Skoghall the real cops took the role of the actors, since they were not legally allowed to fulfill their duties as policemen in Sweden. It all turned out the way I had imagined, but worse. The American cops were looked upon as movie stars. They were asked to sign autographs and to participate in radio and television shows, and the newspapers carried long articles discussing their activities on an almost daily basis. Schools called me and asked me to bring the cops over, since they couldn't get anything productive done: the students just talked about the American cops. What took place was both fascinating and scary.

Two other projects, created by Alfredo Jaar and Paco Cao, might illustrate the concept of generosity a little more clearly. Alfredo Jaar had a large exhibition hall, constructed of wood and paper, erected in the middle of the town square.

The paper came from the local paper mill, which Skoghall is built around. The exhibition hall was open for twenty-four hours and showed a group exhibition with fifteen young Swedish artists. When the exhibition closed, the structure and its contents were set alight and burned to the ground. Alfredo wanted to offer the residents of Skoghall the experience of having a community exhibition hall. Through the gift of the exhibition hall, with all the effort it took to build, and at the same time by its destruction, he hoped to create a deeper sense of loss, so that people would realize how much they missed art and culture in their everyday lives. The discussions around Alfredo's project very soon polarized into two sides. One group thought it was crazy to burn such wonderful wood; it could have been used for a more reasonable purpose. The other group was of the opinion that the exhibition hall should have remained there as a permanent art venue.

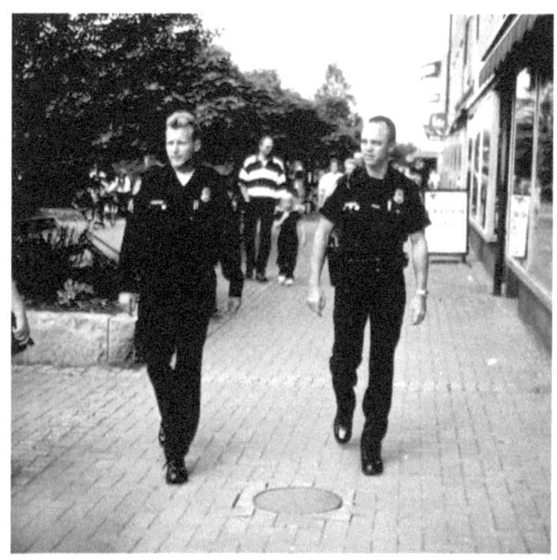

Jörgen Svensson *PUBLIC SAFETY* 2000

Paco Cao deposited his body as a work of art to a Spanish museum sometime in the mid-nineties. In order for Paco Cao to be part of the *Public Safety* project, the council in Skoghall had to write a letter requesting to borrow him. Paco's idea was to be transported from Spain to Skoghall as a work of art, that is, without a passport. This entailed huge difficulties and many very funny incidents, especially with the passport authorities. When Paco Cao arrived in Skoghall, he offered the residents the opportunity to borrow him. Whoever was interested had to sign a contract, promising to keep him protected from rain and cold and also to refrain from harming him in any way. Several residents took up his invitation.

Public Safety turned out to have significant influence on the little community. After the project was finished, the public architect drafted a new plan for the community, which was totally inspired by the project. The residents also chose Alfredo's exhibition hall to be the most beautiful building in the community and submitted it to an architectural contest. Recently the mayor of the community stepped down after twelve years in office. A journalist asked him, what he considered most important and memorable during those years. He answered, "*Public Safety*."

The media have been immensely important to me. With the help of newspapers, television, and radio, I have been able to create the imaginary space I have needed to put my projects into a context. I was initially very reserved, but perhaps also a little afraid of the consequences of using the media as tools in my projects. There were two reasons for this fear. On the one hand, the traditional artist's role versus the outsider's, on the other, the fear of losing control. Many of my projects could easily have turned into spectacular stunts. There would have been a huge risk of the projects being dismissed as stunts had I not considered the media useful tools. Since I carefully monitored the information given to the media, I controlled the interpretation of my projects. Instead of being a threat, the media became collaborators, helping with the effort to disseminate information about the projects.

In my experience, the kind of art projects that I have described here, and that could be considered "social sculptures," are better realized outside the traditional framework of galleries and museums. When meeting with an audience that is unaware of the established codes, the more direct and intimate communication that this kind of work requires is generated.

In conclusion, I would like to add a few words concerning the "generous" aspects of this kind of project. If one looks upon it from an international point of view, the broader phenomenon is really about food, people meeting each other, and an opportunity for increased communication. These are all very basic and fundamental needs in human life. Perhaps the fact that projects like these are emerging indicates a recognition of the importance of these basic needs in our society and current time. If this is the case, these kinds of projects carry an important message by both identifying these needs and, sometimes, even fulfilling them.

RECIPROCAL GENEROSITY

Mary Jane Jacob

This word—*generosity*—that is taking different shapes throughout this publication and seeking a form in recent art practice, has simultaneously well-intentioned and problematic connotations: positioned on two sides of a moral equation, each seemingly dependent on a uneven power relationship between parties. Inserting the question "for whom is the generous act intended?" can raise disturbing implications of beneficence along a route from haves to have-nots. Does this need to be so?

To give and to help; to provoke, catalyze, and enable; to be of service, to be responsible, to better and to improve, to contribute to betterment; to give food . . . to give "voice." In the social contract that is the art experience, the audience member, or viewer, is a recipient of what the artist makes: the artist gives, the audience receives. Exactly how generous the artist is, is determined by the usevalue of the thing received: Can I eat it, wear it, trade it, collect it? Does it give me a platform or exposure for my cause, further my way of life or that of those in my community?

I am moved to think about the personal, unspoken, unseen, uncountable and unknowable, latent, or even unrealized benefits offered by art. This demands trusting in the processes that art objects, installations, and actions set in motion, and recognizing the timeframe that an art experience can occupy. An effect that can be launched with as little as one work of art, one moment, can span as much as a lifetime. When museum director J. Carter Brown reflected on his mentor Bernard Berenson, he located this quality of art in the idea of "living life as a work of art." According to Brown, the elder art historian "found, at the end of his life, that his great experiences came in his daily walk, which he did at the end of the day up behind *I Tatti*, where, he said, the fruits of a lifetime of looking at art objects allowed him to look at nature in a newly meaningful way."[1] Was Berenson experiencing the essential generosity of art, a generosity that does not have as its product a gift, or thing given, but rather exists as art's intrinsic goal of giving meaning to life?

By contrast, generous art as a free commodity became commonplace in museums and public spaces in the 1990s, being catapulted into mainstream art consciousness by Felix Gonzalez-Torres's candy piles and poster stacks and Rirkrit Tiravanija's food-events. Other artists of a more social reform variety provided ideas, solutions, and structures for change. This is seen in, say, Iñigo Manglano-Ovalle's *Tele-Vecindario: Street-Level Video* (1993), a program of youth training in technical and critical skills and outdoor media installation, or Christine Hill's 1997 *Volksboutique* installation-cum-used-clothing-store. Both projects also provided forums for discussion and social exchange. Indebted to the 1970s democracy-in-art movements that led to free or cheap artists' books, mail art, performance-exchanges, and other give-aways, as well as politically motivated practices manifested as performative social actions, these works are a new generation of engagement and, here, fall within the realm of generous art.

The full breadth of this art-as-offering—from a meal to a skill—is perhaps most succinctly foreshadowed in the catalytic and generous art of Gordon Matta-Clark. Not only was Matta-Clark key in the pioneering of the SoHo district of New York with the collaborative restaurant/art project *Food* (1971), but he also designed a scheme of social purpose with *A Resource Center and Environmental Youth Program for Loisaida* (1977). Initiated at the end of his short life and never fully realized, it was to have been a recycling facility where local residents could receive cash for certain materials, or acquire used goods at modest prices. The local youths maintaining it would have acquired practical vocational skills and a critical ecological consciousness in return for their labor.

For me, it is easier to see the good side of generous art in social examples. I admire artistic routes that are two-way streets. At times I wonder what motivates other artists and what they get from the generous processes they initiate. Personally, in knee-jerk fashion, I am halted from disregarding a "generous" artwork as just another gimmick when the thing given away gains importance by being useful to someone in need. Why feed another art group and call it art? Yet I realize that I have used the same method myself in several projects. Still, for me, the aims of the work distinguish the practice and are at the conceptual core of works I produce, though I may not recognize them clearly in the intentions of others.

So when Suzanne Lacy staged *Dinner at Jane's* in 1993 as part of her project *Full Circle* for the experimental public art program "Culture in Action,"[2] it was not to offer food, but to create both a metaphoric image and a conducive mode for exchange. This gathering of fourteen female world leaders whose service to their communities parallels the global import of the work of Jane Addams and her circle met in the very room where their turn-of-the-century cohorts met to share a meal and reshape society.[3] When the Italian team of Federica Thiene and Stefania Mantovani organized *Chow for "Conversations on Culture,"* they crafted menus and sites for a two-week series of dinners according to the evening's theme. The inspiring settings played a fundamental role in these discussions on art and social subjects, designed in collaboration with Michael Brenson as a major discursive thread. They were also one of a series of international artists' projects comprising "Conversations at The Castle," which I curated for the Arts Festival of Atlanta as a counterpoint to the 1996 Olympics.[4]

While artists in this publication have spoken about their work and practice, my understanding of "generosity" centers around examples of artworks brought about through my curatorial practice. Motivating my engagement with this concept is a critique of the arts institution's relationship to its audience. My interest arises from the class implications of the prevailing concept of the "art audience" that is so embedded in our professional practice. Museums by mandate and mission operate from a position of power (called variously "knowledge," "tradition," "authority," or "prestige"). Charged with giving, the receiver—their audiences—is seen as being in need, lacking, or deficient. Museums offer enlightenment, education, experience, and entertainment.[5] Even as museums have claimed to open their doors to the masses, there is little expectation that among the offerings they will take seriously, and in a sustained way, the critical issues of contemporary art. A driving question for me, as I initially moved from the context of museum gallery to public site in 1990, was: How can artists be more generous and encourage an experience of their art that is more open, allowing "others" entry and equally appreciating their experiences? How can art be an exchange?

My critique is exercised through exhibition programs—as I like to call my work, since "exhibition" seems too confined to visual presentations, and does not encompass the active exchanges that I feel exhibitions can, and should, engender—in which artists are commissioned to undertake projects, and posit questions, around a place and a set of circumstances. A complex of core questions develops in the process. In the end they are embodied in the work and, at best, they emerge from the work with greater clarity as questions of public urgency. Thus, these works offer not only art experiences, but also new ways of thinking about audience. They seek to challenge the premises of the institutional mindset about "audience" in ways that can shift our perception of the public's relationship to contemporary art.

I am interested in developing a consciousness of a wider public as a *valid* audience for avant-garde and critical contemporary art and ideas. Testing the concept of audience, I have found it necessary to locate exhibition programs in meaningful local contexts outside museums. Removing as much as possible the institution as the "middle man," or mediator, of art has allowed me to decrease the distance between art and audience. Another basic strategy is identifying what the non-art-world, non-art-professional audience *knows*, hence what they bring to the art experience. Rather than subscribing to a deficiency model, I do not believe such audiences are lacking, that they are empty vessels that we need to fill with art history and art criticism information. In fact, in commissioning public projects, such audience members are always the initial resources that inform the work. At times they co-produce it. They offer ideas and bring issues to bear that give the works meaning. They reflect on the work after it is created and elaborate its interpretation as well as inspire further steps in the artist's work, in mine, and theirs with regard to the issues with which the work seeks to grapple. Thus, I believe we can learn from these audiences and, by listening to them, find out how they can contribute, and even at times surpass, our own narrative of the work of art.

While the artist, the artwork, the arts institution, or art vehicle has been nearly always cast in the role of bestowing, it is perhaps in these moments of exchange that the deepest sense of generosity exists. So is there another equation for art in which both artist and audience each give and receive, in equal—or unequal—parts? And, if so, don't we need to consider more fully the identities of the recipients of the art experience since they play an important role, too, in this process. Acknowledging, identifying, meeting the audience face-to-face, we begin to eliminate the barriers of distance, difference, and power, that anonymity otherwise allows.

Can generosity be a reciprocal practice? Can we reconsider the division between artist and audience? Chogyam Trungpa wrote: "The basic problem in artistic endeavor is the tendency to split the artist from the audience and then try to send a message from one to the other . . . No matter how well-intentioned or technically accomplished such approaches may be, they inevitably become clumsy and aggressive toward others and toward oneself . . . [I]n meditative art, the artist embodies the viewer as well as the creator of the works. Vision is not separate from operation . . . We give up aggression, both toward ourselves, that we have to make a special effort to impress people, and toward others, that we can put something over on them."[6]

In Chicago, for "Culture in Action," the collaborative group Haha extended their ranks to include others from inside and outside the art world, enlisting them to volunteer in the AIDS healthcare network, each participant engaged in the generous act of giving and receiving. Their operations were centered in a storefront installation, *Flood,* which was dominated by a hydroponics garden. *Flood* participants tended the garden, too, donating the regularly harvested, toxic-free produce to an AIDS hospice—a beneficial outcome of art. But the spirit and practice of this art project extended beyond to the youth and surrounding community, through education programs on safe sex and hydroponics, and to the *Flood* members themselves, who shared and aired, in weekly discussions, their experiences in a field which they had (at least temporarily) adopted and reflected upon social aid systems. Thus, generosity became the medium, or methodology, and the subject, or product, of this project. How can we be of service to others with food and with our time, and what do we, the giver, get in exchange as volunteers?

All the works in "Conversations at The Castle" were acts of generous conversation—an exchange between artists and audience. Visitors offered German artist Regina Frank, for example, a personal thought through email (still at that time a novel, foreign mode of communication) and in return she "gave" them a glass bead, sewing it within a kimono that was the focal point of the installation (its cloth made from the pulp of all the books dear to the artists in her lifetime) so that it became a cloak of communication. Senegalese artist Ery Camara and the Brazilian-Swiss team of Mauricio Dias and Walter Riedweg each took up residence locally and worked with community groups on collaboratively produced installations. Other works, like *Chow*, had less tangible results. The Irwin group traveled from Atlanta by RV to cities across the United States, facilitating exchanges between a Russian artist who joined them on board and American artists at each location. Irishman Maurice O'Connell divided his residency into two parts: six weeks of talking to social service workers, and lending an ear; and then six weeks at the exhibition headquarters, The Castle, ensconced in his own office for his created-for-the-occasion agency, "Brothers for Others," where visitors could come to chat.

Generosity exists in exchanges, like conversations, and within temporal experiences shared by a social or communal body, which are conceived as art, crafted by artists, though these generous acts might not look like art, or in fact be art but become art-like moments. In exhibition programs, I often find that art is the means of facilitating a dialogue or exchange in which all parties have something to contribute, and gain. Everyone is in possession of something valuable and it is critical to respect their knowledge, as we gain from it in order to ensure that it will not be exploited, coopted, or devalued, once offered. A mutual relationship to facilitate generosity has often, for me, taken the form of listening, speaking, and reflecting. The openness upon which these interactions depend—a generosity with the other—is possible only when trust has been developed by getting to know, one-to-one, what is of deepest concern to others and what they hold dear. So for "Evoking History," a multi-year curatorial project that I co-curated with Tumelo Mosaka for the Spoleto Festival USA in Charleston, South Carolina, the exhibition aspect is threaded together by "stakeholder forums." These are comprised of local persons from different walks of life who have a stake in the artists' objects because the issues they evoke matter to their lives. Perhaps most importantly, it is within the creation of open exchanges that an understanding of others can begin to be engendered and the potential for change can arise.

Discursive exchanges can even approach or be art themselves. By this I do not mean because they are couched in artful trappings (props and plates, settings and table settings) that look like art. I do, however, mean experience that embodies what art can do. This is revealed when New York critic and writer Michael Brenson, reflecting on a moment in the 2001 installment of "Evoking History," spoke of the "participatory audience" that we cultivated and included at the table:

> Their belief in art is probably connected to their sense of its ability to actually deal with or accommodate that history . . . So for them

> to keep struggling and imagining and re-imagining themselves and their worlds, there have to be ways in which they can continually work with that history and explore and expand it. Art can be indispensable here—particularly your way of working—because, within the complex textures of historical situations, it makes room for process. It encourages not holding onto one's history for dear life, but exposing as well as asserting it, letting one's responses and beliefs be engaged by others, and also testing it and stretching its limits so that it is possible to grow.

Then, in speaking of the meeting staged at the end of a passage through ideas and art, a weekend-long conversation between these local stakeholders and national visitors—in and about Charleston—Brenson asked me:

> Would you say that the discussion that took place over two or three hours on the porch at I'On last June was an art experience? . . . It was an experience, and it was made possible by art. We needed to pass through [the work of artists] Lonnie Graham, Neill Bogan, and Ping Chong. Their engagements with the amazing and often painful histories of Charleston, and by implication of the United States, created a ground or texture that allowed this opening up and this beginning of trust to happen. It didn't feel to me fundamentally different from a really important art experience. I don't know where I would draw the line and I'm not sure I would want to.[7]

So does this discussion qualify as generous art?

Another participant at that forum was former Charleston resident and playwright-poet-author Kendra Hamilton, who wrote six months later:

> So I never got to tell you how I felt. But that experience seems to have completely healed the wounds that I've been carrying around in my heart from growing up in that sick and seductive city since childhood. When I return to Charleston now, to visit my family or do research, it's without that dull ache that used to start throbbing as soon as the pine barrens gave way to the low marshy flats surrounding the city. That is a gift that you have given. And I only wish there were something I could do to repay you.

How do we locate the gifts that art—and the public programs and personal exchanges that surround it—can bring?

With so much to gain in the process, I have departed from the conventional curatorial model of presenter and arbiter of quality, trying to locate my practice in the task of articulator of art within visual and social terrains. In developing this position, I am inspired by cultural critic Lewis Hyde's metaphorical comparison of the artist to the legendary figure of the trickster, the boundary-crosser and "jointworker" who shifts the joints or workings of society.[8] "The possibility of playing with the joints of creation [is] the possibility of art," Hyde writes. Thus, the artist or trickster-artist "chang[es] the manner in which nature, community, and spirit are joined to one another," shifting patterns in relation to one another, dismantling the hierarchy, decentering it, and making evident the divisions or joints of society, keeping those lines or joints flexible, porous, and receptive to change, rearticulating them, and even bridging or translating differences. I like to extend this concept to the role of curator. For those of us who value the place of audience in art and in the practice of exhibitions, taking on this role has value. It evokes the possibility of change in the culture, so that through exhibitions it might be possible to shift ideas and work the joints of what art "is," who the audience are, and what their place is in art.

Opening the process of art-making to others previously held at a distance is demanding. It involves inserting them into the process and being accountable to them, while they—having become thoughtfully and constructively engaged—become accountable to us and to the art. It is not a passive giving and receiving, and responsibilities exist for each party involved. But the dialogue that is engendered—whether art or part of the process of making—is evidence that in the experience of art, we all have something to gain. The more openly and generously we listen to each other, and encourage other perceptions, the more we will hear, and the greater the work of art will resound.

Notes

1. Recorded at the June 2001 consortium meeting of "Awake: Art, Buddhism, and the Dimensions of Consciousness"; see http://www.artand buddhism.org.

2. Inigo Manglano-Ovalle's *Tele-Vecindario: Street-Level Vide* was also part of "Culture in Action"; see Mary Jane Jacob et al., *Culture in Action* (Seattle: Bay Press, 1995).

3. See Jacob et al., *Culture in Action*.

4. See Mary Jane Jacob and Michael Brenson, eds., *Conversations at The Castle: Changing Audiences and Contemporary Art* (Cambridge: MIT Press, 1998).

5. These are the four current meanings of *education* in museums identified and discussed by Lisa C. Roberts in *From Knowledge to Narrative* (Washington, D.C.: Smithsonian Institution Press, 1997).

6. Chogyam Trungpa, *Dharma Art* (Boston: Shambhala Publications, 1996).

7. *Reflections on Evoking History: Listening Across Cultures and Communities* (Charleston, South Carolina: Spoleto Festival USA, 2002), 42–43.

8. Hyde establishes this link etymologically through a lineage of words with the ancient root **-ar*, from the Latin *articulus*. He assembles a large group of related terms whose original meaning encompassed "to join," "to fit," "to *make*." Artisan is an **-ar* word meaning a joiner or maker of things. The Latin noun *ars* from the same root

means arts or a work of art. Also from the same root comes *articulate*, which meant joining bones together or, in today's usage, words well-joined or a "joint-worker" who shifts the joints or workings of society. See chapter 11, "Trickster Arts and Works of *Artus*," in Lewis Hyde, *Trickster Makes This World: Mischief, Myth, and Art* (New York: North Point Press, 1998).

A GIVEN

Ben Kinmont

Free is an alternative economy accessible and a means to empowerment. From waffles to clothes, I have given in order to find out what it would feel like and to see. After all, what would happen if an economy other than the professional capitalism of the art world were pursued? To fade together and become.

After twelve years of these projects, I now wonder about this point of disappearance. Most of my friends with whom I discussed ideas of interaction, value, and generosity have followed their art practice out of the area of art. Social workers, yogis, and hermits they have become, which in a sense is quite beautiful. I am reminded again of the idea that art about life is not so important for what it does for art but for what it does for life. But perhaps this was already happening. Perhaps this is simply to acknowledge a space in between where exchange is a reciprocal act of shaping a given.

Waffles for an Opening

For a two-month period people came to our house for waffle breakfasts. I was thinking about whether it was safe for my family, how many would come, and who was trusting most. My biggest surprise was how my friends didn't come, but strangers did. We signed the paper plates as a thanks for coming and I started to see it as the gift sculpture object.

Archive begun 1991. White Columns and my home over thirty-one days. Four hundred thirty-two people took invitations. Thirty-two people ate waffles. Project can be repeated. Bill Arning Collection, New York.

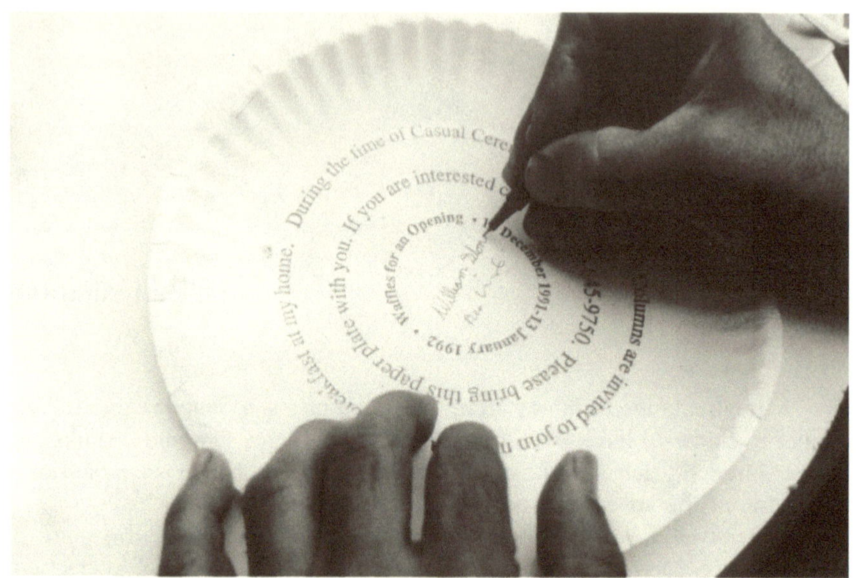

During the time of Casual Ceremony visitors to White Columns are invited to join me for a waffle breakfast at my home. If you are interested call me at 212-645-9750. Please bring this paper plate with you. **Waffles for an Opening • 13 December 1991-13 January 1992 •**

Ben Kinmont *Waffles for an Opening* 1991/1992

I need you

While on the street, their time was to describe the space in between; their trust was to give me their signature and a means of contacting them. I fulfilled my promise by giving them the proceeds of the archive's sale. One participant put the check in a frame whereas another, who was living in a shelter at the time but had since moved on, never received his mail.

Archive begun 1992. 96th and Broadway, 16th and Eighth Avenue, and Murray and Broadway. Four hours and forty-one minutes on the street. Seven hundred fifty catalytic texts given. Fifty-eight people stopped and spoke with me. Sixteen gave me their signatures and addresses, each being mailed a $40.00 check one year later. Project cannot be repeated. Caroline Bourgeois Collection, Paris.

```
--------------------------
CLERK #02
DATE: 01/12/94 04:24:01 PM
--------------------------
MO #4975392366
100 MO - DOM              40.00
101 MO FEE-DM               .75
MO #4975392367
100 MO - DOM              40.00
101 MO FEE-DM               .75
MO #4975392368
100 MO - DOM              40.00
101 MO FEE-DM               .75
MO #4975392369
100 MO - DOM              40.00
101 MO FEE-DM               .75
MO #4975392370
100 MO - DOM              40.00
101 MO FEE-DM               .75
MO #4975392371
100 MO - DOM              40.00
101 MO FEE-DM               .75
MO #4975392372
100 MO - DOM              40.00
101 MO FEE-DM               .75
MO #4975392373
100 MO - DOM              40.00
101 MO FEE-DM               .75
MO #4975392374
100 MO - DOM              40.00
101 MO FEE-DM               .75
MO #4975392375
100 MO - DOM              40.00
101 MO FEE-DM               .75
MO #4975392376
100 MO - DOM              40.00
101 MO FEE-DM               .75
MO #4975392377
100 MO - DOM              40.00
101 MO FEE-DM               .75
MO #4975392378
100 MO - DOM              40.00
101 MO FEE-DM               .75
MO #4975392379
100 MO - DOM              40.00
101 MO FEE-DM               .75
MO #4975392380
100 MO - DOM              40.00
101 MO FEE-DM               .75
MO #4975392381
100 MO - DOM              40.00
101 MO FEE-DM               .75
090 POSTAGE                1.29
090 POSTAGE                 .25
090 POSTAGE               10.44
090 POSTAGE                2.50
109 PVI                    1.34
```

I NEED YOU TO HELP ME MAKE A SCULPTURE.
In between people there exists a space where communication occurs between the self and an other. For many, this space goes undetected even though it forms the basis of cultural differences, personal relationships and understanding.

I NEED YOU TO SHARE **with me your ideas on this space in order to make a sculpture. How would you describe this space in between people?**

PLEASE TALK WITH ME **now; but if you do not wish to, thank you anyway for participating by taking a flyer.**

If you share your ideas with me and provide me with your signature and a means of contacting you, you will be a partial owner of this sculpture in its final form, be notified upon its exhibition and, if it is sold, receive a portion of the money earned.

Ben Kinmont c/o Sandra Gering Gallery, 476 Broome St., New York, N.Y., 10012.
1992.

Ben Kinmont catalytic text for *I Need You* 1992

For you for me for painting

My biggest was the feeling of giving away four years of paintings. Only my collectors knew where but anybody passing by could have one. During the distribution, we reauthored each painting, putting our signatures to their backs. Then, when talking with the participants one year later, each had a different story to tell about what had happened.

Archive begun 1993. Wall Street and Broadway and in Sandra Gering Gallery. Twenty-three paintings offered. Twenty-one given away. Eight went to strangers who happened to be passing by. Thirteen went to previous collectors. Only one of the collectors has continued to purchase work. The two paintings left unclaimed went into the archive. Project cannot be repeated. Jedermann Collection, N.A.

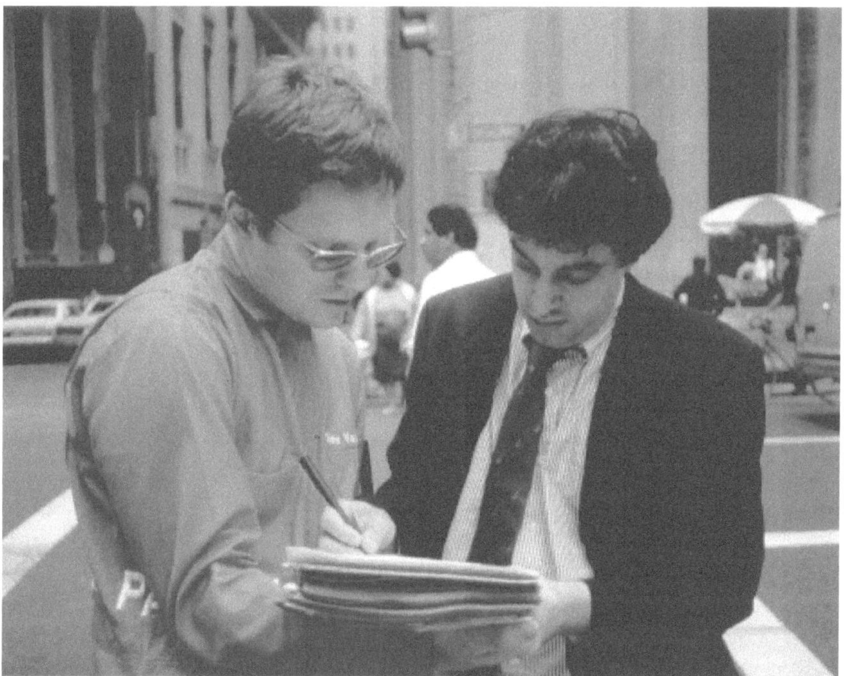

Ben Kinmont *For you for me for painting* 1993

Artist's Offer:

We are here to give away 23 paintings by Ben Kinmont. He is represented by galleries in New York and Cologne and has been successful in selling these paintings. We are here to help him givesomething back for the support you havegiven him. If you would like a painting, you must speak NOW with one of the people handing out the flyers.

Explanation:

Several people will go out onto the street and hand out flyers offering free paintings. Each person will wear a special suit which designates them as participants in the performance. The only people who will know the time and location beforehand are my colle({19rs. The purpose of the project is to give away 23 paintings, paintings which I have painted over the last four years and mean a great deal to me. In a sculptural sense, the project will investi gate the possibilities of giving. Collectors will mix with people who just happen to be passing by as they take a flyer and select a painting. Both collectors and passersby will participate in an art transaction which begins out in the open on a street comer and ends in a SoHo gallery. More impor tantly, the project will place painting, the artist, and the dealer in a situation of enerosity, one where a new social and economic context is created and into which a viewer can re-orient his or her experience of a painting.

This text seems to be corrupted. I checked the word file and these errors are there as well. There are added spaces, missing letters, and other weirdness...please read carefully!

FOR YOU FOR ME FOR PAINTING by Ben Kinmont

Artist's Offer:

We are here to give away 23 paintings by Ben Kinmont. He is represented by galleries in New York and Cologne and has been successful in selling these paintings. We are here to help him give something back for the support you have given him. If you would like a painting, you must speak NOW with one of the people handing out the flyers.

Explanation:

Several people will go out onto the street and hand out flyers offering free paintings. Each person will wear a special suit which designates them as participants in the performance. The only people who will know the time and location beforehand are my collectors. The purpose of the project is to give away 23 paintings, paintings which I have painted over the last four years and mean a great deal to me. In a sculptural sense, the project will investigate the possibilities of giving. Collectors will mix with people who just happen to be passing by as they take a flyer and select a painting. Both collectors and passersby will participate in an art transaction which begins out in the open on a street corner and ends in a SoHo gallery. More importantly, the project will place painting, the artist, and the dealer in a situation of generosity, one where a new social and economic context is created and into which a viewer can re-orient his or her experience of a painting.

NYC.
1993.

Ben Kinmont catalytic text for *For you for me for painting* 1993

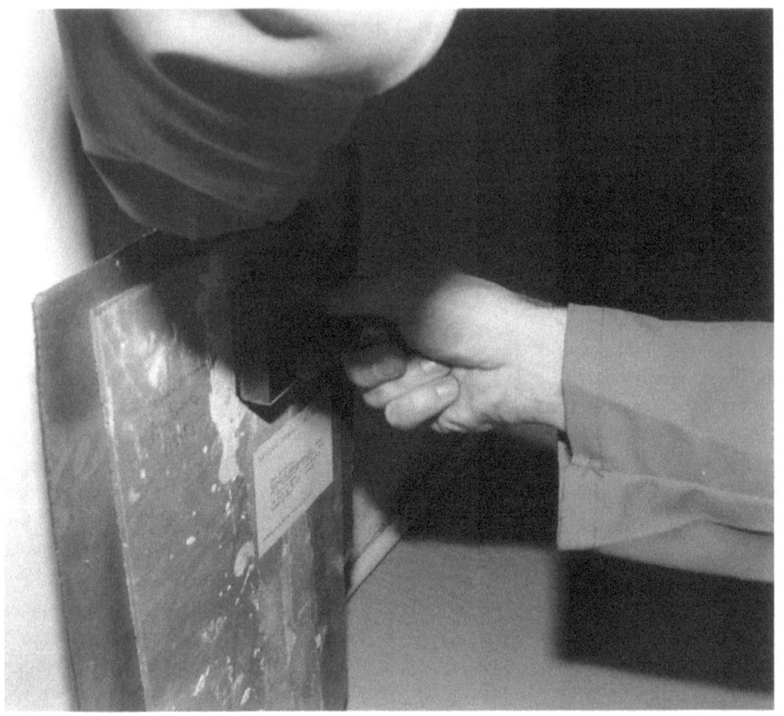

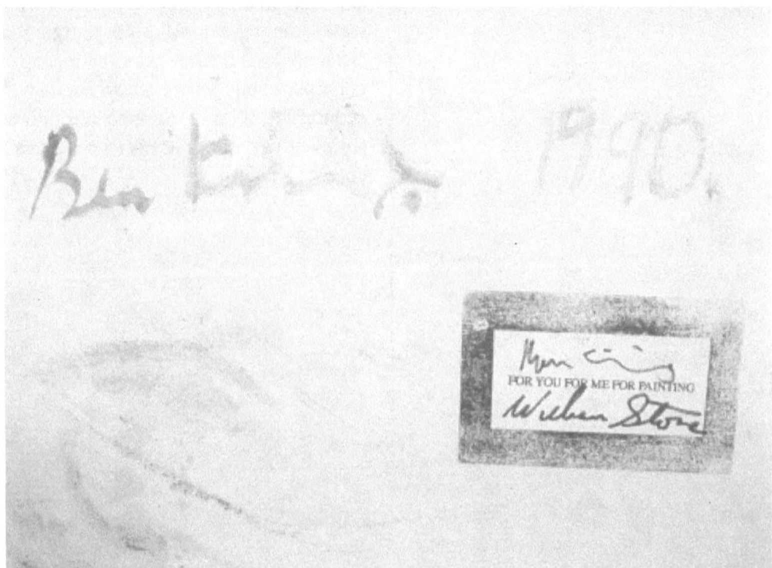

Ben Kinmont *For you for me for painting* 1993

Somebody's SoHo

Your philanthropy is our sculpture. Being invited to participate in a group show that had to occur within SoHo, I pointed out the efforts of six community health organizations that maintained SoHo addresses. For six days some friends and I sat at tables in the Grammercy Hotel Art Fair, the New Museum, Lucky Strike Restaurant, and Our Blessed Lady of Pompeii street fair. The organizer of the street fair understood the project better than anyone else and offered us a table gratis next to the Office of the Mayor and the church's Senior Citizen's Club. It worked best in this context.

Archive begun 1995. Friends in Deed, Housing Works, Children's Hope Foundation, Gilda's Club, God's Love We Deliver, and the SoHo Partnership participated. Thirty-two hundred flyers and brochures given. Project can be repeated.

Somebody's SoHo seeks to bring attention to various SoHo organizations that provide assistance to people in need. The information below describes the services these charitable organizations provide and the ways in which you can support their activities. In an art historical context, the purpose of the project is to introduce the idea of philanthropy as an active sculpture in our community.

Participating organizations are: Children's Hope Foundation, Friends in Deed, Gilda's Club, God's Love We Deliver, Housing Works, and the SoHo Partnership.

your philanthropy is our sculpture

Ben Kinmont catalytic text for *Somebody's Soho* 1995

Exchange

People coming into agnes b. could trade the shirt off their backs for any shirt in the store. Most who I approached thought I was a nuisance and looked to the staff for assistance; when it became clear that I was in earnest, they smiled and quickly found a shirt. Once the shirt was chosen, the participant and I signed a new label printed with the project's title. Then, I removed the store's label and price tag, and sewed our cosigned label onto the new shirt. Next I sewed the store's label and price tag onto the old shirt and then hung it onto the store's racks, as a new agnes b. shirt for sale. While this was going on, participants used the video camera to document the exchange. By the end, half of the people coming in were there by word of mouth. The number of shirts given was determined by how long it took me to do the seam-ripping and sewing.

Archive begun 1995. agnes b. pour hommes, New York City, for three days. The store's seamstress and twenty customers participated. Twenty shirts worth $2,934.00 given. Project can be repeated.

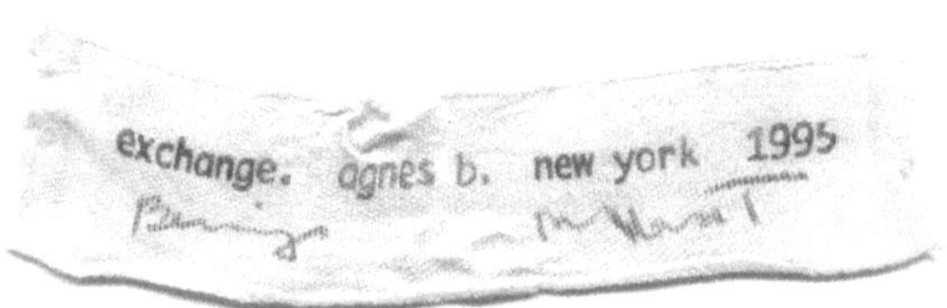

Ben Kinmont *Exchange* 1995

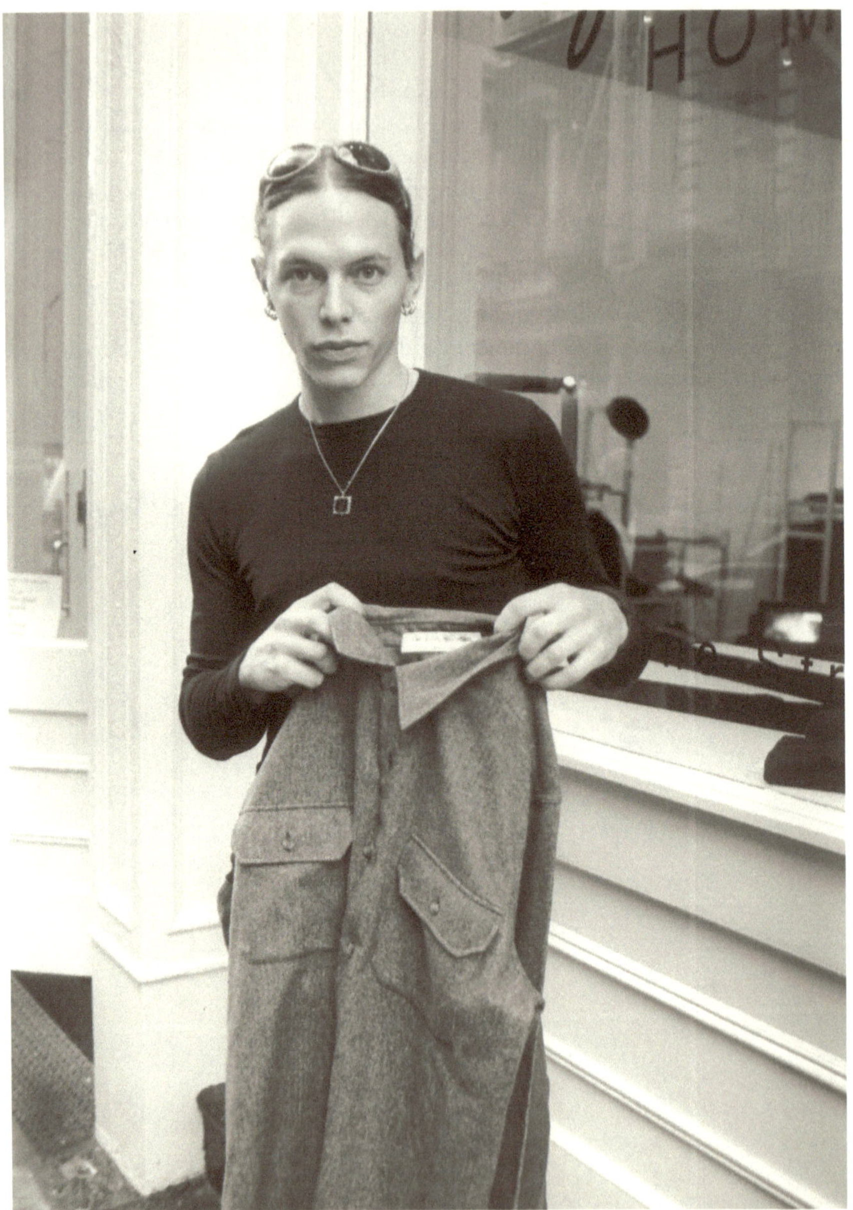

Ben Kinmont *Exchange* 1995

A CALL FOR SOCIALITY

Jeanne van Heeswijk

Imagine walking along a street and passing a heap of garbage. In the middle of the pile of broken furniture, clothes and torn up paper, some green leaves are sticking out. Would you stop and look for the plant? Would you pick it out? The Rotterdam based sculptor Rolf Engelen did just this one day, over five years ago, and this formed the start of The Second Chance Plant. The Second Chance Plant saves unloved plants that have been put out with the garbage—plants that aren't beautiful enough, that are too big or that people are tired of. These plants are brought in to a conservatory and provided with a new pot, fresh earth, and fertilizer. When the plants have recuperated, a new owner is sought who is willing to adopt the plant. As the project continued, people who were stuck with a plant they wanted to get rid of could call The Second Chance Plant. In an interview about The Second Chance Plant, Rolf Engelen told me that he actually doesn't like plants at all. But from the moment he was struck by the idea that you could not place any living species out by the garbage—he felt obliged to take on the role of rescuer. He sees his role not just as a project but as an attitude, that is an integral part of his profession as an artist.

The unselfish nature of The Second Chance Plant crossed my mind when I was invited to speak at the "Generosity Projects" symposium that was the impetus for this volume. Would I call this a "Generosity Project"? Thinking about this gave rise to questions about the problematic nature of generosity as a concept, especially when applied to art. As an artist whose work has been created in public spaces and communities, these questions have become overly apparent when working with the projects I have been involved with over the last ten years.

First of all, I do not like the term generosity projects. It is, in my opinion, an oxymoron. The Oxford English Dictionary defines generosity as "**1** excellence or nobility of birth. **2** courage, nobility of conduct. Now only magnanimity, willingness to forgive." Collins Dictionary of the American Language also gives a third meaning: "**3** willingness to give or share." These definitions reinforce an association in the word generosity that echoes a colonial past, as it involves a

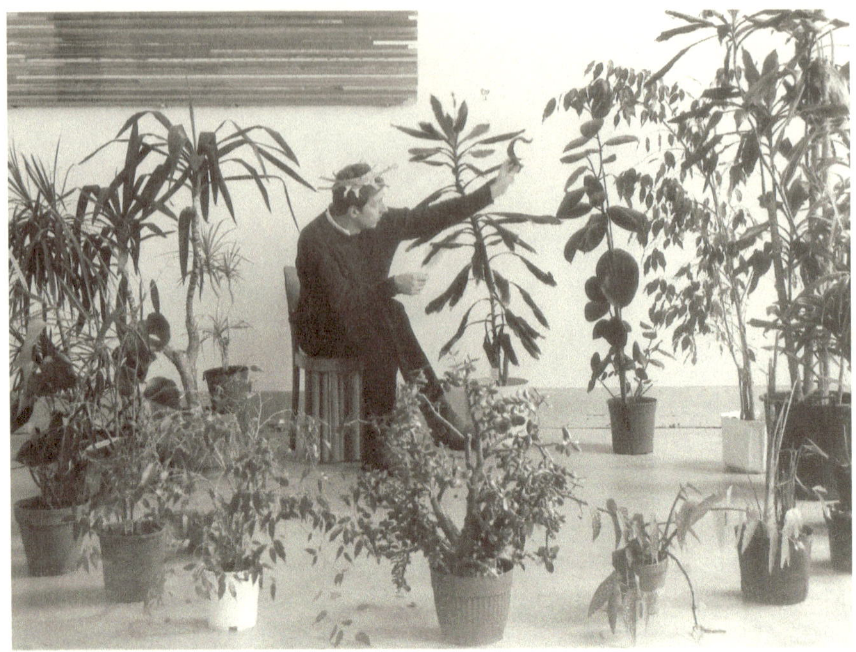

Jeanne van Heeswijk The Second Change Plant 1997–present photo: Rolf Engelen

certain hierarchy in relating to the other. Generosity can mean an act of good will, but this act can also contain a strong feeling of guilt, since giving has not always been free of moral or ethical dilemmas or the commercial messages that may be attached to it. Recently this became again apparent when the U.S. military dropped food packages above Afghanistan. The package contained "All-American" products such as peanut butter. The common joke "get peanut butter in the desert, try to whistle" took on new meaning in this context, with its strange mix of generosity, cultural framework, and American business.

The use of "generosity" as applied to "generosity projects" through the agency of a conference about "generosity in art" seems to me even more problematic, as it implies that one can stage generosity or an act of generosity or even do it as an artistic practice. One could question the role of the artist in creating such projects, and why there is such a need for them. In a conversation I had with writer and critical theorist Reinaldo Laddage while preparing the catalogue for the project "Face Your World" at the Wexner Center for the Arts, he pointed out that in America you could see interesting parallels between the withdrawal of government from many areas of public life and the demand for projects that deal with public space. This, in turn, has generated new career opportunities for artists.[1]

Philosopher and poet Maaike Engelen addressed the same issue in her article "Creative Urge Annex: A Zeal for Improvement":

> It's very lucrative to call oneself an artist nowadays, and then just to go on doing what one wants to do, whatever it may be. Whether it's helping the homeless, preaching in public, or spading over vegetable gardens for the neighborhood. Anything goes and gets subsidies as long as it is called art and has a public . . . So maybe a criticism could be that the artist behaves as a missionary in pursuit of converts and that she conceives of art as a possibility to mold this missionary urge. All very well, this longing for a putsch for a better world. Where acting is the central point, not listening. The good must be realized, must be attained. The responsibility is ours. That's all very well, but it's by now obvious enough how much misery good intentions can cause. The point is not everyone shares them; it remains a struggle.[2]

As an artist, I am aware that my motives are sometimes ambiguous; after all, I want to change the things that I think are important to change. In my practice, I am genuinely concerned with the creation of spaces within which any person may speak. The key concepts underlying my work are *acting, meeting,* and *communicating.* These are all activities that demand that both the viewer and the initiator take on levels of responsibility. In order to facilitate such an engagement, I try to create "intermediate spaces" through my work. I see the arrangement and/or rearrangement of space—and here space can also be understood metaphorically (space in your head, space in your heart, space to share)—as a condition or possibility for bringing about changes, and preferably improvements, in social structures.

In my practice, a work is created in collaboration with the community it is addressing and the projects are dependent upon the community's continued involvement for their sustainability. As I strongly believe in the multiplicity of thought rather than in the singularity of my own ideas, my work is never considered to be something over which I have sole authorship, as that appellation has to be ascribed to all of the participants who were involved in its creation. It is essential to the projects that I step into the community and become part of it. As Rick Lowe of Project Row Houses pointed out in his lecture at the "Engaged Art, Engaged Buddhism" conference, "When I became part of the audience myself, I began to learn to shift from creation in splendid isolation to collaboration. I had to develop the ability 'to listen' on how to interject my creative energy."[3]

This might seem a simple act to perform, but over the course of my practice, I have learned how difficult it can be. In 1994, I went to work in Oud-Beijerland, a small Dutch community, on a commissioned intervention in an existing public site, the new Oud-Beijerland town hall. Because of the specific make-up of its community—mainly strictly Protestant—the citizens wanted, as part of the 1 percent regulation (a law that demands that 1 percent of the total sum to build a new public building will be spend on art), an artwork that was more applied and serving. The strictly Protestant community leads a sober life in honor of God. They have dress codes for women (long skirts, no trousers), birth control is not allowed, and they refrain from television and other such distractions of modern society.

There was a general perception of art as being something rather frivolous, something without any real connection to the community. Furthermore, the postmodern architecture of the new building had already made them feel somewhat alienated. From this set of starting points, we were asked to start a process to give the new building a greater local significance by responding to functional and aesthetic needs. These needs only became apparent through a series of interactions with the town hall's users.

By asking such questions as: Can a local town hall still embody a sense of community? Or, are there still collective narratives and can they be made present in the building? I encouraged people to be involved in what I saw as the start of processes that would continue and through which they would have further control over their environment in the future. This process was long and sometimes painful, as we had to learn about each other's ideas and different viewpoints, and it is this process of learning that embodies the concept of sociality.

Sociality, a term introduced by the English sociologist Scott Lash in his essay "Difference or Sociality," is a process through which human beings can learn to design their own environment and where communication is an exchange between two individuals.[4] The first step in this act of communication is to place our own subjectivity at risk. At the heart of Lash's idea of sociality is the return to point zero, the moment where the "I" ends and "the other" begins.[5] However, what particularly matters in such a conversation is that in order to (partly) abandon one's identity, one must arrive at the conversation with a clear idea of just what one's own identity is. It is impossible to encounter the other without identity since in any encounter both parties have to have something to relinquish. Moreover, one has to possess a private set of values, norms, and metaphors as an impetus for a dialogue, because these personally held portions of our self-image are what we must be willing to both defend and, possibly, let go of. Let's face it: if a conversation is addressing only "pre-fab" metaphors and generic beliefs and opinions, there would really be very little to discuss, as there would be very little that is actually at stake.

In my dialogues with Oud-Beijerland residents we discussed notions such as art being serving versus being frivolous, restricted identities, and definitions of home. For me a major question was, What does it mean to serve a community that very clearly has different viewpoints of life? In the process we all had to relinquish our preconceptions of each other's ways of living and learn to combine different identities in a concept of home. Within the project entitled A House for the Community, we (myself in dialogue with members of the community) created spaces in the new town hall of Oud-Beijerland that we named "habitats" or "atmospheric zones," in which we planted seeds, both real and metaphorical. These seeds are still being tended today by those who both work within and visit the building. A House for the Community consisted of four zones, called "Polder," "Community," "Collaboration" and "Culture." For each zone, interventions were made in the architecture of the building (and, of course, none of this would have been possible without the support of the architect, Victor de Leeuw). "Polder" allowed for the creation of an inner garden, which functions as a model for the current ecological management of the region, while an orchard was planted on the outside of the building, representing the historical, natural environment instead of the planned parking lot. For "Community," we built an "engagement room." This special room was overlooked in the design of the new building because the registration of marriage, birth, and death is nowadays mostly processed at the central information desk. In Oud-Beijerland, however, family matters are considered to be of great importance and thus a special, private room needed to be created where these intersections of personal life and bureaucratic procedure could take place. After a careful process of negotiation, a kiosk was placed in the main hall. The kiosk, an octagon made from vitrine-like segments, offered the over 120 clubs and associations that make up Oud-Beijerland's community a space in which to present themselves on a six-month rotation schedule. When sitting inside the kiosk to register, one sees oneself surrounded by the community as the presentations in the vitrines project a mosaic pattern on the milkglass backside of these segments. "Collaboration" consisted of a new design program for the information desks and the canteen, emphasizing the need for the town hall's employees to learn more about each other and their work activities. Finally, in "Culture," a program was established for four years in which artists were invited to make additions to the different zones. All these habitats were anchored in a specially designed signposting system. By making use of existing budget allocations related to the building process, it was possible to take the project beyond the small amount of funding reserved for art, and today it is still up and running. Different community groups are creating presentations in the kiosk; the Society for the Protection of the Hoeksewaards Landscape uses the inner garden as a model, organizing talks and visits to it. The city government has created a part-time post for art, making it part of it's program, and each year different artists are asked to contribute their ideas to the project. The intense years of not only working with the community to integrate an art project into their lives but devising an official city governmental structure to give it ongoing support paid off.

At present, eight years later, I am about to finish my involvement, not because the project is finished but because I am no longer needed. The original intention to create a house for the community has been realized not through finding enough money to continue but by establishing a state of mind that moves responsibility for the building and its surroundings from the municipal authority and puts it in the hands of the people who use the building. These people have come to feel that an integral part of using the building is not just simply the carrying out or requesting of administrative services, but also the creation of a communal atmosphere. They view contemporary art as a natural component in this process of creating communal property—a home.

Working in Oud-Beijerland made me aware of the need to transform ways of working in, and with, public spaces. I shifted my focus from the art object to the art objective. I started to see art as a tool in a process of communication, making visible and enhancing cultural production. As I see it, cultural production is the sum total of activities with which people express their identity and with which they attempt to come to grips with their environment, as well as with the ways in which they express the relationship between their identity and their environment. Similar to a craftsman who uses tools for a specific production, I bring in a set of aesthetic questions and a body of knowledge that begin a process of inquiry in a social space, when applied to the situation at hand. This process of dialogue enables people to build their environment in such a way that they become aware of the importance of their stake in the community as a whole.

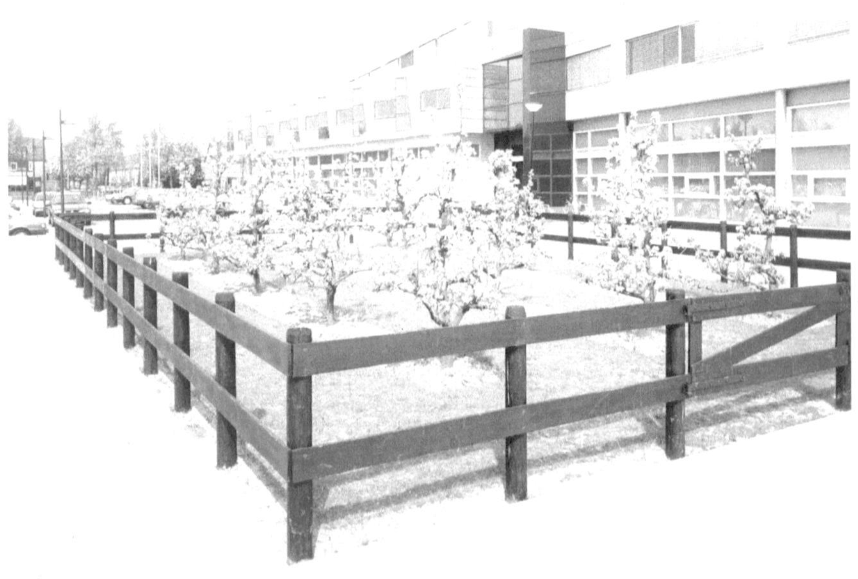

Jeanne van Heeswijk A House for the Community, The Orchard (part of the Polder in front of the Town Hall) 1994–2002 photo: Rolf Goedewaagen

When asked in 1995 to think about a sculpture plan for the Westwijk in Vlaardingen, I initially refused the commission because I didn't see sense in putting a series of sculptures in an area that was designated an area in need of urgent regeneration, Having learned from the process in Oud-Beijerland, I wondered, while looking at the plans for this major regeneration scheme, how the local inhabitants would be involved in what appeared to be the total transformation of the social tissue of their area. If the planned changes, such as increasing housing in the now green areas or taking away the community facilities and small shopping strip in the four neighborhoods and replacing them with one central mall, were carried out, would the results be beneficial to the social climate? Would they positively affect the existing social networks, as the plans proclaimed? All of these questions seemed relevant given that at this moment in time there were a lot of people stressing the importance of local decentralized networks versus a center in city-planning initiatives.

Instead of creating a plan for a public sculpture, as I was asked to do, I proposed to accompany the whole process of transformation over the ten-year period to come, and engage with the process of change in the Westwijk. Under the title *Until We Meet Again*, I began a series of projects, each of which had the intent of involving the residents in discussing and shaping the changes that were going to take place during the period of redevelopment. To enable this, I effectively became a "re-granting authority," re-distributing my artistic commission to other artists, who were given (sub)commissions to investigate, support, question, and stimulate the process of change in the Westwijk. Their projects were formulated to create opportunities for real encounters through the means of temporary sculptures, social projects, installations, and happenings. These projects were to be made in active cooperation with the local residents so that they could contribute to the initiation of new connections and directions necessary for forming new social structures and networks in the Westwijk. They had the overarching concept of creating spaces where people can really meet each other, while at the same time creating a breathing space for art.

The modernist architect Van Thijen designed the Westwijk (an area now consisting of sixteen thousand inhabitants) in the fifties in reaction to the cramped nineteenth-century housing districts. He wanted to create a built environment for the working class with a lot of air and light, open views, and a lot of green that at same time would contribute to the formation of a social unity and the support of urban culture. He divided the Westwijk into four manageable neighborhoods, each with its own character, separated by green belts. He hoped to facilitate the coexistence of different lifestyles through building a mix of multifamily/multistoried buildings and single-family houses, all built with straightforward architectural proportions and divided by smaller green belts that create a clear division between the various types of housing blocks and contain shopping strips, community facilities, playgrounds, schools, and sport centers.[6]

By present-day standards the quality of the houses is insufficient. Because of the limited architectural variety the turnover in the district is large. Consequently the composition of the population changes constantly. Although a large part of the population is still made up of inhabitants that settled in the district from the very beginning, their children have grown up and moved to other districts because is not possible to have a housing career (a phrase used to describe the way in which people move from renting to owning their own home) within the area. Because of their size, their level of conveniences, and the relatively low rent, the vacant flats attract mainly young families, many of non-Dutch descent, with low incomes, often from welfare. These new residents tend to have lifestyles that differ from those of the older ones, and the ignorance of each other's habits leads to prejudice, noninteraction, and sometimes even clashes. Furthermore, the support for social and cultural facilities is dropping through the steady decline in population in the Westwijk. In response to the turnover and social problems a major gentrification of the area was started in 1995 and is scheduled to come to a conclusion by 2005. The original spatial and urban structure will be preserved, but the number of houses (mainly single family houses) will increase. To this extent the smaller green belts, housing the community facilities and shopping strips, are being dismantled in favor of a newly created district center.

Until We Meet Again, in close collaboration with the community, critically monitors and questions the changes the Westwijk is undergoing and reacts by means of temporary sculptures, projects, installations, and happenings. One of the eight available commissions for *Until We Meet Again* was given to Advies Groep 2005, an advisory board composed of local inhabitants, to enable them to shape one specific element completely themselves. One major element of the redevelopment plan was to centralize all the shops into the future "heart" of the district. Thus, the various shopping strips located in the four neighborhoods as originally designed by Van Thijen are being dismantled. Due to this, the amount of walking to basic services in the district has been dramatically increased and changed. Where one once had to walk ten minutes to a local shop, now the distance is doubled. Advies Groep 2005 distributed a questionnaire in the district asking people to mark the future route they would walk to the new center. All the routes were put on top of each other. This process revealed the points where future routes would entwine. These junctions could be envisioned as the places where residents would encounter each other and suggested places where people might stop to rest. In collaboration with artist Kamiel Verschuren, Advies Groep 2005 is now designing these junction points to make them interesting places to stay, linger, and congregate. The first meeting place will be completed in the end of 2004.

Also due to the dismantling of the shopping strips, one particular strip, located at the Floris de Vijfdelaan, was vacant and boarded up at the time and awaited a new use. Because of the long-term critical involvement of *Until We*

Meet Again with the changes the district is undergoing, Stichting Waterweg Wonen (the district's largest housing association and the owner of the fifteen vacant shops) approached *Until We Meet Again* to think about a new use for the area. They commissioned me to conceive of a new, temporary, function for this strip. Until recently it housed neighborhood shops, including a supermarket, a bakery, a flower shop, and a drugstore, but at present the shopping strip is no longer tied to direct economic production. However, cultural production is also of importance in the maintenance of our society. The idea of having a site switch or transform from one mode of production to another is analogous to the process of giving form and content to the environment one lives in and analogous to the transformation that underlies the creation of art objectives. Setting up places where this cultural production can occur is essential to the development of a breeding ground for culture in the broadest sense of the word, so it became clear that the shopping strip could be used as a location for a shift in modes of production to occur. Thus transformed, the space could continue to contribute to life and community in the Westwijk.

As a result, the shopping strip at the Floris de Vijfdelaan was established as a cultural zone in the Westwijk, opening May 23, 2002, and lasting for two years. *De Strip*, as this project has been titled, consisted of an exhibition program, an artist's program, and a community program. Priority was given to the presentation of the diverse cultural identities that make up the area, and space was offered for the various residents to meet each other. Part of the program for *De Strip* consisted of the opening of a branch of Boijmans Van Beuningen Museum in three of the former shops. Using selections from their collections of applied and modern art, the museum committed itself to set up five exhibitions, alongside which they also opened a museum cafe and a bookshop. In the former supermarket, MAMA (Showroom for Media and Moving Art) hosted a series of workshops on youth culture. Besides these large efforts, studios and small workplaces were created in the strip where artists and craftsmen could work for a period of three months. Instead of paying rent they agreed to open their workspaces twice a week for interested visitors or to give workshops. Nearby to this, the *Uit en Thuis* (going out and staying home) video-magazine offered the people of the area the possibility to watch and to create videos. The video magazine, the artists' studios, and the museum café spaces were available for a lecture and performance program organized by the inhabitants of the Westwijk themselves. The project also published a bimonthly newsletter in the style of a comic strip. In this "strip," the projects agenda was announced and the ups and downs of *De Strip* and the Westwijk were discussed.

Using dialogue and interventions to help the community become an active part of Westwijk's ten-year process of change has made it possible, once the processes started, to work outward into a larger social and political context as well. The city took notice of *De Strip* and recognized a need for an area of cultural production and is at present shaping the conditions through which this

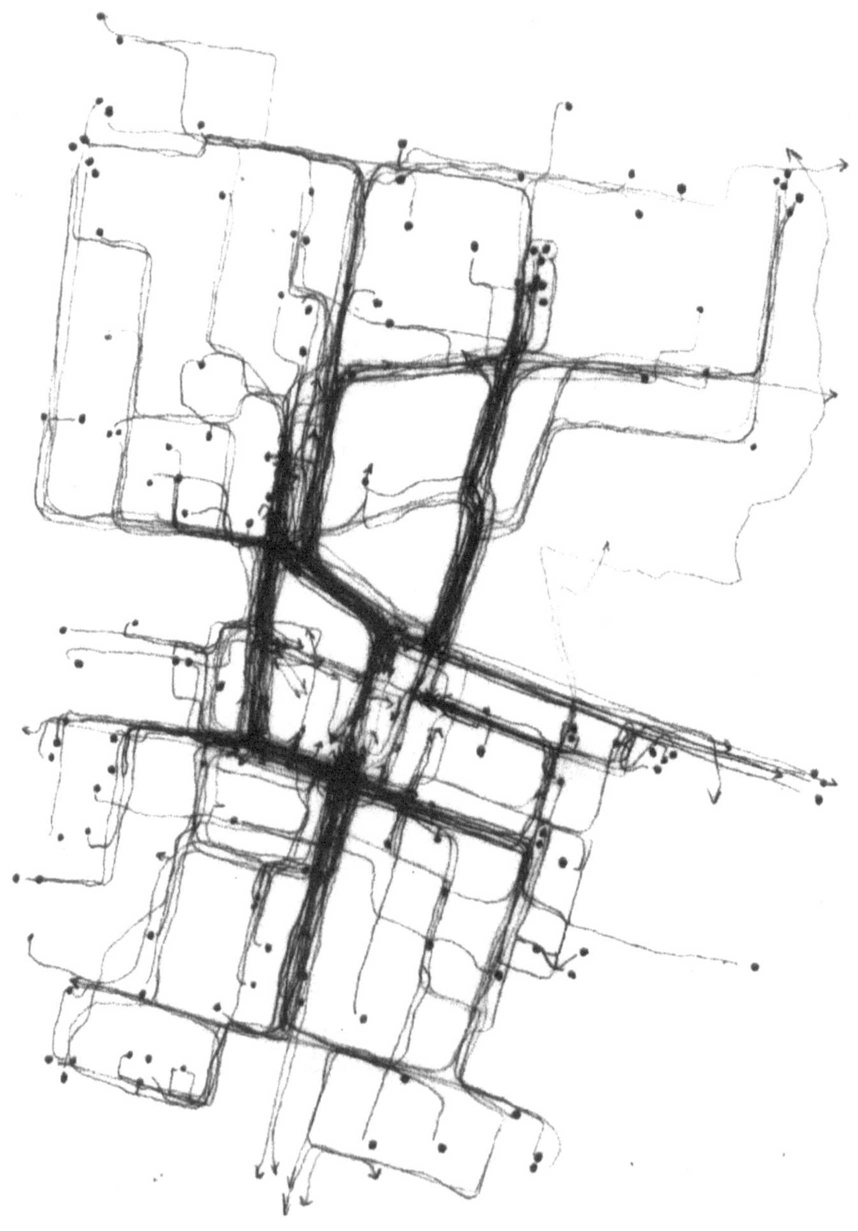

Jeanne van Heeswijk *Until We Meet Again* 2005 (map showing the new meeting points in Westwijk) photo by the author

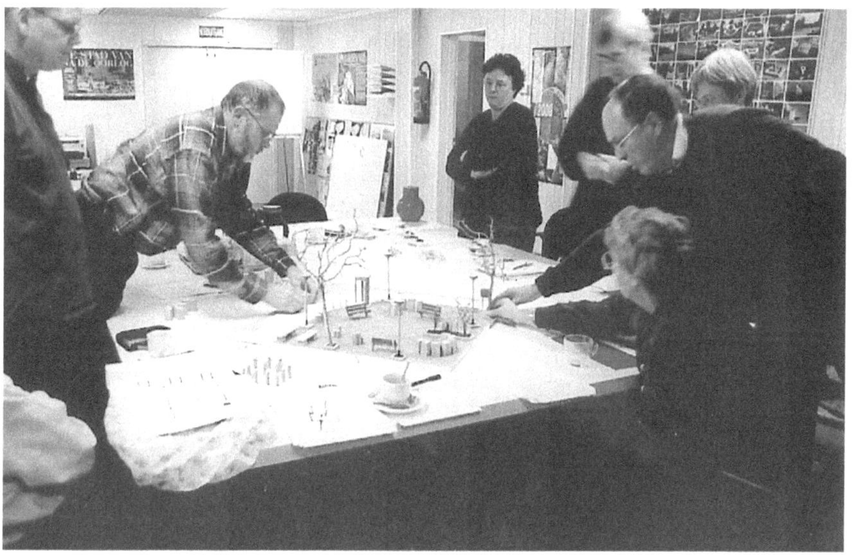

Jeanne van Heeswijk *Until We Meet Again* Advies Groep 2005 discussing with Kamiel Verschuren the creation of a square made out of street furniture 2002 photo by the author

cultural zone might have a more permanent character. They have even looked into ways to avoid completely dismantling the other three shopping strips in the district. I have found that when communities start to shape themselves, start to articulate their own voices and aesthetics, and begin to self-organize, it becomes clear that they know what they really want. As artists, we might manage to pass on tools, in the form of aesthetic questions, that allow them to reshape their world in the process.

If one could make a wish in relation to projects that fall into the category of "generosity projects," one would wish that the energy generated through people acting out in their own environment could lead to a network of support, a critical reading of one's own surroundings and an involvement in the changes that take place. Thus, what I am suggesting here is that our continued efforts to think about possibilities for collective action under the rubric of "generosity projects" is doomed to fail if we do not undertake a critical analysis of the sedimentary meanings of the word *generosity*. As a rubric for action, "generosity projects" implies a kind of topdown distribution of resources and implies a hierarchy of relations between people.

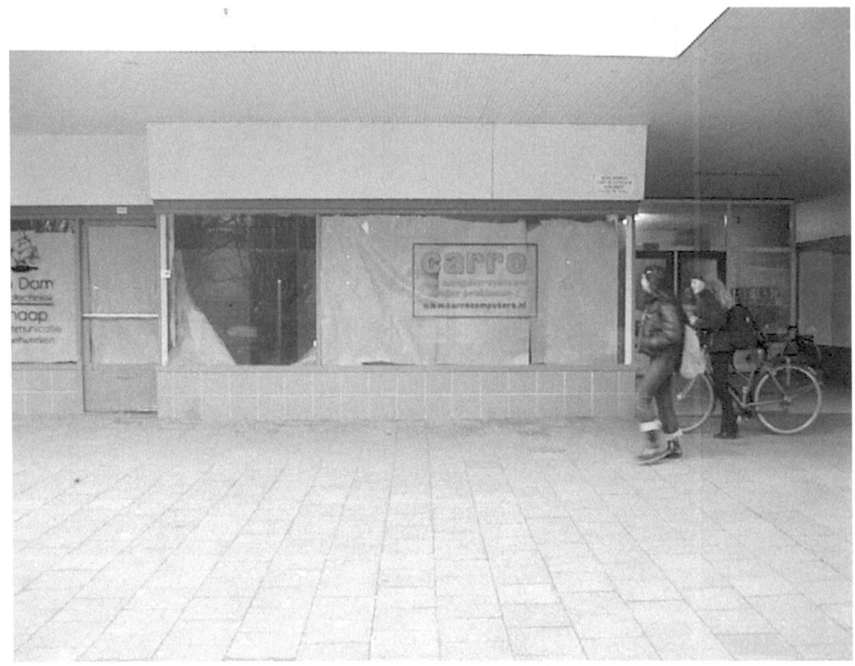

Jeanne van Heeswijk *Until We Meet Again* The Floriside Vijfaelaan Shopping Strip, vacant due to regeneration 2002 photo by the author

My suggestion instead is that we make a "call for sociality" by reformulating the rubric of generosity and think about how various models of sociality—nonhierarchical forms of distribution of resources—can uncover possibilities for social action and how these models can inform artistic practice. It would mean maximizing the potential within communities for open dialogue, communication, and collective action. The key then would be to create and implement an infrastructure or a network of support, which could foster such a dialogue and create the conditions for a critical discourse that illuminates the possibilities for social change. For this we need continuously to go back, to listen again and again and to create an understanding that public space actually means a shared space, to which everyone's contributions make a difference.

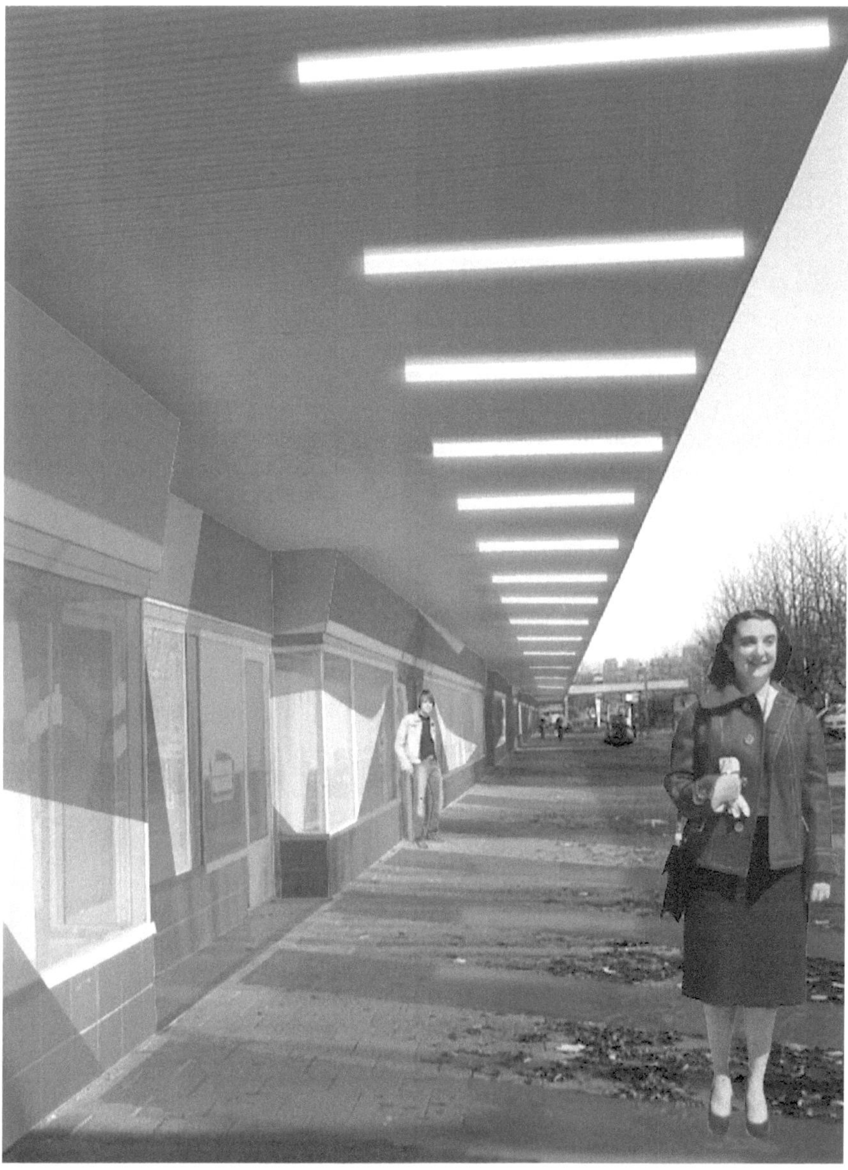

Jeanne van Heeswijk *Until We Meet Again* Plan for the façade of *De Strip* 2002 photo by the author

Notes

With special thanks to Steve Hunt

1. Reinaldo Laddaga is Assistant Professor in the Department of Romance Languages at the University of Pennsylvania, where he teaches contemporary literature and art, and critical theory. *Face Your World* ran from June 17 to August 16, 2002, in Columbus, Ohio. The accompanying catalogue, *Jeanne van Heeswijk: Face Your World—Notations*, edited by Carlos Basualdo, was published by Artimo (Amsterdam) in 2003.

2. Maaike Engelen, *Creative Urge Annex: A Zeal for Improvement* (Amsterdam: Mama Cash, 2001), 1–16.

3. "Engaged Art, Engaged Buddhism," Muir Beach, California, February 7–9, 2002.

4. Scott Lash goes on to suggest that "we can find an escape route through focusing on non-representative forms. By actively creating meaning through dialogue and intersubjective communication, we may be able to find a way out of the productivity system, which makes us passive receivers, rather than active producers of meaning. The first step is to place our own subjectivity at risk." Scott Lash, "Difference or Sociality," in *Towards a Theory of the Image*, ed. Jon Thompson (Maastricht, The Netherlands: Jan van Eyck Academie, 1996), 112–29.

5. See Jeanne van Heeswijk, "How Are They Going to Peruse This?" in *Dürfen die das?* ed. Stella Rollig and Eva Strum (Vienna: Turia and Kant, 2002), 82–83.

6. Van Thijen's Westwijk, as it was completely built and executed according to rigid, theoretical plans, is a good example of modernist city planning.

CONTRIBUTORS

Bill Arning is the director of the Contemporary Arts Museum Houston. After arriving in Texas in 2009, Arning organized solo exhibitions of Marc Swanson, Matthew Day Jackson, and the late Stan VanDerBeek. Jackson and VanDerBeek were jointly organized with the MIT List Visual Arts Center, where Arning was exhibitions curator from 2000 to 2009. At MIT he organized shows of AA Bronso, Cerith Wyn Evans, and a retrospective of Kate Ericson and Mel Ziegler. From 1985 to 1996, Arning was director of White Columns in New York City, where he organized groundbreaking first solo shows for many of the best-known artists of his generation, including John Currin, Marilyn Minter, Andres Serrano, Richard Phillips, Cady Noland, and Jim Hodges. Arning has written on art for journals such as *Artforum*, *Art in America*, and *Parkett*, as well as multitudes of international museum publications. Arning is currently co-curating, with Elissa Auther and the MCA Denver, a career survey of renowned painter Marilyn Minter, which is scheduled to open in 2015.

Peter Coyote has performed as an actor for some of the world's most distinguished filmmakers, including Barry Levinson, Roman Polanski, Pedro Almodovar, Steven Spielberg, Walter Hill, Martin Ritt, Steven Soderberg, Diane Kurys, Sidney Pollack, and Jean Paul Rappeneau. He is an Emmy Award–winning narrator of over 120 documentary films, including Ken Burns's *The National Parks*, *Prohibition*, *The West*, and *Dust Bowl*. Coyote is the author of a memoir of the 1960s counter-culture, *Sleeping Where I Fall*, which received universally excellent reviews, appeared on three bestseller lists, sold five printings in hardback, and was rereleased with a new cover and afterword in May 2009. A chapter from that book, "Carla's Story," won the 1993/94 Pushcart Prize for excellence in nonfiction. He is currently working on a new book about politics. From 1975 to 1983, Coyote was a member of the Literature Panel of the National Endowment of the Arts and then chairman of the California State Arts Council. During his chairmanship and tenure, expenditures on the arts rose from $1 million to $16 million annually. He is an ordained Zen Buddhist priest who has been practicing for thirty-eight years. He is and has been engaged in political and social causes since his early teens.

Kate Fowle is the chief curator at Garage Center for Contemporary Culture in Moscow and director-at-large at Independent Curators International (ICI) in New York, where she was executive director from 2009 to 2013. Prior to this, she was the inaugural international curator at Ullens Center for Contemporary Art in Beijing. In 2001, Fowle co-founded the Master's Program in Curatorial Practice at California College of the Arts in San Francisco, and was Chair from 2002 to 2007. Before moving to the United States, she was co-director of Smith + Fowle in London (1996–2001) and curator at the Towner Art Gallery in Eastbourne (1993–96).

Mary Jane Jacob is a curator who, through hundreds of exhibitions, site-specifc and community-based projects, and public programs, has actively worked with artists to expand the practice and public discourse of art as a shared process. Her study into the nature of the art experience has lead to the anthologies *Buddha Mind in Contemporary Art, Learning Mind: Experience into Art*, and *Chicago Makes Modern: How Creative Minds Changed Society*. As professor and executive director of Exhibitions and Exhibition Studies at the School of the Art Institute of Chicago, she is currently spearheading a major research project on Chicago social practice.

Ben Kinmont is an artist, publisher, and antiquarian bookseller. Occupying a space somewhere between conceptual art and "social sculpture," Kinmont's work is based in real-time exchanges such as meals, conversations, and gestures. In 1996 he began his publishing project, Antinomian Press, which focuses on ephemera and archival material, often distributed for free. Kinmont also has an ongoing antiquarian bookselling business, begun in 1998, that specializes in books and manuscripts about domestic economy and food. He currently lives in Sebastopol, California.

Elyse Mallouk is an artist and writer with a longstanding interest in socially engaged practices. She is a founding editor of *Landfill Quarterly*, an online archive, print journal, and subscription service that chronicles and redistributes ephemera produced by socially engaged artworks. She holds an MFA and an MA in Visual and Critical Studies from California College of the Arts, and has independently contributed writing to several exhibition catalogues and online publications. Based in New York, she is currently Digital Content Manager at the Whitney Museum of American Art.

Francis McIlveen writes: "I have expanded my practice to the real world. Since 2003, I have been using the Community Land Trust model to convert private property into a community-owned and -controlled asset. This radical model inverts the basic legal and economic premises of property ownership—land serves working class people and communities. Housing, community centers, and gardens are no longer subject to the whims of absentee investors who treat them as commodities. Control is localized. Governance and economics are participatory. For more information see http://www.cltnetwork.org/."

Cesare Pietroiusti is an artist living in Rome. Through performative actions, his practice explores the relations between the logics of economy, exchange, and art's perceived worth. Trained as a medical doctor, Pietroiusti studied Psychiatry in the late 1970s. His artist's book *Pensieri non-funzionali / Non-Functional Thoughts* documents most of his projects, both realized and unrealized (www.nonfunctionalthoughts.net). Co-founder of many artist-run projects, Pietroiusti has been a professor of studio practice at the University of Venice (IUAV) since 2004 and is MFA faculty professor at the Art Institute of Boston at Lesley University (2009–present).

Ted Purves is a writer and artist based in Berkeley, California. His public projects and writings are centered on investigating the practice of art in the world, particularly as it addresses issues of localism and power, systems of exchange, and critical occupations of social forms. He produces socially based projects in collaboration with Susanne Cockrell under the umbrella name of Fieldfaring (www.fieldfaring.org). Their most recent project, The Red Bank Pawpaw Circle, a large public planting project, was completed in Cincinnati, Ohio, in Fall 2012. Purves was founder of the MFA concentration in Social Practice at California College of the Arts in 2005, and is currently the chair of the MFA Fine Arts Program.

Matthew Rana is an artist and writer. His projects, publications, readings, and performances have been presented at SITE Santa Fe, SFMOMA, Museé de l'Objet, and the Biennale de Belleville, among others. He is a contributor to *Art Agenda* and *frieze* and, since 2010, has been a member of the Paris-based group Speech & What Archive. Matthew currently lives and works in Gothenburg, Sweden, where he is a lecturer in Fine Art at Valand Academy.

Shane Aslan Selzer is an artist, writer, and organizer whose practice develops micro communities where artists can expand on larger social issues such as generosity, exchange, and failure. Selzer uses historical research to make personal interventions into social and material archives. Her work has been exhibited at numerous venues including The Suburban, Oak Park, Illinois; Andrew Kreps Gallery and P.S.1 MoMA, New York City; The Poor Farm, Manawa, Wisconsin; and The Bag Factory, Johannesburg, South Africa. She is currently a fellow at A Blade of Grass in New York City.

Jörgen Svensson has worked and exhibited both within Sweden and internationally. He has been described as an avant/pioneer of project-based, sociopolitical art. His most significant projects take place in general public forum, but his work also includes film, music, painting, books, and radio plays. For many years he worked as a professor at various art academies in Scandinavia. and he is represented in many of the largest museums in Sweden, including the Museum of Modern Art in Stockholm and the Gothenburg Art Museum. In 1998, he was the first person in Sweden to receive a Fulbright Scholarship at the PhD level within the field of art.

Jeanne van Heeswijk is a visual artist who creates contexts for interaction in public spaces. Her projects distinguish themselves through a strong social involvement. Through her work, Van Heeswijk stimulates and develops cultural production and creates new public (meeting) spaces or remodels existing ones. To achieve this, she often works closely with artists, designers, architects, software developers, shopkeepers, governments, and citizens. Van Heeswijk regularly lectures on topics such as urban renewal, participation, and cultural production. Her work has been featured in internationally renowned biennials such as those of Liverpool, Busan, Taipei, Shanghai, and Venice. She was awarded the 2011 Leonore Annenberg Prize for Art and Social Change and the 2012 Curry Stone Design Prize for Social Design Pioneers.

Jacob Wick is a conceptual artist, composer/improvisor, and writer based in Los Angeles. Although he rejects the notion that all of his work, through all genres, must cohere into a sensible whole, he is generally interested in looking at or through the space that opens when an object or an idea begins to move away from itself. For the 2013 Hidden City Philadelphia Festival, he worked with the Think Tank that has yet to be named to open Germantown City Hall, an installation of an open civic space within a disused town hall building.

INDEX

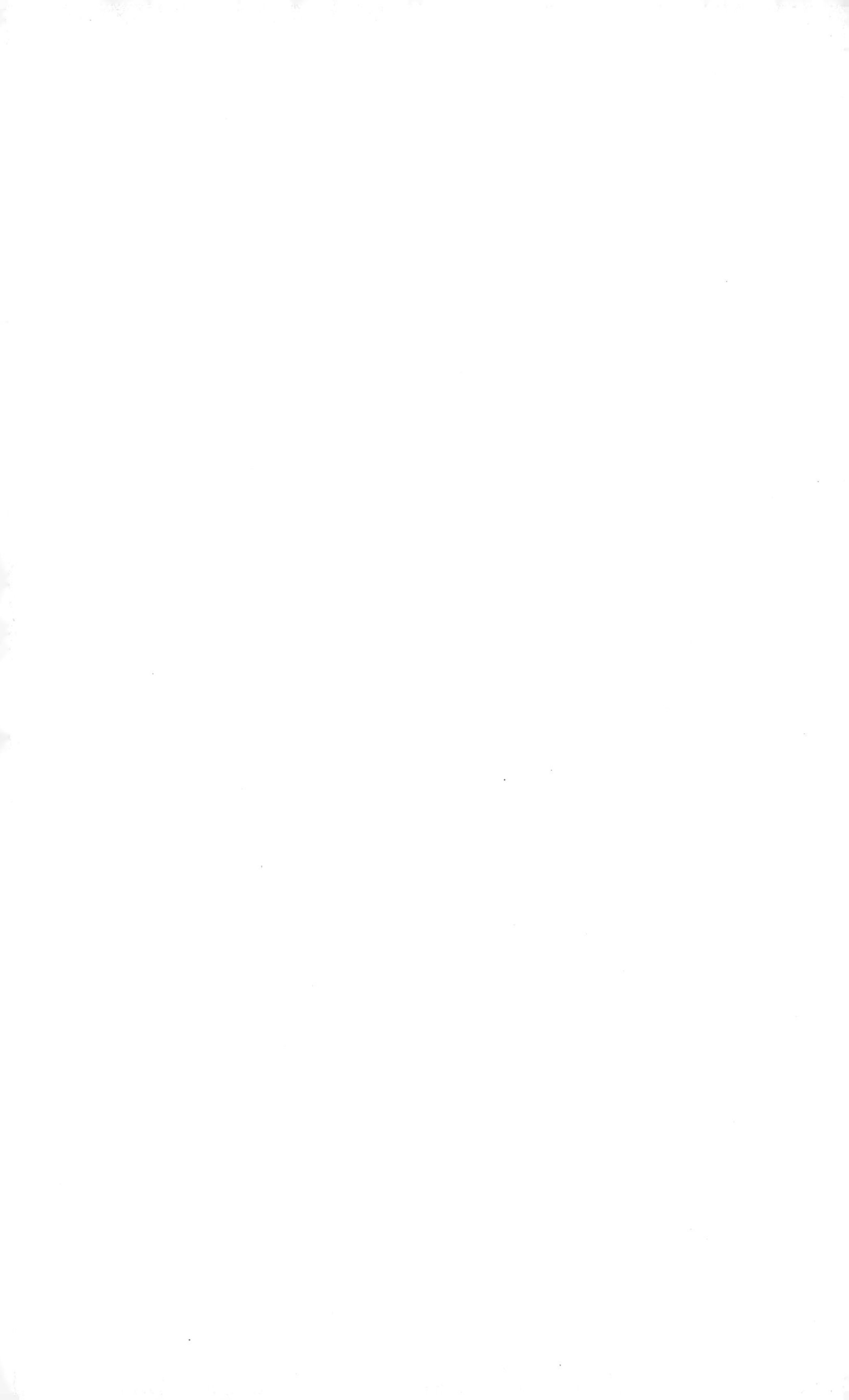

www.ingramcontent.com/pod-product-compliance
Lightning Source LLC
LaVergne TN
LVHW100921110826
845155LV00035B/35

* 9 7 8 1 4 3 8 4 5 3 1 4 9 *